THE POLITICS OF PUBLIC PENSIONS

The Politics of Public Pensions

PARTIES, STATE GOVERNMENTS, AND UNIONS

Carolyn Abott

Columbia University Press
New York

Columbia University Press
Publishers Since 1893
New York   Chichester, West Sussex

Copyright © 2025 Columbia University Press
All rights reserved

Library of Congress Cataloging-in-Publication Data
Names: Abott, Carolyn, author.
Title: The politics of public pensions : parties, state governments, and unions / Carolyn Abott.
Other titles: Parties, state governments, and unions
Description: First edition. | New York : Columbia University Press, [2025] | Includes index.
Identifiers: LCCN 2024047907 | ISBN 9780231214223 (hardback) |
ISBN 9780231214230 (trade paperback) | ISBN 9780231560252 (ebook)
Subjects: LCSH: State governments—Officials and employees—Pensions—
United States—States. | Pension trusts—United States—States—Finance. |
Government employee unions—Political activity—United States. |
Political parties—United States—States.
Classification: LCC JK2474 .A37 2025 | DDC 331.25/240973—dc23/eng/20250305

Printed in the United States of America

Cover design: Chang Jae Lee
Cover image: © AP Photo/Andy Manis

GPSR Authorized Representative: Easy Access System Europe,
Mustamäe tee 50, 10621 Tallinn, Estonia, gpsr.requests@easproject.com

For my grandfather, who never doubted me.

Contents

Acknowledgments

The completion of this book would not have been possible without the unwavering support and encouragement of many individuals and institutions.

First and foremost, I express my deepest gratitude to Nolan McCarty. His generosity and guidance began even before my admission to graduate school, graciously responding to my emails as an eager undergraduate seeking direction on grant writing. His support continued throughout my time at Princeton University, and his encouragement to apply for assistance from the Russell Sage Foundation was pivotal to the inception of this project. Our collaboration on that initial pension project was formative in my development as a political scientist, providing me with essential research experience. I am profoundly grateful for his time, kindness, and unwavering faith in me over the years. I am also sincerely thankful to Brandice Canes-Wrone and Chuck Cameron for their invaluable advice and support. Brandice consistently encouraged me to connect my work to broader questions in political science, while Chuck's theoretical insight and healthy skepticism significantly enriched my research. Their exceptional feedback and guidance greatly benefited the work presented here. I am also indebted to Marty Gilens and Tali Mendelberg for their mentorship and encouragement during my time at Princeton.

I owe a special thanks to my fellow scholars at Princeton, whose camaraderie and support were indispensable. The many discussions we shared, whether over lunchtime salads or happy hour cocktails, were instrumental in shaping my understanding of political science. I am particularly grateful to the participants of the Gradutae Research Seminar in American Politics and Nolan's institutions research group, including Alex Acs, Mike Barber, Alex Bolton, Ben Fifield, PJ Gardner, Mary Kroger, Asya Magazinnik, Lauren Mattioli, and Sharece Thrower. Presenting my research in such intellectually stimulating environments was immensely beneficial, and I deeply appreciate their contributions to my academic journey.

After leaving Princeton, I was fortunate to spend two years at the Ohio State University, where I worked on the Education Governance and Accountability Project. I am incredibly grateful for my time there, where I received incredible support and encouragement from Stéphane Lavertu, Vlad Kogan, and Zac Peskowitz. Their mentorship was indispensable, providing several rounds of detailed feedback on various chapters of this book. They went above and beyond, even organizing a practice job talk during a federal holiday to ensure I was thoroughly prepared for a last-minute flyout. Their dedication and commitment to my professional development was instrumental in shaping this research and advancing my career. I am deeply appreciative of their guidance and the intellectually stimulating environment they fostered at Ohio State.

I am also thankful to my colleagues at Baruch College for their continuous support, especially Stephanie Golob, Els de Graauw, David Jones, and Jessica Lang, and to the Professional Staff Congress and the City University of New York for the financial assistance that made the completion of this book possible. Additionally, I extend my thanks to the government department at St. John's University, particularly Fred Cocozzelli for his guidance as an early assistant professor, and Diane Heith for her mentorship and generous advice during the book proposal stage.

Participants at workshops and conferences provided critical feedback and encouragement, including Chris Berry, Tony Bertelli, Thad Calabrese, James Clinger, Steve Rogers, Jack Santucci, Akheil Singla, Charlie Steindel, and Pengju Zhang. The Faculty Fellowship Publication Program through the City University of New York furnished me with essential financial assistance to complete the book along with a group of fabulous colleagues who provided advice on the introduction and chapter 5 of this book: Thank you to Casey Boland, Chloe Choi, Seon Mi Kim, Nafiz Shuva, Monica Stantonkoko, and, most of all, Lina Newton.

Alisha Sukhram provided exceptional research assistance. Her dedication and hard work significantly contributed to the quality of this book. I also extend my heartfelt thanks to the rotating cast of Princeton undergraduates who laboriously copied and coded pension data from old, sometimes nearly illegible, financial reports.

I am deeply appreciative of Stephen Wesley at Columbia University Press for his invaluable guidance and support in bringing this book to publication amid a global pandemic, a move, a job change, and the birth of a child. I am also grateful to the anonymous reviewers for their insightful and constructive feedback.

To my parents, I offer my deepest thanks for instilling in me the importance of asking questions. Their willingness to provide on-call childcare and food preparation is and was a gesture of support that I will never be able to adequately express my gratitude for.

Finally, I thank my husband, Simon. His unwavering support and reassurances were essential during the final phases of this project. Thank you for being my rock, for making breakfast for the kids, and for your enduring love.

And to Henry and Lila: thank you being an endless source of joy and inspiration, and for always wanting to understand what all the numbers on the computer screen mean.

THE POLITICS OF PUBLIC PENSIONS

Introduction

In 2011, the Democratic state treasurer of Rhode Island, Gina Raimondo, proposed the first public pension overhaul in the history of U.S. public labor that would cut benefits for current workers and retirees. At the time, the state pension funding ratio—that is, pension assets divided by pension liabilities—had slipped to somewhere south of 40 percent. This meant that Rhode Island's pension assets would cover less than 40 percent of its liabilities if they had to be paid out right away. On average, other states had self-reported funding ratios closer to 75 percent. Ranking states' self-reported funding ratios placed Rhode Island close to the bottom of all fifty states. On top of Raimondo's Democratic affiliation, Democrats controlled 78 percent of the Rhode Island state Senate, 87 percent of the state House of Representatives, and the governor's mansion in the year that the pension reform took place.[1] In a state that has incredibly strong public sector unions—nearly two-thirds of state workers were unionized in 2011—the popular and scholarly narrative would not have predicted that sweeping pension overhaul would have come out of a strong, unified Democratic state government.[2] Yet it was under newly unified Democratic control, and *not* under the Republican leadership that had characterized the state for the sixteen years prior to 2011, that this ambitious and ultimately successful reform was undertaken. How did this happen?

Fiscal sustainability is an esoteric concept. For many, fiscal sustainability is defined through a lens of "I know it when I see it." There is a natural inclination to compare government finances with personal finances. This is wrongheaded for several reasons, chief among them that individuals and families cannot raise revenue through taxes, issue debt, or print money. Although governments in the United States are subject to budget constraints, much in the way that individuals and families are, the malleability of those budget constraints varies widely across different levels of government. The federal government, for instance, has the weakest budget constraint in that it can borrow and print money with few limits, whereas small, single-purpose local governments have some of the hardest budget constraints. These types of governments typically are not able to raise taxes and are prohibited by Article I of the Constitution from coining their own currency. For this reason, the federal government in the modern era has never had a fiscal crisis,[3] whereas local governments regularly experience fiscal crises over the course of an economic business cycle.

Beyond the abstraction away from personal finances, fiscal sustainability can be difficult to grasp because it is unclear—even to scholars—what sustainability means in the very long run. Given that most governments have infinite time horizons, how should we calculate exactly how much debt is too much debt? What are the symptoms of too much debt? What benchmarks can we use to pinpoint when a government might go over the sustainability cliff? Some economists like to use the metric of how fast debt is growing relative to how fast the local economy (and thus, the local tax base) is growing. Others, including political scientists, often point to how fast debt is growing relative to the rest of the budget. The lack of a universally accepted measure of a "good amount of debt"—or, even more contentious, a good "type" of debt—has made our understanding of fiscal sustainability even murkier.

Often, when politicians and voters raise concerns about fiscal sustainability or debt growth, they are really thinking about—and motivated by—tax burden. This is a distinct concept. Solvency, which is the degree to which the government can pay its bills, depends on government revenue (much but not all of which comes from taxes) being adequate to sustain government spending. Taxes can be high while spending is high or while spending is low; neither scenario is problematic for fiscal sustainability as long as spending remains lower than taxes. The same is true of low taxes (or moderate taxes, or indeed any level of taxes). The same is also true of various levels of government spending, often referred to as the size of government; a "large" public sector is not necessarily any more or less fiscally sustainable than a small one. When there *is* a mismatch of revenue to spending, however, governments must borrow and issue debt.[4] With this debt that arises from budget imbalances comes the potential for fiscal unsustainability, less transparency about spending, a redistribution of resources from future to current generations, and confusion about exactly how public finances are being managed.

In the United States, state public sector pensions are a microcosm of this dynamic. Although the politics and particulars of public sector pensions have always been contentious, the Great Recession of 2008 and subsequent financial market turmoil increased the prominence of pensions in the debate about the proper role and size of government and public sector unions.[5] Popular media accounts painted the conflict—which exploded into the public consciousness with demonstrations in Wisconsin in 2011 in which public sector workers around the country mobilized to protect pension benefits and collective bargaining rights—with clearly partisan brushstrokes: Democratic lawmakers were for the unions, and Republican lawmakers were for the taxpayers. A central aim of this book is to show that this is a grossly simplified version of events, and mostly mischaracterized.

In actuality, the goals of the Democratic Party and those of public sector unions are not identical and are indeed at times at odds with one another. Without doubt, public sector unions have historically enjoyed a less hostile relationship with Democrats than with Republicans, but the Democratic Party has a host of political and policy considerations other than those prioritized by unions—including pension benefits. More than anything else, the Democratic Party—like the Republican Party—prioritizes winning elections for its members and maintaining control of state governments.[6] Public sector unions care about elections only implicitly, inasmuch as their preferred party pursues their preferred agenda. This is the key distinction between interest groups and political parties and is also why the Democratic Party sometimes pursues policies that are not in the immediate best interests of public labor.

The Politics of State Pensions

Harold Lasswell famously wrote that politics is the study of who gets what, when, and how.[7] This book directly tackles the question about the relationship between politics and policy—the who, what, when, and how—in the context of public sector pensions.

Public employee pensions are an ideal policy in which to explore Lasswell's dictum. For one, they are as close to a pure transfer between groups of voters as exists in the United States. Although public employees of course provide essential services to taxpayers, any (fully funded) increase in the generosity of public employee pension benefits must mean a decrease in the take-home pay of taxpayers who are not public employees. Conversely, a decrease in generosity to public employees is a net gain to other taxpayers' bottom line, holding all else equal.[8]

Public employee pensions are also a type of policy that requires the support of future taxpayers who do not yet exist. With the exception of the very few state public sector pensions that are funded at or above 100 percent, the vast majority of underfunded employee pensions generate debt, levying an implicit tax on future generations. When pensions are underfunded, the "who, what, when, how" questions are how we assess the distributional consequences of politics and policy not just between classes of state residents but also between *generations* of state residents. As a result, pension policy also speaks to issues surrounding fiscal sustainability.

This book argues that Democratically controlled governments are not—typically—more generous than Republicans toward public sector pensions. Strong public sector labor (as typified by strong public sector unions) and unified Democratic state government reduce the likelihood of passing expansionary pension legislation, reduce the size of pension liabilities, and increase the overall funding levels of pension systems. The reasons for this are manifold.

Compared with scenarios in which Democratic lawmakers inherit a relatively unorganized workforce and scenarios in which Republican lawmakers must contend with hostile unions, the Democratic Party and unions have overlapping—though not identical—goals. Although all partisan governments suffer from the temptation to kick the fiscal can down the road, generating debt for future taxpayers, only one type of partisan government—Republican—can credibly commit to allowing a pension fund to default.[9] Because of this, public sector unions recognize that heavily subsidized pension benefit increases will only be *paid for* (i.e., funded) by Democratic governments even though both Republicans and Democrats may be willing to increase unfunded benefits. Unorganized workers care little about the electoral ramifications that Democrats face as a result of this one-sided partisan bailout, but strong unions recognize the serious dangers of having Democrats unilaterally increase taxes to fund their pensions. In other words, public sector unions can internalize the externalities associated with increased pension benefits for their members when working with Democratic governments because the external costs imposed on taxpayers and the governing party *matter to unions when Democrats bear them.*

As a result, lawmakers are less concerned with the fiscal health of the state—and are more willing to provide scarce resources to private (i.e., labor) interests through policy change—when interest groups and political parties are fractured than when well-organized groups cooperate with strong, centralized political parties. This finding is a result of the discipline that strong groups and parties can exert on their individual members to pursue the policy choices that are best for the group or party in the medium and long term. Rather than a zero-sum game in which fractured interests compete voraciously over a fixed set of resources, strong political parties can coopt well-organized constituencies into the party infrastructure such that they work to achieve an optimal, cooperative equilibrium. Within the context of a Democratic-controlled government, public sector unions are not pluralist interest groups; they are instead part and parcel of the Democratic Party establishment apparatus. This idea—that factions can move from being external group actors hoping to influence elections and political parties from the outside to being incorporated into the party structure depending on which party is in control of government—is novel. This theme runs throughout the book.

The Evidence

The biggest hurdle necessary to overcome when discussing public pension policy is data. Although there tends to be lots of it, the data necessary for evaluating pension growth and sustainability is decentralized and stored in documents that are not easily accessible (this is discussed at length in chapter 2). In addition, the data that has been constructed by state governments is characterized by a number of actuarial assumptions and projections that are liable to political and financial manipulation. These subjective assumptions may also be accompanied by omissions and changes to data that may be politically motivated. The Governmental Accounting Standards Board (GASB) moved to improve data reliability by attempting to standardize some methods and assumptions by issuing new accounting standards in 2012,[10] but these standards did not go into effect until 2014 and have been inconsistently adopted.[11]

To accurately assess pension policy, then, I needed to construct standardized measures of liabilities and assets grounded in objectively chosen actuarial assumptions. To do this, I hand collected seventeen years' worth of state pension financial reports and reconstructed pension data that could be compared across place and time. Using this unbiased data, I show that the fiscal sustainability of pensions has clearly declined over time. The average liability per state resident increased by more than $10,000 ($6,742 in constant dollars) between 1995 and 2011. The average unfunded liability—the portion that has yet to be paid for—per state resident increased nearly $6,000 ($4,480 in constant dollars). But this change over time is dwarfed by cross-state differences. In 2008, for example, Vermont's pension liability stood at a little under $5,000 per capita while Colorado's was more than $40,000. In the same year, Vermont had a $2,625 per capita unfunded liability, while Colorado's was more than $32,000. Figure 0.1 shows the average state per capita liability and unfunded liability across time, and figures 0.2 and 0.3 present a snapshot of all state pension finances in 2008. Figures 0.4 and 0.5 present this information by individual states.

For these reasons, in this book, I primarily focus on the causes and consequences of this large interstate variation in public pension finances. I explore, for instance, whether certain types of political and administrative environments are more likely to lead to significant gaps in financial disclosure, or what I term *fiscal malfeasance*. Unions, like other groups who seek to receive funding from the government, have much to gain from creative accounting. The smaller the perceived spending of the pension plan—and the more fiscally sustainable—the more room unions have to negotiate for more generous benefits. This is especially important if voters and good government groups have access to easily interpretable data. I tested these theories using the data collected from detailed financial reports of 130 different pension plans. I linked their self-reported funding levels to their revised funding

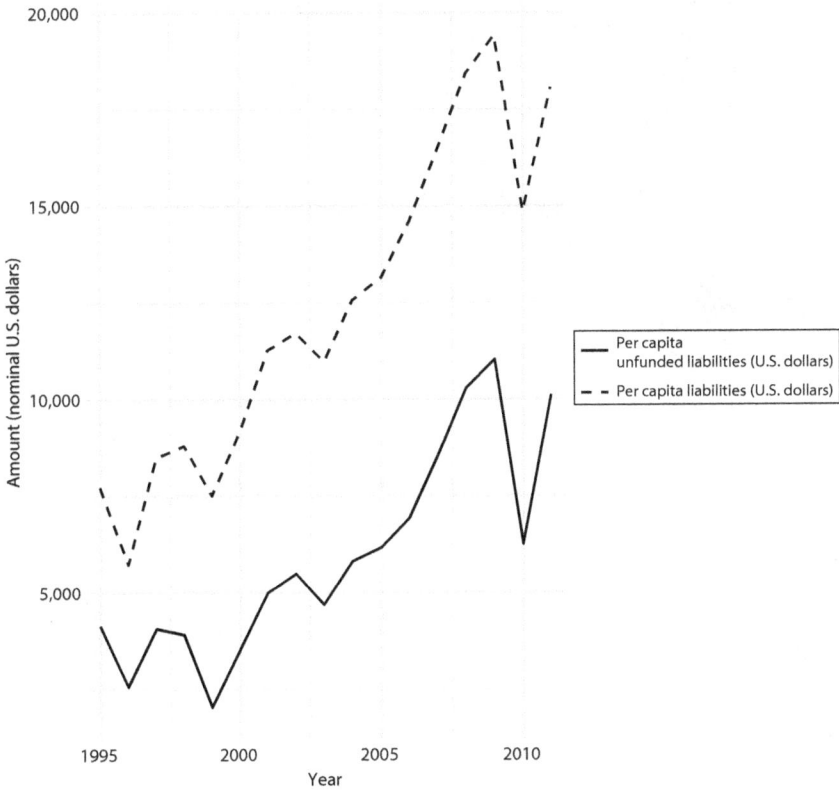

Figure 0.1 Average standardized per capita liabilities and unfunded liabilities over time (in nominal U.S. dollars). The dashed liabilities line should be considered only as illustrative, as my unbalanced panel makes it difficult to compare per capita pension obligations over time. Throughout this analysis, I use changes in per capita pension liabilities (from one year to the next, within a given pension plan) only when discussing relationships. The unfunded liabilities column in this figure does not suffer from the same threat from my unbalanced panel, as the liabilities are reported in the context of the plan's assets. This makes a comparison over time more appropriate.

Source: Author's dataset.

levels and that difference in funding levels to the administrative structure of the pension, the strength of the union, and the overall transparency of state reporting practices. I also collected data on the strength of state political parties, public sector union activity and size, state fiscal transparency, and state debt and credit ratings, allowing me to ask a number of other questions about public sector pensions in their role as state redistributive policy.

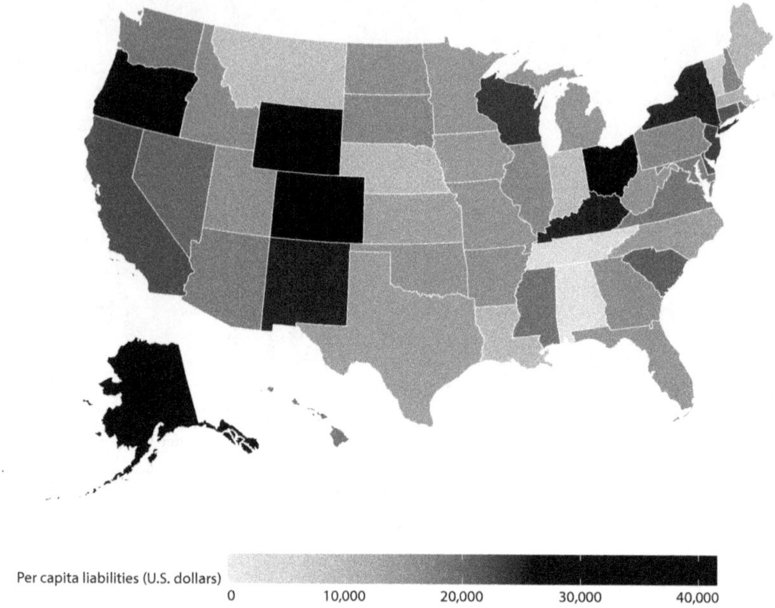

Figure 0.2 Standardized per capita liabilities across states in 2008 (in nominal U.S. dollars). Liabilities for Tennessee are not included because the state was not able to provide data for 2008. Liabilities for Alabama are also missing because no data for any year could be procured for that state.

Source: Author's dataset.

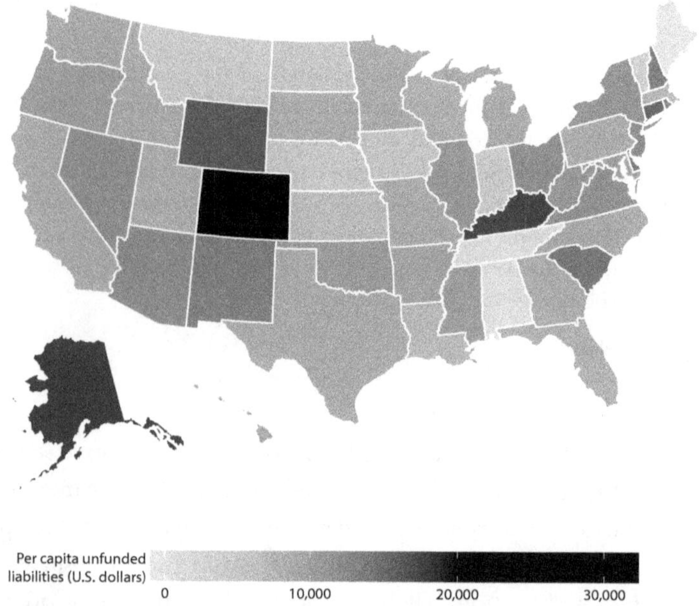

Figure 0.3 Standardized per capita unfunded liabilities across states in 2008 (in nominal U.S. dollars). Unfunded liabilities for Tennessee are not included because the state was not able to provide data for 2008. Unfunded liabilities for Alabama are also missing because no data for any year could be procured for that state.

Source: Author's dataset.

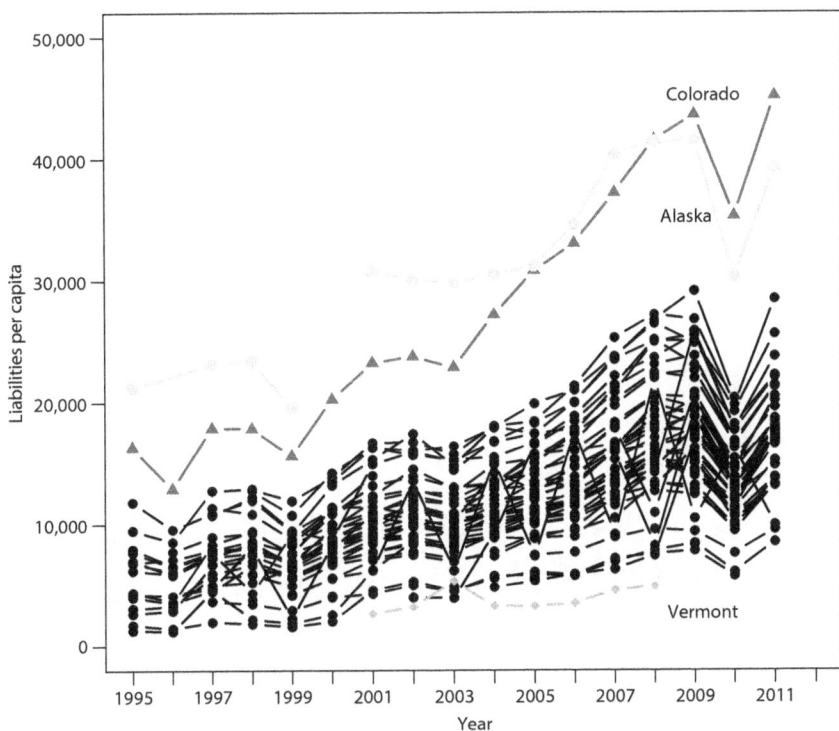

Figure 0.4 Standardized per capita liabilities over time (in nominal U.S. dollars). The large dip in liabilities in 2010 is a function of deflation in that year increasing the discount rate (via lower cost of living adjustments). Liabilities are reported in nominal U.S. dollars and come from the author's calculations. Colorado and Alaska are highlighted as the two states with the largest per capita liabilities over time, while Vermont is highlighted for having the lowest.

Source: Author's dataset.

Plan of the Book

Chapter 1 provides the theoretical framework of the book. In this chapter, I outline the key ways in which public sector unions are different from traditional interest groups. The first, and perhaps most well-known, manner in which public sector unions are distinct is in their ability to elect their own employers and bring government to a standstill through strikes.[12] The second, and less discussed difference, is how public sector unions interact with the political environment. Whereas most private interest groups spend a

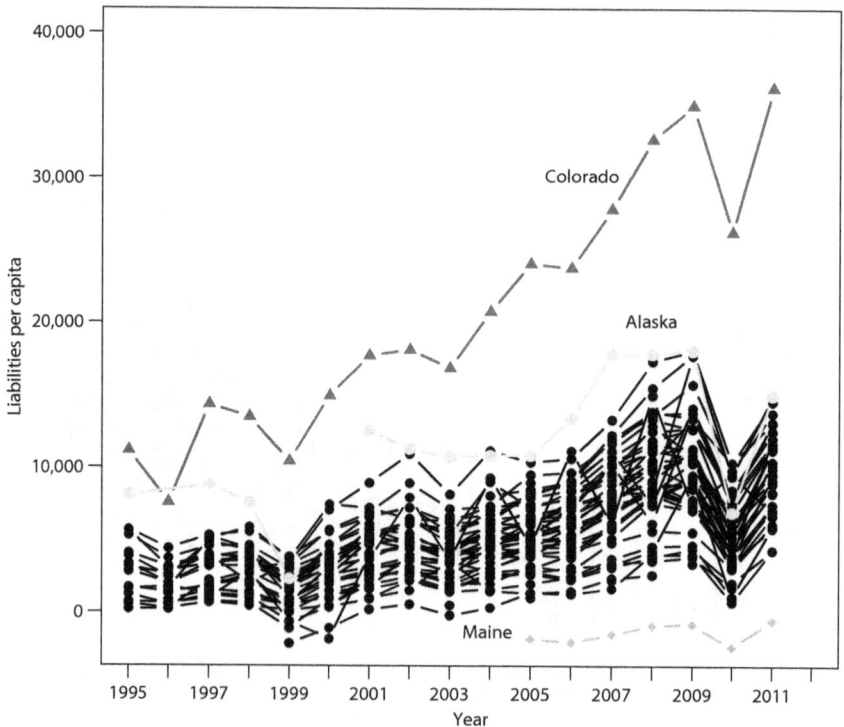

Figure 0.5 Standardized per capita unfunded liabilities over time (in nominal U.S. dollars). The large dip in liabilities in 2010 is a function of deflation in that year increasing the discount rate (via lower cost of living adjustments). Liabilities reported in nominal U.S. dollars and come from the author's calculations. Colorado and Alaska are highlighted as the two states with the largest per capita unfunded liabilities over time, while Maine is highlighted for having the lowest (and is in fact overfunded over my sample period).

Source: Author's dataset.

majority of their political dollars on lobbying, both public and private sector unions spend more of their resources on electing or reelecting Democrats to office.[13] This is true even of the more stereotypically conservative police and fire unions. In the minds of unions, the best way to achieve their political objectives is by electing Democrats to office. Joseph McCartin stresses that the history of public sector labor success in the United States was dependent on and the result of an intimate alliance between the Democratic Party and public sector unions.[14] Although the relationship between private sector unions and Democrats may have indeed been a "barren marriage," there would have been no public sector unions at all had the Democratic

Party not been there to support them.[15] That said, Democrats were not and are not willing to support public unions at the expense of losing control of government. As McCartin further details, political and fiscal crises have thrown this relationship into sharp relief again and again, emphasizing that "each side in that relationship knew well how much it needed the other."[16] If it is politically necessary, Democrats are willing to make sure that public sector unions take one for the team.

In this chapter, I also emphasize the paramount influence of a fiscally constrained environment over the union-party relationship. State governments—much like local governments—face sharp resource constraints in ways that the federal government does not.[17] This creates an environment in which private groups compete over fixed resources in a more or less zero-sum game. For example, if public sector workers are granted an increase in compensation, taxpayers must pay for that increase—either now or in the future. The longer taxpayers put off paying for that increase in compensation, the stronger the likelihood that the state government will experience some sort of fiscal reckoning or crisis.

Finally, I provide an overview of the historical experiences of these types of resource-constrained governments under different types of party systems: reform systems and strong party or machine systems. During eras of political reform, in which state and local political parties were weak or nonexistent, electoral coalitions were fragile and transitory. These coalitions required the appeasement of many different types of private interests, including both business and labor. As a result, taxes were often decreased in deference to the business community, while social services were maintained or even increased. This sort of fractured policymaking almost always ended in fiscal crisis and a return to austerity. In response to the politically unpopular austerity, political machines were able to regain power and centralize the policymaking process. Because of their innate strength and natural and permanent electoral coalitions, machines were able to—at least temporarily—ignore the demands of those outside their coalition and, as a result, maintain fiscal integrity.[18] Considered together, I argue that well-organized public workers will act like an electorally permanent piece of Democratic coalitions when Democratic parties are strong but transform into a traditional interest group—engaged in fractured, competitive political maneuvering—when Republicans are in power. This results in fiscal stability and well-managed pensions in the first case, and fiscal crisis in the latter.

Chapter 2 includes the first of several empirical investigations. Armed with an original and comprehensive dataset that standardizes and removes problematic biases from pension data across states and years, I show that Democrats are not more generous in their pension policy than Republicans.[19] This is contrary to both the dominant popular and academic narrative.[20] The presence of strong unions and a strongly Democratic state government—the true recipe for fiscal disaster, according to popular accounts—actually reduces the likelihood of passing expansionary pension legislation, decreases the size of unfunded pension liabilities, and increases the size of the contribution rate. Unions accept a decline in pension solvency from Republican governments in exchange for an increase in the size of their benefits, whereas Democratic governments offer an improvement in solvency in exchange for no change or a decrease in the size of workers' benefits. Organized state workers realize that because any prior benefit increase will only be *paid for* by Democratic governments, they must balance their desire for greater pension benefits against electoral consequences for Democrats who are stereotypically perceived as profligate and belonging to the party of higher taxes. Strong unions recognize the serious electoral and systematic dangers of having Democrats unilaterally increase taxes to fund union pensions, but unorganized workers care little about the electoral ramifications of this one-sided partisan bailout by Democrats. The crux of this argument is that, unlike many other interest groups, public sector unions not only care about pensions but also about *other things*—especially things that involve deeply existential threats to their very survival, like unified Republican control of the state.

In chapter 3, I investigate the mechanics and justifications for the labor policy decisions explored in the previous chapters. Both governments and unions face a distinct trade-off when making decisions about how to present financial information—and how much of it—to the general public, as these representations are used to justify real changes to pension policy. On the one hand, pension finance is so opaque that even states with strong transparency laws can easily get away with making unreasonable assumptions about the solvency of their plans. On the other hand, stakeholders in states that have fewer requirements for publishing state financial information to the general public will have little incentive to misreport key pension information that is easily manipulated by actuarial assumptions: After all, if no one is going to see the data, why go to any effort to manipulate it?

Just like decisions surrounding actual pension solvency, choices made about how to report pension solvency are politically fraught and often caught in the crosshairs of various stakeholders' incentives. In the chapter, I explore how certain types of political and administrative environments are more likely to lead to significant gaps in financial disclosure. Although their alignment with strong Democratic parties tempers their pension demands from the legislature, unions still have much to gain from creative accounting. The greater the perceived funding level of the pension plan, the more room unions have to negotiate for more generous benefits. This type of creative accounting alters the perceived budget constraint of pensions, allowing unions more wiggle room in their negotiations, regardless of with whom those negotiations take place. The greatest predictor of this fiscal gimmickry is the strength of the labor union and the accessibility of state financial data. The more access voters and good government groups have to financial data, and the stronger unions are, the more likely the pension board will be to make less conservative assumptions and overreport their funding levels. Overreporting behavior is also more likely to occur on pension boards on which state workers have a greater amount of influence in the decision-making and policy process. This finding is in line with previous work on this topic.[21]

In chapter 4, I address the consequences of the "what, when, and how" of pension policy. If fiscal sustainability is a trade-off with partisan responsiveness to the materialist demands of interest groups, are there differences in policy outcomes if a state prioritizes one over the other? Does fiscal sustainability matter in concrete terms, in ways that affect voters and residents in tangible ways? Do expansions in pension benefits, funded or not, crowd out other state spending? Does pension debt? Work to date has shown that pension debt does not substantively affect the state economy, and overall debt does not substantively affect the national economy, but comparably less has been done on the effect of pensions on the size and composition of state budgets.[22] Do increases in pension benefits and pension debt materially affect service solvency?[23] Although I do not find any first-order effects of pension debt on line-item expenditure categories, newly generated pension debt affects contemporaneous budgets by increasing the cost of borrowing for state governments. Increases in credit ratings and interest burdens that are associated with new pension debt have direct and clear consequences for state politics and the value of a state's tax dollar, even in the absence of any first-order impacts on line-item spending in the budget.

Chapter 5 is a historical investigation of three states' pension systems: New Jersey, New York, and Kentucky. In this chapter, I take a deep dive into how the fortunes of these three states' pensions diverged so remarkably. The selection of these states is intentional, with each representing one of the regime types identified in chapter 1: New Jersey as a pluralist state with strong unions and extended periods of Republican state control; New York as a coalitional state, also home to robust public unions but more frequently governed by a centralized Democratic Party; and Kentucky as a disorganized state, historically dominated by Democrats but more recently characterized by Republican control and weak public labor organization.

Despite their economic and political similarities, New York and New Jersey have experienced vastly different outcomes in managing their pension plans. New York's pension system is among the best funded in the country, whereas New Jersey's system is one of the worst. I show that this divergence can be traced back to decisions made about both funding and benefits and is largely attributable to differences in partisan control of the state government. Kentucky, the third state analyzed in this chapter, exemplifies the consequences of weak public sector union activity and a legislature characterized by divided government.[24] The Kentucky case provides an excellent example of what can happen when public labor is unorganized and marginalized, lacking long-run time horizons and unmoored from institutional and organizational concerns for the fiscal sustainability of the state—that is, negligence of the pension system even when external fiscal conditions necessitate attention.

In chapter 6, I take a closer look at the relationships among pension policy, electoral outcomes, and anti-public-sector labor laws. The political dynamic in states that have recently passed such measures—Indiana, Wisconsin, Michigan, Ohio, and Illinois—are examples of coalitional politics gone awry. As traditional strongholds of manufacturing and union labor, it was unexpected that the Midwest would so abruptly end its love affair with the organized worker. But the postindustrial collapse of the region brought instability to capital and labor in the private sector, sending deep convulsions into the political environs. This conflict is encapsulated perfectly within the struggle over pension promises to public workers. In this chapter, I investigate how budget crises, underfunded pensions, and hostile political relations between state governments and workers came to dominate this traditionally labor-friendly region during the beginning of the twenty-first century and, ultimately, the way in which pension policy played a leading role in the existential crises of public sector unions in these states. I also demonstrate how tax increases and unfunded pension expansions led to a decline in the electoral fortunes of incumbents, particularly Democratic incumbents.

Finally, in the conclusion, I summarize the novel claims and arguments made over the course of the book: First, fiscal sustainability is absolutely dependent on stable political coalitions and centralized budgeting authority, particularly in an era marked by nationalized political conflict and a belief in a soft or nonexistent budget constraint at the state level; and, second, well-organized public sector workers and Democratic state governments will be less likely than other types of governing coalitions to pursue unfunded pension benefit expansions. I also consider the future of public sector labor politics in the wake of *Janus v. AFSCME*, the Supreme Court case that ruled labor unions collecting fees from nonunion members constituted a violation of their First Amendment rights.[25] I argue that the ban on the legal enforcement of agency fees has not and will not destroy the public sector union—at least in blue states. As Patrick Flavin and Michael Hartney argue, states that have mandatory collective bargaining laws—predominantly Democratic strongholds—have already created the mechanism whereby public sector workers can overcome the collective action problem.[26] As such, it is not the ban on the agency fee in *Janus* that creates the greatest existential threat to public sector unions; it is the ban on collective bargaining. A number of states have already passed or are attempting to pass anti-collective-bargaining laws to deal with what the public perceives as overly powerful public sector unions. In contrast, private sector unionism has been in decline for decades for reasons largely unrelated to changes in bargaining laws. Only time will tell whether public sector unionism will follow suit in the wake of the spate of antilabor legislation. Last, I offer some predictions for both the future of public sector pensions and public sector unions, as well as insight into how good government groups and GASB reforms might affect the fiscal outlook of states. I also caution the policymaker against pinning their hopes on financial documents and to instead dig deeper into big picture expenditure and revenue patterns, to truly familiarize themselves with the political context in which budget decisions are made, and to fully understand the way in which the assumptions that go into making forecasts are politically motivated.

CHAPTER I

Public Sector Unions, Pensions, and Partisanship

Interest Groups and the States

Interest group capture of the policymaking process has been a fear of scholars since at least the time of Elmer Schattschneider.[1] Many scholars have since learned, however, well-organized interest groups get the type of policy they want only under specific political arrangements, such as when the benefits are concentrated and the costs diffuse, when voters are at an informational disadvantage, or when legislatures need help governing.[2] Careful studies of interest groups and the likelihood of their success have been conducted almost entirely within the context of either national or local policymaking; barring some exceptions, states have largely been left out of this literature.[3]

Within states, interest groups must contend with all of the constraints that groups at the national level must face as well as with a constraint that is typical at the local level—scarce resources. The national government has a nearly limitless ability to generate resources for policy-driven interest groups, *if they so choose.* They can do this not only by allocating budgetary resources differently (in a zero-sum scenario, in which one group loses out to another group) but also by raising revenue, issuing debt, and printing money (i.e., by increasing the size of the fiscal pie). Like local governments, states have less capacity to raise revenue than the national government, are severely constrained in their borrowing ability relative to the national government, and are constitutionally prohibited from coining their own currency. As a result, the dynamics of navigating the demands of interest groups are quite different. State policymakers must balance their policy and electoral concerns—which are often closely tied to the policy concerns of interest groups—against the harsh reality of a government faced with ever scarcer resources.

This raises two questions: When are the policy demands of private interest groups more important than fiscal sustainability? When does a state government choose to heed the needs of those interest groups and when does it choose to ignore them? The short answer to both of these questions is when political parties are weak. The structure and strength of the political party plays an essential role in determining the types of policies private interest groups can successfully achieve, and the types of policies that groups advocate for in the first place.

Looking to political parties to try to understand interest groups is not a new endeavor. The UCLA school of political parties, for example, views the party and the interest group as one and the same, and as being primarily policy centric.[4] This view stands in stark contrast to John Aldrich's conception of the party as a candidate-driven and electorally focused institution.[5] Raymond La Raja and Brian Schaffner posit a middle ground, hypothesizing that the party is likely to consist of both UCLA-like "purists" and Aldrich-like "pragmatists" to one degree or another.[6] This type of political party that exists as a battleground between those who want specific policies and those just want to govern also has roots in earlier work on urban and regime politics. For much of the late nineteenth and twentieth centuries, Northeastern and Midwestern cities were dominated by Democratic Party machines. These machines did not—ostensibly—care about policy. The machine and its supporters cared only about winning elections and reaping the rewards that were a direct consequence of governing. In the purest form of this machine, these rewards were graft and patronage jobs. In the late twentieth and early twenty-first century, these rewards have come to look somewhat different, but in many cases, they still involve a wink, a nod, and a large constituency of employment-motivated voters. Political monopolies in the United States are not dead; they have simply evolved into something more modern.[7] A large part of this modernization has been the public sector union.

State Democratic Parties do not view public sector unions as ordinary interest groups. This has been well argued by Terry Moe.[8] My conclusions, however, are quite different. As in Paul Frymer's work on the role of African Americans in the Democratic Party, a staunchly loyal constituency of the

Democratic Party like public sector unions is *not* given special treatment; extra attention is not paid to these narrowly defined interests.[9] State Democrats view public sector unions as a structural component of their party. Democratic Parties are at no risk of losing union votes or support, much like traditional machines were at no risk of losing the loyalties of working-class immigrants. This was and is because of tools at the governing coalition's disposal: friendlier collective bargaining negotiations, economic rents allocated to union leaders, and all sorts of workplace protections. As a result, Democrats are not compelled to provide unions with additional carrots for their support. Similarly, union leaders can get rank-and-file members to acquiesce to sometimes-unpopular Democratic policy decisions because of the specter of the stick: Republican control of state government. Much like the reform coalitions that coalesced in opposition to the urban machines and their method of controlling the public employment environment, state Republicans are ideologically opposed to the existence of public sector unions. Under Republican control, public sector unions are treated like any other ideologically hostile interest group: with contempt, but also with an understanding that their governing coalition may depend on their tacit support. Interest group politics require budgetary compromise, and as such, public sector labor in strong union states can extract distributional concessions from Republican governments in exchange for changes to other policies.[10] In the case of public sector pensions, this typically meant tax cuts through pension contribution holidays accompanied by expansions in unfunded benefits for annuitants. This approach has allowed state Republicans to pursue their party's primary political agenda (i.e., encouraging business interests through lower spending and taxes) by kicking the pension funding can down the road and keeping unions from crying foul at the same time. During the reform era of politics, the story in the cities was the same: patronage jobs were replaced by civil service requirements and corrupt politicians were thrown out of office, but the fiscal commons were ravaged by business interests that demanded lower taxes and by social groups that insisted upon more municipal spending.[11]

As Jessica Trounstine recounts, however, this is not the end of the story: "The debate over the functions of machines presents a false dichotomy. Were machine politicians greedy hacks after the spoils of office or did they truly aid the suffering masses? The distinction implies that politicians should not want to win votes. But the very structure of representative democracy channels the desire for reelection into successful governance."[12]

In other words, both Democrats and Republicans are driven by election concerns. I argue that these election concerns are what make Democratic-union coalitions so distinct relative to other sorts of interest group behavior and that public sector unions are *not* typical interest groups in any sense of the term. Both public sector unions and Democrats want Democrats to stay in office, and they do this by moderating rent-seeking behavior that would otherwise offend the sensibilities of voters. Republicans, in contrast, stay in office by trying to balance the demands of competing interests (public sector unions, among many others) against those of voters. In the latter scenario, voters always lose when the various interest groups are adequately strong.

Much recent work would argue that unions are archetypical of the "purist" element of parties.[13] I challenge the view that public sector unions are singularly driven by their private policy interests. As chapter 2 shows, Democratic state governments are in fact more likely to pursue policies of pension contraction and are less likely to pursue policies of expansion than when Republicans control the legislature. Although individual Democratic legislators may be more likely to vote in favor of expanding pension benefits, legislatures that are overwhelmingly controlled by Democratic majorities are *less* likely to pass legislation that expands benefits *when the public workforce is unionized*.[14] Political parties rely less on external bases of support when they have a firm control of government and have the discipline and luxury of being able to say no to electorally unpopular demands. This strong party form of state government prevents state coffers from being ransacked, just as it has for local governments.

Pension Solvency, Public Sector Unions, and Partisan Government

The fiscal problems of public sector pension plans have been journalistic fodder for more than a decade. According to popular narratives, the combination of a weak financial market and state governments' lack of political will has decimated the assets of hundreds of defined benefit plans across the country.[15] Coupled with expanding liabilities for public sector workers, state-run public sector pension plans have placed an intense financial, political, and fiscal burden on already strained state budgets.

Political talking points notwithstanding, the decision to expand or contract liabilities and the decision to expand or contract assets has not been systematically analyzed—until now.[16] These policy decisions bear directly on both the short-run popularity and long-run sustainability of pension funds and state budgets. By examining individual policy decisions related to the status of pension fiscal positions and analyzing each of them separately, we can assemble a more complete picture of why some states have been able to keep liabilities and assets on an even keel while other states' plans have threatened to upend fiscal outlooks.

The health of public sector pensions involves many factors, but the two main elements of all public sector pensions are how much the pension owes its current and future beneficiaries (the *liabilities*) and how much the pension has saved to pay these beneficiaries (the *assets*).[17] Taken separately, these two components have distributional implications for different classes of taxpayers (pension beneficiaries versus nonbeneficiaries); taken together, however, they have distributional implications for both different classes *and* different generations of taxpayers. For example, if pension liabilities are high relative to total budgetary expenditures, then taxpayer resources are being diverted from other parts of the budget and toward the retirement compensation of public employees.[18] Conversely, if pension liabilities are high relative to pension assets (irrespective of their levels relative to the rest of the budget), the state government is generating debt that future taxpayers must pay back on behalf of their predecessors or face the possibility of insolvency and fiscal crisis.

How might organized workers, governments, or voters respond to the underfunding of public sector pension plans? Unions should want to extract as many concessions as they can from employers and taxpayers by expanding liabilities.[19] As rational interest groups, they should also care about the stability and long-term solvency of the plan and the possibility that the pension fund may be unable to make payments to retirees if it is mismanaged. In other words, unions should care about the financial position of their pension funds—how many assets are socked away relative to the size of benefits. In a perfect world, unions would expand assets at a rate comparable to their liabilities. In the real world, however, unions face scarcity and may be forced to make trade-offs between expanding liabilities and maintaining a given net financial position of the pension.

Elected officials, both Republican and Democrat, also have conflicting incentives regarding the funding of state pension plans. Because long-term liabilities do not enter the general state budget directly, governments can use pensions as piggy banks—both for legal reasons (i.e., to circumvent balanced budget laws) and for political reasons (i.e., to increase spending without increasing taxes). As Truth in Accounting explains, "Only the pension contributions paid to the plans are included in state budgets . . . [the contributions] have nothing to do with the amount of retirement benefits earned by the workers during the budget period. Consequently a state budget calculation may not recognize billions of dollars of retirement costs incurred each year, yet the state is deemed balanced even though current revenue is not set aside to adequately fund these promises."[20] If, however, state pensions were to be so underfunded as to provoke crisis, the government undoubtably would be held electorally responsible.[21] The ramifications of a state pension's insolvency would be felt not only by state workers; the economic and fiscal consequences would be widespread and likely would not even be contained to the state within which the crisis occurred.

Partisan affiliations may also color the government's incentives to adequately fund state pensions. Republicans might hold an ideological commitment to fund the plans, as not doing so would be the moral equivalent of running perpetual deficits.[22] Democrats, however, may also want to keep the plans funded to keep their union-member constituents happy.

As such, theoretical predictions about the behavior of public pension funding rates are ambiguous. Part of the reason for this is the cross-cutting incentives for multiple actors, but an equally significant explanation is the fact that funding rates are a consequence of many decisions made by both employee and employer. Virtually all decisions made regarding the fiscal and financial health of the state pension funds are done at the legislative level, by statute—not through collective bargaining agreements. The primary negotiations over these policies take place in a traditional lawmaking environment, among individual legislators and across parties. The governor can influence policy outcomes through the executive's veto power and as an agenda setter. This is especially important when it comes to budgetary decisions, which almost always originate with the state executive.[23] Unions also have the ability to influence the outcome of the law in much the same way that any type of interest group can influence policymaking—that is, through campaign contributions, lobbying, and electoral mobilization.

For these reasons, we might expect a straightforward relationship between Democrats and the strong public sector unions that donate, work, and vote for them. The stronger the union constituency—in both number and financial strength—the more generous we should expect Democrats to be, and the less concerned we should expect them to be about the ramifications of shifting resources toward public sector pensions. Previous scholars have found little evidence that this is true, however, raising questions about the true motives and incentives of actors.[24] Sarah Anzia and Terry Moe argue that until the Great Recession, pension policy was simply not sufficiently salient to force an opposition group to coalesce around the issue of generous unfunded pension benefits.[25] I argue, instead, that the reason pension policy was not particularly salient until the Great Recession was because unions and Democrats practiced calculated restraint. The Great Recession decimated asset levels and funding ratios for all state pension plans more or less in a nondiscriminatory fashion.[26] This piqued the public's interest, as Anzia and Moe hypothesize, and for good reason. Before and subsequent to the Great Recession, however, funding levels were more likely to rise and fall in line with politically controllable outcomes, like changes in benefit generosity and contribution rates.[27] Some states, in some years, were better at maintaining funding levels than others. If all states and partisans were equally profligate, as Anzia and Moe suggest, the Great Recession would not have been necessary to capture the public's interest in the way that they suggest.

Previously documented null findings about the role of partisanship are directly linked to the unique trade-off that public sector unions face. Public sector unions possess not only the ability to lobby for preferred legislation but also the ability to influence who their future employers are.[28] This trade-off is distinct from that of a traditional interest group. Union efforts to mobilize voters and sabotage unfriendly partisans' policy ambitions influence elections (as do traditional interest groups' efforts), but the winners of the union-influenced elections also control the employment environment for the immediate future. As such, unions would like two potentially conflicting outcomes: first, increases in pension benefits that they are not financially responsible for, and second, control of the state government by Democrats.[29] When these two preferences are in conflict, either because voters do not want to pay for expanded pension benefits or because the budget is already strained, unions must weigh the payoff of extracting increases in unpopular benefits against the cost of Democratic lawmakers potentially being voted out of office. Under these circumstances, do unions blindly demand a more generous policy, or do they moderate their behavior as the political environment dictates, recognizing the electoral externalities inherent in their policy demands and the fact that policy changes often shift the political landscape? Elected officials often use policy to create new types of political constituencies.[30] It is easy to imagine that unions are sophisticated enough to be playing the same policy-as-politics game as their managerial counterparts, and they are strongly motivated to prevent Republicans from taking office.[31] Furthermore, union leaders—in ways distinct from the rank and file—have historically enjoyed distinct privileges associated with Democratic government. In sum, public sector unions have countervailing concerns that can be parsed into two effects on their behavior:

Unconditional effect: Both organized and unorganized public sector workers want better pension benefits and want those benefits to be paid for by taxpayers, although better organized workers will be more successful in achieving their distributional goals.

Conditional effect: Well-organized workers—strong public sector unions—recognize the political consequences of their actions but only **care** when Democrats are in office and when Democrats must pay the price. As a result, unions will temper their demands when Democrats wield more control over state government.

If the unconditional effects outweigh the conditional effects, we should expect to see the strength of public sector unions strongly correlated with expansions in pension benefits that are funded by taxpayers or remain unfunded (as opposed to paid for by increases in employee contributions), regardless of which party controls the government. We should not expect to see a relationship between partisan control and pension benefits and should expect to see a strong, positive relationship between unionization and benefits. I call this hypothesis the Special Interest Group Politics Hypothesis. As discussed, many studies have found evidence in favor of the former condition of the hypothesis (i.e., the lack of a relationship).[32] No studies testing the latter condition of the hypothesis have been conducted, to the best of my knowledge.

Layering the conditional effect on top of the unconditional effect adds a wrinkle to the Special Interest Group Politics Hypothesis, especially if the conditional effect is larger than the unconditional effect. Although the conditional effect does not produce different behavior when Republicans interact with unions, it does have the potential to induce the opposite pattern when Democrats interact with unions. If the conditional effect is powerful enough to overtake the unconditional effect, we should expect strong Democratic governments—when accompanied by strong public sector unionism—to show restraint in passing expansionary pension policy that might otherwise impose higher costs on the public (I discuss what I mean by "strong" in the next section). Although strong public sector unions are more successful in obtaining the policies they prefer, the political cost to Democrats matters more to the unions than the potential gain in benefits. Because Republican governments and unions are subjected only to the unconditional effect, however, their pattern of behavior should look no different than under the special interest group politics hypothesis. As a result, we should expect to see significantly different pension benefit policies under Democratic versus Republican control of government, but only when public sector unions are strong. Specifically, because of pluralist organizational pressures, unions can extract more pension concessions from Republican governments than when they are not unionized. Unions are also more likely to extract concessions from Republican governments than when Democrats control government, because unions' long-term, institutional political goals are well-aligned with those of Democratic legislators and the Democratic Party and, as a result, they are likely to place self-imposed constraints on their distributional claims. When unions are weak, however, we are unlikely to detect any partisan differences in policy. I call this hypothesis the coalitional politics hypothesis.

In some ways, this framework parses theoretical explanations in ways not wholly unsimilar to Anzia and Moe's pre- and post-2008 distinction.[33] In their work, they find that before the Great Recession, the issue of pension policy had not been sufficiently salient to gain attention from voters and, as a result, the scope of the conflict between public sector workers and taxpayers did not expand into partisan politics in ways that Schattschneider predicted until after the economic crisis.[34] If Anzia and Moe are correct, we should find evidence for the Special Interest Group Politics Hypothesis before 2008 but not after.[35] Additionally, although it is not entirely clear what Anzia and Moe's post-2008 Schattsneiderian version of partisan pension politics should look like, we should expect differences in the behavior of political parties. Political parties may diverge in their treatment of pensions in two primary ways: first, they can engage in what Anzia and Moe call "polarization politics" and act more generously toward their natural constituencies (i.e., Democrats will provide more ample benefits to public sector workers), or second, they can act more like neocorporatist employers and employees in which hostile negotiations become a net drag on the government's financial position while friendly negotiations result in compromise, restraint, and a mutual understanding of a "linked fate."[36] The idea that negative fiscal consequences are related to behavior that is more typical of interest group activity—rather than coalitional or intraparty activity—is a common finding in the comparativist literature on consociationalism and neocorporatism.[37] Combined with Schattschneider's classic insight, this concept is the key to the Coalitional Politics Hypothesis.

If this polarization or—in my preferred parlance—constituency effect attenuates or amplifies the conditional effect discussed thus far, then neither the Coalitional Politics Hypothesis nor the Special Interest Group Politics Hypothesis may be correct. Although scholars have not found evidence to support the claim that Democrats are more generous than Republicans regarding pension benefits and have not found evidence that unions and Democrats working together are the most likely coalition to expand pension benefits, this is a common refrain in the popular media.[38] This claim suggests that—holding all else equal—Democrats are more likely to be hospitable to public sector worker demands, because they are a natural constituency of the labor wing of the Democratic Party. Additionally, the attenuation of this conditional effect will be more pronounced for public sector workers who share an ideological affinity, such as teachers, than for those who may not, such as police officers. If we were to completely supplant the conditional effect with this constituency effect, we should expect to see public sector workers get more from the government when Democrats are in power and get even more when they are organized into unions (as a result of the unconditional effect). In contrast, it is also plausible that the constituency effect may amplify the conditional effect. For example, if teachers are closer to the Democratic Party in terms of constituent characteristics than police officers, teacher unions are also likely to form a closer coalitional relationship to the Democratic Party than police unions and also may care much more than the police do about keeping the Democratic Party in power. As such, we may see a large difference in the way that partisans formulate policy for different types of pension plans, or we may not.

Table 1.1 presents a two-by-two table that depicts the different regime types and the expected fiscal behavior of the regime if the Special Interest Group Politics Hypothesis were correct. Under this hypothesis, the unconditional effect is stronger than the conditional effect in all regimes. As a result, state governments controlled by either political party are likely to heed workers' desires for larger pensions when workers are well organized into unions (top row). Conversely, neither party is likely to increase pension benefits when public sector workers are unorganized (bottom row).

TABLE 1.1

Regime type and expected fiscal behavior under the Special Interest Group Politics Hypothesis.

		Dominant party	
		Republican	*Democratic*
Public sector workforce	*Organized*	Increase benefits, decrease taxpayer-funded contributions (*less sustainable*)	Increase benefits, maintain taxpayer-funded contributions (*less sustainable*)
	Unorganized	Maintain benefits, maintain taxpayer-funded contributions (*no change*)	Comparison group

The Coalitional Politics Hypothesis is represented in table 1.2. In the bottom row, the state public sector workforce is, again, not unionized. In this scenario, the unconditional effect reigns supreme under both types of partisan dominance. But because workers are unorganized and less powerful than their unionized counterparts, both Democrats and Republicans will not likely heed the demands of these voters and instead will decrease pension benefit generosity. Partisans in this scenario can afford to do this because public workers are relatively weak and unorganized and thus unlikely to influence the outcomes of elections. This is true under both hypotheses and in both table 1.1 and table 1.2. I call this type of regime *disorganized*.

The top row of table 1.2 shows where these two hypotheses diverge. This row presents the two different partisan regimes in a strong public sector union state. Here, the conditional effect is likely to overwhelm the unconditional effect. During periods of Republican control, strong unions want to extract as much as possible from the state government. Republicans are willing to give into union demands of increased pension benefits to decrease funding—and taxes—for those benefits (see more on the issue of funding). This approach will have a clear and unmitigated draw on the fiscal sustainability of the pension. Both the unions and the Republican government are willing to draw on this sustainability to reach at least one of their two preferred outcomes. In this case, fiscal sustainability is the price of compromise in a competitive group system. I refer to this type of political regime as *pluralist*.

TABLE 1.2

Regime type and expected fiscal behavior under the Coalitional Politics Hypothesis.

| | | Dominant party | |
		Republican	Democratic
Public sector workforce	*Organized*	Mixed strategy: increase benefits, decrease taxpayer-funded contributions (*less sustainable*) OR Attempt to eliminate public sector unions	Decrease benefits, maintain taxpayer-funded contributions (*more sustainable*)
	Unorganized	Maintain benefits, maintain taxpayer-funded contributions (*no change*)	Comparison group

Note: The bottom row of the table describes two scenarios in which the governing regime would be classified as a "disorganized state." The top-left cell, characterized by well-organized state workers and Republican rule, is classified under my schema as a "pluralist state." The top-right cell, characterized by well-organized workers and strong Democratic rule, is classified as a "coalitional state."

A ticking timebomb is lurking in the background, however. In the past decade, Republican governments have flirted with a second strategy in dealing with strong public sector workforces. This strategy involves destroying the pluralist system altogether, stripping public sector unions of their right to exist, and turning the system into one of disorganization. Although Republican state governments have had only mixed success with this (mixed) strategy, a point to which I return to in chapter 5, this existential threat is a possibility that public sector unions must keep in the back of their minds as they strategize and negotiate with different types of partisan regimes.

Democratic regimes can stave off the demands from strong public sector unions in ways that Republican governments cannot: strong Democratic governments do not need to compromise with unions because public sector unions are a component of the party. If, for example, a Democratic government wanted to decrease pension benefits and the union resisted, the union would have no recourse other than to try to get Republicans elected in the next election cycle. This move, of course, would come with its own risks, including not only potential increases in pension benefits at the expense of solvency but also a possible annihilation of the union itself through a ban on collective bargaining, prohibition of agency fees, or wholesale cuts to the public workforce. As a result, strong public sector unions and strong Democratic government tend to work as partners, forming and acting as a coalition rather than as pluralist cogs. Consequently, I refer to this regime as *coalitional*.

Much of this theoretical framework can be traced back to Clarence Stone, who argues that although pluralism applies within some governance contexts, it is often regime politics that can best explain political and policy outcomes.[39] Stone's research occurred primarily within a local, nonpartisan context, but other examples of the Coalitional Politics Hypothesis are at work within a varied body of literature. For example, evidence found in the public administration reform literature has suggested that political machines—an extreme version of strong party government—are more fiscally conservative than Progressive-era types of good governments that encourage the sophistication and growth of professional bureaucrats and the suppression of strong political parties. Ester Fuchs finds that the machine politics of Chicago during the twentieth century allowed the city to fiscally recover from economic crises in ways that the more reform-minded New York was unable to.[40] This failure to recover in New York was largely due to the necessity of assembling electorally fragile coalitions that could only be bolstered by increasing spending. Chicago politicians, in contrast, could rely entirely on the party to win elections. At the state level, David Primo and James Snyder find similar evidence that spending is lower when parties are strong, whereas Christopher Berry finds that strong state parties prevent municipalities from overfishing common-pool tax resources.[41] Although these studies emphasize either the strength of parties or the strength of interest groups, they do not explore their interaction. The Coalitional Politics Hypothesis states that *if* interest groups are strong, elected officials will display more fiscal restraint when the party that the group relies on is also strong. The party needs the interest group less for electoral and policy success and the interest group needs them more for rent-seeking activities.

The electoral politics of this logic is important. Though there is little evidence to suggest that voters pay close attention to public pension policymaking, and as such, they are likely to bear the diffuse costs of pension benefits that accrue to state workers, any underfunded pension policy will also shift public goods spending away from nonworkers or increase the state's debt load (which is likely to have contemporaneous consequences through credit ratings and bond markets, as discussed in chapter 6).[42] Both of these outcomes are the result of either zero-sum or negative-sum interactions among workers, nonworker voters, and future taxpayers, and they are inherently deleterious to the welfare of taxpayer-voters who are not employed by the state.[43] Furthermore, expansions in unfunded benefits are not a negligible part of the budget; average unfunded liabilities relative to total state expenditures grew from 105 percent in 1995 to 143 percent in 2011, a jump of 36 percent.[44] As such, simple retrospective voting as suggested by Morris Fiorina is adequate to motivate both unions and strong Democratic governments to restrain themselves from gutting state budgets in favor of unfunded pension expansions.[45] If Democratic fiscal performance is perceived as inadequate by voters, Democratic lawmakers can simply be replaced by Republicans. Neither the incumbent Democrats nor the unions that depend on their beneficence want to see this happen.

In sum, I argue against previous findings that partisan and interest group politics play little role in public sector pension policymaking. On the contrary, pension policy—much like budgetary policy—is politically fraught on all levels. Every state dollar spent on pensions is a dollar not spent on other public goods, either now or in the future. Whether Democratic state governments and unions collude to expand pension liabilities in an effort to placate constituencies and fulfill ideological commitments (in what Anzia and Moe call "polarization politics") or whether they recognize that they are both playing a repeated game of electoral politics in which forbearance has its virtues is investigated in the next chapter.[46]

Strong Unions and Strong Parties

Until now, the most important adjective used in the foregoing explanation—"strong"—has remained undefined. The strength of each actor is key to this story of unconditional versus conditional motivations and interest group versus coalitional politics. When both public sector workers are well organized into strong unions and Democratic partisans within the state government are also strong, the Coalitional Politics Hypothesis predicts that pension benefits will be reduced (or expanded less quickly) relative to scenarios in which either or both workers are poorly organized and Democrats are weak. (Recall that the Special Interest Group Politics Hypothesis predicts that Democratic strength will make no difference in pension benefit policy, but that union strength does.) As such, the way we conceive of public sector worker strength and of partisan strength is of the utmost importance.

The political strength and importance of public sector workers may vary in both qualitative and quantitative ways. First and foremost is the size of the state public labor force—both in absolute terms but, more important, in terms that are relative to the overall employed workforce. When workers are more numerous, they possess political strength primarily as a voting bloc. Once those numerous workers are well organized into unions, however, that strength is multiplied by their ability to mobilize said workers along with their family, friends, and associates. Unions also possess the power of the purse through political action committees (PACs), the socialization and persuasion of individual members to give to preferred candidates, and lobbying.[47] The legal environment within the state is also crucial when gauging the political strength of public sector workers and the strength of their formal and informal bargaining powers. The contours of collective bargaining laws, public worker strike laws, and right to work laws all greatly influence the manner in which unions and workers operate within the state's political realm. Patrick Flavin and Michael T. Hartney, for example, discuss how access to some of these key union privileges—particularly collective bargaining laws—politically empower the institutional features not only of unions but also of individual members.[48] They find that unionized teachers are more likely to try to influence others' voting behavior, work for a political campaign, publicly express their support for a candidate, donate money to a campaign, and attend a political rally—and that this likelihood increases about 50 percent when unionized teachers reside in states with mandatory collective bargaining laws. Although all types of workers—public and private—are more politically active if they belong to a union, this effect is an order of magnitude larger for public sector workers, particularly teachers. I return to this point, and the *extra-special* relationship between teachers and the Democratic Party, at the end of this chapter and in subsequent chapters of the book.

In sum, politically strong public sector workers means strong public sector unions, which means strength in numbers, strength in membership rates, financial largesse, and legal protections. Some state unions, in some years, have more strength in one of these dimensions than in others and at other points in time. This variation affords us the opportunity to observe the role that union—and public sector worker—strength plays in pension policy.

And what of parties? What makes a political party strong at a moment in time? First, the party must be in control of government to some degree or another. This may mean control of one or both houses of the state legislature, supermajority control of one or both houses of the state legislature, control of the governor's mansion, or all of the above. Fully unified state government with supermajorities in both houses is by far the most uncommon of these scenarios, but both politicos and scholars would roundly agree that is also the most preferred form of government for a given political party (and, conversely, the most detested for the party out of power). Within each of these categories, however, quantitative differences affect the sheer political strength of a governing party. Moving from majority to supermajority status is empowering, but so too are more marginal increases in legislative seats. The organizational sophistication of the state party is also exceedingly important in assessing the size of a party's political muscle and a topic on which David Mayhew wrote a magisterial encyclopedia.[49] He has argued that among the spectrum of political organization, classic political machines—which he refers to as Traditional Party Organizations (TPOs)—are the most powerful and successful in getting what they want and in staying in control of government. True political machines at the state level more or less ceased to exist after the middle of the twentieth century, but the culture and institutions of these organizations have lived on in many states.[50] Similarly, the lack of traditional organization in many places like California has resulted in persistent Progressive-era political institutions like nonpartisan elections, initiatives, and referenda and in the type of hyperpluralism in which interest groups act largely independently of political parties.

Finally, note what is *not* a good indicator of strong or weak political parties—that is, persistent control over time. Although low levels of competition for control of government may certainly be good for a party's ability to win elections, they are typically endemic to one-party states and, consequently, associated with a high degree of intraparty conflict.[51] When the external enemy is eliminated, internal enemies loom larger and natural factions arise. As such, a Democratic Party that faces no electoral threat from a Republican Party is more likely to be disorganized, factional, and personality driven (this is also true, naturally, if the names of the parties are reversed). Parties that are most likely to find themselves in a position of strength in regard to governing and policymaking but nevertheless deeply concerned with electoral prospects are those that win supermajorities in the legislature by narrow margins in many or all electoral districts. For this reason, typical measures of party competition do not quite capture the electoral environment and how it directly influences the governing one.[52]

The ideal way to empirically operationalize the strength of political parties—by recreating and updating Mayhew's detailed investigations—is, in many ways, beyond the scope of this work and the capacity of historical data. Other scholars, however, have adapted Mayhew's classification scheme for contemporary purposes, and I utilize their measures in many of my empirical analyses.[53] I also use other less-than-perfect measures, including whether a party has unified or divided control of the state government, whether it has split control of the legislature, the percentage of legislative seats a party holds, the degree of legislative turnover within the past half-century, how ideologically polarized the two major parties are from one another, and the degree of ideological dispersion within the party.

Who Pays?

Understanding the politics of public sector pension funding is tricky for many reasons, but perhaps none more so than the fact that overall funding policy is determined by not one but multiple policy decisions. These decisions can be sorted into two broad categories: those that influence the size of a pension's liabilities and those that influence the size of a pension's assets.

Pension liabilities are accumulated over time as employees work and (typically) contribute a portion of their salaries to the pension plan's funds. This functions differently from a public 403(b) or private 401(k) plan in which the employee's contributions are placed in an individual account that is earmarked specifically for the worker who has paid into it. In a public, defined benefit pension plan, the government promises to pay participating workers' pensions after retirement. The generation of state pension liabilities and their size are primarily influenced by policy decisions about the eligible retirement age, the pension benefit formula, cost-of-living adjustments (COLAs), and actuarial assumptions about things like life expectancy and salary growth. Decreasing the age at which workers can retire and qualify for pension benefits, increasing the generosity of the pension benefit formula and size of COLAs, and increasing expectations about life expectancy and salary growth will all increase the pension plan's overall liabilities.[54] Making subsequent changes to any of these policy levers in the opposite direction will lower pension liabilities. Nearly all of these decisions, with the exception of the actuarial assumptions, are determined at the statutory level through the state legislature.[55]

Although liability-side decisions are typically the most transparent and publicized (apart from the ways in which actuarial assumptions are determined), asset-side decisions are equally—if not more—politically fraught. State legislatures set policy that determines whether pensions will be funded now or in the future (or, more ominously, whether pensions will spin into default). This funding can come from employer (i.e., state agencies, school districts) contributions, employee contributions, or state general fund revenue.[56] Where the funding comes from—and whether it comes at all—is a political bargaining chip over which political parties and public sector workers can haggle. Workers would like to see their pensions be well funded by taxpayers, but they may very well be willing to sacrifice funding for larger pensions. Similarly, certain governing regimes may be willing to give workers larger pensions as long as their constituents do not have to pay for them.

Remember, however, two key facts about funding: First, most public sector workers and unions do not believe that the state can legally choose to *not* fund public pensions if the state's financial situation were to become truly dire. This is not without reason; recent high-profile bankruptcy court cases have confirmed that, although public sector workers may face some competition from general obligation bondholders for resources in the face of default, workers are entitled to legal privilege during fiscal emergencies.[57] This means that workers should expect to have their pensions protected even when faced with increasing plan insolvency and that plan insolvency is problematic only in the eyes of public sector workers to the extent that it is accompanied by general state insolvency.[58] As a result, it is plausible that public sector unions would be willing to trade contributions to the pension system for increases in—or at least maintenance of—pension benefits.

Second, the two major political parties do indeed have ideological differences over the solvency of pensions. Neither party, it must be mentioned, is the party of antideficits. Instead, Republicans have thrown their ideological weight behind the idea of "starve the beast" in which government can shrink simply by failing to fund it.[59] The liability side, in this ideological construct, is nearly beside the point because it is in fact a consequence of the asset side. The Democratic Party, in contrast, has a much greater ideological commitment to maintaining funding of its preferred social spending—including benefits for public sector workers—such that they are not bankrupted through ideological negligence. Democrats, consequently, are far more likely to shift general taxpayer revenue into the coffers of public pension systems. As a result, the party potentially faces the ire of voters who would prefer to see a more obvious return to their tax dollars. This issue of pension default was at the core of debates between party leaders about the value of extending the federal bankruptcy code to state governments during the COVID-19 fiscal and economic crisis. Republican leaders, exemplified by Senate Majority Leader Mitch McConnell (R-KY), pushed so hard to allow state governments to file for bankruptcy rather than have the federal government "bail them out" precisely so that state governments could abrogate pension contracts with public sector workers and essentially dissolve pension funds. Only the special legal status of federal bankruptcy protection could allow state governments to take such a drastic step; however, the political logic of Republicans that would underfund or defer payments to pension systems in return for increasing workers' benefits is clear—whether or not the state is experiencing acute fiscal crisis.[60] The converse of this logic—that Democrats are more likely to increase or maintain funding for pensions—follows naturally. This dynamic is reflected in both tables 1.1 and 1.2 and the data, as explored in subsequent chapters, bear out these differences in funding patterns across political party control.

Different Types of Workers and Natural Constituencies

A final addendum to the theoretical framework laid out in this chapter involves the natural heterogeneity of public sector workers. It is wrong to discuss public employees as monoliths, even those that are well organized into large, politically cohesive unions. The first difference that comes to mind is that of one between occupational classifications—the political distinctions between a public school teacher and a uniformed worker, such as a police or correctional officer, for instance. But differences across states— some with workers who are more sympathetic to the Democratic Party than in others—and within occupations (e.g., older teachers may be more entrenched within the union and its working relationship with Democrats than younger teachers) are also likely. Although we have no concrete data on how strong individual worker attachment is toward each party broken down by public sector occupation (i.e., police officers versus teachers), we do have data on the behavior of the unions that represent these workers. Popular perceptions would paint teachers' unions as overwhelmingly Democratic and police officers' unions as less so, but the data are less clear. Teacher organizations do donate more to Democratic candidates' campaigns but do also sometimes give to Republicans. Police unions, in contrast, also give more to Democrats than to Republicans, but they do so at rates that are less lopsided than those of teachers.[61] Of course, who these individuals vote for, or who they tell their friends to vote for, is beyond the scope of our current knowledge.[62]

Data limitations notwithstanding, the financial behavior of different unions should offer us some clues about the working relationship with the two parties. Teachers are clearly more entrenched within the Democratic Party apparatus—certainly financially, probably electorally, and almost definitely ideologically—and we should expect their relationship to more closely mimic one in line with the Coalitional Politics Hypothesis than police officers or general state employees. As the group of workers grows closer to the Democratic Party and becomes a more essential component of the party, we should find far more cooperation and avoidance of outcomes that could directly harm the party. As the group of workers drifts away from the party, we are likely to see more concessions that are not necessarily in the long-term interest of the party. This logic, in fact, can help explain why Democratic-run cities often make more political and financial concessions to police officers than to teachers. Think of the defund the police movement in the wake of the 2020 George Floyd protests: How many Democratic-run cities pulled significant funding? And yet how many of those same Democratic-run cities forced teachers to take buyouts and put educational staff on furlough in response to the COVID-19 fiscal crisis?

This dynamic extends beyond financial decisions as well. In 2021 in New York City, one of the most—if not *the* most—powerful public sector union towns in the country, Democratic Mayor Bill DeBlasio made a surprise announcement mandating vaccines for all municipal employees.[63] No labor leaders were consulted or warned of this mandate in advance. Even if workers were ideologically predisposed to favor such a mandate, unions were incensed that not only did no bargaining occur over this change in workplace condition but also that they were never even given the courtesy of a phone call alerting them of the new policy. They found out, like every other resident of New York City, by watching the mayor's press conference. The Correction Officers' Benevolent Association (COBA NYC)—by far the most hostile of all the public sector unions to the Democratic Party in New York—threatened to sue; the New York City Police Benevolent Association (NYC PBA)—the leaders of which are openly supportive of Republicans but who's rank and file are far more politically split than the COBA—kept their mouth shut; and the United Federation of Teachers (UFT) offered its reluctant support. To be sure, *none* of the unions were happy with the way the issue had been handled. But the clear heterogeneity in the pushback was very much related to the closeness of the workers to the Democratic Party. We should expect the same to be true of public sector pension policy and of any policy decision that is in tension with the preferences of workers and the broader public.

Public sector unions are interest groups—but they are not *just* interest groups. Joseph Schlesinger wrote that one of the most important pursuits of political party research is to understand and differentiate the goals of party activists from the goals of political parties and their candidates for office.[64] Party activists or "purists" are motivated by policy (and possibly ideology) and do not care which party is in office so long as they achieve their goals.[65] The establishment of the political party is home to the second kind of benefit seeker, however.[66] These benefit seekers are elected officials, party operatives, and those who are otherwise motivated primarily by career concerns and the nonideological (but perhaps distributive) rewards of controlling government. These "pragmatists" care far more about the label of the political party in power than the interest groups that seek to influence them. I argue that although archetypes of these classifications exist in the U.S. government—with a group such as the National Rifle Association as "purist" and party leadership as "pragmatic"—a considerable gray area exists in the benefit seeker spectrum. Public sector unions exist in this zone as a synthesis between purist interest groups and pragmatic party operatives in the sense that they have policy goals but are not prepared to pursue them at all costs.

The theoretical framework of this book highlights both the distinction between and the cooption of public sector unions by the Democratic Party. To be sure, I am not the first to point out Democratic pushback of union demands. The Democratic Party of the 1970s and 1980s, for example, was forced into an escalating series of confrontations with public sector unions over expanding influence and largesse.[67] This escalation is best exemplified by Democratic, default-era New York City forcing the teachers' union to use pension assets to purchase worthless municipal bonds.[68] More recently, Illinois governor and Democrat Pat Quinn attempted to rein in the galloping hole in pension funding by raising employee contribution rates. The unions, failing to see the potential consequences of their behavior, resisted and removed their support from Quinn. Quinn, in turn, proposed a hugely unpopular telecommunications tax to help fill the gap in funding. As a result, Quinn lost his reelection bid to Republican Bruce Rauner to much remorse and gnashing of teeth by the unions.[69]

Subsequent chapters systematically quantify and expand on these anecdotes and show that although the direct link between expansive pension policy, fiscal bailouts, and success at the polls is important to elected lawmakers, the secondary effects of these policy decisions—such as raising taxes on voters—loom especially large in the electoral arena.

CHAPTER II

The Size and Fiscal Sustainability of State Pensions

In the previous chapter, I provided the theoretical linkages between pensions, unions, and parties. In this chapter, I show, empirically, how the political process affects both the size of pension liabilities and the size of pension debt. Liabilities can be large or small relative to gross state product (GSP), on a per capita basis, or on a per employee basis relative to other plans or other years. Liabilities can also be large or small relative to the assets that the state has managed to sock away for the pension. When liabilities are large relative to assets, compared with other plans or other years, the pension is relatively poorly funded and is generating more debt than in other plan years.

The key consideration in this case is that the size of pensions and their fundedness are different concepts. Unions would like to have both large and well-funded pension benefits; they are unlikely to have this option, however. Large, well-funded benefits shift resources from other sectors of government and out of the hands of taxpayers *today*. Large, poorly funded benefits, however, do not require resources until *tomorrow*. Both unions and political parties can (and do) trade off of this potentially deferred cost to government.

In chapter 1, I presented two competing hypotheses about the relationships among pensions, unions, and parties:

Special interest group politics: No relationship exists between partisan control and pension benefits and a strong, positive relationship exists between unionization and benefits.

Coalitional politics: Pension benefit policies will be different during Democratic versus Republican control of government, but only when public sector unions are strong. Specifically, unions will extract greater pension concessions from Republican governments compared with when they are not unionized. They will also extract greater concessions compared with when Democrats control government. There are no partisan differences in policy when unions are weak.

The Special Interest Group Politics Hypothesis is cleaner, more intuitive, and more easily testable. But the reality may indeed be messier—as it often is—than we would like. Although popular accounts of the pension debate often assume the Special Interest Group Politics Hypothesis to be true, previous scholarly work has found considerable support for the Coalitional Politics Hypothesis, instead. Roderick Kiewiet, for instance, finds no effect whatsoever of unionization or ideology on pension funding—a fact that he finds downright puzzling, especially when compared with their effects on other types of worker compensation.[1] Daniel DiSalvo and Jeffrey Kucik, although not explicitly looking at pensions or pension debt, find that the size of other postemployment benefit (OPEB) liabilities for state workers is not a simple function of the governing political party but rather is a more complicated interaction between party and union strength in which Republicans increase the generosity of OPEBs as unions grow stronger.[2]

In this chapter, I provide evidence that fiscal sustainability at the state level is best achieved when policymaking is highly centralized, a finding that is in line with a long tradition of municipal finance literature.[3] Governments act more fiscally responsible when the policymaking environment is not fragmented by a bevy of pluralist interest groups and when electoral coalitions are stable. Although it is possible that strong, monopolistic government—as in the heyday of machine politics—will provide larger benefits to a narrower coalition, it does not do so recklessly and without regard for the long-term fiscal horizon. Strong coalitions want to hold onto the reins of power for as long as possible and will not provide unsustainable resources to their constituents if doing so threatens their control of government. I next investigate this dynamic within the context of public sector pensions.

Data

To test my two competing hypotheses, I need a way to operationalize the size of pension benefits, the funding status of pensions, the strength of public sector unions, and the strength of each state political party.

Reliable data measuring the size of pension liabilities—which is a shorthand way to think of the kind of benefits that the media usually talk about—are incredibly difficult to acquire for a variety of reasons. The first reason is somewhat prosaic: pension data are reported at the plan level and are not aggregated into any sort of repository. I was able to acquire financial documents for 130 distinct, state-financed pension plans only by visiting individual state department websites and—in the pursuit of more historical data—by calling and emailing individual pension offices and state agencies. Through my own data-collection efforts, I estimate I was able to collect at least one year's worth of data for 96 percent of state-administered pension plans in forty-nine states and across seventeen years.[4] (Seventeen years was about the upper limit of data that state offices had retained, and many documents that needed to be scanned and manually coded were becoming illegible beyond that point.)

The second, more challenging, reason for why reliable data are so hard to come by has to do with the fact that pension finances are not governed by federal law. No legal body audits state pensions, sets reporting standards, or mandates specific actuarial assumptions. Although the Governmental Accounting Standards Board (GASB) issued loose guidelines over the period of my study (1995 to 2011, and subsequently tightened their guidelines in 2012), these suggestions were just that—and were unenforceable in any real way. As a result, states set their own rules about how to report pension data, often changing them from year to year when it best suited them.[5] Thus, data are subject to what most scholars now believe is clear and obvious self-reporting bias.[6]

Collecting individual plan data by hand, however, allowed me to standardize a number of key assumptions—varying across both time and place—and recalculate the final liability number that was being reported by these pension plans and states. This standardization, following Robert Novy-Marx and Joshua Rauh's somewhat-controversial algorithm, allowed me to remove the politically motivated bias inherent in the act of self-reporting.[7] That said, although Novy-Marx and Rauh's calculations allowed me to tremendously improve the raw data, they do not represent an objective or true way to construct these liabilities. The liabilities could be calculated in many other ways, and many different assumptions could be made. The value of Novy-Marx and Rauh is that the data and calculations involved are (comparably) less demanding than other methods used to construct the liabilities and—most important for the purposes of my research questions—the data can be compared across plans, states, and years. I provide more details of the calculations in the Methodological Appendix.

After I calculated the standardized size of the liabilities, it was considerably easier to calculate the funding ratio of the pensions. As a reminder, the funding ratio (just one of many ways to calculate how well funded a pension plan is) shows how many dollars a pension has relative to the dollars that the pension will have to pay plan members' benefits over a thirty-year period, or actuarially valued assets divided by actuarially accrued liabilities. Calculating the size of pension liabilities give us the denominator in the funding ratio (i.e., the actuarially accrued liabilities), which means that all we need to do is standardize the calculation of actuarially valued assets. This calculation is much more straightforward and requires that only two assumptions be standardized: the expected rate of return on assets over the next thirty years and how long is reasonable to smooth losses and gains. Most pension plans assumed a rate of return of 7.5 percent over this period, although some assumed rates as low as 5 percent and others as high as 9 percent. Assuming a uniform rate of return—which is reasonable, given that these pensions have access to an identical set of investment opportunities—and a uniform period of smoothing (most plans assumed five years) further helps to remove any self-reporting bias inherent in the unstandardized calculations. Alternative ways to operationalize the fundedness or solvency of a pension plan include taking unfunded liabilities (i.e., liabilities minus assets) and dividing that number by plan assets (i.e., how many assets as a percentage of existing assets does the plan need to cover all liabilities?), calculating unfunded liabilities per plan member or per state resident, and calculating unfunded liabilities as a percentage of state expenditures or revenue. Additionally, for much of the analysis that follows, these numbers are aggregated from the plan level up to the state level. But having the calculations available at the plan level allows for some degree of heterogeneity analysis.

Getting an accurate sense of what is moving the fundedness of a given pension plan, however, is more complex than first glance might suggest. As the previous discussion indicates, funding status is a function of two separate variables: assets and liabilities. The funding ratio and financial sustainability of the plan may decrease if assets decrease (e.g., because of a temporary financial market event) or if liabilities increase (e.g., because of an expansion in pension benefits). The ratio may also not change if assets are decreasing at the same rate that liabilities are decreasing or vice versa. This is quite complicated, especially because much of the movement in these numbers may be temporary and a result of forces outside of political control (most notably, the stock market or economic environment). Given this wrinkle, I also collected data on exactly what state legislatures and unions were *doing* during this time period in relation to pension sustainability: passing or not passing statutory changes to benefits, employee contribution rates, employer contribution rates, and cost of living adjustments (COLAs).[8] I collected these data from the National Conference of State Legislatures, which provided extensive summaries of all passed state legislation relating to pension reform for the years 1999 to 2011. Data were hardcoded as $\{-1, 1\}$ to reflect whether or not a state had passed legislation that would result in a contraction or expansion of liabilities and were hardcoded as 0 if they passed no legislation in the individual policy arena. Figure 2.1 summarizes trends in average legislative policy over time.

Because I am interested in operationalizing the change in the pension's financial sustainability, I am ultimately interested in the *net* expansion or contraction of liabilities. If a state passes legislation that raises the benefit replacement rate, for example, but also passes legislation increasing employee contribution rates that offset the replacement rate increase, the state would not, on net, be liable for any increase in pension obligations. If state workers pay for their pensions solely through their contributions and the interest earned on already existing assets, the government should have no qualms about increasing the generosity of replacement rates or COLAs. It is only when workers receive expanded benefits that do not "pay for themselves" that voters should sit up and take notice, intervening if they deem necessary. If these sort of unfunded benefit enhancements occur with adequate regularity, the pension will be forced to make a choice: undergo a potentially painful adjustment to the liability or to the asset side of the ledger. Either the workers or the taxpayers will have to pay; remember that, like in local politics, there are no free lunches in state politics.

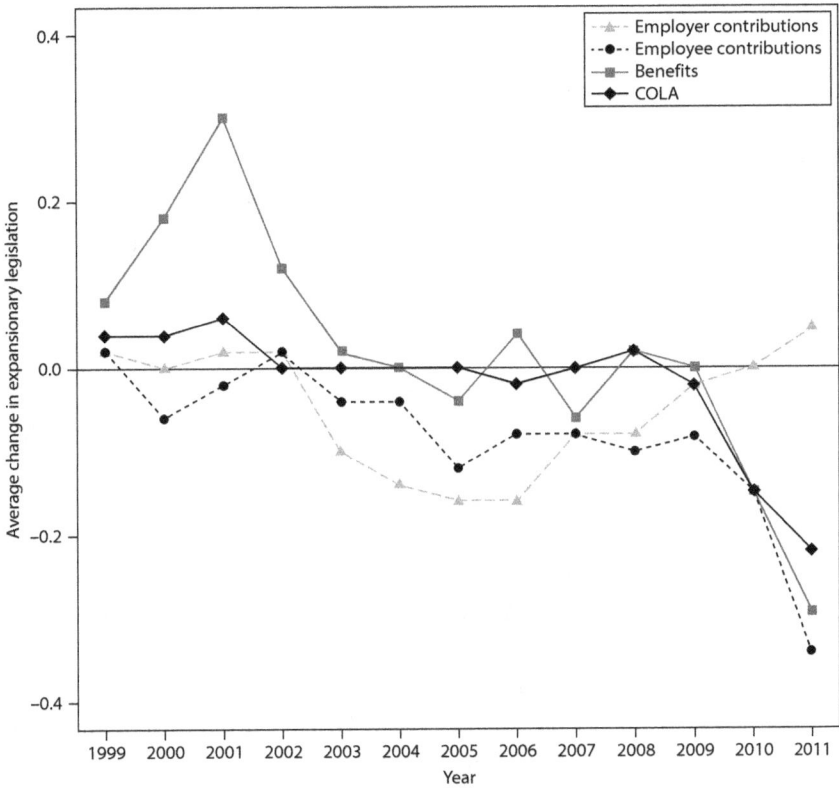

Figure 2.1 Average pension reform involving benefit changes across states, by year. Increases (decreases) on the graph correspond to increases (decreases) in benefit allowances, increases (decreases) in COLAs, and decreases (increases) in contribution rates, all of which are expected to expand (contract) liabilities and worsen (improve) the pensions' fiscal positions.

Source: National Conference of State Legislatures (1999–2011, 2011).

I presume that benefits that are expanded with a payment plan in mind—even if symbolic—will face far less scrutiny from voters. Expanding benefits at the same time as increasing employee contributions is less likely to have an impact on the possibility of fiscal crisis. Thus, expanding benefits are less likely to increase the likelihood that voters will face an increased tax bill (or service cuts) at some point in the future or default of the pension fund. This operationalization of pension sustainability, then, is constructed as the count of passed legislation that increases (or decreases) pension benefit generosity less the count of passed legislation that increases (or decreases) employee or employer contribution rates.[9] In the data, this variable takes on the value $\{-4, -3, -2, -1, 0, 1, 2, 3\}$. A negative realization of the variable lowers default risk but corresponds to a decrease in state worker utility. A positive value is a net benefit for employees but increases default risk.

Measuring the independent or predictor variables for the analysis is similarly no easy task. Most research on public sector unions measures the strength of those unions based solely on their unionization rate calculated from figures provided by Barry Hirsch and David MacPherson.[10] I believe that financial strength, proxied by the size of political campaign contributions, is also an important indicator of the power unions exert over state politics.[11] I combine these two measures—the percent of the public workforce that belongs to a union and how much public sector unions contribute to state elections—into a single index that is then normalized across space and time.[12] I also include data on how strong workforce protections are in the state, including whether the state has a duty to collectively bargain with unions, whether the state is a right to work state, and whether public sector unions are legally allowed to strike.

Finally, I operationalize the strength of state political parties in a variety of ways. The first—and perhaps most straightforward—method of doing this is by looking at the percentage of state legislative seats a political party holds in a given year. This is the measure that Olle Folke, Shigeo Hirano, and James Snyder use in their study of patronage and electoral outcomes and the measure that DiSalvo and Kucik use in their study of OPEB liabilities.[13] This operationalization makes intuitive sense: The more seats a state party holds in the legislature, the less likely they are to lose majority control and, consequently, statutory power. Of course, we would also like to know something about the degree of ideological and voting homogeneity within the state legislative party, a measure that is provided by Boris Shor and Nolan McCarty in their study of state-level polarization.[14] They find that the more homogeneous a party is, the more it can impose the party's median preference over the entire legislature.

Other studies of partisan legislative behavior have used dummy variables to indicate whether a legislative chamber is controlled by a given party, whether the chambers are controlled by different parties (split government), or whether the legislature and the governor's office are controlled by different parties (divided government). I present the results of this operationalization in addition to the one discussed previously but note that providing a binary indicator of whether the chamber is controlled by Democrats elides much of the details about how strong that control is. I also use David Mayhew's measure of state party organization and Terry Clark and Vincent Hoffmann-Martinot's updated version of this measure as a robustness check on the main analysis.[15] I elaborate on the details of these variables and analysis in the next section.

Analysis

The Size of Pension Liabilities

I now turn to analyzing the data and testing my two hypotheses, beginning with an analysis of the first dependent variable—that is, the size of pension liabilities. The size of liabilities—standardized as either a percentage of GSP or on a per capita basis—can also be thought of as a "cost" to government, as in Sarah Anzia and Terry Moe's framework.[16] In that work, Anzia and Moe investigate the extent to which unionization drives up wages, employment, and fringe benefits.[17] They rightly point out the comparable opacity (and, consequently, political advantage) of increasing things like health care benefits and pensions. Like them, I use a linear model to gauge the impact of union strength on the relevant policy outcome—in this case, the size of pension liabilities. Unlike them, however, I look at *changes* in the size of liabilities rather than their absolute size (more on this below). I also interact union strength with legislative party strength to better understand whether unionization alone can explain larger pension benefits or whether party and unionization work in complicated and interrelated ways to determine worker benefits. Finally, I include a host of socioeconomic control variables in the regression to consider changes not accounted for by taking first differences of the independent and dependent variables.

Because my data come from an unbalanced panel in which historical data collection yielded plan documents in some years but not in others and because a number of gradual reforms and policy changes (most notably the slow move toward defined contribution plans and away from traditional defined benefit pension systems) makes determining actual coverage difficult, it makes the most sense for identification purposes to analyze changes in the size of pension liabilities within a plan rather than the absolute size of liabilities. Because of data collection issues, it is also possible that my unbalanced panel creates a situation in which I have plan documents for three pension systems within a given state and year but documents for only two systems in that state the previous year.[18] This specification is a blessing in disguise, however. The ability to analyze changes in liabilities allows us to better understand how these *changes* in unionization and partisan control actually affect outcomes instead of simply relating cross-sectional snapshots to each other. In the latter case, most of the effects of politics have already been baked into the sheer size of pension benefits.[19]

To appropriately assess the impact of both union activity and partisan strength on pension liabilities—and to eventually test my original hypotheses—it is important to interact these two variables with each other rather than include them additively in my empirical model. Focusing on the interaction between parties and public sector unions is one of the greatest contributions of this research and is one that has previously been sidelined empirically. This condition on the model, however, makes interpreting regression coefficients and tables difficult. To understand the true impact of union strength on pension liabilities, for instance, we need to add multiple coefficients together and determine where and when the sum of these coefficients are statistically significant and where and when they are not. For this reason, graphs are much more helpful in interpreting interactive regressions than tables, which is why I show the results rather than simply list them. The results I present are first difference models with the main predictors being an interaction between the lagged change in the share of Democratic legislative seats and the lagged union strength index. I control for a double lag of the change variable, a lag of the dependent variable (change in per capita liabilities), the lagged party of the governor, and lagged versions of the following: total taxes per capita, logged general expenditures, the percent of all workers employed by the state, the pension's funding ratio, logged population, per capita personal income, logged nominal GSP, and the state unemployment rate. Other than the main predictor variables, unemployment is the largest and most regularly significant predictor of a (negative) change in per capita pension liabilities. For example, a 1 percentage point increase in unemployment tends to decrease per capita liabilities on average around $125, depending on the model.

Figure 2.2 depicts the marginal effect of a 1 percentage point increase in the percent of state legislative seats held by the Democratic Party and

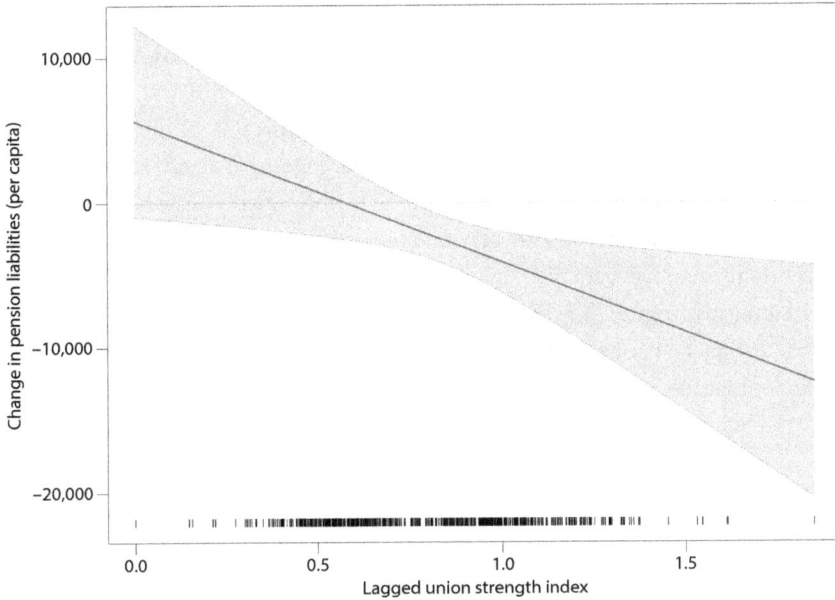

Figure 2.2 The marginal effect of a change in Democratic seats on per capita pension liabilities. Effects plotted using data from the second column of table 2.3.

Source: Klarner (2013b, 2013c); U.S. Census Bureau and Bureau of Labor Statistics, Current Population Survey (1995–2012); Hirsch and Macpherson (2023); Author's dataset; U.S. Bureau of Labor Statistics (1995–2012); U.S Bureau of Economic Analysis (1995–2012); U.S. Census Bureau, Census of Governments (1995–2012); Hou and Smith (2006); Valletta and Freeman (1988); Shor and McCarty (2011).

illustrates how that effect varies as state union strength varies. A positive change in Democratic seat shares is associated with a decrease in the pension plan's per capita liabilities when union strength is near its average or higher (the median of the index across state-years is 0.8). When union strength is below average, I do not find a detectable statistically significant effect of changes to the partisan composition of the legislature. The point estimate is positive, however, implying an *increase* in per capita liabilities, when unions are adequately weak. This, then, is clear: As legislatures become more Democratic, the absolute size of the burden of pensions on state residents *decreases* as long as public sector unions are a relevant and important power player.[20] Legislatures need to get buy-in from unions to engage in these cuts to per capita liabilities, and only strong Democratic state parties have the leverage to put down their foot. To be fair, the average year-over-year change in Democratic seat shares in the data is only 0.6 percent. This translates to a measly $20 cut in per capita liabilities when union strength is at its average.[21] For an average state with a population of six million people, however, this is not an insignificant amount of money—about $120 million or 6.5 percent of a given year's general fund expenditures. Additionally, this cut in liabilities is for each individual pension plan. In my dataset, states can have up to ten distinct pension plan systems that issue individual financial data.[22]

In contrast, figure 2.3 shows that a change in union strength is not as impactful as a change in partisan legislative seat shares (figure 2.2). If the state legislature is more or less split, increasing union strength does give

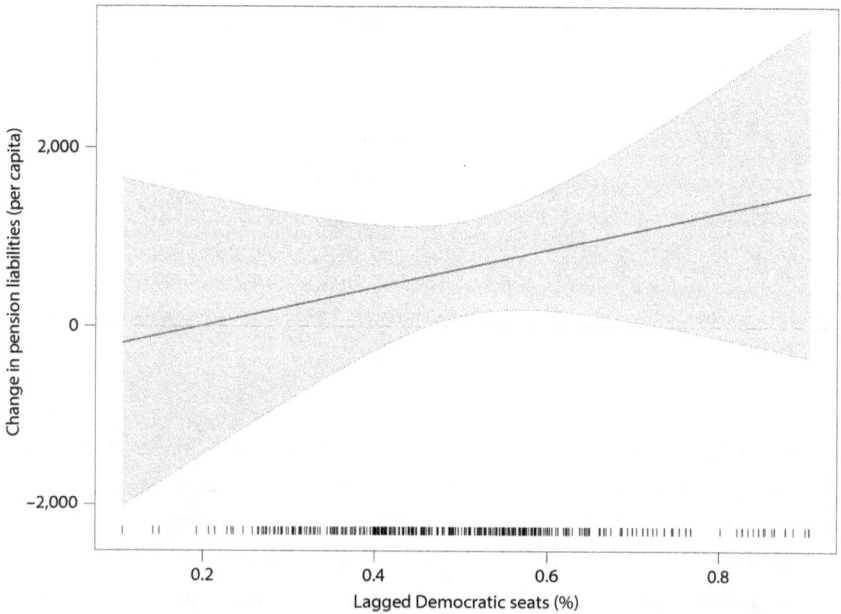

Figure 2.3 The marginal effect of a change in union strength on per capita pension liabilities. Effects plotted using data from the second column of table 2.3.

Source: Klarner (2013b, 2013c); U.S. Census Bureau and Bureau of Labor Statistics, Current Population Survey (1995–2012); Hirsch and Macpherson (2023); Author's dataset; U.S. Bureau of Labor Statistics (1995–2012); U.S. Bureau of Economic Analysis (1995–2012); U.S. Census Bureau (1995–2012); U.S. Census Bureau, Census of Governments (1995–2012); Hou and Smith (2006); Valletta and Freeman (1988); Shor and McCarty (2011).

pensions a bit of a boost: per capita liabilities go up about $5 with a split legislature and an average increase in union strength (0.0084 improvement in the index). But this relationship breaks down on either side of partisan legislative control—that is, changes in the strength of the state's public sector unions has no effect on liabilities when either party is in firm control of the legislature. Intuitively, this makes sense. It is easy for a legislature to switch gears after an election swings control towards one party or the other. Conversely, changes in public labors' organizational capacity, financial resources, and human capital take time to feel and be felt.

Every state-run pension system is one of a kind. Some states have one plan that covers every nonfederal public employee in the state; others have plans just for judges, teachers, and uniformed workers.[23] Figure 2.4 analyzes this relationship between liabilities and the interaction of unionization and partisanship, but it breaks the data into different pension plan types: it includes date for pension plans that cover general state employees or a mix of general, teacher, judge, and uniformed worker (panel A); the other panels depict (B through D) this relationship for teacher-only plans, judge-only plans, and uniformed worker-only plans. Although liabilities for pension plans that cover general state employees or a mix of the public workforce do react to an increase in Democratic legislators, judge-only and uniformed worker-only plans exhibit virtually no relationship between liabilities and politics. The teacher-only plans are truly driving this relationship. This makes sense from a conventional wisdom standpoint. Although my measure of union strength is a statewide index, popular accounts of public sector unions acknowledge that public sector workers are not a monolith.[24] Uniformed workers are believed to be more ideologically conservative and less supportive of Democrats relative to teachers. This popular account does somewhat stand up in the data—uniformed workers unions tend to split their campaign donations across state party lines, whereas teachers unions give overwhelmingly to only Democrats—but we also know that Republicans tend to treat uniformed workers very differently from, say, teachers.[25] In 2011, Governor Scott Walker of Wisconsin, for example, successfully stripped all state workers of the right to collectively bargain *except* for state troopers, local firefighters, and local police.[26] As such, it is not terribly surprising to find that teachers unions and state Democrats are more likely to agree to coalitional policy changes than police unions and state Democrats.

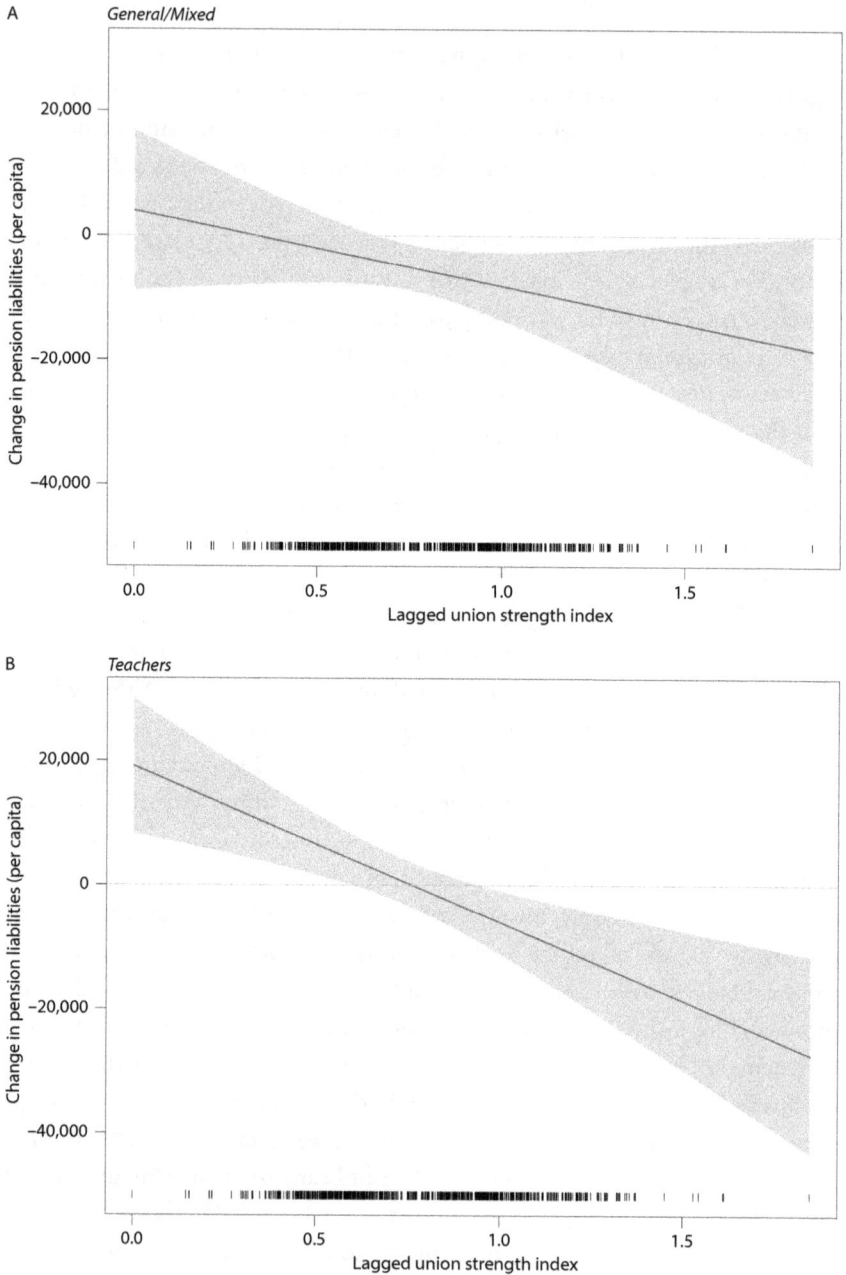

Figure 2.4 The marginal effect of a change in Democratic seats on per capita pension liabilities across different occupational plans (four panels). The full model estimates are reported in the Methodological Appendix. Panel (*a*) depicts the marginal effect of a change in Democratic legislative seats for general or mixed employee plans; panel (*b*) depicts the marginal effect for teacher plans; panel (*c*) depicts the marginal effect for uniformed employee plans (e.g., police officers, fire protection); and panel (*d*) depicts the marginal effect for plans that cover judges.

C   *Uniformed workers*

(chart: y-axis "Change in pension liabilities (per capita)" with values 20,000, 0, −20,000, −40,000; x-axis "Lagged union strength index" with values 0.0, 0.5, 1.0, 1.5)

D   *Judges*

(chart: y-axis "Change in pension liabilities (per capita)" with values 20,000, 0, −20,000, −40,000; x-axis "Lagged union strength index" with values 0.0, 0.5, 1.0, 1.5)

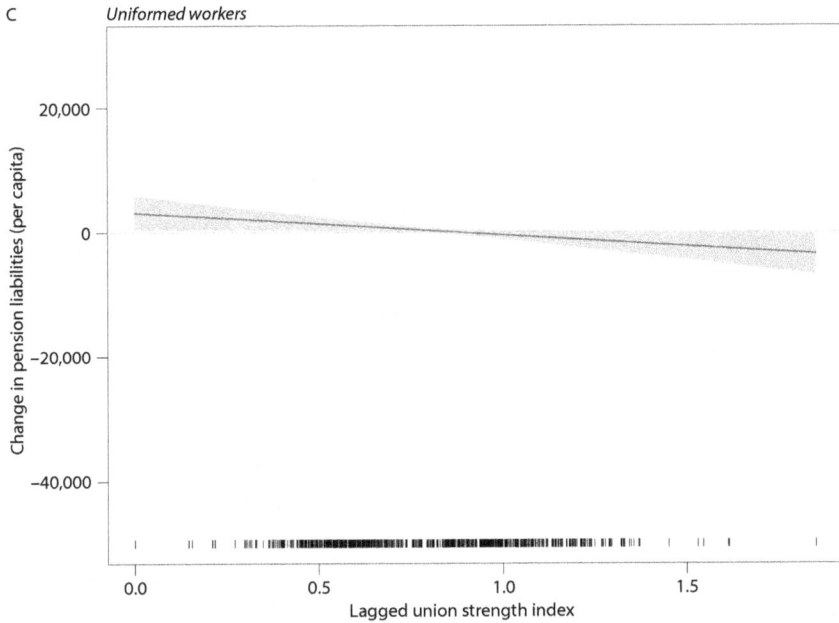

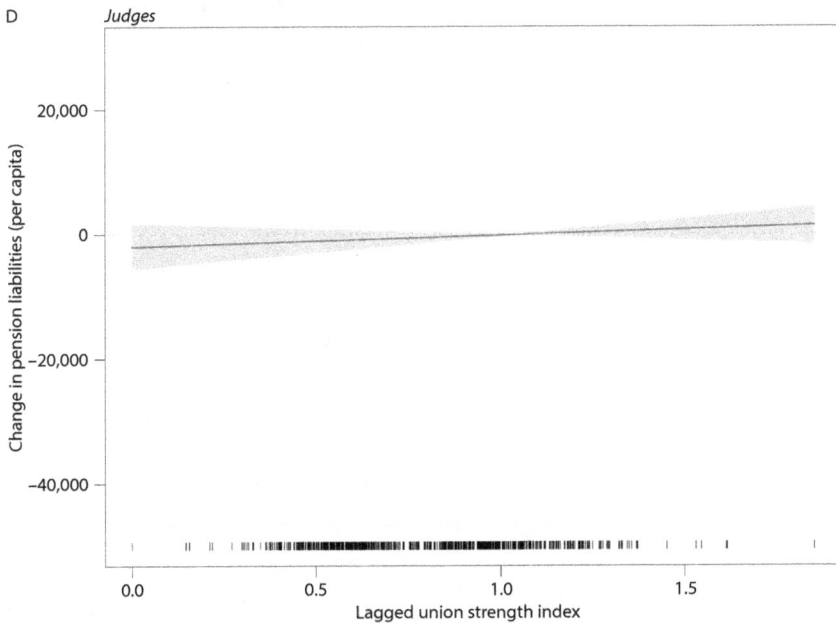

Figure 2.4 (continued)

Source: Klarner (2013b, 2013c); U.S. Census Bureau and Bureau of Labor Statistics, Current Population Survey (1995–2012); Hirsch and Macpherson (2023); Author's dataset; U.S. Bureau of Labor Statistics (1995–2012); U.S. Bureau of Economic Analysis (1995–2012); U.S. Census Bureau (1995–2012); U.S. Census Bureau, Census of Governments (1995–2012); Hou and Smith (2006); Valletta and Freeman (1988); Shor and McCarty (2011).

I next analyzed the data that speak directly to questions of fiscal solvency and financial sustainability. When do pensions generate debt? Why do they generate debt? The answers, as the data show, involve political expediency, fragmented decision-making, and an alignment (or disalignment) of relevant time horizons for various political groups.

To understand the dynamics of pension funding decisions, I first turn to the actual legislative outputs: what I call *net pension legislation*. The main dependent variable is an indicator of the *net* expansion or contraction in liabilities. In the data, this variable can take on any discrete value between −4 and 3. Again, a negative realization of the variable corresponds to a decrease in state worker utility as either their benefits are decreasing or their contributions are increasing. In contrast, a negative value also decreases financial risk to the plan and to the state. A positive value is a net benefit for employees but increases financial risk.

Although the dependent variable takes on discrete values only, the use of a nonlinear statistical model (such as an ordered probit) would present an inferential challenge because of the panel nature of the data.[27] As a result, I use a linear probability model for the following analysis. As a robustness check, I contrast my main findings with results from an ordered probit and a rare events logit model, the results of which are largely in line with my main findings and are contained in the Methodological Appendix.

Table 2.1 presents estimates from four regressions analyzing the effect of the key predictor variables on the likelihood of passing expansionary pension legislation. The first model pools all observations together into an ordinary least squares regression that controls for previous expansions in pension benefits (*Lagged Pension Policy*), the financial health of the pension in the previous year (*Lagged Funding Ratio*), an index of labor friendliness (*Bargaining Index*), and the percentage of full-time workers who are employed by the state (*State Worker Concentration*). The second model controls for state and year fixed effects. Both models include a host of economic control variables, as in the previous analyses. The coefficient on *Union Strength* is statistically significant and greater than zero in both of my models. The combination of this coefficient with the coefficients from either interaction, however, is never greater than zero as the coefficient on *Union Strength × Avg. Dems* is large and negative in both models, even after the inclusion of state and year

TABLE 2.1

Linear probability model of net expansionary pension legislation

	(1)	(2)
Avg. dems.	0.71	1.92
	(0.65)	(1.20)
Union strength	0.92★★	1.45★
	(0.46)	(0.75)
Democratic governor	−0.12	−0.24
	(0.14)	(0.18)
Bargaining index	−0.00	
	(0.01)	
State worker concentration	1.39	0.32
	(1.11)	(3.99)
Avg. dems. × union strength	−1.68★	−3.01★★
	(0.88)	(1.31)
Dem. gov. × union strength	0.06	0.16
	(0.19)	(0.20)
Lagged pension policy	−0.08	−0.09
	(0.07)	(0.07)
Lagged funding ratio	0.05	−0.08
	(0.26)	(0.28)
No. obs.	545	545
State fixed effects		✓
Year fixed effects		✓
Economic controls	✓	✓

Source: National Conference of State Legislatures (1999–2011); Klarner (2013b, 2013c); U.S. Census Bureau and Bureau of Labor Statistics, Current Population Survey (1995–2012); Hirsch and Macpherson (2023); Author's dataset; U.S. Bureau of Labor Statistics (1995–2012); U.S Bureau of Economic Analysis (1995–2012); U.S. Census Bureau, Census of Governments (1995–2012); Hou and Smith (2006); Valletta and Freeman (1988); Shor and McCarty (2011).

Note: Control variables and intercept not reported for purposes of brevity. Robust standard errors clustered by state reported in parentheses. Economic controls and data sources are described in the text and Methodological Appendix. ***$p < 0.01$, **$p < 0.05$, *$p < 0.1$.

fixed effects. Although *Union Strength* × *Dem. Gov.* is not statistically significant, this is not surprising considering that pension legislation falls within the purview of the state legislature. These results fail to provide evidence in favor of the Special Interest Group Politics Hypothesis.[28] On the contrary, these findings suggest that the Coalitional Politics Hypothesis is a more accurate description of reality.

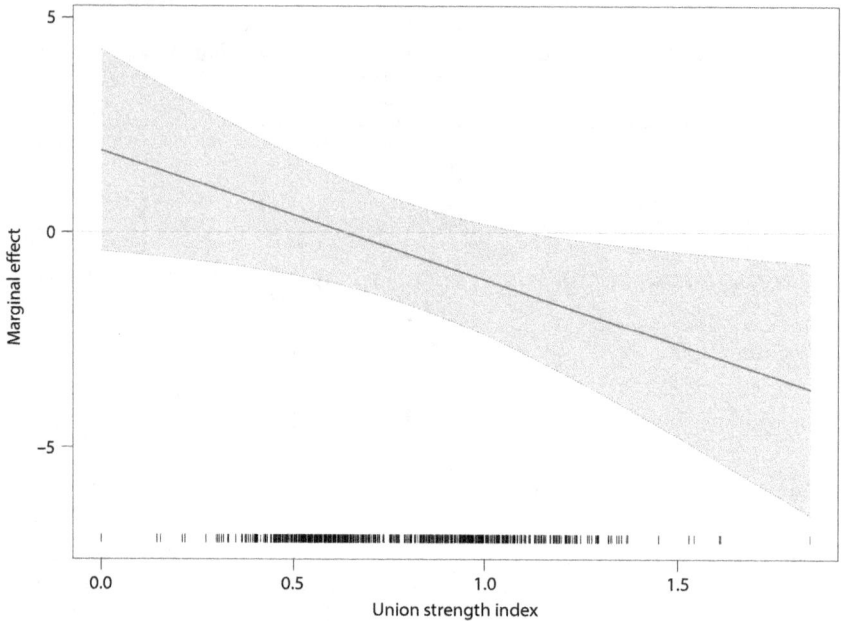

Figure 2.5 The marginal effect of a change in Democratic seats on pension legislation. Effects plotted from model 2 of table 2.1.

Source: National Conference of State Legislatures (1999–2011, 2011); Klarner (2013b, 2013c); U.S. Census Bureau and Bureau of Labor Statistics, Current Population Survey (1995–2012); Hirsch and Macpherson (2023); Author's dataset; U.S. Bureau of Labor Statistics (1995–2012); U.S. Bureau of Economic Analysis (1995–2012); U.S. Census Bureau, Census of Governments (1995–2012); Hou and Smith (2006); Valletta and Freeman (1988); Shor and McCarty (2011).

The results in table 2.1 show that pension policy generosity is tempered by the combination of Democratic legislators and strong unions. Changes in the likelihood of policy change are related to changes in the percent of Democrats in the legislature, but only when unions are strong. Consider figure 2.5. When my index of union strength in a state-year is less than 1.11, or at about the halfway mark, changes to the partisan composition of the legislature have no marginal effect on the likelihood of passing expansionary or contractionary pension legislation. When the union strength index is greater than 1.11, however, partisans have a strong impact on policy. As more Democrats populate the legislature under regimes of high unionization rates and union campaign activity, the more likely it is that the government will

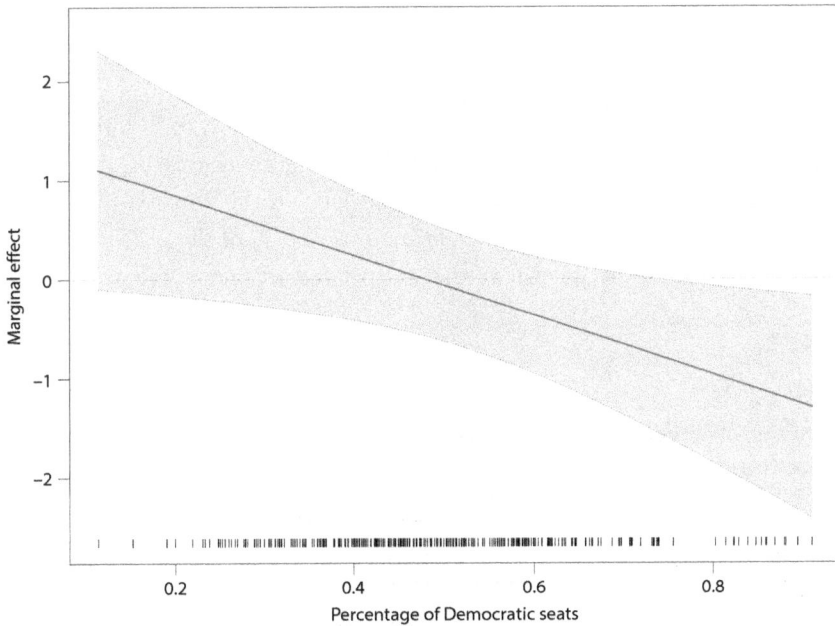

Figure 2.6 Marginal effect of a change in union strength on pension legislation. Effects plotted from model 2 of table 2.1.

Source: National Conference of State Legislatures (1999–2011, 2011); Klarner (2013b, 2013c); U.S. Census Bureau and Bureau of Labor Statistics, Current Population Survey (1995–2012); Hirsch and Macpherson (2023); Author's dataset; U.S. Bureau of Labor Statistics (1995–2012); U.S. Bureau of Economic Analysis (1995–2012); U.S. Census Bureau, Census of Governments (1995–2012); Hou and Smith (2006); Valletta and Freeman (1988); Shor and McCarty (2011).

pass contractionary pension policy, and the less likely it is that the government will pass expansionary policy.

Figure 2.6 paints a similar picture. Increasing the strength of public sector unions decreases the likelihood of expansionary pension policy when at least 71 percent of the state legislature is populated by Democrats. Additionally, although not statistically significant, a marginal increase in the strength of the union *increases* the likelihood of passing legislation that would expand the unfunded liabilities of the state pension system when at least 52 percent of the state legislature is controlled by Republicans. Well-organized workers, finding themselves in a fragmented political environment with no insider advantage, must wield their political power as interest groups—rather than doing so through and within a party apparatus—when Republicans rule the roost.

Table 2.2 looks at alternative measures of party strength and competition. Model 1 uses Mayhew's classification of party organizations in the fifty states, where a higher value of the index is indicative of a stronger state party.[29] Mayhew considers states that fall into his top-two classifications as having traditional party organizations (TPO) of the classic political machine flavor. Although these classifications were generated using data

TABLE 2.2

Linear probability model of net expansionary pension legislation with party organization measures

	Traditional party organization	Strong party organization
Avg. dems.	0.70	1.38
	(1.73)	(1.82)
Union strength	−0.42	0.46
	(1.05)	(1.41)
Avg. dems. × union strength	−0.19	1.06
	(2.05)	(2.16)
Party strength × union strength	4.78**	0.07
	(2.38)	(0.06)
Avg. dems. × party strength	6.09	0.15
	(3.71)	(0.10)
Avg. dems. × party strength × union strength	−10.05**	−0.20**
	(4.75)	(0.10)
No. obs.	545	451
State fixed effects	✓	✓
Year fixed effects	✓	✓
Economic controls	✓	✓

Source: National Conference of State Legislatures (1999–2011, 2011); Klarner (2013b, 2013c); U.S. Census Bureau and Bureau of Labor Statistics, Current Population Survey (1995–2012); Hirsch and Macpherson (2023); Author's dataset, U.S. Bureau of Labor Statistics (1995–2012); U.S. Bureau of Economic Analysis (1995–2012); U.S. Census Bureau, Census of Governments (1995–2012); Hou and Smith (2006); Valletta and Freeman (1988); Shor and McCarty (2011); Mayhew (1986); Clark and Hoffmann-Martinot (1998).

Note: Control variables and intercept not reported for purposes of brevity. Robust standard errors clustered by state reported in parentheses. *TPO* takes on a value of 1 if a state has a traditional party organization and 0 otherwise, while *SPO* is a continuous variable that increases as the state's political party organization becomes stronger. Data sources are described in the text and Methodological Appendix. ***$p < 0.01$, **$p < 0.05$, *$p < 0.1$.

from the 1960s and have not been updated since, they do remain the standard in analyzing state party structure and have been utilized in a variety of contemporary scholarly work.[30] As such, I created a dummy indicator for states that are considered to have (or have had) TPOs and interacted it with the other variables of interest. I assume that TPO states will see larger swings in legislative output as union strength and Democratic control waxes and wanes. The results of the fixed effects regression are as expected. Strong unions in TPO states are successful in getting expansionary legislation passed when Republicans control the legislature but push for less legislation once Democrats take over. For instance, in 2011, in New York, a TPO state, would have been likely to pass about one contractionary piece of legislation (point estimate of −1.26, with 95 percent confidence of being between −2.04 and −0.48) if Democrats had controlled 75 percent of legislative seats and unions had been about as strong as the upper percentile of unions in my sample.[31]

The second model of table 2.2 uses an alternative measure of state party strength, strong party organization (SPO), borrowed from Clark and Hoffmann-Martinot and aggregated by Berry.[32] Although Clark and Hoffmann-Martinot's measure also has a number of drawbacks, including the omission of observations for a number of states, the results are largely in line with the TPO model and provide additional evidence for the importance of party organization in exercising fiscal restraint.

The analysis of changes in my revised pension obligation data in table 2.3 compares the relationship between Democrat-union regimes and unfunded liabilities (column 1) to one focused on the sheer size of pension liabilities (column 2). The coefficients are remarkably similar in size and statistical significance, suggesting that coalitional politics matters more in determining liability size than it does in determining asset size (column 3). The coefficients that are statistically significant in both column 1 and 2 appear to play no role in column 3, which suggests that the growth or the shrinkage in pension assets follows a remarkably different process than that of liabilities. Asset growth appears to be apolitical in many ways and, in fact, previous work has found very little variation in asset growth across states in a given year.[33] In contrast, an increase in the number of Democrats in the state legislature is associated with a considerable decrease in both unfunded and total obligations. In the case of unfunded liabilities (column 1), a 1 percentage point increase in the number of Democrats in the state legislature decreases per capita unfunded liabilities by $171.04 if union strength is held

TABLE 2.3

Linear regression on change in pension obligations and assets

	Unfunded liabilities (U.S. dollars, per capita)	Liabilities (U.S. dollars, per capita)	Assets (U.S dollars, pe capita)
Intercept	4403.42* (2459.45)	5798.67* (3398.65)	1619.15 (1054.14)
Change in avg. dems.	−3567.13*** (661.51)	−3578.34*** (692.17)	−94.91 (73.55)
Change in union strength	−535.32** (235.75)	−613.00** (218.66)	−11.44 (23.63)
Chg. − avg. dems. × union strength	−13536.50** (6001.41)	−10532.49** (5248.92)	−847.81 (674.87)
Dem. governor	98.14 (135.73)	104.30 (131.06)	12.01 (19.52)
Lagged avg. dems.	900.87 (724.40)	261.71 (1036.79)	−271.09 (325.27)
Lagged union strength	221.50 (525.90)	−102.29 (696.63)	−93.10 (194.74)
Lagged dem. governor	−55.41 (124.39)	−62.13 (123.06)	−9.33 (19.51)
Lagged − avg. dems. × union strength	−978.22 (1011.85)	−398.71 (1311.90)	205.33 (380.85)
Lagged funding ratio	385.00*** (123.93)	409.77*** (140.64)	41.39 (31.35)
State worker rate	1653.20 (2350.25)	795.61 (2954.13)	−1169.48 (877.64)
Total taxes, per capita	0.15*** (0.05)	0.13** (0.06)	−0.01 (0.01)
General expenditures, per capita	0.04 (0.03)	0.01 (0.04)	0.04** (0.02)
Logged population	620.56** (274.64)	712.38* (372.24)	122.51 (108.52)
Personal income, per capita	0.03*** (0.01)	0.03*** (0.01)	−0.00 (0.00)
Logged nominal GSP	−576.39** (261.87)	−667.91* (353.49)	−126.17 (103.52)
Unemployment	−133.89*** 14.48	−129.67*** (17.17)	−16.78*** (5.00)
No. obs.	1,506	1,516	1,506

Source: Klarner (2013b, 2013c); U.S. Census Bureau and Bureau of Labor Statistics, Current Population Survey (1995–2012); Hirsch ar Macpherson (2023); Author's dataset, U.S. Bureau of Labor Statistics (1995–2012); U.S. Bureau of Economic Analysis (1995–2012); U. Census Bureau, Census of Governments (1995–2012); Hou and Smith (2006); Valletta and Freeman (1988); Shor and McCarty (2011).

Note: Robust standard errors clustered by pension plan reported in parentheses. The first dependent variable is the change in unfunde pension liabilities, per capita. The second dependent variable is the change in total pension liabilities, per capita. The third dependent variable is the change in actuarially adjusted assets, per capita. All change variables are calculated from year t to year t − 1. Lagged variabl are from t − 1. ***$p < 0.01$, **$p < 0.05$, *$p < 0.1$.

constant. If, however, unions experienced an increase in strength equal to the sample average, but Democrats did not lose or win any seats, then per capita unfunded obligations would decrease on average by $91.64. Looking at the sheer size of pension liabilities (column 2), a 1 percentage point increase in the number of Democrats in the state legislature decreases total per capita obligations by $141.11 if union strength does not change, and by $72.58 if unions experience an increase in strength equal to the sample average. These numbers in table 2.3 imply that coalitional politics not only have led to large reductions in liability size but also that it is more difficult to use politics to increase asset returns or to encourage employers to increase contributions. In this sense, it is quite remarkable that coalitional politics can move the size of unfunded liabilities to the degree that it does. This reduction comes almost entirely from decreases in the sheer size of obligations.

It is also worth mentioning the role of other variables in the regressions contained in table 2.3. Particularly noteworthy is the large, positive, statistically significant coefficient on the lagged funding ratio in the first two columns. Over the period of my sample, average pension plan funding ratios after my standardization adjustment were just over 55 percent. Plans that were funded at the average rate experienced, on average, an increase in liabilities of $228.45 per capita and an increase in unfunded liabilities of $214.64 per capita each year. The better funded the plan, however, the larger the annual increase in liabilities. For plans that were poorly funded at the 25th percentile of the distribution (37 percent), liabilities increased by considerably less: $151.41 in liabilities per capita and $142.46 in unfunded liabilities per capita. In contrast, plans at the top 75th percentile of funding (69.1 percent) felt that they were in a rosy enough financial position to increase per capita liabilities by $283.11 and to increase per capita unfunded liabilities by $266. These results are in line with previous work that finds that poorly funded plans try to close the gap in liabilities and assets by cutting workers' benefits rather than by increasing employer or state-level contributions to the plan and that well-funded plans are more generous toward workers because they can afford to be so.[34] This finding puts a large hole in popular narratives that blame worker largesse for poorly funded pension plans. Poorly funded plans, instead, are those that exhibit greater restraint in liability growth and, although not statistically significant in my model in table 2.3, include those that fail to increase the size of the asset pool.

Government Contributions to the State Pension System

In the previous section, I demonstrated that politics—particularly *coalitional politics*—exerts a strong influence on changes to the size of public sector pension benefits and related debt. Increases in the percentage of Democrats in the state legislature and increases in the strength of public sector unions are associated with significant contractions (all else equal) in the size of both total and unfunded pension liabilities. These same politics, however, appear to play no role in the change in pension assets. As briefly discussed, this finding is unsurprising. In all states and nearly all years,[35] the process for investing plan assets is remarkably insulated from the legislature and typically outsourced to an external private manager.[36]

Although returns to the preexisting pool of assets should be reasonably uncorrelated with politics, the change in contributory behavior toward that pool is unlikely to be. This section focuses on public (i.e., nonemployee) contributions to pension funds. These contributions can come from local or state employers or may be appropriated directly by the state legislature. When the state directly contributes to the pension system, these funds invariably come from state general revenue that is otherwise diverted from operational expenses in the name of better pension funding. The state is the sole guarantor of state pension funds—not pensioners and not individual employers (be they school districts, counties, or state agencies). In a sense, then, nonemployer state payouts to pension funds can be considered bailouts because they are being provided to a substate entity that should—in theory—be able to pay for benefits solely through employee contributions, employer contributions, and returns on investments. When a pension fund fails to do so and, as a result, receives transfers from the flow of general state revenue, public workers are accumulating net benefits at an additional cost to taxpayers. If large or frequent enough, these transfers may begin to crowd out other budgetary expenditures.[37]

To test the idea that the size and likelihood of these contributions are the result of partisan and interest group politics, I run a fixed effects regression modeling the size of the contributions appropriated to the state pension system.[38] These models, shown in table 2.4, contain the same variables as the regressions that model the size of liabilities and assets with the addition of an interaction between the presence of a Democratic governor and the strength of the state's public sector unions. I include this additional interaction to account for the governor's outsize role in budgetary decisions

TABLE 2.4

Linear regression on pension contributions

	Annual required contribution	General expenditures ($1,000)
Intercept	24.00 (18.12)	830.27 (676.34)
Avg. dems.	1.32 (0.86)	16.84 (24.70)
Union strength	0.34 (0.44)	3.91 (13.77)
Avg. dems. × union strength	−1.22 (1.05)	0.12 (26.52)
Dem. governor	0.21* (0.13)	11.43*** (3.89)
Dem. governor × union strength	−0.15 (0.14)	−14.07*** (5.28)
Lagged funding ratio	0.23* (0.13)	−2.76 (6.23)
State worker rate	−2.79 (3.49)	−41.28 (68.42)
Total taxes, per capita	0.00 (0.00)	(0.00) (0.00)
General expenditures, per capita	0.00 (0.00)	−0.00 (0.00)
Logged population	−1.81 (1.50)	−40.21 (47.93)
Personal income, per capita	0.00 (0.00)	0.00 (0.00)
Logged nominal gross state product	−0.01 (0.57)	−12.95 (20.16)
Unemployment	−0.94 (3.89)	151.87 (118.19)
No. obs.	411	416
State fixed effects	✓	✓
Year fixed effects	✓	✓

Source: Klarner (2013b, 2013c); U.S. Census Bureau and Bureau of Labor Statistics, Current Population Survey (1995–2012); Hirsch and Macpherson (2023); Author's dataset; U.S. Bureau of Labor Statistics (1995–2012); U.S. Bureau of Economic Analysis (1995–2012); U.S. Census Bureau, Census of Governments (1995–2012); Hou and Smith (2006); Valletta and Freeman (1988); Shor and McCarty (2011).

Note: Robust standard errors clustered by state reported in parentheses. The first dependent variable is the ratio of the amount paid by the state to the pension relative to the revised "required" amount (the ARC) less employee and employer contributions. The second dependent variable is the ratio of the state payment relative to general expenditures. ***$p < 0.01$, **$p < 0.05$, *$p < 0.1$.

(e.g., how general revenue is appropriated) relative to policy decisions (e.g., changes to a pension benefit formula).[39]

The models contained in table 2.4 are linear fixed effects regressions that test whether Democrats are more likely than Republicans to provide bailouts to pension funds. The dependent variable used in the first model is the ratio of the actual state payment, in nominal U.S. dollars, relative to the revised annual required contribution (ARC). The ARC is akin to a mortgage payment for the state—that is, it is the amount the state would need to pay every year to fully amortize current pension debt over the following thirty years. This number, perhaps even more so than the funding ratio, is exceedingly politicized and manipulated from year to year and from state to state. Figure 2.7 demonstrates this with startling clarity. The black line is the distribution of state payments relative to the gap between self-reported (and self-calculated) ARC and employee and employer contributions for individual state-years. In other words, the black line plots what state legislatures directly appropriate to the pension system as a percentage of the remaining ARC after employee and employer contributions. Note that this distribution is not normal, with a remarkable spike at one. Pension plans are consistently reporting, year after year, that the state legislature is contributing 100 percent of what is necessary to fully amortize the unfunded liabilities after employees and employers contribute their share. This is implausible for myriad reasons, the most obvious of which is that many states report $0 in contributions over several years. It is highly unlikely that contributions from employees and employers were calculated so precisely as to typically meet the ARC without any additional assistance from the legislature or without contributing more than the required amount. The leftover ARC, if it was not being manipulated, should not be so highly clustered around zero. The gray line in figure 2.7 recalculates the ARC using my measure of revised and standardized actuarial liabilities and subtracting employee and employer contributions. Dividing payments from the state legislature to the pension system by this measure and plotting the distribution (the gray line) presents a much more normal distribution with a more reasonable median pension contribution of 35 percent.

The second model in table 2.4 reconsiders the dependent variable by analyzing the size of the state's pension payment relative to general expenditures for the year. This second specification considers the possibility that voters and public sector unions care more about the size of transfers being made from one sector of the government to another (voters to workers)

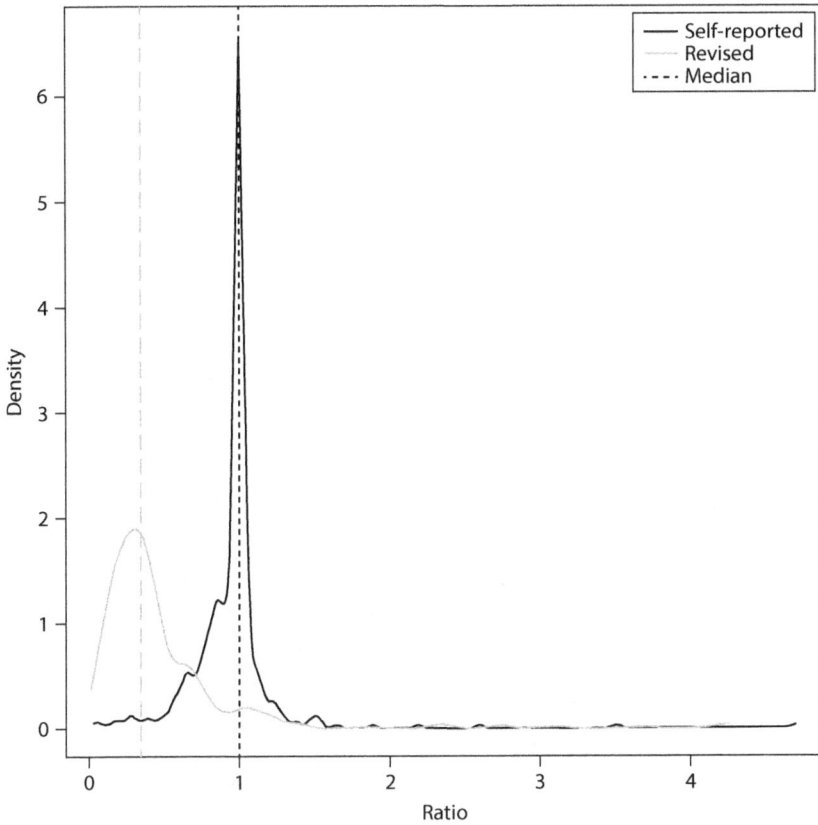

Figure 2.7 Distribution of self-reported versus revised contribution rates. This rate is the percentage of the ARC (less employee and employer contributions) paid off by the state government in a given year. Data sources are described in the text and the Methodological Appendix.

Source: Author's dataset; Public Plans Data (2001–2022).

than the size of the transfers being made from one generation to another (i.e., the size of the pension debt the government is paying off, or the contribution rate).

The impact of having a Democratic governor in office is statistically significant across both model specifications in table 2.4, although the partisanship of the governor is mediated by union strength in the second model. Democratic governors increase the contribution rates (the dollar size of the state's payment relative to the revised ARC) of their states by an astonishing

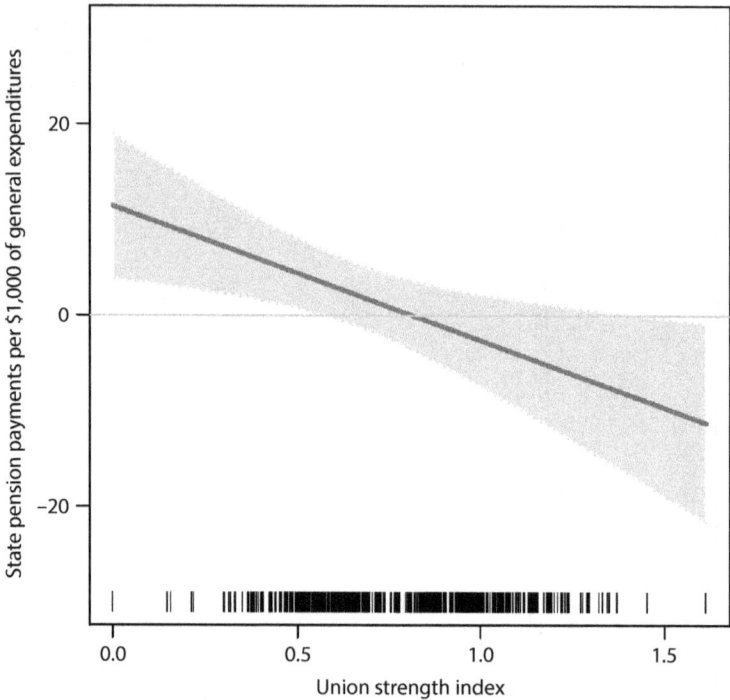

Figure 2.8 Marginal effect of a Democratic governor on state pension contributions, relative to general expenditures. Effects plotted from model 2 of table 2.4.

Source: Klarner (2013b, 2013c); U.S. Census Bureau and Bureau of Labor Statistics, Current Population Survey (1995–2012); Hirsch and Macpherson (2023); Author's dataset; U.S. Bureau of Labor Statistics (1995–2012); U.S. Bureau of Economic Analysis (1995–2012); U.S. Census Bureau, Census of Governments (1995–2012); Hou and Smith (2006); Valletta and Freeman (1988); Shor and McCarty (2011).

21 percentage points relative to Republican governors. This pattern is similar but slightly more complicated when looking at the percentage of general use funds allocated to pensions. Although strong unions appear to prevent Democratic governors—and only Democratic governors—from transferring large payments to the pension fund that could potentially hurt their reelection chances, Democratic governors still allocate more on net when unions are relatively weak (when the index is below its midpoint). Figure 2.8 depicts the marginal effect of the partisanship of the governor across different labor regimes. Finally, although legislative partisanship does not have an impact on pension payment behavior, it is not surprising that the executive

plays a larger role in this case than the legislature, and also plays a larger role than in passing pension legislation, because the budget is often commandeered by the governor's agenda setting and bargaining power.[40] In most states, the governor proposes the initial budget, and it is up to a legislative committee to agree on changes to it or to introduce it to the legislature as is. For this reason, the governor plays a much larger role in budgetary policymaking than in the process to legislate statutory changes to pension benefits.

At first glance, the results suggest a curious thing: Democratic governors are more likely to "bail out" a state pension fund through the transfer of general use funds, but legislatures with large Democratic majorities, operating in conjunction with highly unionized workforces, are less likely to pass the type of expansionary policy that would make a bailout necessary in the first place. These results, however, are indeed in line with the Coalitional Politics Hypothesis: Knowing that bailouts are costly to Democrats and taxpayers, and that Democrats are more likely than Republicans to pursue them, unions and friendly copartisans restrain themselves during the policymaking stage to prevent situations in which Democrats have to make costly transfers. The electoral implications of the Coalitional Politics Hypothesis are further discussed in chapter 5.

Budgetary Crowd-out and Voters

In the years since I first collected this data, the conversation appears to have shifted from a concern over the sustainability of pension liabilities and pension debt to a concern over what I call *budgetary crowd-out*. That is, pundits and policymakers are now less worried about the possibility of pension default as they were during the Great Recession and in the early days of the COVID-19 pandemic. Now they are more worried that certain states are spending too much of their resources on pension maintenance at the expense of other spending (or, as is implied, tax breaks). This shift appears to have begun with the publication of several papers demonstrating that the sustainability of pension debt—like other types of public debt—is best evaluated by comparing it to local economic growth. Work by Jamie Lenney, Byron Lutz, and Louise Sheiner, along with that of Charles Steindel, has shown that virtually no state is on an unsustainable path when using the metric of pension debt growth relative to economic growth.[41] No state is likely to see their pension debt growth exceed their economic growth, even after varying the assumptions

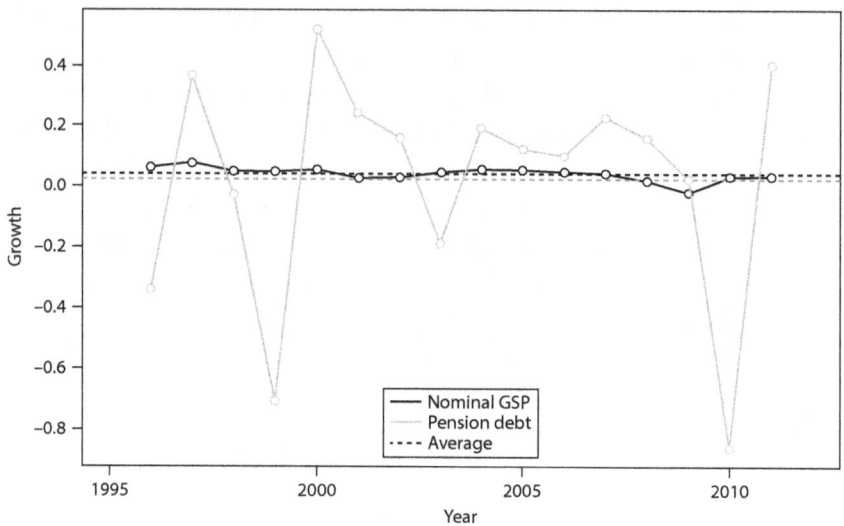

Figure 2.9 Growth in nominal gross state product and pension debt, over time.

Source: Author's dataset; U.S Bureau of Economic Analysis (1995–2012).

that are key to the models. Figure 2.9 plots median pension debt over time as a percentage of the state's nominal GSP. Although debt has indeed increased since the late 1990s, it has not outpaced nominal GSP. Over the sample's time period, GSP grew on average at an annual rate of 4.4 percent, whereas (recalculated) pension debt grew at a rate of 2.6 percent per year.

That is not to say, however, that there are no tangible consequences to the growth in pension debt. Roderick Kiewiet and Matthew McCubbins outline the problems inherent to having an ever-expanding portion of the government's budget devoted to legacy costs (i.e., retirement and medical expenses). They argue that such a "fiscal ice age" creates a climate in which tax dollars can purchase far fewer government services like transportation and education.[42] Figure 2.10 plots these costs across time as a portion of the state's general expenditures. Both pension debt as a percent of GSP and the standardized ARC as a percent of general expenditures have risen over the past fifteen years, but actual state payments as a percent of general expenditures have remained steady with a modest increase beginning in 2005. As a result, payments to the nation's public pension system have stayed below 4 percent of overall budgets and were unlikely to substantively crowd-out other spending *in practice*. The ballooning ARC tells another story,

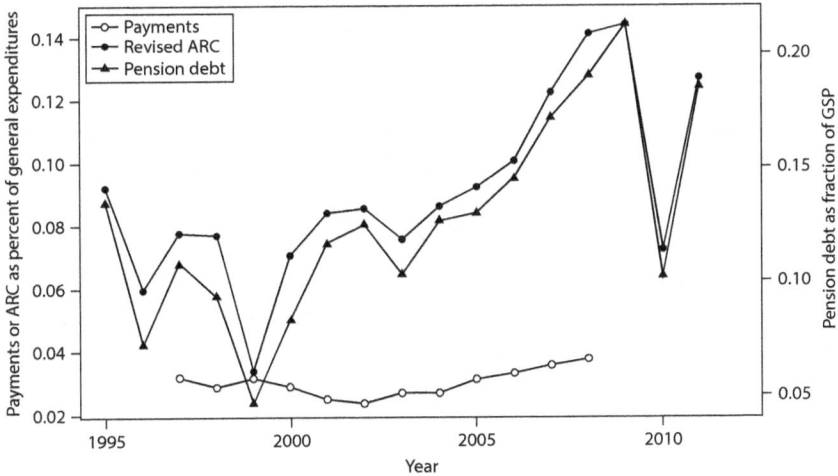

Figure 2.10 Pension payments and revised annual required contribution relative to general expenditures (left axis) and pension debt relative to gross state product (right axis), over time.

Source: Author's dataset; U.S Bureau of Economic Analysis (1995–2012); U.S. Census Bureau, Census of Governments (1995–2012).

however. Over time, states should have committed an increasingly greater percent of budgetary resources toward the pension system if they wanted to meet the goal of thirty-year amortization. Although states did begin to contribute more, on average, beginning in 2005, the political will to redirect resources toward paying down debt and achieving full amortization simply did not exist.

Therefore, states have not, on average, decreased education funding (for instance) to pay for retirement benefits, but they have consistently and persistently failed to meet amortization goals. It is worth asking: So what? Thirty-year amortization is a completely arbitrary goal based on the loan structure of conventional mortgages. State governments are neither individuals nor families; they are long-lived institutions with near-infinite horizons. Thus, the appropriate metric for determining the sustainability of pension debt is likely not whether they will pay it off within thirty years, but whether it is growing faster than the state can manage it. As Steindel rightly points out, baby boomer retirements have now peaked, and we are likely to see state pensions become smaller and more solvent as states phase out defined benefit plans altogether.[43] I return to the question of pension payments in my discussion of the electoral consequences of pension politics in chapter 6.

Understanding the dynamics of public spending—and underfunding—is no easy feat. Many moving parts are involved, oftentimes operating in opposing directions. Revised data on state pensions clearly show, however, that liabilities drive the size and fundedness of retirement plans and are strongly associated with political variables. Strong unions, working in concert with large Democratic legislative majorities, work to limit the growth of both the absolute size of pension liabilities and the size of pension debt. This effect is not perceivable if unions operate in the absence of Democratic majorities or vice versa: the key is cooperative, coalitional politics between the party and the constituent group that acts as a component of the party when it is in power and as a pluralist interest group when the party is out of power. This claim is bolstered by the fact that this relationship is evidenced most strongly in teacher pensions and not at all in judge pensions. The relationship is also evident but weaker in general employee pensions—general employees' unions being traditionally Democratic but not as strongly Democratic as teachers' unions; this is also true for uniformed worker pensions. As mentioned, the relationship is not at all perceptible in judge pensions, which is unsurprising given the fact that judges are not unionized, although at least one attempt was made to create a judges' union in the country in the past ten years.[44]

The decision of whether and how to fund the pension liabilities that already exist, however, is less cut and dry. Some evidence suggests that Democratic governors are more likely than Republican governors to appropriate funds to pay down the pensions' ARC, but they—like Republicans—are more hesitant to increase the size of pension payments relative to the overall budget. In fact, even as overall pension debt—and the size of the ARC— has climbed over time relative to the size of general expenditures, state governments have only barely increased their payments as a percentage of the budget. This is good news for those concerned about the possibility of legacy debt eating up larger and larger shares of state spending, leaving less room for crucial government services like education and transportation. Crucially, although this behavior may seem to be nothing more than kicking the pension debt can down the road, it does appear to be sustainable for now as pension debt growth has remained below state economic growth since the mid-1990s.

CHAPTER III

The Paradox of Financial Transparency

M uch work on good government assumes that greater access to information will lead to greater accountability and an overall improvement in outcomes.[1] Other research, however, finds that there are caveats to how much good transparency can do. Andrea Prat, for instance, finds that when a lawmaker's policy decisions—rather than the consequences of that decision—are well known, the decision is less likely to be correct, and the voter is less able to sort competent lawmakers from incompetent ones.[2] Justin Fox extends this analysis to ideologically biased versus unbiased elected officials with similar results.[3] Scott Ashworth and Kenneth Shotts find that in certain information environments transparency through media exposure can lead to increases in pandering by incumbent politicians.[4] In this chapter, I show that, in public sector pension policy, the context in which transparency occurs is important. The variation in the nature of information environments explains much about why and when state governments are more honest about the state of their pension finances than others. In this chapter, I also explain why I needed to hand-collect raw pension data from states rather than rely on their self-reported summary statistics in the analysis I conduct throughout the book.

Asymmetries in information environments have long been known to favor interest group activity at the expense of voters.[5] There is, as I show next, a clear distinction between having information and understanding information. From a technically complex policy standpoint, information accessibility—or *transparency*—will not mean much to the average voter if that information cannot be understood or if it is incorrect. This information may hold great value to more sophisticated interest groups, however, that possess the processing ability to understand data that are presented in even the most complicated ways. Because of these differences in data-processing abilities and the costs to untangle complex data, greater transparency can exacerbate informational asymmetries among different groups in the electorate.[6] Consider two extremes: If a government does not allow any information to be accessible to those outside of the bureaucracy or legislature, both voters and interest groups will have equal knowledge and understanding of government performance (i.e., no knowledge or understanding). If, however, a government allows easy access to fiscal or financial data but does not publish it in an easily digestible format (e.g., choosing to release the raw data without any summary statistics), only those with the ability and resources to process what the data "means" will be able to understand how the information relates to good governance. This, is turn, will lead to well-organized and resource-rich groups having an informational upper hand relative to the typical voter.

Transparency alone is not responsible for exacerbating informational asymmetries. The accuracy of and manner in which accessible information is presented—that is, the degree of data *disclosure*—are essential in determining whether or not differences in data-processing abilities matter. When a government is both transparent and engaged in full disclosure, voters' excess costs to understanding the data are less important than when they must put considerable effort into comprehending what is released to the public. Full disclosure is thus essential in facilitating an informed understanding of government performance by voters.

The problem with these sorts of informational asymmetries is twofold. First, interest groups position themselves into a place from which to extract concentrated benefits from voters when they have superior knowledge and understanding of policy outcomes.[7] In contrast, if both interest groups and voters are in the dark about policy, lawmakers do not possess incentives to bias decisions in favor of one constituency over another.[8] Mary Walsh recounts this exact scenario in California, a state well-known for its lack of transparency: Not only were voters blindsided by the size of the pension bill from the California Public Employees Retirement System (CalPERS) that had come due for a tiny pest-control district, but so were the district's employees.[9] Second, fiscal transparency coupled with less-than-full disclosure leads to what is often referred to in the literature as "budget gimmicks." These accounting tricks—making unreasonable assumptions about revenue growth or shifting liabilities from one part of the budget to another, for example—are not as benign as their name implies, however. Beyond concern over damaging democratic and professional norms, these tactics have implications for actual policy: They indirectly influence the trajectory of resource distribution by directly influencing voters' beliefs about who is getting what and how, they determine tax burdens for current and future generations, and they can lead (and have led) to fiscal crises and bankruptcies.[10]

In this chapter, I examine why and how some governments choose to engage in less disclosure than others, and over time. Accurate disclosure of pension finances is likely to go hand in hand with transparency only when the pension's health is quite robust: Pension administrators do not want voters to understand how poorly a public pension is funded if the information must legally be released in a timely and accessible fashion. To get around these transparency requirements, pension boards use budget and accounting gimmicks to increase the cost of processing the "true" value of the data. The presence of well-organized public sector unions exacerbates this effect. Unions, facing lower costs than voters to process the complex data, place additional pressure on pension boards to engage in technically legal but unsavory actuarial reporting. This effect is even stronger when unions have direct control of the board.

Background

In June 2012, the Governmental Accounting Standards Board (GASB) issued two special statements meant to overhaul the way defined benefit public pension obligations were reported by governments. Although little was changed in how governments were advised to calculate liabilities, they issued a very notable recommendation about financial transparency. GASB Statement No. 68, *Accounting and Financial Reporting for Pensions*, states the following:

In financial statements prepared using the economic resources measurement focus and accrual basis of accounting, a single or agent employer that does not have a special funding situation is required to recognize a liability equal to the net pension liability . . . In governmental fund financial statements [prepared using a modified accrual basis of accounting], a net pension liability should be recognized to the extent the liability is normally expected to be liquidated with expendable available financial resources.[11]

GASB's "Frequently Asked Questions" summarizes this recommendation as follows: "The net pension liability will be reported in a single employer's accrual accounting-based financial statements. This is significant because the net pension liability will appear plainly on the face of the financial statements for the first time." If states wish to comply with GASB standards, this means that state governments will now be forced to report their net present value of pension liabilities on their balance sheets—and not just the part of the liability that they are obligated to pay for out of the general fund for the fiscal year.

GASB Statement No. 68 was ostensibly issued to increase the transparency of public pension finances. Putting aside enforceability concerns, encouraging increased transparency without requiring more honest—and standardized—disclosure does little to solve the informational asymmetry between voters and governments in relation to pension finances.[12] Little attempt has been made by GASB or the federal government to standardize disclosure practices.[13] As I will show, transparency and honest disclosure do not necessarily go hand in hand, and in many cases, they are strongly at odds with one another.

There are several dimensions to honest pension finance reporting. The measurement of the present value of the pension liability is perhaps the most politically contentious of these, and the one most likely to be subject to manipulation. Actuaries and pension boards can choose how to report this liability, which is a measure of how much the plan will have to pay to current and future beneficiaries, by selecting different discount rates and accrual methods or different inflation, wage growth, and mortality assumptions. They can also simply report a number they pull out of a hat without justifying their reasoning, depending on how lax or "captured" the board-hired actuary is, and how extensive their Comprehensive Annual Financial Reports (CAFRs) are required to be by law. Asset valuations, however, can also be manipulated and dishonestly reported. This is usually done by assuming a much larger rate of return than reasonable market forecasts would suggest or by smoothing market losses over an unusually long time span.

To understand why some public pension plans underestimate their liabilities and overestimate their assets to a greater degree than others, I look at the distance between self-reported funding levels (assets relative to liabilities) and revised, standardized funding levels that are comparable across plans and years. To do this, I pair my dataset of recalculated liabilities and assets with self-reported data provided by the Public Plans Database.[14] This approach allows me to trace the evolution of the gap in disclosure—the difference between what pensions claim they owe versus what they actually owe—over space and time, and the way this gap changes in response to more transparent budgetary processes and the presence of attentive stakeholders.

Although there is a fair amount of literature on budget transparency in the states, this literature is distinct from my concerns with disclosure. The theory that is produced from this literature, however, does complement what I explore. Synthesizing the transparency literature with research on financial disclosure in the private sector, in addition to several novel intuitions, I derive two key hypotheses. First, increased financial transparency should lead to greater effort by pension boards to fudge funding data when actual funding levels worsen and to be more honest when actual funding levels improve—that is, to the extent that pension boards care about voter and government perception of financial stress. Second, the presence of strong unions should pressure pension boards to be less honest in their reporting behavior. Strong unions will be more successful in advocating for increased pension generosity (i.e., increases in benefits or decreases in employee contributions) if they can get voters to believe that the pension is on financially sound footing. Additionally, the cost of determining the true value of the pension's funding status will be lower when workers have greater resources at their disposal. As such, employee- or union-captured boards will have stronger incentives to be dishonest with the public, even if—and often, because—the pension is hemorrhaging funds.

These hypotheses are empirically tested using the data described earlier and are strongly supported by my analysis. The degree to which the government is truthful about the health of a public pension is not just a function of the actual health of the pension but also of the degree of fiscal transparency within the state, the presence of attentive stakeholders, and the administrative structure of the pension board.

Theoretical Framework

Transparency Versus Disclosure

Fiscal transparency and fiscal disclosure, although similar in many ways, are in fact distinct concepts. Transparency, as James Alt, David Dreyer, and Shanna Rose define it, is the degree to which the government provides information about the intentions, actions, and consequences of specific fiscal policies to individual actors.[15] Transparency means visibility of and accessibility to information. Although many public finance scholars have failed to distinguish this concept from disclosure—which I define broadly as "honesty" in reporting practices—financial economists have come to recognize the theoretical differences and have shown how they might act as substitutes rather than complements when agents possess asymmetric information-processing abilities.[16] Take, for example, a company that provides lots of information to its shareholders about its financial position and makes this information easily accessible. Does this company have an incentive to smooth its losses perhaps a bit too generously during a downturn? Or are they going to be as up front as possible about the bad quarter, despite not being legally compelled to do so? If the shareholders are not as good as management at figuring out which tools might have been used to engage in "creative accounting," and how to back out the true numbers, then the answer is the former. If both parties are equally sophisticated and adept at these sorts of gimmicks, however, management will wind up spinning its wheels in an attempt to dupe the shareholders into complacency. If the company had not pursued a policy of transparency in the first place, of course, management would not care either way about which numbers were being reported, because shareholders would probably never see them.

Several agents likely care very much about both the transparency and disclosure of public pension finances. Voters, credit markets, elected officials, and direct stakeholders—like current employees, annuitants, local employers, and pension board members—all have an interest in the degree to which pension data are both available and accurate. Issues relating to transparency and disclosure are relevant only when one set of actors controls more information than another. Regarding pension finances, elected officials and pension board members have the upper hand in this scenario for several reasons. The first is that the pension board is always responsible for publishing the CAFR that summarizes the financial health of the pension plan over the short and long term. The CAFR can be as extensive or as concise as the pension board deems, relative to any guidelines that the state legislature has issued. Second, the pension board is typically responsible for hiring an actuary to compute the summary statistics and details that are reported in the CAFR and have an inordinate amount of leeway in constructing the liability and asset figures. The state government, however, also has the capacity to "regulate" the pension board in the form of issuing rules and choosing actuaries, and it often appoints members to the board. In this sense, both the pension board and state government can exert control over the degree of transparency in pension finances—by deciding how much goes into the CAFR and how easily accessible it is by other actors—and over the degree of disclosure. This is accomplished primarily by giving the actuarial job to a firm that is sympathetic to the pension and administration and by directing the actuary to use certain types of accounting tools (i.e., gimmicks).

Voters, at the other end of the spectrum, are completely at the mercy of pension boards and elected officials in their attempts to obtain accurate pension data. Ease of accessibility to information (i.e., transparency) is likely to influence both their ability to obtain data and their interest in doing so. If there is a glut of information being released about pension finances, chances are that the policy issue will be more salient to voters. Even in a situation in which there is high transparency and saliency, however, it is unlikely that the average voter will be able to distinguish good information from bad. It is in this sense that the degree of disclosure is important. If voters *were* capable of knowing when the information signal was poor, and as equally capable of computing funding ratios as a full-time actuary, disclosure practices would be irrelevant. This is the essence of what it means to say that asymmetric information-processing costs drive attempts to cover up poor pension finance practices, even when governments take all of the legal and politically necessary actions to provide information to voters and other parties.

In between the high information control and low processing costs of pension boards and the low information control and high processing costs of voters lie interest groups and credit markets. Although groups like public sector unions and credit markets do not have well-aligned incentives to ensure that disclosure practices are thorough, they do have a stake in how pensions are financed. Unions, on the one hand, would like to make sure that their members' pensions are financially secure; but not necessarily at the expense of benefits or increased employee contributions. In this way, unions will want to exaggerate pension funding levels, *regardless of their true value*, and to keep accurate information out of the hands of voters and others who might seek to reduce their retirement income. Increased disclosure is a net negative for unions, in that they likely possess the processing skill necessary to compute accurate measures of liabilities and assets, regardless of how honest the pension board's reports are. Accurate disclosure can only be bad for the generosity of pension benefits.[17] State workers who do not enjoy the benefits of a strong union, however, are unlikely to possess the information-processing capabilities necessary to distinguish good information from bad—no matter how plentiful.

Credit markets, in contrast, do not appear to fully possess the processing skills necessary to understand pension financing, much like voters, no matter how sophisticated or organized (chapter 4 explores this in detail).[18] They do, however, have a bit more control over the flow of information relative to voters in that the whims of the market (and the credit rating agencies) can and occasionally do influence a government's decision to release information. California, for instance, recently undertook strong efforts to increase transparency after receiving poor credit ratings from the major rating agencies for several years.[19] For brevity and tractability, however, the markets are absent from most of the foregoing analysis and discussion. I assume that—at least in the very short term—state-level fiscal transparency is fixed and exogenous and that market participants and credit rating agencies have little control over pension board decisions.[20]

Imperfect Information, Bad Signals, and Administrative Capture

Public economists have long been interested in the effects of transparency and disclosure on spending and taxing behavior. Alessandro Gavazza and Alessandro Lizzeri, for example, set up a game theoretic model in which two candidates engage in clientelistic competition between groups of voters that can receive private transfers and subsidies after an election.[21] The authors assume that some groups can observe fiscal policy better than others and that different aspects of policy—revenues versus expenditures, for instance—can differ in their level of transparency. Their results are unambiguous: Increased transparency of who gets what leads to less wasteful transfers, whereas increased transparency of who is being taxed and to what degree does not.[22] The logic of their model is easy to follow; as it becomes more obvious that a group is being given preferential treatment by a candidate, other groups will demand increased transfers as well. Increasing transfers, however, leads to an increase in debt and distortionary taxes. In the extreme case, when transparency is perfect, all groups recognize this dynamic and realize that it is more beneficial for them to demand zero transfers such that they do not have to deal with the deadweight loss of taxation. In this scenario, the government issues no transfers and collects no taxes, so that elections are determined by coin flips or some sort of "ideological attachment."

In the less extreme case of imperfect transparency, a group i observes policy with probability $0 < p_i < 1$ and does not observe policy with probability $0 < 1 - p_i < 1$. When a group does not receive the (supposedly credible) policy signal, it must guess about the distribution of transfers and taxes across the electorate. Gavazza and Lizzeri restrict this belief about policy to be "optimistic." What they mean by this is that when group i receives a deviation in transfers from the average expenditure level, i assumes that this probably means that other groups are also receiving some sort of bonus— but that it is not more generous than the one they receive. Gavazza and Lizzeri argue that this is a reasonable assumption, but they are upfront about how potentially fatal this might be to their model. Remove this assumption and the number of equilibria approaches infinity.

Many good intuitions come out of the work in Gavazza and Lizzeri. Introducing the distinction between transparency and disclosure and the concept of asymmetric information-processing costs augments the model's realism considerably, however. Assume that only two groups in this model are competing for public largesse—public sector workers and voters. Voters, as discussed previously, have very high costs to processing financial data. Public sector workers, in contrast, have lower costs that are decreasing in the strength of the workers' unionization status.

The degree of fiscal transparency in a state is exogenous and fixed. When transparency is very low, voters are unlikely to receive or be capable of obtaining information about policy, and thus they have no opportunity to process it. The probability of receiving any sort of signal about pension finances, p, is near zero.[23] In this case, both voters and workers really do not have much recourse and must assume that no one group is being treated better than the other. Very low transparency is also likely to contribute to low salience of the policy. If no one is talking about pension policy, it will not be on voters' minds.

Although transparency and information access are fixed, the extent of disclosure is not. A pension board can choose either an honest accounting system, which will produce an unbiased estimate of the pension plan's funding status, H, or it can choose a dishonest accounting system, which will produce estimate $H + \omega$, where $\omega > 0$. Because choosing a dishonest accounting system can lead to credit downgrades, tax inefficiencies, poor planning, and possible scandals, a dishonest system requires the pension board pay a cost $c_b > 0$. The pension board receives a sum of the weighted utilities of public sector workers and voters, less this cost, reflecting the composition or extent of "capture" of the board.

Both voters and unions observe a signal with an estimate of either H or $H + \omega$ with probability p. If the board chooses to signal H, or the true value of the pension plan's funding ratio, both voters and unions discover the full size of unfunded transfers to workers. If H is low, implying that pension benefits far outweigh pension contributions from workers and that voters will need to be taxed in the future, workers will pay a cost for voters discovering and understanding the truth, $c_w(H)$.[24] This cost is decreasing in H so that $dc_w/dH < 0$. If, in contrast, the board chooses to signal $H + \omega$, unions pay a cost, c_{audit}, to uncover the size of ω. This cost is decreasing in the degree of organization and financial strength of the union. Voters, however, possess less technical skills and resources than organized workers and cannot distinguish between H and ω at any cost. As a result, they must take the signal at face value. Because voters cannot distinguish between the true accounting system and the dishonest accounting system, workers prefer the dishonest accounting system when the cost of discovering the true value of the funding ratio is sufficiently small, or when $c_{audit} \leq c_w(H)$. This scenario occurs when workers are highly unionized and when the true funding ratio is low. Finally, with probability $1 - p$ both groups observe nothing, or ϕ.

As transparency and information access p increases, the asymmetry of processing costs comes into play. Voters, on the one hand, now care about pension policy and can get to the raw data—but they have no idea what any of it means. Voters must rely on the good faith of the government and pension board and trust that they are not doctoring numbers or calculations. In this sense, the beliefs formed by voters after observing a signal from the government—the CAFR, along with other statements from elected officials—are of the utmost importance.[25] For this reason, I propose my first hypothesis:

Hypothesis 1: Full disclosure will be decreasing in transparency, conditioned on how poor the pension fund's financial position is. Similarly, full disclosure will be increasing in the pension's true funding status when states are transparent about their financial data.

Highly unionized workers, on the other hand, are more likely to be wary of taking the signal at its face value. Utilizing their superior resources, they can extract more accurate information from the signal that the government provides. Because sophisticated and resource-rich unions can accurately and skillfully determine the distinction between H and ω, workers will be better off if ω is large and the signal underplays the true generosity of pension benefits. This way, unions get the information they need from the signal, while convincing voters that workers are not being compensated as well as they are. Similarly, if voters receive a signal that the pension is better funded than it actually is, meaning that there is less debt per capita and fewer transfers are going to state employees than in reality, unions will find themselves in a preferable political position from which they can demand more from taxpayers and elected officials. This leads to my second hypothesis:

Hypothesis 2: Strong unions will prevent full and accurate disclosure of public pension finances when information is readily available to voters, and will be even more likely to do so when the pension is poorly funded.

Finally, for the purposes of this chapter, I assume that pension boards are creatures of the government that can be controlled imperfectly by the state executive, the legislature, and the public sector workers whose retirements they seek to manage. Pension board members have neither interests nor goals that are distinct from their principals. Boards are less likely to reflect employee interests when fewer state workers serve on the board, when the chair of the board is chosen by the executive or legislative branch, and when the individual currently inhabiting the chair's position was originally appointed by the executive or legislative branch. For example, an individual who was picked to serve on the board by state workers, but was chosen to be chair by the governor, is likely to express at least some sympathy toward the executive's preferences. Similarly, an individual who was originally appointed to the board by the governor—such as the state treasurer—but elected to the chair's position by a majority of board members, is also likely to display concern for the executive's interests. If, however, the chair of the board is an employee elected to the position by a majority of members, chances are the chair will exhibit a stronger allegiance to state workers than to the state government. This results in my third hypothesis:

Hypothesis 3: Pension boards will be less likely to engage in full and accurate disclosure when they are controlled by state workers and unions.

Empirical Analysis

I now turn to empirically testing these three hypotheses. I begin by discussing the primary dependent variables of interest.

The first variable is a proxy for financial disclosure and is constructed as the distance between self-reported and recalculated pension plan funding ratios. This variable measures the extent to which a pension plan exaggerates its funding status in a given year. I used the dataset of reconstructed liability and asset measures—which, recall, are free from potential political and reporting bias—from previous chapters and compared the funding ratio that I calculated from these standardized measures to the self-reported funding ratios that the Center for Retirement Research has collected and organized into the Public Plans Database (2001–2013).

Similar to this first measure, I also construct variables that measure the distance between revised and self-reported liabilities per capita, or (*Revised Actuarial Liability − Self-Reported Actuarial Liability*) / *State Population*, and the distance between self-reported and revised actuarially adjusted assets per capita, (*Self-Reported Actuarially Adjusted Assets − Revised Actuarially Adjusted Assets*) / *State Population*. The construction of these variables allows me to examine the disclosure behavior of the expenditure and revenue side of pension finances separately, because I have reason to believe that expenditure transparency and disclosure may be more important than that of revenue to stakeholders.[26] Although the funding status of pension plans and the size of their liabilities are obviously related, the behavior surrounding disclosure of assets is less robust to theoretical predictions and may possibly complicate the empirical analysis of funding status disclosure. All three measures are distributed somewhat similarly.[27] As depicted in figure 3.1, they are constructed such that a larger value of any of the variables implies that disclosure is worse—that is, the pension board is overreporting the funding ratio, underreporting liabilities, or overreporting assets. Note that the median gap in liability reporting is farther to the right of zero than the median gap in asset reporting. The gap in asset reporting is much more tightly clustered around zero, suggesting that the big driver in reporting

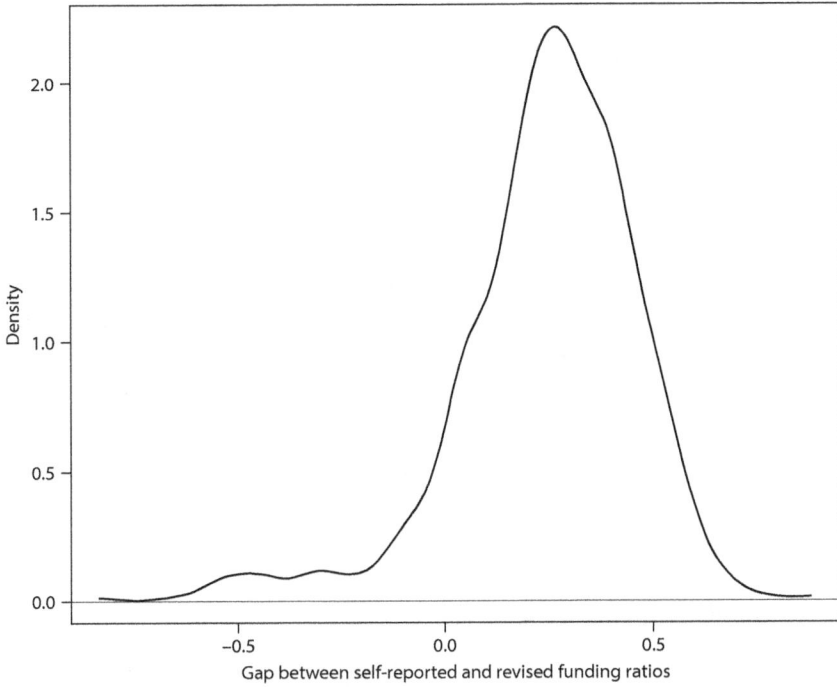

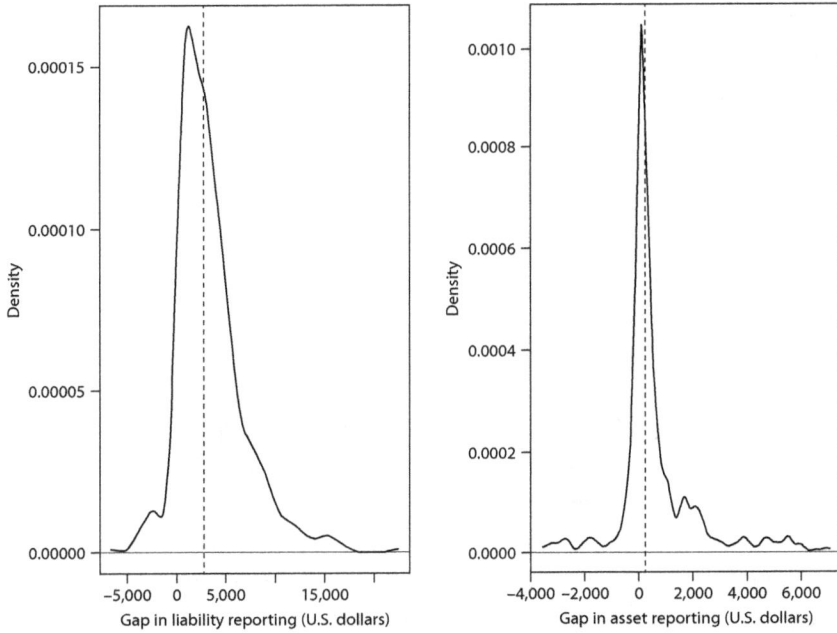

Figure 3.1 Degree of funding discrepancy, by plan-year (two panels). The top panel (a) shows the distribution of the gap between self-reported and revised funding ratios. The bottom panel (b) shows the gap in self-reported and revised liabilities and the gap in self-reported and revised assets. The dashed lines indicate median value of the data. Liability and asset data are per state population.

Source: Public Plans Data (2001–2022); Author's dataset.

behavior is liabilities, much like the way that liabilities are the big driver in pension size and debt (chapter 2).

Fiscal Transparency and Clientelistic Competition

I now turn to investigating my three hypotheses about fiscal transparency and the way stakeholders might seek to influence disclosure of pension finances. Recall that the first hypothesis predicts that financial reporting accuracy will be negatively affected by the ability to easily access data and the saliency of pension policy. For this reason, the main explanatory variable is fiscal transparency. Unfortunately, there is no single agreed-upon measure of fiscal or budgetary transparency.[28] For the purposes of the analysis and hypothesis testing, it is most relevant to quantify the degree to which it is easy to obtain information about pension funding. Furthermore, it is important that the measure used contains no indicator of how accurate that data are. The first measure of transparency I consider is the number of days it takes a state to issue their general budget CAFR, measured from the end of the fiscal year.[29] Although it would be ideal to know the timeliness of *pension* CAFRs, which is unfortunately unavailable, these measures are likely to be closely correlated. Furthermore, using measures of general budget data timeliness rather than pension data timeliness ensures that no direct relationship exists between accurate disclosure of pension finances and the explanatory variable.

The timely release of budget data is perhaps the most important element of fiscal transparency in the way that I have conceived of it. The longer a state takes to release budgetary and financial data, the greater the extent to which policy and political issues will have faded from voters' minds. New Mexico, for example, takes on average 602 days from the end of their fiscal year to release their budgetary data. It is unlikely that voters can even remember what their tax burden felt like by the time they are able to find out exactly how their dollars were spent. Numerous surveys of good government groups and municipal investors associations have confirmed the importance of the timeliness of CAFR release and the uselessness of financial data that is made available long after the fiscal year's end.[30] If voters cannot access information, they cannot assess information. The timeliness of the data has little to do with the accuracy of it, however.[31] Figure 3.2 shows that no simple bivariate relationship exists between "timely" (less than 180

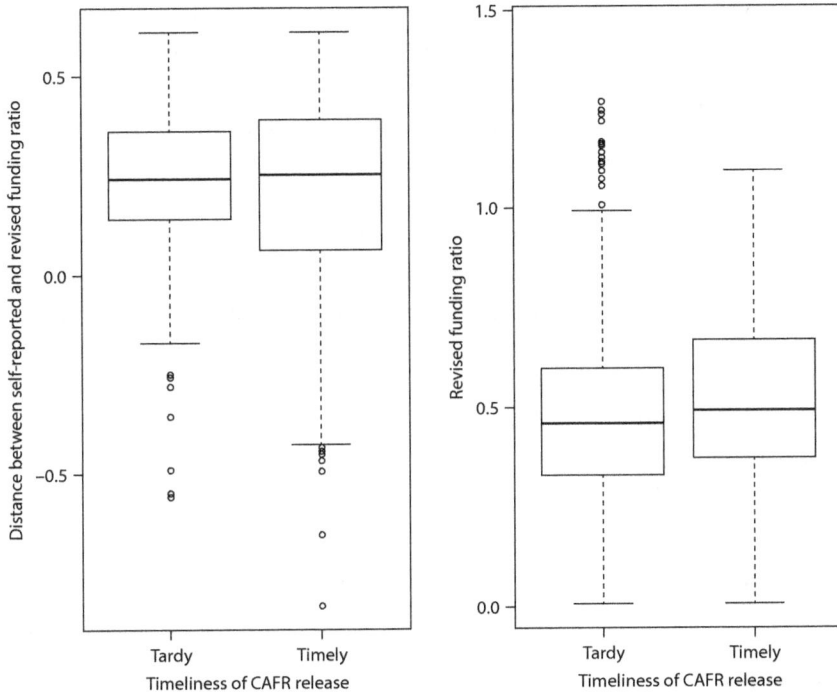

Figure 3.2 Disclosure in low- and high-transparency states. Distributions of the distance between the revised funding ratio and the self-reported funding ratio and of the actual funding ratio in states that issue their CAFRs more than 180 days after the end of the fiscal year (*Tardy*) and in states that issue them in less than 181 days (*Timely*).

Source: Institute for Truth in Accounting (2011); National Association of State Auditors, Comptrollers, and Treasurers (2005–2011); Author's dataset.

days to publish) states, "tardy" (more than 180 days to publish) states, and accurate disclosure. The second panel of figure 3.2 confirms that this is also true of the relationship between timeliness and revised funding status.

In addition to the timeliness of CAFR releases, I also consider ease of access. I operationalize ease of access by the degree to which budgetary data are complete, collected from the Sunshine Review.[32] I also use Alt, Dreyer, and Rose's index of state fiscal transparency, but I am more hesitant to do so given that considerations of accuracy are included in the index.[33] Nevertheless, results from analyses using these alternative measures of transparency are qualitatively similar to those conducted using the timeliness measures and are contained in the Methodological Appendix.

Hypothesis 1 predicts that transparency will have a negative effect on disclosure when conditioned on the funding status of the pension and that a strong funding ratio will have a positive effect on disclosure practices—particularly when governments are transparent. Pension boards will be more likely to fudge the reported numbers when the pension is in financial trouble and will do so to a greater extent when the data are readily available and salient to voters. Table 3.1 reports a series of simple ordinary least squares regressions testing this hypothesis as well as several regressions that use year and region fixed effects to control for any potential omitted variables.

In models 1 and 2 of table 3.1, the transparency measure, *Avg. Days to CAFR Release*, is not statistically related to disclosure. This finding confirms the linear independence of information availability and information accuracy as suggested by figure 3.3. In models 3–5, however, the timeliness of CAFR release is statistically significantly related to the accuracy of reported funding rates and in the expected direction. Both decreases in fiscal transparency and increases in

TABLE 3.1

Linear regression on distance between self-reported and revised funding ratios

	Model 1	Model 2	Model 3	Model 4	Model 5
Avg. days to cAFR release	−0.000 (0.036)	0.011 (0.016)	−0.272*** (0.080)	−0.238** (0.081)	−0.226*** (0.082)
Lagged revised funding ratio (%)			−1.380*** (0.319)	−1.305*** (0.294)	−1.242*** (0.301)
Days × lagged ratio			0.004*** (0.002)	0.004** (0.001)	0.003** (0.002)
No. obs.	613	631	613	613	600
Year fixed effects		✓		✓	✓
Region fixed effects		✓		✓	✓
Economic and demographic controls					✓

Source: Author's dataset; Institute for Truth in Accounting (2011); National Association of State Auditors, Comptrollers and Treasurers (2005–2011); U.S. Bureau of Labor Statistics (1995–2012); U.S Bureau of Economic Analysis (1995–2012); U.S. Census Bureau, Census of Governments (1995–2012).

Note: An increase in *Avg. Days to CAFR Release* indicates that the state is taking longer to release financial information and impeding fiscal transparency. Robust standard errors are clustered by pension plan in parentheses. Estimated intercept is not reported. Controls include unemployment rate, per capita personal income, logged population, and federal transfers as a fraction of general revenue. ***p < 0.01, **p < 0.05, *p < 0.1.

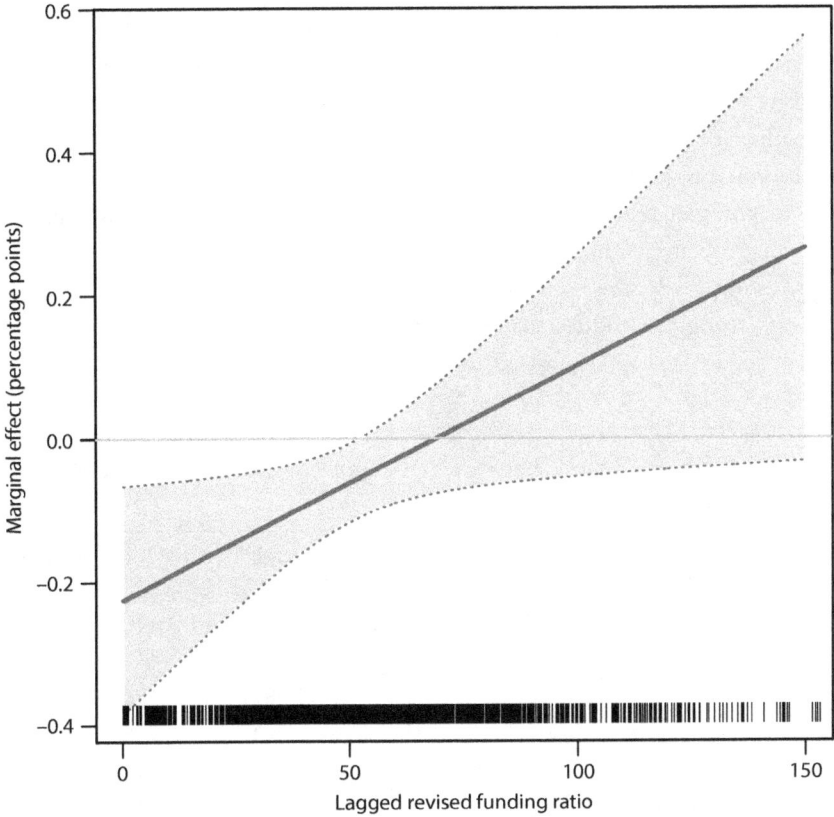

Figure 3.3 Marginal effect of timeliness on disclosure as funding status improves. This figure shows the effect of a one-day increase in the time it takes for a state to release its CAFR on the discrepancy in reporting behavior, as the fiscal position of the pension fund improves. When a pension is funded below 52 percent, an increase in the number of days it takes for a state to release its CAFR (i.e., a decrease in the timeliness of budgetary reporting and a decrease in transparency) results in a decrease in the distance between self-reported and actual funding rates. This effect is attenuated as actual funding status improves. There is no effect of timeliness and transparency on disclosure behavior once the pension is funded above 52 percent. Calculations come from model 5 of table 3.1.

Source: Author's dataset; Institute for Truth in Accounting (2011); National Association of State Auditors, Comptrollers, and Treasurers (2005–2011); U.S. Bureau of Labor Statistics (1995–2012); U.S. Bureau of Economic Analysis (1995–2012); U.S. Census Bureau, Census of Governments (1995–2012).

actual funding status are associated with decreases in reporting inaccuracy, suggesting that pension boards are less compelled to exaggerate how well funded their pensions are when the data are published with less reliability.[34] As the previous year's funding ratio improves, this effect diminishes, as evidenced by the positive interaction between the previous year's funding ratio and the opacity of budgetary data. This attenuation makes sense: As the pension fund's financial position improves, boards will find less reason to be dishonest about it, regardless of whether the pension is subject to particularly transparent or opaque information environments. This dynamic is illustrated in figure 3.3.

Moving on to the hypothesis 2, table 3.2 depicts what happens when union strength is added to the model as an explanatory variable. As

TABLE 3.2

Linear regression on distance between self-reported and revised funding ratios with union strength

	Model 1	Model 2	Model 3	Model 4	Model 5
Union strength	−8.162*	−4.443	12.372	23.236*	28.745**
	(4.836)	(2.986)	(19.251)	(12.331)	(12.337)
Avg. days to CAFR release			0.099	−0.097	−0.083
			(0.086)	(0.091)	(0.086)
Union strength × days			−0.084	−0.118**	−0.132***
			(0.067)	(0.048)	(0.049)
Lagged funding ratio (%)				−1.222***	−1.209***
				(0.262)	(0.249)
Days × lagged ratio				0.003***	0.003**
				(0.001)	(0.001)
No. obs.	610	610	610	598	598
Year fixed effects		✓	✓	✓	✓
State fixed effects		✓			
Region fixed effects			✓	✓	✓
Economic and demographic controls					✓

Source: Author's dataset; Institute for Truth in Accounting (2011); National Association of State Auditors, Comptrollers and Treasurers (2005–2011); U.S. Bureau of Labor Statistics (1995–2012); U.S Bureau of Economic Analysis (1995–2012); U.S. Census Bureau, Census of Governments (1995–2012); Hirsch and Macpherson (2011).

Note: An increase in *Avg. Days to CAFR Release* indicates that the state is taking longer to release financial information and impeding fiscal transparency. Robust standard errors are clustered by pension plan in parentheses. Estimated intercept is not reported. Controls include unemployment rate, per capita personal income, logged population, and federal transfers as a fraction of general revenue. ***$p < 0.01$, **$p < 0.05$, *$p < 0.1$.

in previous chapters, union strength is conceived of as a combination of strength in sheer numbers and strength in financial resources. As can be seen from table 3.2, this index of union strength has a strong, positive impact on dishonest reporting behavior, although the effect is overwhelmed by the transparency indicator. As transparency decreases, the desire and ability of unions to influence beneficial disclosure practices also decreases (or put another way, as transparency increases, the strength of the union matters more for accurate disclosure). Table 3.3 reinforces these findings in a more parsimonious manner. Here, states are split into binary categories of timeliness of CAFR release. States are considered *Timely* if they released their CAFRs less than 181 days after the end of the fiscal year and are considered *Tardy* if they took more than 180 days. These cutoffs are in line with survey respondents' claims about the usefulness of fiscal data once a hypothetical amount of time elapses after the end of the reporting period.[35] In *Timely* states, strong unions have

TABLE 3.3

Linear regression on distance between self-reported and revised funding ratios, split by tardiness versus timeliness

	Timely	Tardy	Timely	Tardy
Union strength	24.100***	6.495	22.774**	7.173
	(8.806)	(4.505)	(8.807)	(5.615)
Lagged funding ratio	−1.096***	−0.340*	−1.102***	−0.369
	(0.036)	(0.204)	(0.033)	(0.230)
Union strength × lagged ratio	−0.359***	−0.102	−0.358***	−0.125
	(0.118)	(0.103)	(0.119)	(0.121)
No. obs.	228	386	228	386
Year fixed effects	✓	✓	✓	✓
State fixed effects	✓	✓	✓	✓
Economic and demographic controls			✓	✓

Source: Author's dataset; Institute for Truth in Accounting (2011); National Association of State Auditors, Comptrollers and Treasurers (2005–2011); U.S. Bureau of Labor Statistics (1995–2012); U.S Bureau of Economic Analysis (1995–2012); U.S. Census Bureau, Census of Governments (1995–2012); Hirsch and Macpherson (2011).

Note: Robust standard errors are clustered by pension plan in parentheses. Estimated intercept is not reported. Controls include unemployment rate, per capita personal income, logged population, and federal transfers as a fraction of general revenue. A CAFR release is classified as *Timely* if it occurred in 180 days or less, and *Tardy* otherwise, in line with previous literature (see Jones et al. 2012; Mead 2011). ***$p < 0.01$, **$p < 0.05$, *$p < 0.1$.

A   Timely CAFR release

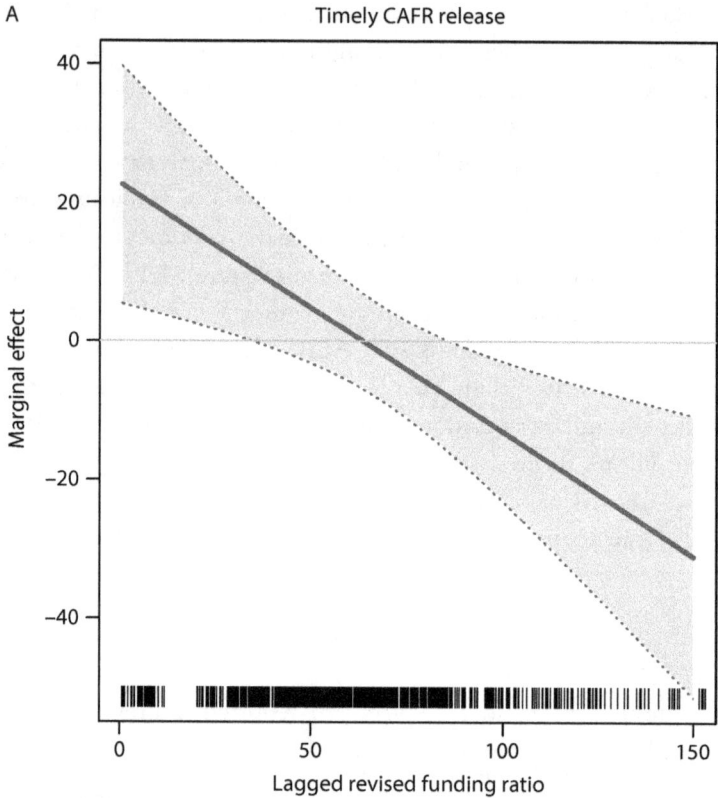

Figure 3.4 Marginal effect of union strength on size of disclosure gap as lagged pension funding ratio increases. This shows the effect of a marginal increase in union strength on the discrepancy in reporting behavior, as the pension plan becomes better funded. When a pension is poorly funded in a transparent state, an increase in union strength increases the gap between the self-reported and actual funding ratio. This trend reverses itself when the pension is well-funded (panel *a*). The strength of the union has no statistical impact on disclosure practices in states that take considerably longer times to release their financial data (panel *b*). Calculations come from models 3 and 4 of table 3.3.

a considerable impact on the size of the gap between self-reported and revised funding ratios of pension plans: A 1 standard deviation increase in the union strength index increases the reporting bias by approximately 12 percentage points, holding the true funding status of the plan constant. In *Tardy* states, however, both unions and—surprisingly—the actual

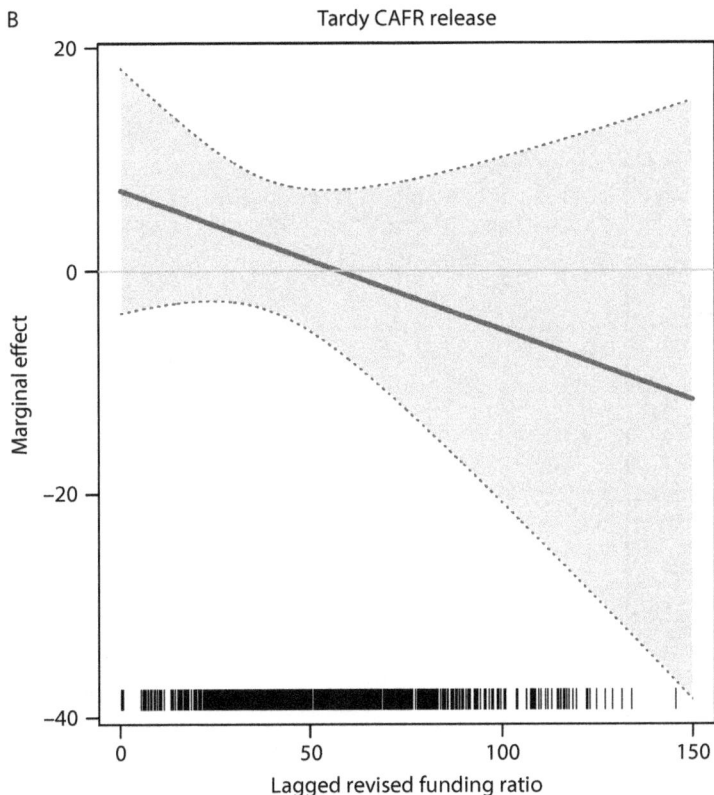

B   Tardy CAFR release

Marginal effect

Lagged revised funding ratio

Figure 3.4 (continued)
Source: Author's dataset; Institute for Truth in Accounting (2011); National Association of State Auditors, Comptrollers, and Treasurers (2005–2011); U.S. Bureau of Labor Statistics (1995–2012); U.S. Bureau of Economic Analysis (1995–2012); U.S. Census Bureau and Bureau of Labor Statistics, Current Population Survey (1995–2012); Hirsch and Macpherson (2023).

health of the pension plan play little role in the board's decision to distort financial reporting. These effects are depicted visually in figures 3.4 and 3.5. In states that release their CAFRs within 180 days, distortions in financial reporting become larger as unions grow stronger and pension health worsens (see figure 3.4a), while improvements in pension funding lead to more honest reporting (see figure 3.5a). This is not true in states that take longer than 180 days from the end of the fiscal year to issue their CAFRs (see the figures 3.4b and 3.5b).

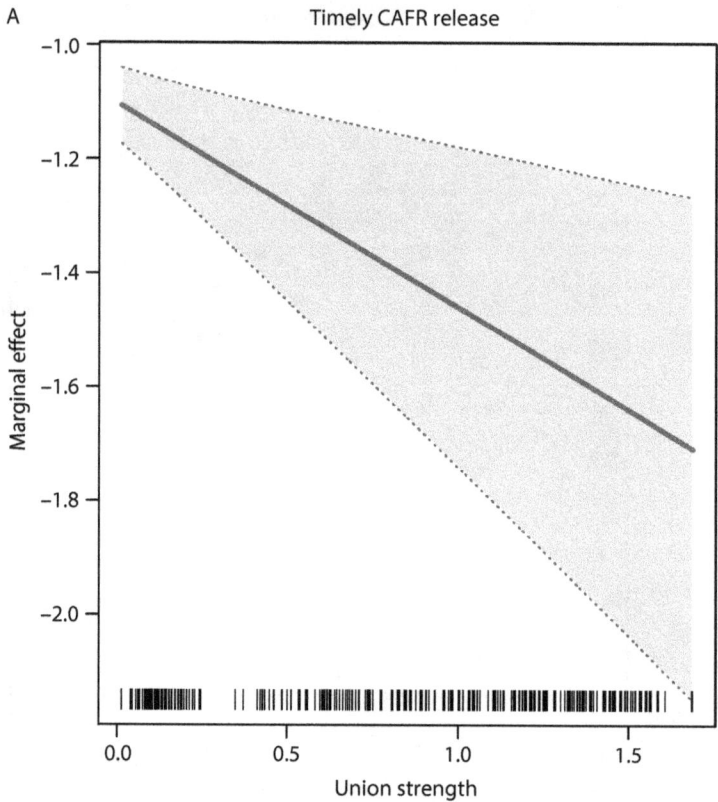

A   Timely CAFR release

Figure 3.5 Marginal effect of lagged funding ratio on size of disclosure gap as union strength increases (two panels). This shows the effect of a marginal increase in a pension plan's revised funding ratio on the discrepancy in reporting behavior, as the state's unions becomes stronger. In transparent states, a marginal increase in the funding ratio decreases the gap between the self-reported and actual funding ratio. This effect is amplified as unions grow stronger (panel *a*). In states that take considerably longer to release financial reports, the actual funding status of the pension has no statistical impact on disclosure practices (panel *b*). Calculations come from models 3 and 4 of table 3.3.

Attentive Stakeholders and Captured Government

Several scholars have presented evidence to suggest that employee-administered pension boards routinely manipulate actuarial assumptions to undermine the solvency of their funds or to allow governments to defer payments in exchange for increased benefits.[36] Although my theory posits alternative explanations for these patterns in the data, it similarly predicts that pension

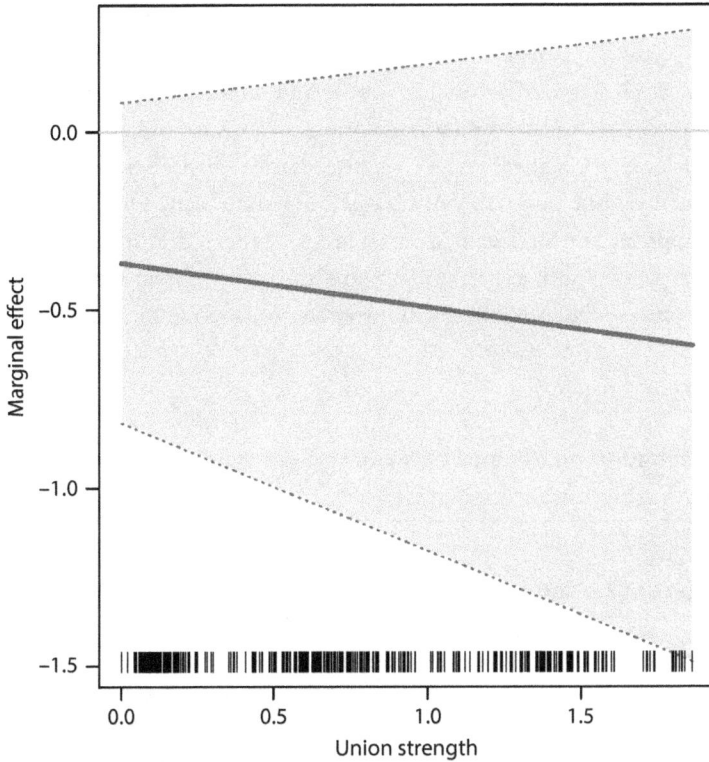

B   Tardy CAFR release

Figure 3.5 (continued)
Source: Author's dataset; Institute for Truth in Accounting (2011); National Association of State Auditors, Comptrollers, and Treasurers (2005–2011); U.S. Bureau of Labor Statistics (1995–2012); U.S. Bureau of Economic Analysis (1995–2012); U.S. Census Bureau and Bureau of Labor Statistics, Current Population Survey (1995–2012); Hirsch and Macpherson (2023).

boards will be less likely to engage in full disclosure when they are con-trolled or captured by state workers (hypothesis 3). To test this hypothesis, I constructed a new dataset containing information about the administra-tive structure of each pension plan board that manages state funds. The key independent variables in the following analyses are whether the chair of the board was picked by the government or elected by a majority of board members and whether the individual currently serving as chair is an employee or annuitant covered by the pension. I also investigate whether the percent of employees currently sitting on the board influences disclosure practices. Table 3.4 displays the results of a series of linear regressions that predict the distance between self-reported and revised funding ratios for all pension plans, for pension plans in timely states, and for pension plans in tardy states. All standard errors are robust and clustered by plan.[37]

In table 3.4, *Chair Elected by Board*, *Employee Chair*, and *Percent Employees on Board* have a negative impact on the degree of disclosure the pension board pursues, but they are only statistically significant when conditioned on the appropriate intervening variables. As expected, honest reporting of the most salient and easily understood measure of pension health—the funding ratio—depends on the transparency environment of the state. In

TABLE 3.4

Linear regression on distance between self-reported and revised funding ratios with administrative structure

	Full sample	Timely	Tardy
Chair elected by board	2.099	55.141★★★	−3.329
	(12.130)	(14.901)	(6.556)
Employee chair	−3.027	36.610★★	2.625
	(11.562)	(5.305)	(9.880)
Percent employees on board (%)	0.551★★	0.821★★	0.335
	(0.242)	(0.367)	(0.313)
Lagged funding ratio (%)	−0.333	−0.948★★★	−0.120
	(0.291)	(0.359)	(0.230)
Chair elected by board × lagged ratio	−0.397★★	−0.359★★	0.070
	(0.173)	(0.159)	(0.252)
Employee chair × lagged ratio	0.026	−0.075	−0.202
	(0.177)	(0.151)	(0.157)
Percent employees × lagged ratio	−0.007★	0.001	−0.002
	(0.004)	(0.008)	(0.005)
No. obs.	552	192	359
Year fixed effects	✓	✓	✓
State fixed effects	✓	✓	✓
Economic and demographic controls	✓	✓	✓

Source: Author's dataset; Institute for Truth in Accounting (2011); National Association of State Auditors, Comptrollers and Treasurers (2005–2011); U.S. Bureau of Labor Statistics (1995–2012); U.S Bureau of Economic Analysis (1995–2012); U.S. Census Bureau, Census of Governments (1995–2012).

Note: Robust standard errors are clustered by pension plan in parentheses. Estimated intercept is not reported. Controls include unemployment rate, per capita personal income, logged population, and federal transfers as a fraction of general revenue. ★★★$p < 0.01$, ★★$p < 0.05$, ★$p < 0.1$.

Timely states, pension boards that have chairs elected by a majority of board members rather than appointed by the state government report, on average, funding ratios that are 55 percentage points above their unbiased estimate. Similarly, boards that are chaired by employees or annuitants rather than elected officials or government appointed representatives report ratios that are 37 percentage points above their unbiased estimate. Boards that are composed of 10 percent employees report values that are 8 percentage points above the unbiased measure.[38] Finally, the actual health of the pension plan has a significant impact on the board's reported estimates, but only in states that release their financial reports in a timely manner. In these states, a 1 percentage point decrease in the previous year's revised funding ratio is offset almost completely by a 0.9 percentage point increase in the current year's disclosure gap. If a board is chaired by an individual elected by the other members, this gap expands even faster as the pension's health worsens.

In this chapter, I provided important insight into the political and budgetary determinants of fiscal malfeasance in the U.S. states, furthering the scholarly understanding of fiscal transparency and disclosure in general and of the role that improper accounting and reporting behavior plays in manipulating real policy outcomes in particular. I laid out three hypotheses about what might influence inaccurate reporting behavior and "creative accounting." First, the availability of public financial data, coupled with poor pension performance and organized, attentive state workers, is likely to lead pension boards to report overly optimistic funding ratios. Additionally, pension boards primarily composed of state employees—rather than individuals who represent the government—will be more likely to inaccurately disclose pension finances.

Using my original dataset constructed from the raw data of seventeen years' worth of pension CAFRs, I find overall support for my hypotheses. The transparency of the state and presence of attentive stakeholders are far and away the most important predictors of dishonest reporting. Evidence is strong for the hypothesis that ease of access to financial data is associated with greater attempts by pension boards to fudge reported numbers and that this effect is exacerbated by strong unions and poor funding performance. When pension funding is a transparent and salient issue for voters, effort and incentive to suppress the accuracy of the data available to them is even greater.

Perhaps just as important as the results that support my hypotheses are the results that do not support them. Like the findings of other scholars, I find no evidence of any relationship between partisanship and pension disclosure behavior.[39] This suggests that Democrats are in fact not catering to unions' clientelistic demands to any greater extent than their Republican counterparts. Furthermore, increases in electoral competition and the cost of losing power to partisan rivals (i.e., increases in polarization) have no bearing on reporting accuracy, either. I also find that the disclosure gap in asset performance is more difficult to explain than that of liability growth (reported in the Methodological Appendix). This is not terribly surprising because, as discussed in previous chapters, pension asset management is typically handled in a less politically contentious fashion than that of liabilities. Additionally, the small literature that exists on the transparency and disclosure of the revenue side of public balance sheets offers conflicting predictions.[40] Attentive stakeholders may want to ensure that all groups receive accurate information about asset performance so that voters agree to smooth expenditures efficiently over time. This jump in efficiency and decrease in dead-weight loss may boost the expenditure side of the ledger, if expenditures are not fully transparent and disclosed. This may be the reason that we do not see unions and other interested parties attempting to obfuscate and exaggerate asset reporting, although many other competing hypotheses that cannot be rejected may also explain this curiosity.

The chapter's findings contribute to a conceptualization of the distinction between disclosure and transparency, and how they interact with one another under different political and fiscal regimes. In particular, ease of access to information is not always a boon for good government, to the extent that we believe that the accurate disclosure of financial data is an important characteristic of a robust democracy. So long as one group possesses greater information-processing abilities, increased transparency will make all groups better informed only when the data are accurate and unbiased. If the group that has lower processing costs—in this case, organized workers—is also in a position of power to manipulate the accuracy of the data released, this chapter has provided evidence that disclosure will suffer. When this happens, voters may as well not have any data at all.

Democracy requires multiple constituencies to make decisions about resource allocation on a regular basis. These decisions are often difficult, if not impossible, to make based on any number of dimensions, such as efficiency, preferences, and social responsibility. Without understanding the details of these choices, a community cannot make informed decisions about contemporaneous resource allocation—how much for employees versus how much for taxpayers—or about future resource allocation—which generation pays for what and when. This, of course, is true not only in the context of public sector worker compensation but also in connection to any other type of technically complex policy in which the costs and benefits are not borne equally. To get even close to resolving these issues, all decisionmakers need not only to have all the facts but also to understand them. Pension finance, in this regard, is no exception.

CHAPTER IV

What Does Pension Debt Mean for What States Can Do?

Much has been made over the perceived crisis in public sector pension funding over the past decade and a half. In the wake of the Great Recession in 2008, a number of municipalities (and states) experienced severe financial distress and filed for federal bankruptcy protection in ways that had not been seen since the Great Depression.[1] These local governments often pointed their fingers at unsustainable employee pensions when trying to justify the city's financial woes. In response to the financial crisis and the decline in the global economy, many local governments cut public services, increased taxes, or both.[2] Detroit, Michigan, for example, faced skyrocketing borrowing costs and, at certain points, was cut off from access to credit markets altogether. Emergency Manager Kevyn Orr, appointed by Republican governor of Michigan Rick Snyder, stipulated that Detroit implement substantial reductions to pensions for public sector workers as a precondition for the city's eligibility to seek federal bankruptcy protection.[3] These public employees had never imagined that their pensions were anything but 100 percent secured. In fact, the federal bankruptcy judge later claimed that the deal violated the state constitution and would need to be amended to better preserve the contractual obligations owed to Michigan public workers.[4]

Although states are not legally allowed to use the federal bankruptcy code to default on loans in the way that municipalities are, state-run public pensions have posed and continue to pose a similar threat to service

cutbacks and—often concurrently—increases in borrowing costs.[5] Increases
in borrowing costs have a direct impact on how many dollars it will take to
finance a governmental expenditure. Between 1975 and 2002, for instance,
the spread between the mean of Moody's top-rated bonds (AAA) and the
mean of their low-rated bonds (Baa) was 74.1 basis points.[6] What this means
in practice is that, on average, a state with poorly rated bonds would have to
pay $7.41 million more in interest for every $1 billion of debt issued, relative
to a top-rated state. Even in large states with broad tax bases, this is not an
insignificant premium. When one considers that states with low tax capacity
often receive the worst credit ratings, however, this spread in interest costs
becomes even more important to issues of effective governance and fiscal
sustainability.

There are three ways to measure borrowing costs: by directly calculating
interest costs of new bond issues, by using surveys that poll bond traders
about the price that they think a new state bond issue would hypotheti-
cally command, and by looking at bond ratings from the major credit rating
agencies (i.e., Standard and Poor's, Moody's, and Fitch).[7] As a number of
scholars have discovered, however, bond ratings are the best measure to use
in empirical work that investigates debt costs. Looking only at new bond
issues, for instance, creates potential selection effects that are not easily miti-
gated: States are likely to make the decision to borrow—and how much to
borrow—based on the same criteria that influences their interest costs.[8] The
incidence of new bond issues is thus likely to be strongly conflated with
the cost of borrowing. Using surveys, with the Chubb Insurance Company's
Relative Value survey being the one most often employed, creates other
sorts of issues, the most obvious of which is that bond traders may be wrong,
and in systematic ways. It is not clear, ultimately, whether bond traders are
equipped to give point estimates of borrowing costs for states, particularly
for those that are not currently issuing debt. Most of all, evidence suggests
that credit ratings, in and of themselves, do in fact influence borrowing
costs.[9] For these reasons, there is good reason to study credit ratings agencies
and their decisions—both as indicators and determinants of interest costs.

Much like the U.S. federal government, state governments have the
authority to issue bonds to pay for all sorts of public projects.[10] When bonds
are not issued to finance a specific long-term capital project that will be able
to generate its own revenue (such as a toll road), they are referred to as
general obligation (GO) bonds and are meant to be paid for through the
state's general power of taxation. Every time a state issues GO bonds, the

two major credit ratings agencies, Standard and Poor's (S&P) and Moody's, evaluate the riskiness of the bond issue and assign it a letter grade meant to connote the likelihood of a state defaulting on the bond. The rating does not just reflect the worthiness of the project or projects that the bond is meant to finance; the rating acts as an indicator of the state's general fiscal and financial soundness. S&P delineates their rating criteria of state GO bonds as follows:[11]

- Economy
- Management
- Financial performance and flexibility
- Debt burden

According to the published S&P criteria, pension liabilities and obligations fall under both of the last two areas of analysis and are considered to be an essential component of GO debt ratings. Most important when evaluating the risk of pension liabilities to GO bonds are

- growth in assets;
- growth in liabilities;
- pension funded ratio (i.e., the ratio of assets to liabilities);
- contribution rate (i.e., the amount of dollars contributed to the fund by public employers relative to the annual required contribution, ARC); and
- unfunded pension liabilities as a percentage of total plan assets (the unfunded actuarial accrued liabilities, or UAAL).[12]

There is no debate that bond spreads are higher for issues with lower ratings, and some limited evidence suggests that credit ratings are in fact causally related to the cost of borrowing for state governments.[13] Ultimately, these two characteristics—credit ratings and interest costs—are strongly related to one another. In this chapter, I explore (1) whether the credit ratings agencies used self-reported, politically manipulated pension data to inform their evaluations of GO risk or whether they used a more sophisticated analysis that considers potential misreporting by state-run pension administrative boards, and (2) whether these key financial decisions—the fundedness of the pension plans and the credit rating of the state—affected the lived experience of state residents through their effects on the contemporaneous budget. While chapter 6 provides evidence that expansionary pension legislation increases tax burdens despite state pension contributions not eating up greater portions of state budgets over my sample period (as discussed in chapter 2), I preface these findings by exploring what the actual consequences are of expanding and underfunding pensions: the cost of borrowing. Using historical S&P's ratings collected by the Pew Trusts and my revised pension data, I run a series of simple empirical models to see whether self-reported or revised data are better at predicting one-year ahead GO ratings.[14] The self-reported data outperform the revised data in terms of explanatory power, though the revised data are better at predicting actual interest costs. Additionally, the cost of borrowing has a significant and notable impact on the types of services that states expend resources on.

Borrowing Costs, Credit Ratings, and Pensions

There is good reason to imagine that bondholders, and prospective bondholders, would care deeply about pension funding. Although the law is still unclear about the question of whether state GO bondholders or state pensioners would be paid out first in the event of a state fiscal crisis, it is clear that GO bondholders and pensioners would be legally entitled to payouts before other creditors.[15] In this sense, it is natural for GO bondholders to see state pensioners as rivals in the case of default. Recent legal rulings in municipal financial reorganizations have underscored this uncertainty, despite substate governments having access to the federal bankruptcy code.[16] If pension liabilities are large, and underfunded, bondholders may view public employee pensions as a threat to future loan payments and as the impetus to increase their assessment of the riskiness of purchasing GO bonds. As a result, interest and other borrowing costs are likely to increase for states with less-than-stellar pension balance sheets.

Even if bondholders and pensioners were not in competition over payouts in the event of a state fiscal crisis, however, creditors should care about unfunded pension liabilities simply because they represent a form of (off-budget) debt. Any entity—state, municipal, corporate, or individual—is certain to see an increase in their borrowing costs as their debt load relative to earning power increases.[17] As the debt burden increases for the state relative to their total revenue or to their gross state product, for instance, it will be increasingly difficult for the state to both pay off loans and continue providing day-to-day public services. As a result, creditors will believe that the likelihood of default on payments is greater. This is similar to the logic behind why tax and expenditure limits have been found to increase and decrease borrowing costs for states, respectively.[18]

Given the concerns that prospective creditors might have, credit rating agencies should rationally take public pension size and fundedness into account when assigning grades to state GO debt. That S&P explicitly states that state pension funding is a critical component of GO debt ratings certainly lends credence to this hypothesis.[19] Furthermore, previous work has found strong links between political and institutional variables and credit ratings, including work on tax and expenditure limits, public management quality, political uncertainty, and political corruption.[20] If these political and fiscal variables influence credit ratings—and thus borrowing costs—it seems likely that public pensions would also play a role.

Thus far, the importance of pensions has received little attention. A body of research does show how private pension management affects corporate debt ratings, but Alicia Munnell, Jean-Pierre Aubry, and Laura Quinby are the only scholars to have systematically investigated the relationship between public pensions and public credit ratings.[21] Their work found that, in conflict with my previous argument, public pensions actually had no significant relationship to credit ratings, and only a mild influence on bond yields. Their analysis differs from mine in a number of important ways, however. First, the research does not limit the analysis to GO bonds. Although they add a dummy indicator for GO bonds, there is reason to believe that bondholders and credit rating agencies think of the relationship between GO bonds and pensions and revenue bonds and pensions as wholly different. As discussed previously, GO bondholders expect to be in competition with pensioners in the event of fiscal catastrophe; revenue bond loans are repaid through the revenue-generating capacity of the entity that issues the bond (i.e., through tolls or other fees), and bondholders should *never* expect to receive payments that have been generated through the taxation power of the state. For this reason, revenue bonds are viewed as riskier than GO bonds and command both higher yields and less favorable credit ratings, characteristics confirmed by the negative coefficient on the GO dummy in Munnell, Aubry, and Quinby's paper. The second and more problematic concern is the way in which the authors operationalize the pension variable. The authors use the percentage of the pension plans' self-reported ARC actually paid as an indicator of the funds' riskiness or threat to fiscal stability. This is not an ideal measure to use for several reasons. The first problem is that the percentage of ARC paid out is a flow measure, whereas pension fundedness (and size) is a stock measure. Using the percentage of ARC paid by the state legislature as a measure of fiscal risk is like using the national deficit rather than the national debt when evaluating the fiscal sustainability of the U.S. government. Although these two measures are often conflated in casual discourse, bondholders are more sophisticated in their understanding of the difference. For this reason alone, it is not terribly surprising that the researchers could not find any effects on credit ratings and found only a small impact on bond yields. The second problem with using the authors' ARC measure is that this variable is actually not an indicator of pension fundedness but rather of the quality of public management. As previously discussed, the percent of ARC paid out is a flow measure and there is little relationship between the yearly contribution rate and the overall fundedness of a plan. The yearly contribution rate *is* likely to be related to the quality of fiscal management in the state and a host of other political variables, however, as discussed in chapter 2. In my dataset of forty-nine states from 1997 to 2008, 75 percent of state-years contributed *more than 85 percent of their ARC*, whereas 88 percent of states claimed to have contributed *100 percent or more of their yearly required contribution*. There is, it appears, virtually no variation in this measure; of course no link to borrowing costs was uncovered. This clustering of self-reported contribution rates suggests something more sinister, however: States are picking ARC targets that can be handily met (in the extreme, a number of states over a number of years picked $0 as their ARC and subsequently reported a 100 percent contribution rate when they, obviously, met their ARC target quite easily).

I next address these issues by building my own model and using measures of "pension threat" that are more appropriate for understanding whether poor fiscal and financial performance of pensions can be held responsible for increased costs of doing business for states. The following analysis also addresses whether pensions can be held responsible for contemporary changes to spending patterns and whether pension maintenance is crowding out other state spending.

Data

The empirical analysis in this chapter required the collection of additional data to match the variables that S&P claims to consider when calculating

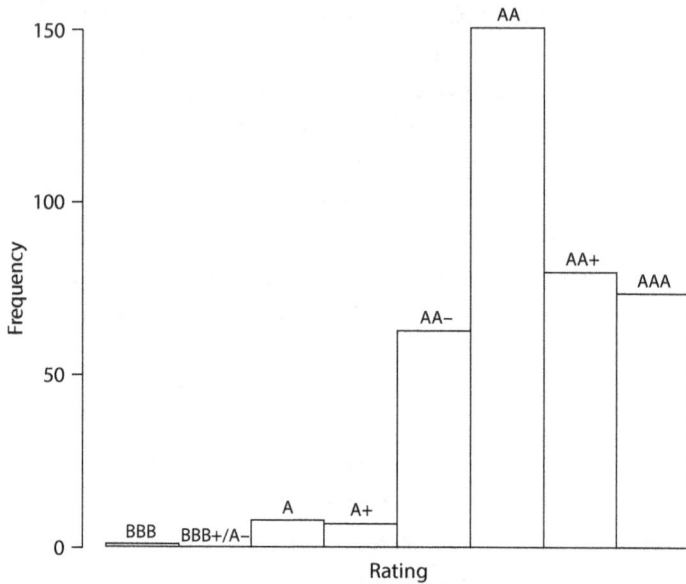

Figure 4.1 S&P's credit ratings of U.S. state general obligation debt from 2001–2012.

Source: Prah, Rotmil, and Fehr (2014).

their ratings. First and foremost, I had to collect the credit ratings themselves. S&P's credit ratings of state GO bonds were collected from Pew and span all fifty states from 2001 to 2012.[22] The lowest rating over this time period was a BBB given to California in 2003. Many states received S&P's highest rating of AAA, often several years in a row. The median rating over this time period was AA, which is the third highest rating a state could receive. Figure 4.1 shows the distribution of the S&P's ratings over state-years.

Second, I needed to measure the cost to state governments of borrowing (issuing debt). Rather than directly calculate total borrowing costs of new bond issues, which poses potential problems of selection bias and requires a large financial investment, I collected data on the total cost of interest payments relative to total debt outstanding from the U.S. Census of Governments.[23] This measure does not perfectly capture the cost of borrowing additional funds for government business purposes, but total relative interest costs for the state government is a concrete indicator of how costly debt is, overall, for a state in a given year. This measure also takes into account any refinancing opportunities that the state chooses to avail itself of. Figure 4.2 depicts the normal distribution of relative interest costs over state-years.

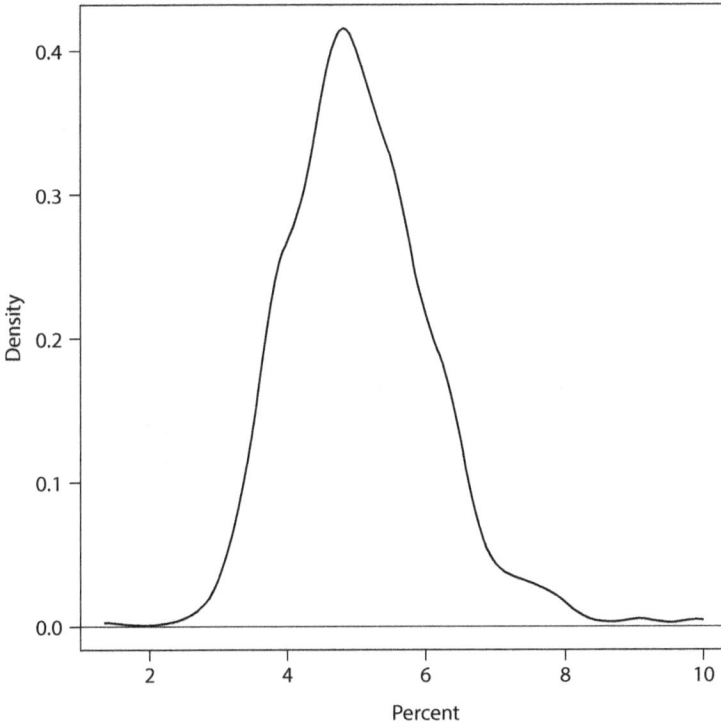

Figure 4.2 Distribution of interest costs as a fraction of state debt across state-years, 1995–2011. States with the highest interest costs relative to general expenditures (over 6 percent for more than one year in the sample) were Connecticut, Delaware, Massachusetts, New Hampshire, and Rhode Island. States with the highest nonpension debt loads relative to general expenditures (over 100 percent for more than one year in the sample) were Connecticut, Delaware, Illinois, New Hampshire, New Jersey, and Rhode Island.

Source: U.S. Census Bureau, Census of Governments (1995–2012).

Third, I also collected data on states' self-reported pension liabilities and assets. In addition to collecting S&P's credit ratings for state GO debt, the Pew Center on the States compiled a comprehensive dataset of state-level pension liabilities and assets over twelve years.[24] I use this self-reported data to ask the question of whether credit rating agencies and borrowing costs are responsive to states' self-reported funding ratios or contribution rates.

In addition to these newly collected data, I bring a variety of data we have seen in previous chapters to the analysis that follows. These data include indicators of the state economy from the U.S. Bureau of Labor

Statistics and the Bureau of Economic Analysis; state government partisan composition from Carl Klarner; state polarization data from Boris Shor and Nolan McCarty; budgetary data from the U.S. Census of Governments; and, in models without state fixed effects, indicators of legal limits on state debt and deficits from Yilin Hou and Daniel Smith.[25]

After I identified whether credit rating agencies and investors take *self-reported* pension data into account when evaluating debt riskiness, I go one step further and investigate whether they are taking standardized pension liability and asset data into account by using my revised measure of pension liabilities and assets. As discussed in previous chapters, self-reported data are unreliable for a number of reasons and can be manipulated with differing degrees of ease from state to state and from year to year. States also might self-report with a direct eye toward the credit rating agencies, as the impact of pensions on borrowing costs is surely one of the most important consequences of data disclosure. With this in mind, the following analysis investigates whether rating agencies and creditors are sophisticated enough to distinguish between the "pretty" numbers that states control and self-report and the more realistic numbers that have been calculated objectively.

Empirical Model

Suppose the relationship between the S&P's belief in the likelihood of default and a series of economic, financial, and political indicators can be summarized as follows:

$$y_{st}^* = \beta_1 \, Funding\,Ratio_{s,\,t-1} + \beta_2 \, Contribution\,Rate_{s,\,t-1}$$
$$+ \beta_3 \, Liab\,Growth_{s,\,t-1} + \beta_4 \, Asset\,Growth_{s,\,t-1} + \gamma \mathbf{X}_{s,\,t-1} + \varepsilon_{st}$$

Note that *FundingRatio* is constructed as the fraction of plan assets to total liabilities, that is, *Assets/Liabilities*. I also rerun the model using the state-aggregated UAAL, that is, $(Liabilities - Assets)/Assets = 1/FundingRatio - 1$, and obtain qualitatively similar results. *ContributionRate* is the number of dollars contributed by public employers relative to either the self-reported ARC or the ARC I constructed using the new liability and asset calculations I created by hand. *LiabGrowth* and *AssetGrowth* are liability and asset growth rates, respectively, observed from periods $t - 2$ to $t - 1$; $\mathbf{X}_{s,\,t-1}$ is a vector of control variables previously described; and ε_{st} is an error term.

Assume that we cannot directly observe $y\star$ but instead we observe one of the nine possible ratings that S&P assigns to the state's GO debt in year t.[26] These responses are modeled as follows:

$$y = \begin{cases} 0 & \text{if } y\star \leq \mu_1, \\ 1 & \text{if } \mu_1 < y\star \leq \mu_2, \\ 2 & \text{if } \mu_2 < y\star \leq \mu_3, \\ 3 & \text{if } \mu_3 < y\star \leq \mu_4, \\ 4 & \text{if } \mu_4 < y\star \leq \mu_5, \\ 5 & \text{if } \mu_5 < y\star \leq \mu_6, \\ 6 & \text{if } \mu_6 < y\star \leq \mu_7, \\ 7 & \text{if } \mu_7 < y\star \leq \mu_8, \\ 8 & \text{if } \mu_8 < y\star \end{cases}$$

and an ordered probit is run to estimate the coefficients of the regression on the latent dependent variable.

Alternatively, I can use a linear probability model (ordinary least squares, OLS) to estimate the likelihood that S&P assigns a state's debt a particular grade in year t without much fear that the marginal effects will differ markedly from those of a correctly specified nonlinear model.[27] OLS, apart from possessing the luxury of easily interpretable coefficients, also allows me to make the specification more robust by including fixed effects and robust clustered standard errors. OLS does not allow for, however, the possibility of qualitative differences between certain notches of credit ratings, that is, going from an AA− to an AA is treated the same as going from an AA+ to an AAA in a linear probability model, whereas there is no presumption of equivalence in an ordered probit. Both specifications are reported in the results.

Finally, I run a fixed effects linear model to test whether interest costs—constructed as interest payments relative to total outstanding debt—are influenced by pension concerns in patterns similar to the S&P's credit ratings.

$$Interest\ Costs_{st} = \beta_1\ Funding\ Ratio_{s,\,t-1} + \beta_2\ Contribution\ Rate_{s,\,t-1}$$
$$+ \beta_3\ Liab\ Growth_{s,\,t-1} + \beta_4\ Asset\ Growth_{s,\,t-1} + \gamma \mathbf{X}_{s,\,t-1} + v_{s,\,t-1,\,r} + \varepsilon_{st}$$

Here, the variables are defined as in equations (4.1), and I variously include fixed effects for states, years, and regions, as each specification indicates. All standard errors are robust and clustered by state.

Results

Ordered Probit Results

This section includes the results from four regressions estimating the effect of revised versus self-reported pension data on the S&P GO credit rating decision. The first two models, depicted in table 4.1, are specified in the same way except that model 1 uses my revised measures of fundedness and contribution rates, while model 2 uses numbers that are self-reported in state financial documents. Using the S&P's criteria for evaluating GO debt as guidance, I also included a number of economic and financial controls as previously described. Although not explicitly included on the list of criteria, I controlled for political factors in GO credit ratings as well by including binary indicators of partisan control of government and a measure of polarization.

The pension fundedness measure is statistically significant only in model 2, and in the correct direction, which implies that an increase in the self-reported funding ratio increases the likelihood of receiving a higher credit rating from S&P. The revised, standardized funding ratio has no relationship to the credit score. Note that the coefficient on the revised funding ratio variable in model 1 has a standard error that is actually smaller than that of the self-reported funding ratio in model 2. Model 1's coefficient is not statistically significant because the point estimate is so close to zero. The predicted probabilities for each category of observed credit rating are presented in figure 4.3.

Model 3 in table 4.2 is identical to model 1 in table 4.1 except that I substitute the revised funding ratio and contribution rate for my measure of revised excess liabilities. The same is true of the relationship between model 2 and model 4, except in that I am using self-reported numbers. In contrast to the first two models, the unfunded liability measures—both revised and self-reported—are clearly statistically significant, and in the correct direction. The magnitude of the self-reported coefficient in model 4, however, is more than four times as large as the revised coefficient in model 1, and the overall fit of model 4 is superior to that of model 3. The predicted probabilities are plotted in figure 4.4.

Notably, the contribution rates have no impact on credit ratings, however, in line with Munnell, Aubry, and Quinby's findings. All other pension funding variables are statistically significant in my analyses with the exception of the revised funding ratio. This is important if we care about the

TABLE 4.1

Ordered probit regression of fundedness on S&P general obligation credit ratings (0 = BBB, 8 = AAA)

	Model 1	Model 2
Revised funding ratio	−0.110	
	(0.356)	
Revised contribution rate	−0.002	
	(0.035)	
Revised liability growth	−0.140	
	(0.298)	
Revised asset growth	0.146	
	(0.366)	
Unemployment rate	−30.029★★★	−27.926★★★
	(5.677)	(5.690)
Per capita income (U.S. dollars, thousands)	0.044★★★	0.053★★★
	(0.014)	(0.013)
Real gross state product growth	−3.159★	−3.029
	(1.859)	(1.860)
Debt-to-revenue	−1.049★★★	−1.051★★★
	(0.268)	(0.251)
Surplus-to-expenditures	−1.954★★	−1.820★
	(0.948)	(0.958)
Legal debt cap	0.325★★	0.447★★★
	(0.132)	(0.130)
Transfers-to-expenditures	−4.923★★★	−4.404★★★
	(1.308)	(1.234)
Dem. governor	0.014	0.019
	(0.119)	(0.115)
Dem. senate	−0.095	−0.042
	(0.149)	(0.142)
Dem. house	−0.637★★★	−0.594★★★
	(0.144)	(0.140)
Avg. polarization	−0.436★★★	−0.543★★★
	(0.142)	(0.143)
Self-reported funding ratio		1.026★★
		(0.426)
Self-reported contribution rate		−0.012
		(0.175)
Self-reported liability growth		−2.618
		(1.688)
Self-reported asset growth		0.010
		(0.933)

(continued)

TABLE 4.1

(*continued*)

	Model 1	Model 2
AIC	982.706	1030.697
BIC	1067.643	1117.031
Log likelihood	−469.353	−493.349
Deviance	938.706	986.697
No. obs.	351	374

Source: Prah, Rotmil, and Fehr (2014); Author's dataset; Public Plans Data (2001–2022); U.S. Bureau of Labor Statistics (1995–2012); U.S. Bureau of Economic Analysis (1995–2012); U.S. Census Bureau (1995–2012); Klarner (2013b, 2013c); Shor (2020).

Note: AIC, Akaike information criterion; BIC, Bayesian information criterion. ★★★$p < 0.01$, ★★$p < 0.05$, ★$p < 0.01$.

consequences of both accurate and inaccurate disclosure of pension finances on issues like costs of borrowing—pension balance *matters* for both the man on the street and the man in the state capitol. I next present a number of additional models to bolster my claims.

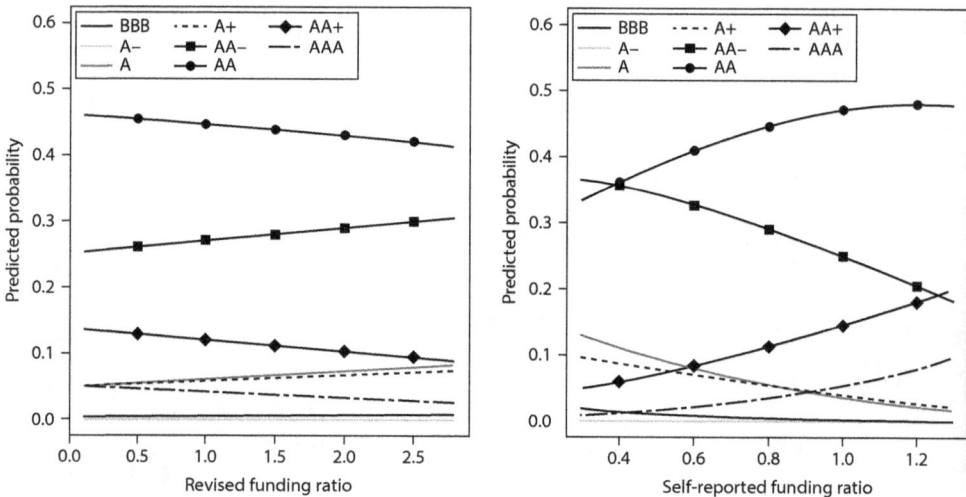

Figure 4.3 Predicted probabilities of credit rating assignments using funding ratio as predictor. Effects plotted from model 1 (left-hand panel) and model 2 (right-hand panel) of table 4.1.

Source: Prah, Rotmil, and Fehr (2014); Author's dataset; Public Plans Data (2001–2022); U.S. Bureau of Labor Statistics (1995–2012); U.S. Bureau of Economic Analysis (1995–2012); U.S. Census Bureau, Census of Governments (1995–2012); Klarner (2013b, 2013c); Shor (2020).

TABLE 4.2

Ordered probit regression of excess liabilities on S&P general obligation credit ratings (0 = BBB, 8 = AAA)

	Model 3	Model 4
Revised excess liabilities	−0.171**	
	(0.076)	
Revised liability growth	−0.053	
	(0.253)	
Revised asset growth	−0.046	
	(0.314)	
Unemployment rate	−12.780***	26.851***
	(3.160)	(5.681)
Per capita income (U.S. dollars, thousands)	0.066***	0.051***
	(0.011)	(0.013)
Real gross state product growth	−3.034**	−3.019
	(1.525)	(1.841)
Debt-to-revenue	−1.362***	−0.979***
	(0.237)	(0.251)
Surplus-to-expenditures	−1.807**	−1.804*
	(0.841)	(0.957)
Legal debt cap	0.287**	0.426***
	(0.116)	(0.128)
Transfer-to-expenditures	−3.175***	−4.468***
	(1.061)	(1.217)
Dem. governor	0.002	0.026
	(0.107)	(0.115)
Dem. senate	0.050	−0.038
	(0.134)	(0.142)
Dem. house	−0.598***	−0.592***
	(0.132)	(0.140)
Avg. polarization	−0.508***	−0.556***
	(0.122)	(0.143)
Self-reported excess liabilities		−0.716***
		(0.269)
Self-reported liability growth		−2.303
		(1.630)
Self-reported asset growth		0.186
		(0.914)
AIC	1250.246	1030.027
BIC	1336.068	1112.492
Log likelihood	−604.123	−494.013
Deviance	1208.246	988.027
No. obs.	440	375

Source: Prah, Rotmil, and Fehr (2014); Author's dataset; Public Plans Data (2001–2022); U.S. Bureau of Labor Statistics (1995–2012); U.S. Bureau of Economic Analysis (1995–2012); U.S. Census Bureau (1995–2012); Klarner (2013b, 2013c); Shor (2020).

Note: AIC, Akaike information criterion; BIC, Bayesian information criterion. ***p < 0.01, **p < 0.05, *p < 0.01.

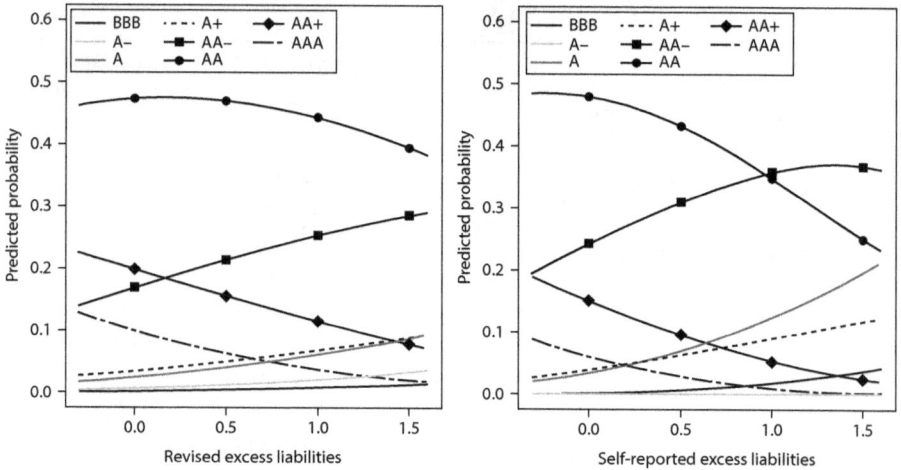

Figure 4.4 Predicted probabilities of credit rating assignments using excess liabilities as predictor. Effects plotted from model 3 (left-hand panel) and model 4 (right-hand panel) from table 4.2.

Source: Prah, Rotmil, and Fehr (2014); Author's dataset; Public Plans Data (2001–2022); U.S. Bureau of Labor Statistics (1995–2012); U.S. Bureau of Economic Analysis (1995–2012); U.S. Census Bureau, Census of Governments (1995–2012); Klarner (2013b, 2013c); Shor (2020).

Linear Probability Model Results

To ensure that my results are robust, I present a linear probability model of S&P's grades that incorporates fixed effects and robust clustered standard errors. In table 4.3 and table 4.4, I present a simple OLS model predicting credit grades as a function of funding ratios. As shown in models 5–7, the revised funding ratio remains statistically insignificant, which is in line with the results from the ordered probit model. Models 9 and 10 also support results from the previous section, indicating that the self-reported funding ratio has a statistically significant positive relationship to one-year-ahead credit ratings even after controlling for year, region, and state fixed effects. Interestingly, my measure of general fund balance (the *Surplus-to-Expenditures* variable in tables 4.3 and 4.4) switches signs in both model 7 and model 10 relative to the ordered probit, but remains insignificant in the other four linear probability models in tables 4.3 and 4.4. Munnell, Aubry, and Quinby also found the general fund balance to be statistically negatively related to credit ratings in their probit and simple OLS regressions. This peculiarity disappears after I control for unobserved across-state and across-year variation using fixed effects.[28]

TABLE 4.3

Linear probability model of revised fundedness and S&P general obligation credit ratings (0 = BBB, 8 = AAA)

	Model 5	Model 6	Model 7
Revised funding ratio	−0.036	0.546	0.166
	(0.732)	(0.927)	(0.526)
Revised contribution rate	−0.001	0.017	−0.011
	(0.028)	(0.031)	(0.013)
Revised liability growth	−0.155	0.108	0.051
	(0.175)	(0.141)	(0.065)
Revised asset growth	0.174	0.034	−0.090
	(0.244)	(0.182)	(0.069)
Unemployment rate	−29.850***	−35.000***	−18.055**
	(9.118)	(11.701)	(7.041)
Per capita income	0.044**	0.030	0.122***
(U.S. dollars, thousands)	(0.020)	(0.033)	(0.045)
Real gross state product	−3.095*	−2.177	−1.333
growth	(1.733)	(2.023)	(1.241)
Debt-to-revenue	−9.08*	−0.399	0.588
	(0.499)	(0.638)	(0.539)
Surplus-to-expenditures	−1.808	−0.692	0.662*
	(1.463)	(1.318)	(0.396)
Legal debt cap	0.410	0.449	
	(0.309)	(0.342)	
Transfers-to-expenditures	−4.451*	−5.444***	0.339
	(2.354)	(2.636)	(1.845)
Dem. governor	0.013	−0.029	−0.209*
	(0.167)	(0.171)	(0.106)
Dem. senate	−0.154	−0.193	0.095
	(0.278)	(0.286)	(0.113)
Dem. house	−0.622**	−0.587**	−0.158
	(0.284)	(0.274)	(0.097)
Avg. polarization	−0.483	−0.170	1.015**
	(0.448)	(0.454)	(0.495)
Year fixed effects		✓	✓
Region fixed effects		✓	
State fixed effects			✓
R^2	0.275	0.322	0.895
Adj. R^2	0.242	0.265	0.869
No. obs.	351	351	351

Source: Prah, Rotmil, and Fehr (2014); Author's dataset; Public Plans Data (2001–2022); U.S. Bureau of Labor Statistics (1995–2012); U.S. Bureau of Economic Analysis (1995–2012); U.S. Census Bureau (1995–2012); Klarner (2013b, 2013c); Shor (2020).

Note: ***$p < 0.01$, **$p < 0.05$, *$p < 0.01$. Estimated intercept not reported. Robust state-clustered standard errors reported in parentheses.

TABLE 4.4

Linear probability model of self-reported fundedness and S&P general obligation credit ratings (0 = BBB, 8 = AAA)

	Model 8	Model 9	Model 10
Self-reported funding ratio	0.991	1.513*	0.828*
	(0.663)	(0.828)	(0.459)
Self-reported contribution rate	−0.020	0.019	−0.028
	(0.158)	(0.173)	(0.067)
Self-reported liability growth	−2.671	−1.982	−0.084
	(2.188)	(1.700)	(0.576)
Self-reported asset growth	0.169	0.231	−0.527
	(0.739)	(0.810)	(0.584)
Unemployment rate	−27.454***	−31.952***	−16.698**
	(9.585)	(11.332)	(6.917)
Per capita income (U.S. dollars, thousands)	0.051**	0.031	0.128***
	(0.020)	(0.032)	(0.043)
Real gross state product growth	−2.874	−1.427	−1.433
	(1.817)	(1.980)	(1.267)
Debt-to-revenue	−0.853*	−0.355	0.715
	(0.456)	(0.563)	(0.542)
Surplus-to-expenditures	−1.706	−0.605	0.757**
	(1.403)	(1.257)	(0.380)
Legal debt gap	0.503	0.502	
	(0.327)	(0.351)	
Transfers-to-expenditures	−3.859*	−5.105**	0.086
	(2.091)	(2.429)	(1.562)
Dem. governor	0.014	−0.019	−0.211**
	(0.152)	(0.146)	(0.099)
Dem. senate	−0.100	−0.145	0.001
	(0.275)	(0.282)	(0.109)
Dem. house	−0.568**	−0.485*	−0.164*
	(0.270)	(0.263)	(0.093)
Avg. polarization	−0.567	−0.271	0.860*
	(0.427)	(0.417)	(0.440)
Year fixed effects		✓	✓
Region fixed effects		✓	
State fixed effects			✓
R^2	0.290	0.342	0.893
Adj. R^2	0.261	0.291	0.869
No. obs.	374	374	374

Source: Prah, Rotmil, and Fehr (2014); Author's dataset; Public Plans Data (2001–2022); U.S. Bureau of Labor Statistics (1995–2012); U.S. Bureau of Economic Analysis (1995–2012); U.S. Census Bureau (1995–2012); Klarner (2013b, 2013c); Shor (2020).

Note: ***$p < 0.01$, **$p < 0.05$, *$p < 0.01$. Estimated intercept not reported. Robust state-clustered standard errors reported in parentheses.

The patterns in models 11–16 (tables 4.5 and 4.6) are similar to those described previously. Instead of funding ratios, however, I used state-aggregated UAALs (i.e., excess liabilities) as the key operative predictor variable. In two of the three models (11 to 13), the revised measures are statistically significant and correctly signed as in the ordered probit, although the self-reported variables are (in two of the three models, 14 to 16) greater in absolute size—again, as in the ordered probit. These models show that the ordered probit results are generally robust to a number of specifications, providing further evidence that pension fundedness has a clear and direct impact on crediting rating agencies' decisions.

Interest Costs

I next investigate the relationship between interest costs (rather than credit ratings) and pension debt through a series of OLS and fixed effects regressions of various indicators of pension funding. As an informal measure of state borrowing costs, the outcome variable is constructed as the ratio of total interest payments for the year to total outstanding debt. This serves as a kind of effective interest rate at which the state is borrowing. When this measure increases, states are paying more in interest for a fixed amount of borrowed principal (debt)—that is, borrowing costs are greater. Although this measure is not as ideal as the credit rating agency grades from the previous analysis (as discussed in the beginning of the chapter), these regressions serve as an additional check on the behavior of market participants. Furthermore, because there is not a one-to-one relationship between state GO credit grades and interest cost, creditors (who are actually purchasing the debt) may behave differently than credit rating agencies (which are simply evaluating the debt).[29]

The first set of models, included in table 4.7 and table 4.8, uses the revised pension data to examine whether any statistical relationship exists between the size or financial position of the state's pension system and the interest cost of carrying and issuing nonpension debt. Table 4.7 uses the revised funding ratio as the operable funding measure and Table 4.8 uses my revised excess liabilities variable, but neither of these funding measures offer any appreciable insight into the behavior of creditors in the sense that interest costs are statistically unrelated to both. In fact, no measure of funding status—revised or self-reported, as presented in table 4.9 and table 4.10—bears any statistical relationship to interest costs. The factors that have the largest impact on the

TABLE 4.5

Linear probability model of revised excess liabilities and S&P general obligation credit ratings (0 = BBB, 8 = AAA)

	Model 11	Model 12	Model 13
Revised excess liabilities	−0.152	−0.368★	−0.332★★
	(0.171)	(0.196)	(0.137)
Revised liability growth	−0.082	0.167	0.091
	(0.142)	(0.163)	(0.108)
Revised asset growth	−0.002	−0.111	−0.056
	(0.193)	(0.174)	(0.108)
Unemployment rate	−13.751★★	−32.095★★★	−18.225★★★
	(5.343)	(9.562)	(6.953)
Per capita income (U.S. dollars, thousands)	0.067★★	0.025	0.112★★★
	(0.021)	(0.028)	(0.043)
Real gross state product growth	−3.181★★	−3.188★★	−1.781★
	(1.250)	(1.616)	(1.070)
Debt-to-revenue	−1.253★★★	−0.398	−0.064
	(0.469)	(0.629)	(0.467)
Surplus-to-expenditures	−1.666	0.221	−0.155
	(1.207)	(1.150)	(0.670)
Legal debt cap	0.378	0.502	
	(0.304)	(0.336)	
Transfer-to-expenditures	−2.935	−5.989★★★	−0.811
	(1.829)	(2.277)	(1.790)
Dem. governor	0.024	0.004	−0.161
	(0.178)	(0.186)	(0.102)
Dem. senate	−0.038	−0.099	−0.032
	(0.256)	(0.274)	(0.138)
Dem. house	−0.610★★	−0.518★★	−0.002
	(0.284)	(0.256)	(0.106)
Avg. polarization	−0.598	−0.247	0.825
	(0.505)	(0.496)	(0.590)
Year fixed effects		✓	✓
Region fixed effects		✓	
State fixed effects			✓
R^2	0.242	0.342	0.867
Adj. R^2	0.217	0.295	0.841
No. obs.	440	440	440

Source: Prah, Rotmil, and Fehr (2014); Author's dataset; Public Plans Data (2001–2022); U.S. Bureau of Labor Statistics (1995–2012); U.S. Bureau of Economic Analysis (1995–2012); U.S. Census Bureau (1995–2012); Klarner (2013b, 2013c); Shor (2020).

Note: ★★★$p < 0.01$, ★★$p < 0.05$, ★$p < 0.01$. Estimated intercept not reported. Robust state-clustered standard errors reported in parentheses.

TABLE 4.6

Linear probability model of self-reported excess liabilities and S&P general obligation credit ratings (0 = BBB, 8 = AAA)

	Model 14	Model 15	Model 16
Self-reported excess liabilities	−0.667★	−0.945★★	−0.242
	(0.369)	(0.429)	(0.298)
Self-reported liability growth	−2.339	−2.039	−0.235
	(1.967)	(1.690)	(0.578)
Revised self-reported asset growth	−0.350	0.370	−0.396
	(0.722)	(0.828)	(0.576)
Unemployment rate	−26.334★★	−31.129★★★	−17.277★★
	(9.505)	(11.264)	(7.009)
Per capita income (U.S. dollars, thousands)	0.048★★	0.031	0.123★★★
	(0.019)	(0.032)	(0.042)
Real gross state product growth	−2.913★★	−1.507	−1.402
	(1.706)	(1.924)	(1.246)
Debt-to-revenue	−0.818★	−0.355	−0.681
	(0.452)	(0.550)	(0.530)
Surplus-to-expenditures	−1.644	−0.588	−0.773★★
	(1.364)	(1.236)	(0.374)
Legal debt cap	0.483	0.485	
	(0.316)	(0.342)	
Transfer-to-expenditures	−3.927★	−5.123★★★	−0.057
	(2.008)	(2.324)	(1.553)
Dem. governor	0.021	0.010	−0.213★★
	(0.155)	(0.148)	(0.101)
Dem. senate	−0.101	−0.145	0.013
	(0.274)	(0.280)	(0.106)
Dem. house	−0.565★★	−0.482★	−0.182★
	(0.271)	(0.265)	(0.093)
Avg. polarization	−0.574	−0.283	0.797★
	(0.429)	(0.418)	(0.422)
Year fixed effects		✓	✓
Region fixed effects		✓	
State fixed effects			✓
R^2	0.290	0.343	0.893
Adj. R^2	0.262	0.292	0.868
No. obs.	375	375	375

Source: Prah, Rotmil, and Fehr (2014); Author's dataset; Public Plans Data (2001–2022); U.S. Bureau of Labor Statistics (1995–2012); U.S. Bureau of Economic Analysis (1995–2012); U.S. Census Bureau (1995–2012); Klarner (2013b, 2013c); Shor (2020).

Note: ★★★$p < 0.01$, ★★$p < 0.05$, ★$p < 0.01$. Estimated intercept not reported. Robust state-clustered standard errors reported in parentheses.

TABLE 4.7

Ordinary least squares and fixed effects regression of revised funding ratio on state nonpension debt interest costs (in basis points)

	Model 17 (1)	Model 18 (2)	Model 19 (3)
Revised funding ratio	−26.434	−36.888	12.612
	(42.716)	(45.914)	(77.181)
Revised contribution rate	−6.713★★★	−6.457★★★	−5.430★★★
	(0.529)	(0.572)	(0.777)
Revised liability growth	58.573★★★	54.206★★	65.574★★★
	(18.995)	(22.152)	(19.938)
Revised asset growth	−25.405★	−30.580★	−39.269★★★
	(14.714)	(15.576)	(11.892)
Unemployment rate	−1,422.415★★	−481.599	−418.429
	(598.508)	(888.735)	(784.682)
Per capita income (U.S. dollars, thousands)	−4.080★★★	1.954	−3.333
	(1.388)	(1.963)	(4.929)
Real gross state product growth	−233.252★★	32.379	130.891
	(117.501)	(170.251)	(154.255)
Debt-to-revenue	−20.910	−28.193	−107.069
	(32.196)	(35.791)	(65.491)
Surplus-to-expenditures	169.232★★	53.335	29.970
	(81.054)	(77.186)	(87.014)
Legal debt cap	−17.574	−13.949	
	(16.392)	(15.372)	
Transfers-to-expenditures	−415.936★★★	−101.749	−192.478
	(157.929)	(158.293)	(332.530)
Dem. governor	−34.680★★	−32.103★★	3.950
	(14.436)	(15.265)	(13.998)
Dem. senate	10.564	14.409	8.335
	(16.540)	(14.526)	(14.311)
Dem. house	−1.716	−11.976	−18.771
	(16.012)	(16.739)	(16.682)
Avg. polarization	6.094	5.216	16.576
	(20.287)	(25.112)	(41.614)
Year fixed effects	No	Yes	Yes
Region fixed effects	No	Yes	No
State fixed effects	No	No	Yes
No. obs.	422	422	422
R^2	0.238	0.339	0.629
Adj. R^2	0.210	0.291	0.555

Source: Prah, Rotmil, and Fehr (2014); Author's dataset; Public Plans Data (2001–2022); U.S. Bureau of Labor Statistics (1995–2012); U.S. Bureau of Economic Analysis (1995–2012); U.S. Census Bureau (1995–2012); Klarner (2013b, 2013c); Shor (2020).

Note: ★★★$p < 0.01$, ★★$p < 0.05$, ★$p < 0.01$. Estimated intercept not reported. Robust state-clustered standard errors reported in parentheses.

TABLE 4.8

Ordinary least squares and fixed effects regression of revised excess liabilities on state nonpension debt interest costs (in basis points)

	Model 18 (1)	Model 19 (2)	Model 20 (3)
Revised excess liabilities	8.545 (11.112)	7.923 (10.276)	−34.596★★ (17.178)
Revised contribution rate	−6.638★★★ (0.513)	−6.390★★★ (0.580)	−5.447★★★ (0.772)
Revised liability growth	58.235★★★ (19.145)	54.722★★ (21.813)	72.629★★★ (17.679)
Revised asset growth	−25.068★ (14.836)	−31.086★★ (15.462)	−47.165★★★ (11.149)
Unemployment rate	−1,397.229★★ (597.546)	−465.586 (896.271)	−311.192 (789.106)
Per capita income (U.S. dollars, thousands)	−4.074★★★ (1.378)	1.962 (1.968)	−3.083 (4.988)
Real gross state product growth	−228.233★ (116.959)	33.181 (172.672)	114.891 (144.287)
Debt-to-revenue	−21.452 (32.264)	−26.098 (35.317)	−121.737★ (63.259)
Surplus-to-expenditures	165.813★★ (80.099)	52.770 (76.577)	11.699 (84.005)
Legal debt cap	−18.126 (16.344)	−13.747 (15.375)	
Transfers-to-expenditures	−419.531★★★ (155.831)	−108.181 (154.594)	−166.898 (327.597)
Dem. governor	−35.151★★ (14.341)	−33.220★★ (14.709)	4.046 (14.392)
Dem. senate	10.056 (16.324)	14.340 (14.548)	7.183 (14.497)
Dem. house	−2.107 (15.966)	−12.113 (16.752)	−20.027 (15.966)
Avg. polarization	5.346 (19.865)	3.859 (24.669)	8.760 (44.304)
Year fixed effects	No	Yes	Yes
Region fixed effects	No	Yes	No
State fixed effects	No	No	Yes
No. obs.	422	422	422
R^2	0.239	0.339	0.633
Adj. R^2	0.211	0.290	0.560

Source: Prah, Rotmil, and Fehr (2014); Author's dataset; Public Plans Data (2001–2022); U.S. Bureau of Labor Statistics (1995–2012); U.S. Bureau of Economic Analysis (1995–2012); U.S. Census Bureau (1995–2012); Klarner (2013b, 2013c); Shor (2020).

Note: ★★★$p < 0.01$, ★★$p < 0.05$, ★$p < 0.01$. Estimated intercept not reported. Robust state-clustered standard errors reported in parentheses.

TABLE 4.9

Ordinary least squares and fixed effects regression of self-reported funding ratio on state nonpension debt interest costs (in basis points)

	Model 21 (1)	Model 22 (2)	Model 23 (3)
Self-reported funding ratio	17.877 (59.704)	−75.782 (52.463)	61.195 (93.338)
Self-reported contribution rate	−1.430 (24.324)	−10.124 (23.839)	−27.749★ (14.760)
Self-reported liability growth	−14.274 (137.169)	−164.445 (117.081)	−119.381 (115.447)
Self-reported asset growth	51.079 (75.545)	40.753 (71.605)	68.736 (62.483)
Unemployment rate	−1,381.723★★ (634.968)	−643.595 (881.777)	−64.721 (912.517)
Per capita income (U.S. dollars, thousands)	−2.908★★ (1.392)	2.211 (1.827)	−0.301 (5.713)
Real gross state product growth	−252.848★ (131.330)	124.853 (198.534)	205.289 (167.931)
Debt-to-revenue	−16.845 (31.830)	−31.731 (37.949)	−112.639 (71.681)
Surplus-to-expenditures	114.613 (82.086)	−10.473 (82.020)	−18.045 (77.677)
Legal debt cap	−17.368 (16.504)	−13.417 (15.579)	
Transfer-to-expenditures	−305.669★ (160.727)	−26.303 (148.020)	−121.418 (296.485)
Dem. governor	−29.925★★ (14.769)	−27.290★ (14.905)	1.379 (16.232)
Dem. senate	9.683 (16.196)	9.029 (14.264)	3.951 (16.653)
Dem. house	−4.931 (16.062)	−19.542 (16.415)	−16.817 (18.092)
Avg. polarization	3.292 (20.928)	13.105 (23.736)	44.229 (52.371)
Year fixed effects	No	Yes	Yes
Region fixed effects	No	Yes	No
State fixed effects	No	No	Yes
No. obs.	435	435	435
R^2	0.134	0.244	0.567
Adj. R^2	0.103	0.192	0.483

Source: Prah, Rotmil, and Fehr (2014); Author's dataset; Public Plans Data (2001–2022); U.S. Bureau of Labor Statistics (1995–2012); U.S. Bureau of Economic Analysis (1995–2012); U.S. Census Bureau (1995–2012); Klarner (2013b, 2013c); Shor (2020).

Note: ★★★$p < 0.01$, ★★$p < 0.05$, ★$p < 0.01$. Estimated intercept not reported. Robust state-clustered standard errors reported in parentheses.

TABLE 4.10

Ordinary least squares and fixed effects regression of self-reported excess liabilities on state nonpension debt interest costs (in basis points)

	Model 24 (1)	Model 25 (2)	Model 26 (3)
Self-reported excess liabilities	−3.992 (38.167)	46.477 (33.924)	8.095 (51.221)
Self-reported contribution rate	−1.158 (23.984)	−10.717 (23.447)	−25.546★ (14.024)
Self-reported liability growth	−16.545 (137.222)	−157.483 (117.056)	−151.473 (113.390)
Self-reported asset growth	54.808 (75.785)	33.860 (71.801)	94.685★ (55.560)
Unemployment rate	−1,398.038★★ (639.966)	−691.737 (892.737)	−229.321 (910.949)
Per capita income (U.S. dollars, thousands)	−2.979★★ (1.365)	2.182 (1.823)	−1.195 (5.534)
Real gross state product growth	−256.557★ (132.568)	122.962 (197.714)	202.905 (167.739)
Debt-to-revenue	−17.746 (31.627)	−30.957 (37.761)	−114.377 (74.811)
Surplus-to-expenditures	113.457 (81.788)	−9.283 (82.041)	−14.280 (76.818)
Legal debt cap	−18.279 (16.433)	−12.518 (15.803)	
Transfer-to-expenditures	−310.289★ (159.491)	−24.675 (148.165)	−128.278 (293.388)
Dem. governor	−29.875★★ (14.769)	−27.758★ (14.825)	0.550 (16.675)
Dem. senate	9.214 (16.329)	9.268 (14.299)	4.652 (17.179)
Dem. house	−5.395 (16.130)	−19.599 (16.503)	−19.361 (19.060)
Avg. polarization	4.312 (21.177)	13.299 (24.003)	37.007 (50.483)
Year fixed effects	No	Yes	Yes
Region fixed effects	No	Yes	No
State fixed effects	No	No	Yes
No. obs.	435	435	435
R^2	0.134	0.244	0.566
Adj. R^2	0.103	0.192	0.482

Sources: Prah, Rotmil, and Fehr (2014); Author's dataset; Public Plans Data (2001–2022); U.S. Bureau of Labor Statistics (1995–2012); U.S. Bureau of Economic Analysis (1995–2012); U.S. Census Bureau (1995–2012); Klarner (2013b, 2013c); Shor (2020).

Note: ★★★$p < 0.01$, ★★$p < 0.05$, ★$p < 0.01$. Estimated intercept not reported. Robust state-clustered standard errors reported in parentheses.

cost of borrowing for states are pension liability growth, pension asset growth, and, to a much lesser extent, the contribution rate (i.e., the total pension payment made by public employers as a percentage of the ARC). Across all six models shown in table 4.7 and table 4.8, a 10 percent increase in the state's revised pension liability from the previous year (the median in my sample is 9.8 percent) increases the interest on nonpension state debt by approximately 6.1 basis points (i.e., 0.061 of a percentage point). Although this does not appear to be a substantively large effect, it does materially increase the state's cost of doing government business. In my sample, the median total outstanding debt that a state was carrying between 1995 and 2012 was $7.6 billion. A 6.1 basis point increase in the interest rate would be equivalent to an additional $4.6 million in borrowing costs for that state. Conversely, a 10 percent increase in the state's pension assets decreases nonpension interest cost by 3.3 basis points, on average. Clearly, these are not symmetrical effects. Although the overall effect is relatively small, states are punished more for increasing pension liabilities than they are rewarded for increasing pension assets. Creditors appear to be more motivated by the growth in a state's pension obligations than they are by growth in the ability to pay for those obligations.[30]

Table 4.9 and table 4.10 present the same models as shown in table 4.7 and table 4.8 except that they replace the revised pension measures—funding ratio or excess liabilities, contribution rate, liability growth, and asset growth—with the values self-reported by the state pension plans. Neither the funding ratio measure in table 4.9 nor the excess liabilities measure in table 4.10 are statistically significantly related to the state's nonpension debt interest cost, as in tables 4.7 and 4.8. The other self-reported measures of pension financial status, however, are also not statistically significant. This differs from the results in models 17–20 that use my revised data, in which liability growth increases interest cost and asset growth decreases interest cost. These patterns suggest that actual debt purchasers can differentiate between potentially biased, self-reported data and the underlying fundamental values—and that credit ratings may not have much added value in this regard.

Effect on the Budget

Finally, we come to an analysis of how pension obligations and pension debt influence the cost of current spending rather than future spending. Because of data limitations, these results must be more suggestive than those in previous analyses. The evidence, nevertheless, points in one direction: There was no discernible impact of state pension payments on other general fund line-item expenditures in state budgets between the mid-1990s and late-2000s. First, as depicted in figure 2.10 in chapter 2, the median amount states have been putting toward pensions—either in real dollar terms (figure 4.5) or as a proportion of general expenditures (figure 4.6)—has changed very little. This is true despite the fact that state ARCs have been increasing over time. Second, states' expenditure line-items, including education, public welfare (primarily Medicaid and Temporary Assistance to Needy Families), police, highways, and parks, have not decreased in real terms nor as shares of general expenditures

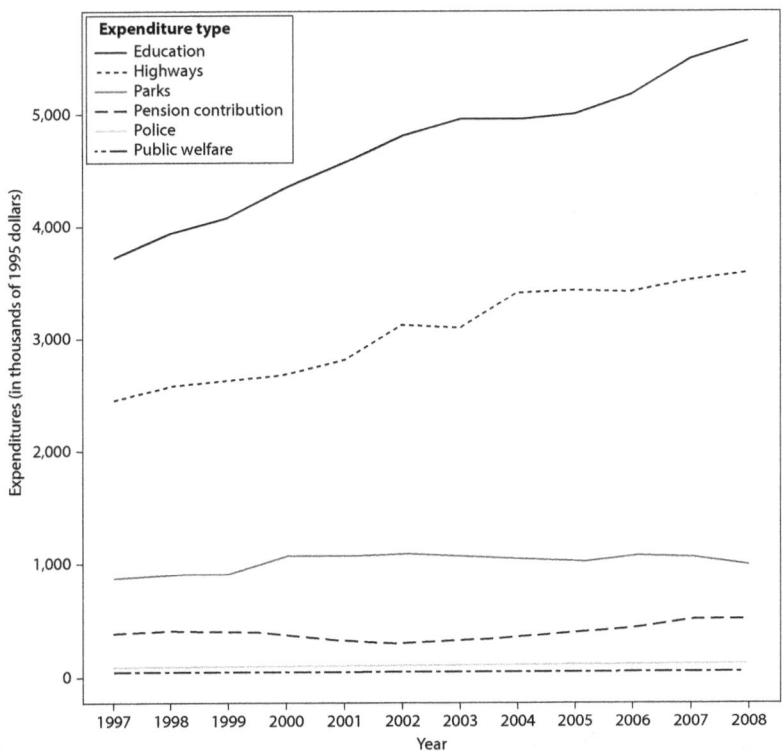

Figure 4.5 Median real spending, over time, by expenditure type. Expenditure types are linked to their visual representation in the legend on the left-hand side of the figure. From top to bottom of the graph, the first line depicts education expenditures; then public welfare expenditures, highway expenditures, pension contributions, and police expenditures; and, last, parks expenditures.

Source: U.S. Census Bureau, Census of Governments (1995–2012).

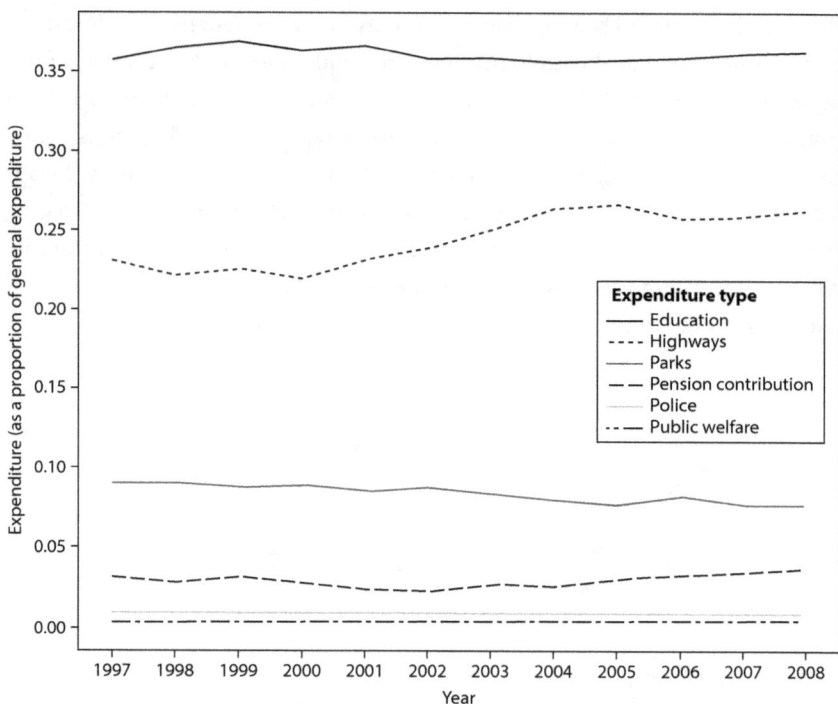

Figure 4.6 Median spending as a proportion of general expenditures, over time, by expenditure type. Expenditure types are linked to their visual representation in the legend on the right-hand side of the figure. From top to bottom of the graph, the first line depicts education expenditures; then public welfare expenditures, highway expenditures, pension contributions, and police expenditures; and, last, parks expenditures.

Source: U.S. Census Bureau, Census of Governments (1995–2012).

over time.[31] This means that, on average, the expansion of pension liabilities over time has not adversely affected the contemporaneous generation of taxpayers in terms of eating up real economic resources or shares of the overall budget. As the previous analysis has shown, however, the impact on borrowing costs—and the calculus of deciding whether or not to issue debt (and how much of it to issue)—may have played at least a partial role in the massive infrastructure underinvestment of the past half-century.[32] We can see evidence of this mechanism in table 4.11, which shows how a change in interest costs is associated with a change in the composition of the state budget. A 1 percentage point increase in my pseudo-interest rate is associated with

TABLE 4.11

Fixed effects regression of interest costs (as a proportion of outstanding debt) on expenditure line items (as a share of general expenditures)

	Highways (1)	Police (2)	Education (3)
Interest as a proportion of nonpension debt	−0.342★★★	0.038★★★	−0.575★★★
	(0.107)	(0.013)	(0.152)
Unemployment rate	−0.215	0.001	0.456
	(0.153)	(0.022)	(0.292)
Per capita income (U.S. dollars, thousands)	−0.001	0.0001	0.001
	(0.001)	(0.0001)	(0.001)
Real gross state product growth	0.013	−0.001	−0.015
	(0.037)	(0.003)	(0.041)
Debt-to-revenue	0.010	−0.001	−0.047
	(0.013)	(0.002)	(0.033)
Surplus-to-expenditure	0.015	−0.001	−0.015
	(0.017)	(0.001)	(0.022)
Dem. governor	−0.006★★	0.0001	−0.002
	(0.003)	(0.0003)	(0.002)
Dem. senate	0.0005	0.0004	−0.0004
	(0.002)	(0.0004)	(0.003)
Dem. house	−0.004	−0.0005	0.011★★★
	(0.004)	(0.001)	(0.004)
Avg. polarization	−0.018★★	−0.002★	−0.014
	(0.008)	(0.001)	(0.011)
Year fixed effects	Yes	Yes	Yes
State fixed effects	Yes	Yes	Yes
No. obs.	5,616	5,616	5,616
R^2	0.844	0.879	0.939
Adj. R^2	0.843	0.878	0.938

Source: U.S. Bureau of Labor Statistics (1995–2012); U.S. Bureau of Economic Analysis (1995–2012); U.S. Census Bureau (1995–2012); Klarner (2013b, 2013c); Shor (2020).

Note: ★★★$p < 0.01$, ★★$p < 0.05$, ★$p < 0.01$. Estimated intercept not reported. Robust state-clustered standard errors reported in parentheses. Other budget categories were examined (not reported for purposes of brevity; results available upon request) but interest costs were not found to have any significant relationship to their compositional size.

a 0.34 percentage point decrease in the share of general expenditures going toward highways and a 0.58 percentage point decrease in the share going toward education.[33] Spending on police as a share of general expenditures, in contrast, increases by 0.04 of a percentage point. Both education spending and highway spending are typically considered to be more of an investment in the future than, say, police spending. This is another avenue in which future generations are affected by the policy choice to generate pension debt and how much of it, much in the same way that those future generations are also affected by the choice to generate different types of nonpension debt.

Issuing debt is a common, recurring, and inherent feature of all levels of U.S. politics. The cost of borrowing is simply part and parcel of the cost of doing government business. Just as when any of the costs of supplying public services becomes prohibitive, if interest on issued debt becomes too expensive for governments to shoulder, they will be forced to either cut back expenses, raise taxes, or both. As such, understanding what drives the distinctly political phenomenon of public borrowing costs—and what drives those drivers, like bond grades issued by credit rating agencies—is essential to mapping the patterns of public finance and even, perhaps, the quality of public and private life.

In this chapter, I sought to determine whether credit rating agencies use self-reported pension data to grade GO debt risk. Exploring this possibility is crucial because politically manipulated data can (and often does, as shown in previous chapters) influence these measures. Self-reported data are often unreliable because of the lack of standardization and reporting bias, which can lead to varying degrees of manipulation across states and over time. In fact, it is plausible that states might self-report with credit rating agencies as their target audience, particularly given the significant impact that credit grades have on borrowing costs. Previous research has shown strong links between political and institutional variables and credit ratings. If these variables can influence credit ratings and borrowing costs, it is likely that public pensions may also play a role.

The evidence outlined in the chapter shows that credit rating agencies are penalizing states that disclose poor pension funding performance, while mostly failing to take into account reporting bias in the state-generated numbers. Self-reported pension funding levels had a statistically significant and positive relationship with S&P GO credit ratings. The coefficients on revised funding ratios were not statistically significant, however, which suggests that S&P places more weight on self-reported data, despite potential inaccuracies. This was the case in both the ordered probit and linear probability models.

This finding, however, does not necessarily suggest that state governments can escape the wrath of the bond markets and lower borrowing costs simply by continuing to use gimmicks in their financial reports. The ratio of yearly interest payments to total outstanding debt is robustly sensitive to revised liability and asset growth, despite being unrelated to the same self-reported measures. As it turns out, creditors might be more sophisticated than credit rating agencies—it is their money on the line, after all. Specifically, a 10 percent increase in pension liabilities correlated with a 6.1 basis point increase in interest costs. This seemingly modest effect can translate to substantial additional borrowing costs, exemplified by the $4.6 million increase for a median state with nonpension debt of $7.6 billion. A similar increase in pension assets decreases interest costs by 3.3 basis points, indicating asymmetric effects. This highlights the sensitivity of creditors to pension fund dynamics and does so in a way that is different from rating agencies.

Finally, I also focused on understanding how the funding status of pension plans and state credit ratings might affect residents' daily lives by imposing strain on budgets directly. I highlighted how pension debt and borrowing costs do and do not alter the types of services a state chooses to fund. My analysis of expenditure line items reveals that although the direct impact of pension expenditures on the largest state budget items (e.g., education and public welfare) is mostly minimal, the indirect impact of pensions through interest costs has played a substantial role in shifting public resources from investments in the future (e.g., highways and education) toward more contemporaneous spending like public safety.

Public pensions, which are creatures of the political process and the bargains that are struck between employer and employee, and the decisions to fund or not fund them has consequences for not just the state workers who directly benefit or the generations to come who will need to fill the funding gap but also for all individuals who either utilize state public services or pay taxes.

CHAPTER V

The Pluralist State, the Coalitional State, and the Disorganized State

Three Examples of Pension Politics

P ublic pensions represent a critical aspect of the social contract between voters, governments, and their employees. Although my quantitative data gets us quite far in understanding the politics of how these social contracts are forged and why, in some cases, they are at risk of abrogation, the data reach back only to the late 1990s. Because many of these pension systems were created more than a century before the beginning of my data, qualitatively exploring the historic trajectories of a sample of these state systems paints a more complete picture of political decisions and fiscal dynamics that can be generalized to similar systems. In this chapter, I present a comprehensive qualitative and historic description of public pensions in three different states: New Jersey, New York, and Kentucky. The qualitative evidence presented in this chapter supports the theoretical claims of chapter 1 and is in line with the findings from my quantitative analysis presented in chapters 2 and 3.

Case studies offer a unique vantage point for examining public pensions. Although my quantitative analyses capture trends in aggregate data, qualitative approaches can allow for a more nuanced exploration of contextual factors, decision-making processes, and complexities in relationships that may be missed by quantitative data alone. Case studies are only as generalizable as their selection allows, however. I selected New Jersey, New York, and Kentucky to represent three of the different regime types described in chapter 1. Recall my classification schema, reproduced here as table 5.1,

TABLE 5.1

Regime type and expected fiscal behavior under the Coalitional Politics
Hypothesis

		Dominant party	
		Republican	*Democratic*
	Organized	Mixed strategy: Increase benefits, decrease taxpayer-funded contributions (*less sustainable*)	Decrease benefits, maintain taxpayer-funded contributions (*more sustainable*)
Public sector workforce		OR Attempt to eliminate public sector unions	
	Unorganized	Maintain benefits, maintain taxpayer-funded contributions (*no change*)	Comparison group

Note: This table is identical to table 1.2 and is reproduced here for ease of reference. The bottom row of the figure describes two scenarios in which the governing regime would be classified as a "disorganized state." Kentucky falls into this row, historically as a Democratically controlled state but more recently as one typically governed by Republicans. The top-left cell, characterized by well-organized state workers and Republican rule, is classified under my schema as a "pluralist state" and describes the politics of New Jersey. The top-right cell, characterized by well-organized workers and strong Democratic rule, is classified as a "coalitional state." New York State is categorized as a coalitional state in my framework.

which shows the different types of regimes: the pluralist state, characterized
by strong public sector labor organization and nondominant Democratic
government control (i.e., Republican control or weak Democratic control);
the coalitional state, also characterized by strong public sector labor organization but coupled with strong Democratic control; and the disorganized
state, characterized by a weak public sector workforce that may experience
either type of partisan control. These three states represent a diverse array
of pension experiences shaped by varying socioeconomic, political, and historical contexts. New Jersey, with its early foray into statewide pension plans
and subsequent challenges, offers a lens into the complexities of establishing sustainable systems amid strong public sector labor interests that have
become unmoored from the long-term institutional interests of the state.
New York, a state also known for its significant public sector organization,
presents a case of pursuing pension reform under different types of gubernatorial administrations. Kentucky, with its distinct socioeconomic profile and
historically lower levels of public sector unionization, offers a window into

the political trade-offs of making public employment attractive enough to retain workers while failing to adequately fund benefits.[1] Collectively, these states represent a microcosm of the broader challenges faced by both governments and public sector workers in managing public pension systems. By examining these cases, I unravel both common and distinct threads, supplementing my quantitative data and analysis and furthering our understanding of the political dynamics at play.

New Jersey and New York: A Tale of Divergence

Similarities Between New Jersey and New York

New York and New Jersey are remarkably similar on paper despite key differences in their governing regimes. This fact helps alleviate concerns about potentially confounding variables in the analysis contained in this chapter.

New York and New Jersey share several similarities because of their geographic proximity and historical ties. Chief among these are their economies, demographics, and physical features. The two states share a 487-mile border.[2] Unsurprisingly, their economies are strongly interdependent. Both states are major players in the northeastern U.S. economy and are part of the larger New York City metropolitan area, which functions as a significant economic hub in the region. Both New York City and Jersey City (although orders of magnitude smaller) serve as significant global financial centers. Apart from finance, both states boast diversified economies with a mix of industries ranging from technology, health care, and manufacturing to transportation and tourism. New York State has the third-largest economy in the country and New Jersey has the ninth-largest economy (New York is the largest on a per capita basis, and New Jersey is the eleventh largest per capita). Both states have a very high cost of living relative to the rest of the country as well as relatively high levels of taxation.[3]

New York and New Jersey also have much in common in terms of culture and demographic diversity, boasting populations that hail from around the world.[4] Both states have densely populated urban centers, as well as suburban and rural areas, with residents from various ethnic, cultural, and socioeconomic backgrounds. The New York City metropolitan area spans across both states, with millions of people commuting between the two for work and other activities. The states have extensive coastlines along the

Atlantic Ocean and are home to many maritime activities and tourism related to the waterfront.

Both New York State and New Jersey rely on a diverse tax base to fund their operations and impose a range of different types of taxes, including income tax, sales tax, property tax, corporate tax, and estate tax.[5] The New York City metropolitan area—not only Manhattan but also parts of northern New Jersey—contributes significantly to both states' tax revenue.[6] This contribution is largely due to the area's financial sector and high property values. Both states have faced challenges related to budgetary constraints and maintaining essential public services while also balancing tax burdens on residents and businesses.[7]

Like their populations, both states have a large and diverse voter base. Although New York is larger than New Jersey and has a more significant impact on the Electoral College, both states are politically significant in national elections. Both states are also solidly Democratic with New Jersey having supported the Democratic presidential candidate in every election since 1992 and New York having supported the Democratic presidential candidate in every election since 1988, but New Jersey has done so by smaller margins. At the state level, Republicans held unified control of the New Jersey legislature from 1992 to 2002 as well as the governor's mansion in eight out of those ten years. The New York State Republican Party, in contrast, has been much weaker in the contemporary era, having not enjoyed unified control of government since a brief period in the 1970s during the gubernatorial reign of Nelson Rockefeller. State Democrats have essentially ruled New York State with impunity since 2006 when Republican George Pataki left the governor's mansion.[8]

Between 1995 and 2012, both New York and New Jersey's state and local workforce made up around 3.5 percent of all employed workers, which was considerably below the national mean of 5 percent (3.5 percent is around the 25th percentile of state workforce rates; Hawaii had the highest average over this period with a state workface rate of 10.3 percent, while Pennsylvania had the lowest with a state workforce rate of 2.8 percent). In absolute terms, however, New York employed the third-largest state and local workforce in the country with 790,000 full-time employees. New Jersey was not far behind with the sixth-largest state and local workforce of 460,000. The sizes of these workforces were more or less proportional to the overall populations of the states; over the sample time period, New York had the third-highest population in the country and New Jersey had the eleventh-highest population.[9]

Both New Jersey and New York have a significant history of public sector unionization, with New York adopting the Public Employees Fair Employment Act—better known as the Taylor Law, which granted collective bargaining rights to public employees—in 1967.[10] New Jersey adopted their own version, called the New Jersey Public Employment Relations Act, in 1968.[11] Unionization rates have varied slightly over time for largely idiosyncratic reasons, but public sector unions have remained considerably powerful since at least the early 1990s. Although the national average public workforce unionization rate hovered around one-quarter between 1995 and 2012, New Jersey's ranged between 47 percent and 67 percent; New York's unionization rate, the highest in the country, hovered between 64 percent and 76 percent. In contrast, over the same period, Kentucky's public workforce was never more than 20 percent unionized. The state with the lowest average unionization rate over the sample period, North Carolina, never had more than 6 percent of their public workforce unionized.[12] Much of the interstate variation in public sector unionization rates has been associated with, although not necessarily caused by, differences in public labor laws. North Carolina, for instance, is a right-to-work state and both North Carolina and Kentucky explicitly prohibit collective bargaining with state public sector employees.[13] Both New York and New Jersey, in contrast, are *not* right-to-work states and have a legal duty to collectively bargain with public employees. New York's and New Jersey's public sector unions represent a wide range of employees, including teachers, health-care workers, transportation workers, law enforcement officers, firefighters, and other types of government workers. Tables 5.1 and 5.2 summarize my quantitative data on unionization, along with data on the partisan composition of state government.

Differences on the Key Variable: Regime Type

Despite the many similarities between New Jersey and New York, the two states have differed significantly in their approach to pension fund management. This serves as the key independent variable—regime type—for purposes of case selection.

New Jersey, as a pluralist regime, has experienced prolonged Republican state control and the power of well-organized public sector unions. New Jersey Republicans have historically conceded to union demands for

TABLE 5.2

Partisan composition of the state government and public sector unionization rate in New Jersey, over time

	General Assembly	State Senate	Governor	Public worker unionization rate
1986	37.5%	57.5%	R	55.1%
1988	47.5%	60.0%	R	55.0%
1990	52.5%	57.5%	D	59.7%
1992	27.5%	32.5%	D	58.8%
1994	33.8%	40.0%	R	62.0%
1996	37.5%	40.0%	R	61.1%
1998	40.0%	40.0%	R	61.4%
2000	43.8%	40.0%	R	58.6%
2002	55.0%	50.0%	R/D	60.5%
2004	58.8%	55.0%	D	59.5%
2006	61.3%	55.0%	D	62.5%
2008	60.0%	57.8%	D	55.0%
2010	58.8%	57.8%	R	56.1%
2012	60.0%	60.0%	R	59.7%
2014	65.0%	60.0%	R	62/1%
2016	65.0%	60.0%	R	56.8%
2018	67.5%	62.5%	D	59.6%
2020	65.0%	62.5%	D	59.2%
2022	57.5%	60.0%	D	57.4%

Source: Klarner (2013b, 2013c); National Conference of State Legislatures (1999–2011); Hirsch and Macpherson (2023).

Note: Legislative data reflect the percent of the chamber that is populated by elected Democrats. Republican control of government is shaded in gray.

pension growth, with the tacit agreement that funding would be redirected
for other purposes. As a result, the state's pensions have seen brisk growth in
unfunded liabilities following years of underfunding while pursuing costly
benefit enhancements. The state has struggled time and again to make contributions coming even close to the annual required contribution (ARC),
and although a Democratic state legislature passed comprehensive pension
reform in 2011 (signed by Republican Governor Chris Christie), the legislation has gone largely unenforced.[14]

TABLE 5.3

Partisan composition of state government and public sector unionization rate in New York, over time

	General Assembly	State Senate	Governor	Comptroller	Public worker unionization rate
1985	61.3%	42.6%	D	R	66.7%
1987	61.3%	42.6%	D	R	67.5%
1989	61.3%	44.3%	D	R	66.1%
1991	63.3%	42.6%	D	R	69.5%
1993	66.7%	42.6%	D	R	70.9%
1995	63.3%	41.0%	R	D	70.1%
1997	63.3%	42.6%	R	D	70.0%
1999	65.3%	42.6%	R	D	70.5%
2001	65.3%	41.0%	R	D	67.6%
2003	68.0%	40.3%	R	D	71.5%
2005	69.3%	43.5%	R	D	69.1%
2007	70.7%	46.8%	D	D	69.6%
2009	71.3%	51.6%	D	D	75.1%
2011	65.3%	48.4%	D	D	75.7%
2013	70.0%	52.4%	D	D	69.9%
2015	70.0%	50.8%	D	D	68.6%
2017	70.1%	50.8%	D	D	67.4%
2019	70.1%	63.5%	D	D	65.5%
2021	70.1%	68.3%	D	D	66.7%

Source: Klarner (2013b, 2013c); National Conference of State Legislatures (1999–2011); Hirsch and Macpherson (2023).

Note: Legislative data reflect the percent of the chamber that is populated by elected Democrats. Republican control of government shaded in gray.

New York, as a coalitional regime, has also been characterized by strong public labor but has more frequently been controlled by a highly disciplined Democratic Party. The state maintains one of the best funded pension plans in the nation, consistently appropriating the entire (self-reported) ARC for every year of my data, whereas New Jersey failed to do so even once. On average, New Jersey paid just 17 percent of its (again, self-reported) ARC, whereas New York paid 100 percent. Using my revised data, New York's track record becomes considerably less rosy with an average payment of only 18 percent of its ARC, but New Jersey's falls to an abysmal 7 percent. In either case, New Jersey is dead last among all forty-nine states in my dataset in terms of paying its ARC.[15] New York has also instituted pension reform, but it has been focused on creating several new "tiers" of benefits for employees who join the pension at different dates rather than on state contributions, which, thus far, have been comparably adequate.

Finally, New Jersey's average annual market growth of its pension assets between 2000 and 2010 was negative: on average, the market value of the state's pension assets shrunk 0.2 percent each year. New Jersey's pension system claimed around $74.9 billion in assets in 2000; however, by 2010, that number had decreased to $70.2 billion. New York's pension assets performed marginally better over the same time period, beginning with $218 billion in assets and ending with $211 billion, despite averaging 0.6 percent of positive growth annually. (The national annual pension asset growth average over this same time period was 5.5 percent.) Expectations were out of line in both states, as well: New Jersey, on average, assumed that pensions would enjoy an 8.5 percent annual market return on its assets, and New York assumed an 8 percent annual return. Overall, although there was not a large disparity in pension asset growth between the two states, it is worth pointing out that New Jersey's pension assets are managed by the state's Treasury Department, the head of whom is appointed by the governor. New York's pension assets, in contrast, are managed by the state comptroller, a statewide elected position that has been occupied by a Democrat since 1994.[16]

In the next section, I investigate the disparities of the two states' pension funds in more detail.

The New Jersey Case

New Jersey established its pension system for public employees in the late nineteenth century. As with most states, New Jersey created different plans for different classes of workers, and on different dates. In 1896, New Jersey set up its first pension plan (the first statewide plan in the nation) for teachers called the Teachers' Retirement Fund. Benefits began to be paid out by the state legislature in 1906 but, having not made any arrangements to *fund* the liabilities of the new pension plan, the Teachers' Retirement Fund almost immediately dissolved into financial insolvency and collapsed soon after.[17] A second teachers' plan was established in 1919, called the Teachers'

Pension and Annuity Fund (TPAF), which required its members to contribute part of their wages to the retirement system (the state provided additional funds).[18] A plan for local police and firefighters, the Police and Firemen's Retirement System (PFRS), was established not long after in 1920. (This plan did not and does not include state police, as the state police force was not established in New Jersey until 1921. The State Police Retirement and Benevolent Fund was established in 1944 and replaced with the State Police Retirement System (SPRS) in 1965.) Like other early pension systems, both plans provided relatively modest benefits, and were primarily designed to attract and retain qualified employees. New Jersey's Public Employees' Retirement System (PERS) was established in 1954 to cover state employees who were not part of the police, fire, or teaching professions. PERS encompasses a wide range of government employees, including administrative personnel, clerical workers, and other civil servants. The establishment of PERS was part of a broader effort to ensure retirement benefits for various segments of the public workforce. New Jersey's youngest pension plan, the Judicial Retirement System (JRS), was established in 1973 and covers members of the state judiciary.[19]

Challenges in funding New Jersey's pension system are not new. The 1970s and 1980s, in particular, were characterized by inadequate contributions and investment losses—and were not distinct to New Jersey. Economic downturns and changes in funding priorities contributed to the underfunding of pension systems across the country. This meant that many state pension systems began to accumulate unfunded liabilities and, as is familiar, many grew deeply concerned about the financial sustainability of the overall public pension system and its potential impact on the broader economy. Speaking in 1976, Senator Thomas Eagleton (D–MO) warned that the U.S. public pension system was a "financial time bomb" and that "cities, states, and the federal government have set up a web of retirement obligations that could have negative consequences for our children's standard of living."[20] A bill allowing the federal government to regulate the financing and administration of state pension systems was introduced in 1975. The bill was essentially a public version of the Employee Retirement Income Security Act (ERISA) that was passed the year before in 1974 and was aptly named the Public Employee Retirement Income Security Act (PERISA). Amid mounting concern, however, PERISA ultimately failed to be passed into law.[21] New Jersey's pension system, along with the other forty-nine states', remains unregulated by the federal government to this day.

With a steady improvement in national asset markets, New Jersey's pension system found itself on better financial footing by the beginning of the 1990s. Democratic Governor Jim Florio, who took office in 1990, had inherited large budget shortfalls from his predecessor and the difficulties of the 1980s, however. It was under Governor Florio's tenure—and a Democratically controlled state legislature—that New Jersey passed the Quality Education Act of 1990 (primarily but not entirely in response to the second *Abbott v. Burke* ruling that mandated that New Jersey change its school district funding formula).[22] The Quality Education Act increased employee and employer (primarily local school districts) contributions to the pension plan, easing the burden and the responsibility of the state in funding employee benefits. The state's teachers union—the New Jersey Education Association (NJEA)—fiercely resisted for reasons that President Betty Kraemer outlined: "In a few scant years, increasing pension costs will eat into the dollars available for programs in schools. Local property taxes will have to rise to support programs, and the cycle of failed funding formulas will begin again."[23] Despite the opposition, Florio and the Democratic legislature passed both the pension funding change and the sales and income tax increases that violated Florio's own version of "read my lips: no new taxes" that he had promoted during his gubernatorial campaign.[24] Now both the teachers *and* the rest of the state's voters were incensed.

In a testament to both the weakness of the state's Democratic Party and the strength of the teachers union, Florio's push to shift the costs of pensions onto local school districts was quickly postponed and then repealed by a faction of Democratic legislators that banded together with Republicans to compel the state to retake responsibility for funding teacher pensions.[25] Disenchanted with the mixed messages of the state's Democratic Party, the NJEA threw its might behind electing Republicans the following year—offering forty-six of its forty-nine endorsements to Republicans—and flipped a Democratic legislature into a veto-proof Republican one.[26] Even Kraemer was incredulous, recounting that "our people are angry and feel they have been betrayed. . . . I never thought I'd be in bed with the Republicans."[27] The teachers were not the only ones who felt wounded by the governor and the party; angry over salary cuts and layoffs, other state public sector unions joined the teachers in shattering the alliance between labor and the state government. A news article from the period described the public fallout: "Union officials say the current campaign, particularly the dissident slate of union candidates, signals a serious rupture in the historic coalition between [public] organized labor and the Democratic Party in New Jersey . . . Democrats see the threat as serious. Steve DeMicco, director of the State Democratic Committee, said, "My long-term concern is the lack of a unified consensus between the unions and the administration. These candidacies may become very real and detract from the issues and the ability of the party to come to some accommodation."[28]

Before the defection of the NJEA and other state employee unions, Republicans had not controlled the New Jersey legislature since 1973. Democrats would not return to power for a decade.[29]

The newly elected Republicans well understood how their electoral fortunes had come to pass, and in 1992, the labor-indebted Republican legislature passed the Pension Revaluation Act. The act used financial gimmicks—perhaps the first of its kind in the nation—to make $1.5 billion in pension assets magically appear on the system's balance sheets. Using these "newly found" assets, the state was able to divert funds meant for pension contributions to other parts of the budget. The financial gimmick ultimately allowed the state to reduce both state and local pension contributions by $1.5 billion over two years. The next year, Florio lost his reelection bid to his NJEA-backed Republican rival, Christine Todd Whitman. Florio later recounted that he had made two cardinal sins: failing to pay adequate mind to the teachers union's preferences, and raising taxes.[30] When Whitman took office in 1994, Republicans held unified control of state government for the first time in more than two decades.

The Florio experience had taught the public sector unions an important lesson: They could get what they want if they were willing to negotiate with a potential enemy. Despite endorsing and actively backing Whitman, the NJEA did not have any misunderstanding about who they were dealing with. The Pension Revaluation Act passed by the Republican legislature in 1992 gave the unions what they wanted (an increased value of their pension benefits through lower employee contributions), but it also came at a price (a more poorly funded pension system, overall). This was the result of compromise. With the Democrats, the compromise had looked different, and the unions had not liked what they had seen. As a result, the unions found new bargaining partners in the form of the Republicans and in particular, Governor Whitman.

Whitman's priority, first and foremost, was to lower taxes. The way she conceived of doing this was by diverting state funds from the pensions—just as Florio had tried to do so under his administration. Rather than divert the funds without making up the difference, as Whitman would go on to do, however, Florio tried to get local employers and employees to contribute more. Not so with Whitman. Whitman's plan, instead, was to stop prefunding cost-of-living adjustments (COLAs), to reduce state contributions further, and to issue pension obligation bonds (POBs).[31]

POBs work like any other government-issued bond; they are debt. POBs, unlike most general obligation debt, however, can be used by governments to arbitrage differences in asset returns. Because government debt is typically considered to be low risk, governments can usually borrow at a lower interest rate than the return they could get from investing the proceeds of the issued debt (e.g., in higher-yield securities like U.S. Treasuries or the stock market). POBs have proven to be too risky for most governments, however, and have largely resulted in net revenue loss for issuers.[32] New Jersey's experience is not an exception. Although Whitman touted the $2.8 billion of issued POBs as a way to improve pension funding during the stock market highs of the late 1990s while simultaneously decreasing local and state contributions (by an additional $1.5 billion), the POBs would go on to balloon to $10 billion in serviceable debt. At the time, however, the NJEA believed this was a good deal for them in exchange for a "nonforfeitable" right to their pensions. The compromise they struck with the Whitman administration meant that it no longer mattered how well or how poorly funded the pension was: retirees would be legally entitled to their benefits no matter what happened to the individual or to the plan. Although this right is implicit in many state pension agreements, the NJEA managed to get this in writing from a Republican administration, further externalizing and abstracting away the costs of pension financial insolvency from the primary stakeholders. As a result, the union dropped its lawsuit against the Whitman administration for underfunding the pension. The NJEA—along with other public sector unions—had decided underfunding was now acceptable.

The financial gimmickry pursued by the Republican state legislature and, later, Governor Whitman, allowed both the government and the public sector unions to claim that the pension system was not just healthy but robust. In turn, that claim—although patently false—bolstered workers' demands for expanded pension benefits. Republican Senate President Donald DiFrancesco said, at the time, "We're talking to the teachers union . . . the way I look at it, if the pension system is healthy, if we can give them some benefit resulting from a good economy, I say give it to them."[33] The Republican state legislature passed a bill expanding pension benefits in 2000, although Whitman vetoed it. Upon Whitman's departure for the George W. Bush administration, the Republican legislature passed the bill a second time. DiFrancesco signed it as acting governor of New Jersey. The bill increased the pension benefit multiplier from 1/60 to 1/55; decreased employee contributions from 4.5 percent to 2.5 percent; and put into law an additional financial gimmick that overvalued pension assets by $5.3 billion. Pleased with the outcome, the teachers union endorsed DiFrancesco in the Republican primary, the first time it had ever endorsed a candidate in a primary for the governor's mansion.

The 2001 elections, however, ushered a blue wave into New Jersey state politics. Democrats took back the General Assembly and governor's mansion and enjoyed split power in the state Senate. The newly elected Democratic Governor McGreevey came into office facing a massive budget shortfall that had been exacerbated—if not created—by years of Whitman tax cuts. The shortfall was nearly 7.5 times the size that Florio had faced a decade earlier.[34] In response, McGreevey increased local employer pension contributions to decrease state contributions, echoing the attempt made by Florio in 1990. A key difference in their approaches, however, was McGreevey's plan to phase in an increase in employer contributions over five years and, having studied his history of previous Democratic governors, to not raise taxes.[35]

In 2004, McGreevey resigned midtenure due to a sex scandal. A series of special commissions and task forces were created by his successors—first acting-governor Richard Codey and then Jon Corzine, both Democrats—to study what was by then perceived as "the pension crisis." Note that these commissions were created and tasked with making recommendations for comprehensive reform well before the Great Recession and the financial crisis of 2008. Although the state failed to adopt the most wide-ranging recommendations, the unified Democratic legislature and governorship did manage to increase employee contributions in 2007 and increase the retirement age in 2008.[36] These were the first contractions in pension benefits observed in New Jersey over both the time period of my quantitative dataset and the longer time period of my qualitative research. Corzine also increased the percent of the ARC that the state contributed to the pension system during his tenure. This increase in pension contributions by the state is, like the contractions in pension benefits, the first such increase observed in my New Jersey data.

Chris Christie, billing himself as a moderate Republican, was elected to the governorship in 2009. Teaming up with the Democratic state legislature, the administration passed the most wide-ranging pension legislation to date. The legislation focused primarily on ramping up funding from the state government to the pension plans. Although some benefits were cut—most notably reversing the increase in the benefit multiplier passed in 2001—they applied only to new state hires. New hires were also to be denied the "nonforfeitable" right to their pension that the NJEA had bargained over with Governor Whitman. Because these pension contractions were forward looking—affecting only a tiny fraction of the public workforce in the short run—the largest immediate impact to the pension's sustainability was on the funding side. The legislation promised that the state would contribute a minimum of one-seventh of the full ARC in 2011 and then "ramp-up" the contribution by one-seventh each fiscal year thereafter, contributing the full ARC by 2018.[37] This "reform" to pension funding held the promise of putting the New Jersey pension system—eventually—onto a sustainable path for the future, but the state proceeded to ignore the statutorily required contributions beginning in 2014. In 2015, the New Jersey Supreme Court sided with Governor Christie—who had been a key proponent in crafting the 2010 funding changes—and ruled in *Burgos v. New Jersey* that the state's failure to comply with the reform law did not, in fact, impair the contractual rights of public employees; the state was free to continue ignoring the law that it had itself passed.[38] Nevertheless, Governor Phil Murphy and the state legislature—both Democratic—paid the ARC in full for the three most recent fiscal years (2021, 2022, and 2023).[39]

Two important points can be concluded from the preceding analysis. First, the contested politics surrounding public pensions in New Jersey are not new, and they are not unique to the contemporary period. Pension politics have been a flashpoint in New Jersey since the founding of the state's pensions. The original teachers fund—the first state fund in the nation—went broke within two decades of its creation. Multiple special commissions and task forces, beyond the ones in the mid-2000s mentioned earlier—have been convened, issued recommendations, been celebrated, and been denounced. The politics have been fraught for as long as these systems have existed. To suggest that the politics are new is to misunderstand the context within which they exist and have existed since the nineteenth century.[40]

Second, Governor Florio—where our story began—has much to be responsible for. Although the outcome may have been the same with another Democratic governor, it was his administration that—within a political environment in which the state's Democratic Party was quite weak and was saddled with large budget shortfalls, the highest property taxes in the nation, and politically difficult-to-implement court rulings surrounding education finance (the *Abbott* mandates) in which the state was compelled to redistribute school aid from wealthy to poorer districts—blew up the party's long-standing alliance with the teachers and state employees. This deterioration in communication and aligned goals, in which Florio and his Democratic state legislature asked the public sector unions to be more directly financially responsible for their pensions to pay for the *Abbott* mandate without raising taxes, was too much for the unions. Once rid of Florio, the unions secured both a "nonforfeitable" right to their benefits (meaning that benefits could never be reduced for current workers or annuitants, only for future hires) and a series of benefit enhancements in exchange for allowing the Republican-controlled state to contribute less to the pension system (facilitated by a number of legislated financial gimmicks that overvalued the assets and undervalued the liabilities). After 2008, this dynamic did not change. Although the Democratic-controlled state legislature and the Republican governor did pursue a number of substantive changes to the benefits and contributions of future plan participants, the state continued to fail to make adequate contributions to the pension system until after the acute phase of the COVID-19 pandemic. This was the case despite the numerous special task forces and commissions called on to present recommendations on how to bolster New Jersey's pension finances and, even more impressively, despite reform legislation that mandated the state drastically change its funding practices.

The New York Case

The core characteristics of New Jersey and New York State's pension system are not dissimilar. Like virtually all state public defined benefits plans, New York's pension system is funded through a combination of employee contributions, local employer contributions, state contributions, and investment returns. Like New Jersey, New York State was an early mover in providing retirement benefits to its employees and, under Governor Al Smith, founded its first two plans in 1920: the New York State Teachers' Retirement System (TRS) and the New York State Employees' Retirement System (ERS). These plans were created by an act of the state legislature after the State Commission on Pensions, convened in 1918, surveyed what other states were doing about the public employee retirement issue. One of the Commission's key contributions to the structure of the state's retirement system was to emphasize the importance of actuarial calculations in estimating the cost and funding of future benefits, having been particularly troubled by the state's assumption of extremely poorly funded local teachers' plans over the previous decade (this plan, the predecessor to the TRS, was called the Teachers' Retirement Fund) as well as the impending collapse of New Jersey's Teachers' Retirement Fund.[41] Both pension plans, as a result, were founded as a contributory plan (whereas the defunct New Jersey Teachers' Retirement Fund had not been) to ensure adequate funding.[42] The New York PFRS was founded considerably later, in 1966. Today, the New York State and Local Retirement System, headed by the New York State comptroller, administers both the ERS and PFRS. The TRS is administered separately (all five of New Jersey's plans are administered individually, with their own trustee boards, like most states). Also unlike New Jersey—or, for that matter, any other state in the country—the statewide elected comptroller is the *sole* trustee of the State and Local Retirement System. Unlike nearly every other public pension system in the United States, it does not have a trustee board.[43]

Between 1959 and 1972, teachers—of which the most has been written and studied—made tremendous gains in New York State. Republican state governments under Governor Nelson Rockefeller "enthusiastically" established a fully noncontributory plan for ERS in 1966 and a fully noncontributory plan for TRS in 1968, while expanding the benefit structure of the plans.[44] With financial clouds on the horizon in the early 1970s, however, and the impending fiscal collapse of New York City, the state began to pull back its largesse with the introduction of a tiered system. The tiered pension system, which grouped state workers according to when they were hired and offered benefits depending on which date range the employee fell into, accomplished multiple goals at once. First, it discriminated against different workers according to the date of their hire, allowing the state to offer less generous benefits to new employees. Second, it allowed the state to recalibrate its pension system's sustainability in a forward-looking way without having to worry about the legality of impinging on the promises made to previous hires: If a potential new employee did not like the terms, no one would force them to accept them. Eventually, the tiered system would grow to encompass six different tiers, each of which had pension benefits that were less generous than the previous tier, and each of which was created in response to large fiscal and economic downturns.

Tier 2 (and by extension, Tier 1) was created in 1973 and made extremely modest pension benefit cuts to future state hires.[45] It was not until a Democratic state government under Governor Hugh Carey created Tier 3 in 1976 that mandatory employee contributions were reintroduced, creating one of the largest and most significant changes to the way the state's pension system was funded.[46] Although a number of benefit enhancements occurred in the late 1990s and early 2000s under Republican Governor George Pataki—including the addition of a COLA for the first time in the history of the New York State pension system and a suspension of Tier 3 and 4's employee contributions after ten years of employment[47]—no other significant reforms would occur after 1976 until the introduction of Tier 5 in the wake of the Great Recession.[48]

As noted earlier, a singular aspect of New York State's pension system is its use of one, statewide elected comptroller to act as trustee, administering benefits and making investment decisions. Since 1994, this position has been occupied by a Democrat, even during periods when other statewide positions have been occupied by Republicans—including the governorship. For this reason, Democratic comptrollers repeatedly found themselves at loggerheads with Governor Pataki. For instance, in 1995, Comptroller H. Carl McCall sued Pataki to prevent him from using $110 million in pension money to help fill a budget shortfall—the same 1995 budget that increased pension benefits for teachers and reduced local employer contributions.[49] Similarly, Comptroller Alan Hevesi (who would later be convicted of "pay-to-play" schemes involving the investment of the pension fund) managed to block Pataki's 2004 attempt to reduce both state contributions and local employer contributions meant to balance the state budget and win political points with local property taxpayers, respectively.[50] Although the Comptroller's job description necessitates vigilance and protection of the pension at all costs, it is notable that this manifested in such a way as to pit Democratic elected officials against a Republican governor intent on reducing the fiscal sustainability of the pension system through benefit enhancements, reduced contributions, and periodic pension raids. The conflict between the comptroller's and governor's office, and the political ambition of both, played an important role in fortifying the fiscal standing of the pension throughout the years of Republican state control.

The end of Republican state control coincided closely with the onset of the Great Recession. When Pataki left office and Democrats gained seats in the State Senate in 2007 (Democrats had had and maintained a supermajority in the General Assembly), the financial ground had already been starting to rumble. As lieutenant governor, Democrat David Paterson inherited the governorship after Eliot Spitzer—mired in a sex scandal—stepped down in March 2008.[51] The transition occurred literally days after Bear Stearns' collapse, sending massive shockwaves throughout the global (and, importantly, state) economy.

As has been well documented elsewhere, the Great Recession and accompanying financial crisis hit state and local government operations extremely hard.[52] Part of this had to do not only with inadequate fiscal stimulus from the federal government but also with balanced budget laws in most states that precluded state and local governments from borrowing money even during economic crisis. As a result, policymakers had to come up with plans to severely curtail expenditures—as increasing taxes, particularly during the worst economic downturn since the Great Depression, was a political non-starter. Governor Paterson believed that the circumstances, borrowing from Governor Carey's playbook three decades earlier during the more localized fiscal crisis, necessitated wholesale reforms of the state pension system.[53] After much back and forth between the unions and the government, a plan to adopt a new tier—Tier 5—that would not affect existing workers (in contrast to what Paterson had initially proposed) was put into place. Although Tier 5 instituted a number of changes that were less generous to new hires than to current workers, the most important was raising the retirement age and requiring new employees to contribute 3.5 percent of their salaries to the fund for the entirety of their careers rather than for only the first ten years. The president of the New York State Public Employees Federation said of the deal, at the time, that "considering the deteriorating condition of the state's finances, this represents a reasonable accommodation," while the president of the Civil Service Employees Association offered that the union "recognizes [that] these are extraordinary times with unprecedented challenges, and we have tried to find ways to help."[54]

Notably, changes to pension benefits affecting uniformed workers—police officer and firefighters—went less smoothly. Uniformed workers had been exempted from Tiers 3 and 4 in the 1970s and 1980s but, to continue the exemption for new hires, the state legislature had to pass a bill each year authorizing the exception to keep newly hired police officer and firefighters in Tier 2. In 2009, on the eve of the passage of the Tier 5 pension reform, Paterson vetoed the reauthorization for the first time. Unions representing uniformed workers, traditionally less close to the Democratic Party in terms of campaign donations, ideology, voting, and electoral mobilization, were nearly apoplectic. The president of the New York State Professional Firefighters Association said that "no previous governor has treated labor so badly" and that "[the firefighters union is] shocked by this veto, which was accomplished without discussion or other communication with those affected."[55] The dynamics of Paterson's Tier 5 reform are very much in line with the quantitative evidence provided in chapter 2 about the heterogenous manner in which different types of unions influence pension policy.

Andrew Cuomo became governor in 2011, continuing the unified Democratic control of government that had begun under Paterson. If the Firefighters Association had felt that Paterson had treated labor worse than any other governor that had come before him, they surely reassessed that claim once Cuomo took over. Cuomo made it clear that he felt Paterson had not done enough to address structural imbalances in the state budget that had been exacerbated and highlighted by a protracted recession. After some tense negotiations with the unions, the most comprehensive pension reform to date was passed by the legislature and signed by Cuomo in March 2012, quickly going into effect only a month later.[56] This reform created the most recent tier for new hires, Tier 6, in which employee contributions are tied to salary—reaching as high as 6 percent for those making more than $100,000.[57] Tier 6 also increased the retirement age for new hires, reduced the maximum pension amount, eliminated most overtime from salary calculations, and increased the vesting period. Although Cuomo had publicly stated that he had preferred to eliminate the defined benefit plan for all new hires entirely, and instead offer a 401(k)-type defined contribution plan, he acknowledged that he was "asking for the moon" and instead settled on the very comprehensive changes to the pension that stakeholders were willing to acquiesce to.[58]

Unlike what unfolded when Democratic Governor Florio attempted to push through pension reform in New Jersey in the 1990s, New York's public sector unions did not abandon Cuomo at the ballot box. Although most labor leaders were indeed irate—Michael Mulgrew, president of the United Federation of Teachers said at the time that the pension legislation was a "sleazy, middle-of-the-night back-room deal"—they also understood what awaited them if they pulled their support from the incumbent Democrat: a victorious Republican.[59] In fact, public labor had remained "neutral" during the 1994 campaign for governor in retaliation against Mario Cuomo—Andrew's father—for opposing labor-friendly legislation during his third term as governor.[60] That election ushered in Republican government under Pataki for more than a decade. Accordingly, the Public Employees Federation stated that "there's no question that the pension vote is going to be a significant consideration when we look at candidates. . . . But it's not going to be a make-it or break-it factor."[61]

Andrew Cuomo ruled the state government with an iron fist.[62] The infamous line "three men in a room in Albany" describing the process by which New York State policy is designed was as appropriate as it ever was during Cuomo's tenure.[63] Despite not getting "the moon" that he had set out for, Cuomo made sure that pension reform—with teeth—happened under his watch. Although a number of public sector unions were displeased with the firm stance against what he, and the voters, perceived as largesse, their nascent attempts to field third-party candidates through the Working Families Party (WFP) proved quixotic. New York State's distinct and idiosyncratic electoral institution of the fusion ballot—a system in which candidates can run on multiple party lines—set Cuomo and the Democratic Party up for potential defeat (or at least embarrassment), but both public labor unions and progressives held the line by refusing to defect from the party in any significant numbers both in 2014 when Zephyr Teachout was *nearly* endorsed by the WFP and in 2018 when Cynthia Nixon actually was. Public labor remained unified behind Cuomo in response to what the progressive wing of the Democratic Party felt was the larger threat: Republicans and a potential return of the State Senate to their control. In fact, Mulgrew—who had been so fiery about Tier 6 reform in 2012—was a key figure in preventing public labor from defecting to Nixon and other state legislature challengers who were endorsed by the WFP. In 2018, he urged other public labor leaders to withdraw from the WFP and refrain from giving donations to WFP-backed candidates, stating "some reckless behavior [is going to] have an unintended consequence of us ending up with a Republican governor. . . . When these elections are over, we will judge any decision we have to make off your behavior if you caused bad things to happen—even though it was not your intent you are responsible for them."[64] Rather than splinter off into a reform party that could be controlled by the WFP's left-wing progressives, prolabor Democrats felt that their efforts would be better off focused on keeping right-leaning Democrats in the Senate from defecting to the Republican Party.[65] As a result, the WFP remained a marginal influence in state politics and the public sector unions had no other option but to remain within the firm fold of the Democratic Party establishment that been responsible for overarching, comprehensive pension reform in New York State.

Kentucky: A Case of Disorganized Politics and Weak Labor

Kentucky is about as different as possible from New Jersey and New York. The state is landlocked, in contrast with the coastal locations of New Jersey and New York; is much poorer (indeed, per capita income is below the national median); and is characterized by lower levels of educational attainment. The state is also more rural, less dense, and less racially diverse. Historically, Kentucky's economy has been dominated by farming and coal, although in recent years, the state has moved toward economic diversification, expanding into the health-care sector especially.[66] The state is more politically conservative than New Jersey and New York, despite the Democratic Party's nearly unbroken domination of Kentucky state politics since the end of the Civil War. Only in recent elections has the state's electorate begun to send Republicans to state office, though the state has supported Republican candidates for national office for considerably longer.[67]

Kentucky's public sector labor is also organized quite differently from that of New Jersey and New York in the sense that it is not really organized at all. Between 1995 and 2008, only about 11 percent of public sector workers belonged to a union in Kentucky. This stands in stark contrast to New Jersey's 59 percent and New York's 71 percent.[68] This disparity in unionization rates existed long before Kentucky's passage of a right-to-work law in 2017 and is more likely a result of the state's history of private sector unionization and its prohibition on public sector collective bargaining.[69] The theoretical framework presented in chapter 1 would suggest that a state with weaker public sector labor would be characterized by comparatively lower state taxpayer contributions to the pension fund, relative to states with better organized public sector labor, stronger unions, and Democratic control of government. The theory also predicts that, in terms of changes to pension benefit generosity, there would be no difference under partisan regimes; the likelihood of passing legislation that made changes to pension benefits in a state like Kentucky with poorly organized public labor would not be affected by whether Republicans or Democrats controlled state government. Because public sector workers who are not unionized have far less say in state politics than those in states who are, Kentucky would be more likely than both New Jersey and New York to underfund its pension system without increasing pension benefits as political compensation to workers.

Although Kentucky's public sector labor strength and organization has differed markedly from that of New Jersey and New York, partisan control of its state government has not looked that different. Despite the South's reputation for conservatism and Republican advantage, much of the region continued to elect members of the Democratic Party—the historic party of the Confederacy—to state and local office well into the 2010s. Kentucky, in fact, has only ever had unified Republican control of government for a brief period of time between 2017 and 2020. The governorship has been controlled by a Republican only a handful of times in the past century, experiencing a long, uninterrupted string of Democratic governorships between 1972 and 2004. The State Senate has been controlled by Republicans since 2000 but only marginally until 2011 (Republicans now heavily dominate the upper chamber). Democrats controlled the State House until 2017. As a result, much of the state's political history until only very recently has been dominated by Democratic policymaking, perhaps much to the surprise of casual observers.[70]

As a relatively young pension system—the TRS of Kentucky began operations in 1940, the Kentucky Employees Retirement System (KERS) was founded in 1956, and the Kentucky SPRS and County Employees Retirement System (CERS) were founded in 1958—much of the administration and structure of the system can be traced to modern political dynamics. TRS literature, for instance, notes that only five people have occupied the executive secretary position—responsible for overseeing day-to-day operations of the pension system—since its inception.[71] In fact, most scholars argue that Kentucky's pension problems are relatively recent, mostly beginning with budget crises of the early 2000s and the realization that the state legislature could defer contributions to the pension system for the indefinite future to plug the holes of more immediate, pressing shortfalls. Repeated and "devastating" market underperformance in the early and mid-2000s exacerbated the inadequacy of Kentucky's pension assets.[72] My data collection confirms these findings: while New Jersey, New York, and Kentucky all had similar average liabilities per state resident over this time period ($15,048, $17,162, and $15,072, respectively) and similar average liabilities per plan member ($196,434, $266,377, and $224,973, respectively), Kentucky's unfunded liabilities as a proportion of its asset base (i.e., liabilities less assets, divided by assets) was, on average, a staggering 139 percent compared with New Jersey's 52 percent and New York's 46 percent. This means that Kentucky would have needed to more than double its pool of assets to cover all of its unfunded liabilities, whereas the other two states needed around an additional half of their assets to cover unfunded liabilities. As shown in figure 5.1, this number increased over time, peaking in 2009 when Kentucky would have needed an astonishing additional 243 percent of its assets to cover its current pension debt. Even at its most unfunded—also in 2009—New Jersey needed only 117 percent of its assets to cover unfunded liabilities while New York needed 81 percent.

Most of Kentucky's pension crisis was a consequence of inaction, a case of the world changing around the state and the state failing to act—drift in Jacob Hacker's model of policy retrenchment.[73] In at least one instance, despite an increase in pension generosity before the peak of Kentucky's

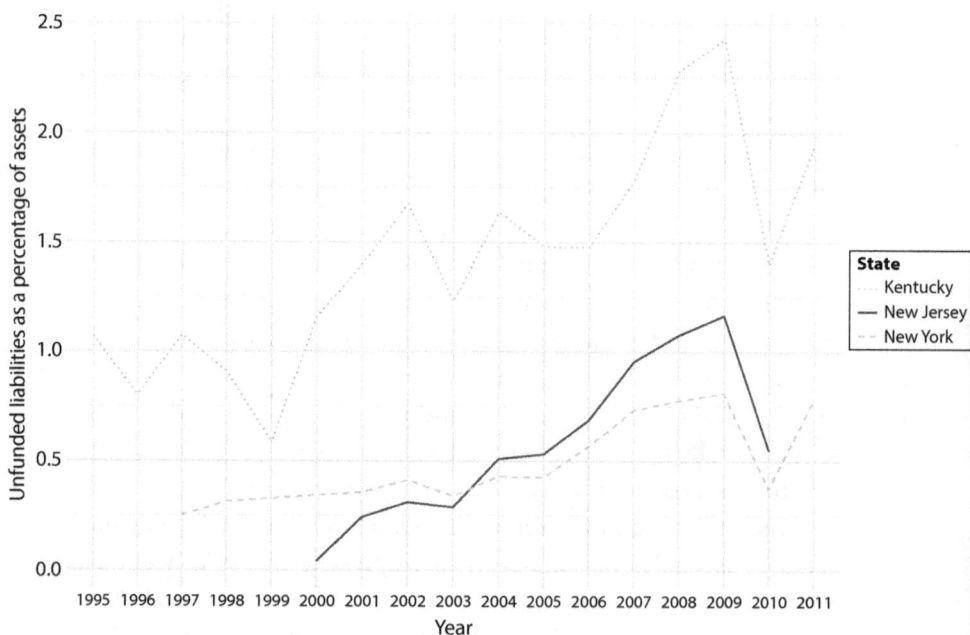

Figure 5.1 Unfunded liabilities as a percentage of assets in Kentucky, New Jersey, and New York, over time. These data come from an original dataset of revised, unbiased actuarial liabilities and assets, the details of which can be found in the Methodological Appendix.

Source: Author's dataset.

pension crisis in 2008–2009—a decrease in employer contributions in 2005 under Republican Governor Ernie Fletcher—Kentucky made virtually no other statutory changes to pension policy between 2000 and 2008. Although Democratic Governor Steve Beshear managed to oversee some minimal reforms in 2008, it was not until 2013—under the same gubernatorial administration—that a comprehensive plan to right the sinking ship was agreed to.[74] Beginning in 2014, the pension system that covered KERS, CERS, and SPRS was closed to all new hires with the exception of uniformed workers (which should again be unsurprising, given the patterns observed in both my quantitative data and the case studies presented in this chapter).[75] New workers would instead be required to join a hybrid pension/401(k)-style plan in which they would be guaranteed a 4 percent return on their contributions and then a percentage of the upside if the plan exceeded its benchmark performance.[76] TRS was not touched until further reforms were passed in 2018, spearheaded by Republican Governor Matt Bevin. Those reforms, however, were swiftly overturned by the Kentucky Supreme Court for improperly using a legislative loophole to push through the extremely politically unpopular—particularly among rank-and-file Republicans—TRS reform.[77] Three years later, in 2021, the General Assembly voted to override Governor Andy Beshear's veto of a second TRS reform bill. The successful reform closed the old TRS to new hires, creating a hybrid plan for teachers who started working after January 1, 2022. The new plan includes both a defined benefit and a defined contribution component and requires new hires to work longer and contribute more to their retirement than those workers covered under the old TRS.[78]

Lessons and Implications

New Jersey and New York's historical experiences in public pension policy are as distinct as my quantitative data suggest. In New Jersey, the pension system underwent a historical struggle for financial stability, grappling with insolvency issues dating back to the late nineteenth century. Plans like the TPAF and the PFRS were later established with relatively modest benefits aimed at attracting and retaining skilled employees.

The 1970s and 1980s marked a period of financial strain and economic challenges in New Jersey, prompting concerns about the sustainability of the pension system. Democratic Governor Florio's initiatives in the 1990s, particularly the Quality Education Act, underscored the political challenges of balancing pension funding responsibilities between state and local entities. Notably, the most heated conflicts between unions and Republicans in New Jersey centered around funding dynamics rather than the statutory expansion or contraction of benefits.

In New York, the narrative similarly unfolded against a backdrop of partisan control shaping pension policies. Democratic Governor Cuomo's tenure brought significant changes, introducing Tier 6 in 2012 and representing a paradigm shift in pension benefits for public employees. The Democratic Party's emphasis on cost-cutting measures left an indelible mark on New York's public pension landscape. Cuomo initially encountered resistance from public sector unions but successfully implemented pension reforms with the 2012 legislation. The intricate dance involving union politics, gubernatorial power, and the Democratic Party's role was evident in Cuomo's ability to navigate and implement change despite opposition.

Although both states faced unique challenges related to pension funding, economic downturns, and the need for reform, they each experienced aspects and degrees of the pluralist state and the coalitional state at different moments in time. New Jersey, marked by a weaker Democratic Party and more sustained Republican control, witnessed more of the pluralist regime over the sample time period. This regime was marked by strong public sector unions successfully pushing for increased pension benefit generosity from Republican administrations and, as a compromise, a decline in state pension funding. New York, in contrast, maintained high levels of state pension funding and cuts to pension benefit generosity during periods of Democratic rule and coalitional decision-making involving public sector unions.

In contrast, Kentucky presented a more divergent case. The state's public sector workforce is less organized than it is in New Jersey and New York, with historically lower unionization rates. The state's pension crisis, beginning in the early 2000s, was exacerbated by a lack of statutory changes to address the growth in unfunded liabilities and a willingness to divert resources from the pension fund to cover general budget shortfalls. Unlike New Jersey and New York, Kentucky's pension problems were largely a consequence of inaction.

It can be a bit less intuitive to understand why a state like Kentucky, characterized by extremely low levels of public sector union activity, might also be plagued by perpetually underfunded pensions like New Jersey. States with lower union activity might tolerate more financially unsustainable pensions because of the difficulty of recruiting workers to public sector jobs when the absence of a strong union has made salaries and working conditions so much less attractive than the private sector, compared with places with stronger union advocacy. Offering more generous pensions grants state governments a bargaining chip to entice workers; one that, unlike salaries and additional hires that enter as operating costs, does not need to be contemporaneously paid for under state budget rules.[79] In this sense, larger and more underfunded pension benefits are not only a political tool to win reelection and engender support from important sectors of the electorate without increasing taxes or cutting other parts of the budget but also a human resources tool to allow the government to adequately staff its offices and continue to provide public services to constituents.

Another, more obvious explanation, is that without union pressure state governments feel less obligated to contribute the full ARC, even if those same state governments never make statutory increases to benefits. In New Jersey, for example, the most intense conflict between unions and the Republicans took place over funding—not over statutory benefit expansions or contractions. Both parties viewed increased pension generosity essentially as a free lunch (the reverse was true in New York as a result of the coalitional dynamic among the unions and the Democrats). In states without strong public labor organizations, workers can act as neither powerful interest groups (as in New Jersey) nor as coalitional members of the Democratic Party (as in New York), allowing state governments to virtually ignore them and use promised benefits as a slush fund to cover budgetary shortfalls.

New Jersey's protracted financial challenges led to failed negotiations between a relatively weak Democratic leadership and influential unions, resulting in compromises on pension funding and benefit expansions and an embrace of state Republicans by public sector labor. The state's subsequent Republican control played a significant role in the contemporary evolution of New Jersey's pension system. This follows my theoretical predictions from chapter 1 about the way in which a pluralist state would operate.

In contrast, New York's story unfolded against the backdrop of Democratic dominance, particularly under Governor Cuomo. Cuomo adeptly navigated the interplay of union politics, gubernatorial authority, and the internal conflicts of the Democratic Party, bringing about substantial pension reforms. Despite initial resistance, Cuomo successfully implemented transformative changes, again in ways that reinforce my theoretical framework.

New York, over the studied time period, exemplifies the complex relationship between public sector unions and Democratic Party governance in a coalitional state.

Kentucky, offering a distinct case marked by weaker public sector labor and historically lower unionization rates, experienced a pension crisis rooted in legislative inaction and opportunistic resource reallocation. The state's ability to tolerate financially unsustainable pensions is likely connected to challenges in recruiting workers, especially in the absence of strong unions. Larger and more underfunded pension benefits are used as both a political strategy for garnering support without raising taxes and a human resources tactic for effective government staffing.

These varied state experiences underscore the nature of public pension policies in which historical decisions, political landscapes, and economic realities converge, and support the theoretical claims discussed throughout this and previous chapters.

CHAPTER VI

Blowing Up the Pluralist Framework

Republicans and Twenty-First-Century Labor Politics

In March 2011, the Wisconsin Budget Repair Bill—better known as Act 10—passed both chambers of the Wisconsin legislature and was signed into law by Republican Governor Scott Walker, its architect and advocate. The bill made substantial changes to public sector pensions in Wisconsin, to the way that health insurance for public employees was funded, and—most significantly—stripped public sector employees of their right to collectively bargain.[1] Outside observers were shocked. Voters and public sector unions were shocked. Governor Walker had not campaigned on destroying the pluralist framework in Wisconsin, a state that once boasted union membership of more than one-third of its labor force and had passed the first public sector collective bargaining law in the country.[2] The country's largest public sector union, the American Federation of State, County, and Municipal Employees (AFSCME) was born in Madison, Wisconsin, in 1932.[3] Republicans had come to accept the price of doing business in a union state—until Walker surprised them all.

Wisconsin, like much of the Midwest, was historically renowned for its manufacturing and strong ties to organized labor—both public and private. Home to industrial giants such as Harley-Davidson and the Miller Brewing Company, Wisconsin's economy, deeply intertwined with manufacturing like much of the Midwest, had long been a bastion of unionized workers. It is no understatement to say that the state's political landscape underwent a seismic shift in the early twenty-first century, challenging its reputation as a labor stronghold.

The transformation of Wisconsin from a labor-friendly to a labor-hostile state and the passage of Act 10 took place amid the economic backdrop of the Midwest's postindustrial collapse. The decline in industries like paper milling and automobile manufacturing decimated Wisconsin's manufacturing sector, not only leading to massive employment dislocation but also creating an atmosphere of economic uncertainty. The resulting budget crises became focal points in the political discourse, with policymakers grappling to address the challenges posed by a shifting economic landscape.

Although the political repercussions from the passage of Act 10 were profound, triggering widespread protests and a (failed) recall election of Governor Walker, none felt the effects more than the public sector unions. A decade after Act 10 was passed, public sector unions have shrunk considerably in Wisconsin, cratering from 44.6 percent of public workers in 1983 to 20.1 percent in 2023.[4] By other accounts, public sector union activity in Wisconsin has contracted by 70 percent.[5] The changes in Wisconsin in the early 2010s fundamentally altered the relationship between the state government and its workers, and several other governors in the Midwest would come to copy Walker's playbook. This included Illinois Republican Governor Bruce Rauner who would take his case all the way to the Supreme Court and who would ultimately be successful in turning the entire nation into a right-to-work state (for public employees) through *Janus v. AFSCME.*[6]

In this chapter, I use both qualitative and quantitative analysis, examining specific data on pension policies, electoral outcomes, and fiscal and economic indicators in Wisconsin and the rest of the country. Although I delve deeply into the specifics of Wisconsin, it serves as a microcosm that reflects larger trends and challenges discussed throughout this book. By examining Wisconsin in detail, we can better understand the broader implications of how expanding pension benefits through legislation has been electorally dangerous for state legislators and how it has been dangerous for governors through its effect on taxes. Strong Democratic governments and public sector unions had found a solution to these electoral consequences by acting coalitionally, internalizing the costs, and successfully balancing public workers' needs with those of elected Democratic officials. Republicans dealing with strong unions, in contrast, had a starker problem, particularly in the wake of *Citizens United v. Federal Election Commission* and the exponential growth in the power of antipublic labor sentiment within the party. As one scholar recounted, the "seemingly decentralized, state-by-state attacks [on the U.S. labor movement] are anything but spontaneous—they are fueled by a shared perspective and agenda. . . . Conservative think tanks and funders have produced draft bills, conducted workshops for new legislators, and poured huge sums of money into advertising, taking advantage of the Supreme Court's 2010 Citizens United decision."[7]

One solution to the strong labor conundrum that Republicans had available to them, depicted in table 1.2, was to entirely eliminate the public sector unions. In the second decade of the twenty-first century, a number of Midwest states, including Wisconsin, tried to do precisely this.

The Cradle of (Public) Labor Civilization

Reflecting on Wisconsin's revolutionary labor history makes it all the more surprising that it banned collective bargaining rights for public union members in 2011 and became the nation's twenty-fifth right-to-work state in 2015. Wisconsin workers established their first private sector union, meant to improve conditions and wages, in 1847.[8] The state quickly became a trailblazer in labor politics through its embrace of the Socialist Party and the progressive, unprecedented reforms codified into state legislation to formally protect workers' rights.[9] This culture of unified labor diffused throughout the industrial Midwest over the next century.

As an outgrowth of the strength of private sector labor and the support of powerful prolabor politicians like Governor Robert La Follette, the origins of the public sector union movement found a natural home in early twentieth-century Wisconsin. Civil servants met with Governor La Follette to plead for their right to organize, which he readily supported. Subsequently, the AFSCME first took shape in Wisconsin in 1932 as the Wisconsin State Administrative, Clerical, Fiscal, and Technical Employees Association (which quickly became known as the Wisconsin State Employees Association). The decision to allow public sector workers to form a union protected them from the consequences of the 1932 elections in which state Democrats rode Franklin D. Roosevelt's coattails into office and looked to replace many public sector workers with their own loyalists by dismantling the state's civil service system.[10] The Wisconsin State Employees' Association, which would evolve into AFSCME once the union was granted a charter from the American Federation of Labor, is one of the earliest examples of a public union representing government workers in America.

Although AFSCME quickly built up local chapters around the country, public sector unionization rates paled in comparison to those of the private sector. These lower rates were largely due to the exclusion of public sector labor from protections put in place by the Wagner Act in 1935. Notably, public sector workers had no recourse to demand collective bargaining from employers. This changed in 1958 when New York City Mayor Robert Wagner, son of Senator Robert Wagner (D-NY) for whom the 1935 law was named, signed an executive order granting collective bargaining rights to city employee unions.[11] Wisconsin passed its own public sector union collective bargaining law a year later—the first state in the nation to do so.[12]

Spurred by the developments in Wisconsin, President John F. Kennedy issued Executive Order No. 10988 in 1962. This executive order served as the federal equivalent of New York City's executive order in 1958 and Wisconsin's state law in 1959, granting federal employees and their unions the right to collective bargaining with their government employers. President Richard Nixon expanded the protections ordered by Kennedy when he issued Executive Order No. 11491 seven years later.[13]

Like most of the country, Wisconsin saw an explosion of public sector unionization rates in the decades following Kennedy's and Nixon's orders. By 1989, 50 percent of all public workers in the state were union members and one out of every five workers in Wisconsin were union affiliated.[14] At the beginning of the twenty-first century, Wisconsin was still home to the tenth-largest concentration of union members in the nation. By the end of the first decade of the new century, however, Wisconsin would experience the largest decline in unionization membership of any state in the country.[15]

Until Walker's tenure as governor, partisanship could do little to explain the rise and fall of union strength in Wisconsin. Between 1970 and Walker's election in 2010, Wisconsin's state government had been relatively balanced in terms of partisan control. The governor's mansion had been evenly controlled by three Democratic administrations and three Republican administrations (inclusive of Walker's). Similarly, the state legislature had been closely divided until 2011, trading off partisan control of both chambers for decades.[16] Periods of previous unified Republican control, however—as under Governor Tommy Thompson in the 1990s—were not marked by any notable attempts to eliminate or undercut the power of public unions in ways that would come to characterize Walker's reign. In fact, when Thompson ran for Senate in 2011, it was widely believed that he would face significant difficulties in Walker's GOP primary because of his record of working with public sector unions. To wit, AFSCME had endorsed Thompson for governor in both 1994 and 1998, and Thompson—likely in reciprocation—successfully pushed for a $4 billion expansion to state pension benefits in 1999.[17] Ed Garvey, the Democratic candidate for governor who ran against Thompson in 1998, recalled in 2011 that "Tommy agreed to decent wages and benefits. His goal was to neutralize labor in terms of his campaign. He was liked by not all of them, but some. Walker [on the other hand] came in trying to destroy labor."[18] As the record now shows, Walker was successful in his mission.

The Role of Pension Policy on Taxes and Electoral Outcomes

Pension Policy and Electoral Outcomes

To understand why Walker and the other Republican Midwestern governors that came after him did what they did, we need to understand why elected officials care about pension policy. Elected officials and political parties care about any type of policy for two primary reasons: first, because interest groups care; and, second, because voters care and will make their preferences known at the ballot box. In previous chapters, I focused on the first reason and the role of unions. In this section, I argue that, while the ruling in *Citizens United* and the general ascendancy of right-wing donor consortia made antilabor interest (and ideological) groups more powerful and effective, acting as an important impetus to the Republican attempt to destroy the pluralist framework, conservatives also worried about the voter side of the equation and their ability to keep taxpayers happy to continue winning elections.[19] Recall that Democrats are electorally protected from the pluralist demands of public sector unions because of their coalitional relationship. Not so for Republicans. Public sector unions, in most cases, do not consider the electoral consequences for Republicans who treat unions "too" well and give them more than is fiscally prudent. This has created a difficult position for Republicans. I provide evidence of the electoral ramifications of passing redistributionary pension policy as a partial explanation—along with the expanded importance of the donor class—for why Republicans wanted a way out of the pluralist framework.

Much of the political behavior literature finds that voters are largely ignorant of state politics and cannot even name their state representative.[20]

I find evidence, however, that at least *some* voters pay attention when a state legislature passes new public pension policy. Part of my theoretical framework relies on the idea that state elected officials and parties face electoral ramifications—perhaps disproportionately for Democrats if voters ascribe issue ownership of pensions to them—if they vote for or support generous pension benefits. These ramifications can stem from directly decreasing the welfare of nonpublic sector employees through changes to the rest of the budget (i.e., decreases in other expenditures or increases in taxes), increasing the cost of doing business for the state through increased borrowing costs (as discussed in depth in chapter 4), or from the implications for the future welfare of residents or their children. Though my sample size is small, limited by necessity to a handful of election years that my data provide coverage for, I find consistent evidence that some important segment of the electorate is regularly paying attention to pension policy.

Using my pension legislation data, state political data from Carl Klarner and budgetary data from the U.S. Census of Governments, I run a series of first-difference models investigating the impact of fiscal and policy decisions on electoral outcomes.[21] Table 6.1 depicts the effects of passing unfunded, expansionary pension policy legislation on the change in the percent of Democrats in the state legislature after an election, the likelihood of partisan control of the state senate changing hands after an election, and the likelihood of control of the state house changing hands. Individual Democratic legislators tend to be asymmetrically punished for the passage of pension legislation, but it does not appear to matter which party was in control when the legislation was passed. Both parties are punished equally in the sense that partisan control of the chamber is likelier to flip after expansionary pension legislation and is not conditional on whether the chamber was controlled by Democrats or Republicans when the law was passed. Passing unfunded, expansionary policy is associated with a 1.8 percent decrease in Democrats across the legislature (first column of table 6.1), independent of which party passed the bill.[22] Additionally, pension legislation is associated with a 10–13 percent increase in the likelihood that the chamber will flip partisan control (second two columns of table 6.1).

Governors face different consequences. Governors are not directly punished by voters for new expansionary pension policy, regardless of whether they happen to be Democratic or Republican. This might seem puzzling at first, given that the governor is so much more visible than individual legislators in state politics. But as V. O. Key put succinctly: "Voters are not fools."[23]

TABLE 6.1

Change in partisan composition of state legislature

	Change in democrats (1)	Change in senate control (2)	Change in house control (3)
Pension policy (election year)	−0.018★★ (0.009)	0.129★★ (0.058)	−0.070 (0.060)
Pension policy (one-period lag from election)	−0.019★ (0.010)	0.045 (0.040)	0.096★★ (0.046)
Percent change in general expenditures, p.c.	0.316★ (0.176)	−0.992 (0.895)	0.072 (0.939)
Percent change in total taxes, p.c.	−0.020 (0.094)	−0.189 (0.460)	−0.969★★ (0.477)
Percent change in total debt, p.c.	−0.047 (0.054)	−0.154 (0.380)	−0.154 (0.480)
Credit rating change	−0.005 (0.014)	−0.089 (0.184)	−0.019 (0.062)
Percent of democrats in legislature	−0.083★ (0.046)		
Dem. governor	−0.004 (0.014)	0.099 (0.064)	0.069 (0.069)
Change in presidential partisan voter index	0.011 (0.010)	0.092★ (0.084)	0.092★ (0.052)
Dem. sen. control		0.125 (0.094)	
Dem. house control			0.052 (0.093)
No. obs.	107	107	107
R^2	0.365	0.233	0.118
Adjusted R^2	0.261	0.107	−0.028

Source: National Conference of State Legislatures (1999–2011); U.S. Census Bureau, Census of Governments (1995–2012); Prah, Rotmil, and Fehr (2014); Klarner (2013b, 2013c); Wolf (2015); U.S. Bureau of Labor Statistics (1995–2012); U.S Bureau of Economic Analysis (1995–2012).

Note: Dependent variable is measured in the year after a state's legislative election. Add one lag to all independent variables (such that policy was realized in the year of the election, unless otherwise indicated). Robust standard errors clustered by state in parentheses. Estimated intercept not reported. Control variables include lagged policy and economic indicators and have not been reported for purposes of brevity. Presidential Partisan Voter Index is a proxy for the partisanship of the state and is measured by comparing the state's Democratic share of the two-party presidential vote against the national average. ★$p < 0.1$; ★★$p < 0.05$; ★★★$p < 0.01$.

Despite the difficulty individual voters face when ascribing accountability to policymakers in a multilayered, complex federal system like the United States, *attentive* audiences are knowledgeable enough to understand how the policymaking process works.[24] Governors play a much smaller role than state legislatures in crafting policy that determines or changes pension benefits.[25] As such, my findings that legislative parties are electorally punished for passing unpopular pension laws, while governors are not, is ultimately heartening for purposes of democratic accountability.

Governors, despite their junior role (in relation to legislators) in legislative politics, play an outsize role in budgetary politics. For a variety of reasons, governors have far more say over and control of state budgets than the substance of policy that must be legislated.[26] In line with this institutional feature, gubernatorial elections are extremely sensitive to previous changes to tax collections. Although governors are not directly electorally affected by the legislature passing new, unfunded pension policy, they are indirectly affected through the legislation's impact on larger tax collections. The one important caveat, however, is that *only Democratic governors* are punished for increased per capita taxes (or, more accurately, failing to decrease per capita taxes enough).

Table 6.2 presents the details of this effect. The first two models look at the likelihood that the governor's mansion is occupied by a Democrat after an election. The first of these two models does not interact the presence of a Democratic governor in the year of the election with the per capita tax change; as the table shows, the only statistically significant variable that predicts the likelihood of a Democratic governor winning the election is whether the office is currently occupied by a Democrat. The second model adds the interaction between party of the incumbent governor and the size of the election year tax change. We can see that the presence of a Democratic governor in office during the election year increases the likelihood of having a Democratic governor after the election, but this effect is significantly moderated by the size of the change in per capita state tax burden. For instance, a 1 percent increase in per capita tax revenue under a Democratic governor reduces the likelihood of a Democrat winning office in the next election by 3.1 percentage points (95 percent confidence interval [CI; −0.6, −5.5]). If, however, a Republican governor oversees a 1 percent increase in per capita tax revenue, that penalty is statistically nonsignificant (although the point estimate is a 0.7 percentage point increase in the likelihood of a Democrat winning the election). Given that the median tax change under Democratic governors in an election year is a 2 percent *decrease*, Democratic

TABLE 6.2

Change in partisan control of governor's mansion

	Likelihood of democratic governor		Likelihood of governing party switch	
	(1)	(2)	(3)	(4)
Pension policy (election year)	0.030 (0.065)	0.009 (0.053)	0.029 (0.088)	0.046 (0.090)
Pension policy (one-period lag from election)	−0.035 (0.067)	−0.022 (0.067)	0.021 (0.056)	0.010 (0.052)
Percent change in general expenditures, p.c.	1.270 (1.496)	1.022 (1.472)	−0.877 (1.352)	−0.670 (1.391)
Percent change in total taxes, p.c.	−1.063 (0.734)	0.693 (0.802)	1.313★ (0.711)	−0.150 (0.851)
Percent change in total debt, p.c.	−0.524 (0.444)	−0.333 (0.501)	−0.008 (0.465)	−0.167 (0.488)
Credit rating change	0.054 (0.059)	0.059 (0.062)	−0.013 (0.098)	−0.018 (0.101)
Percent of democrats in legislature	0.218 (0.440)	0.474 (0.471)	0.298 (0.433)	0.085 (0.428)
Dem. governor	0.323★★★ (0.082)	0.235★★★ (0.088)	0.013 (0.084)	0.087 (0.087)
Change in presidential partisan voter index	−0.089 (0.071)	−0.035 (0.075)	−0.105 (0.073)	−0.150★★ (0.069)
Dem. governor × change in taxes		−3.753★★★ (0.905)		3.127★★★ (0.915)
No. obs.	111	111	111	111
R^2	0.257	0.335	0.152	0.214
Adj. R^2	0.130	0.214	0.007	0.070

Source: National Conference of State Legislatures (1999–2011); U.S. Census Bureau, Census of Governments (1995–2012); Prah, Rotmil, and Fehr (2014); Klarner (2013b, 2013c); Wolf (2015); U.S. Bureau of Labor Statistics (1995–2012); U.S Bureau of Economic Analysis (1995–2012).

Note: Dependent variable is measured in the year after a state's gubernatorial election. Add one lag to all independent variables (such that policy was realized in the year of the election, unless otherwise indicated). Robust standard errors clustered by state in parentheses. Estimated intercept not reported. Control variables include lagged policy and economic indicators and have not been reported for purposes of brevity. Presidential Partisan Voter Index is a proxy for the partisanship of the state and is measured by comparing the state's Democratic share of the two-party presidential vote against the national average. ★$p < 0.1$; ★★$p < 0.05$; ★★★$p < 0.01$.

governors typically set themselves, or other Democratic candidates, up for a 6.1 percentage point bump in the polls.

The second two models shown in table 6.2 speak more directly to the likelihood that the incumbent gubernatorial party retains or loses control of the office after a tax increase or decrease. The third model suggests that no governor should want taxes to increase in an election year, given that the likelihood that they and their party lose control of the state's highest office increases 1.3 percentage points for every 1 percent increase in taxes—regardless of party—while the fourth model emphasizes how much more dire this is for Democratic governors. Democratic governors are hit with an average 3 percentage point increase in the likelihood of a partisan administration change after a 1 percent tax increase (95 percent CI [0.48, 5.47]); again, however, Republican governors do not suffer any statistically significant electoral consequences. This asymmetry in electoral consequences is not unheard of; it is well documented as it relates to the electoral consequences of income and economic growth for different partisan presidential administrations, for instance.[27] Note also that, despite these results suggesting that there is partisanship issue ownership over the area of taxes, Republican and Democratic governors do not pursue markedly different tax policies. As figure 6.1 depicts, both types of governors oversee similar degrees of tax revenue changes during any given year of their tenure. The greatest observable differences in tax collection occur in the extreme tails of the distribution. These extreme-tail differences may be driving the issue ownership assigned by voters to the two parties, but it is not driving the asymmetry in electoral consequences, as removing the outliers does not qualitatively change the results of the analysis.

This discussion has provided evidence that the legislature is punished for passing expansionary, unfunded pension policy, while governors are punished for increasing taxes or not cutting them enough to voters' liking. In this next section, I discuss the ways in which taxes and pension policy are intimately intertwined.

Pension Policy and Taxes

As I have shown, statutory changes to pension policy matter to legislators—and public sector unions, when Democrats are in control—because of their direct relationship to electoral outcomes. Pension policy matters to

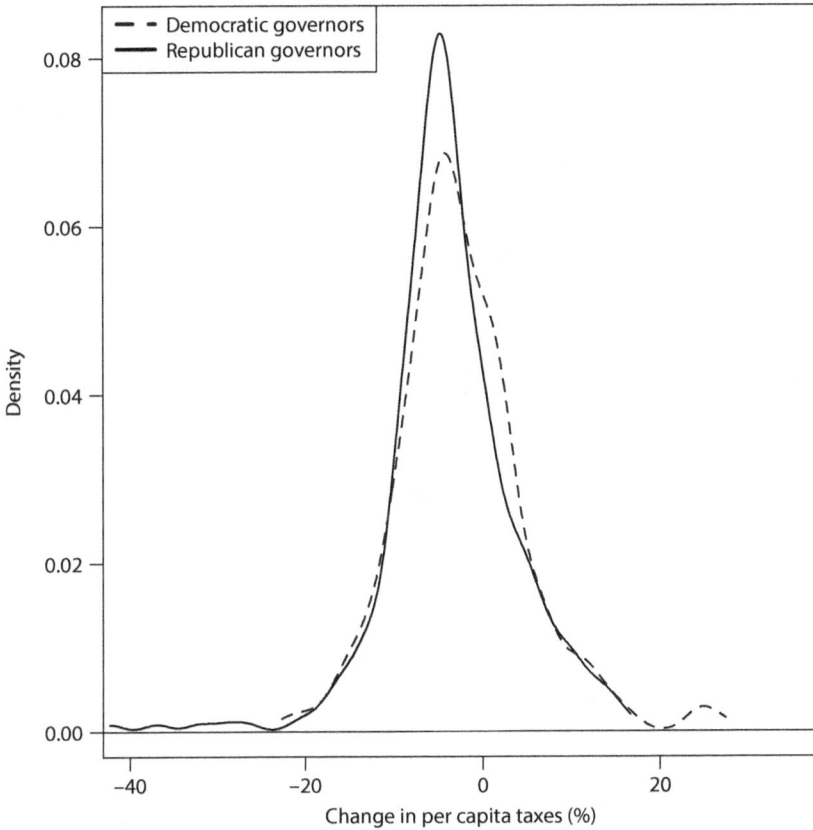

Figure 6.1 Distribution of changes to total taxes, by partisanship of governor. Distributions of year-over-year percentage changes in per capita taxes, subset by party of the governor.

Source: U.S. Census Bureau, Census of Governments (1995–2012); Klarner (2013b, 2013c).

governors, however, because of their impact on tax burdens. Table 6.3 quantifies this relationship, again using a first-difference framework. Expansions in unfunded benefits are strongly associated with increases in per capita tax revenue. Even with a full set of economic, budgetary, and partisan controls, passage of one piece of legislation that increases the generosity of pension policy is associated with a contemporaneous 1.4 percent increase in per capita taxes (95 percent CI [0.01 percent, 2.9 percent]), while passage of one piece of legislation the year prior is associated with a 1.9 percent increase in per capita taxes (95 percent CI [0.7 percent, 3.1 percent]) the following year.

TABLE 6.3
Change in total taxes, per capita

	Percent change in total taxes, p.c.
Pension policy	0.014★★
	(0.007)
Pension policy (one-period lag)	0.019★★
	(0.006)
Pension policy (two-period lag)	0.002
	(0.008)
Percent change in general expenditures, p.c.	0.636★★★
	(0.244)
Percent change in total debt, p.c.	−0.030
	(0.040)
Credit rating change	−0.016
	(0.015)
Lagged total taxes, p.c.	0.0001★★★
	(0.0002)
Change in percent of democrats in legislature	0.295★★
	(0.131)
Dem. governor	0.020★
	(0.012)
Change in partisanship of governor	0.036★★
	(0.016)
Dem. governor after partisan switch of office	−0.056★★★
	(0.021)
No. obs.	397
R^2	0.252
Adj. R^2	0.218

Source: National Conference of State Legislatures (1999–2011); U.S. Census Bureau, Census of Governments (1995–2012); Prah, Rotmil, and Fehr (2014); Klarner (2013b, 2013c); Wolf (2015); U.S. Bureau of Labor Statistics (1995–2012); U.S Bureau of Economic Analysis (1995–2012).

Note: Dependent variable is measured as the percent change in per capita total taxes from one year prior. Robust standard errors clustered by state in parentheses. Estimated intercept not reported. Control variables include lagged policy and economic indicators and have not been reported for purposes of brevity. ★$p < 0.1$; ★★$p < 0.05$; ★★★$p < 0.01$.

The same budgetary data suggest that pension policy changes do not affect aggregate general expenditures in the same way, although expenditures slightly increase by 0.5 percent three years after a pension bill is passed (statistically significant only at the 90 percent confidence level, not reported).

Data availability makes it difficult to show the impact on the *composition* of expenditures, but see chapter 4 for a discussion of the growth (or, rather, lack thereof) of state appropriations to the pension system as a percentage of expenditures.

These results provide evidence of the link between pension policy—an area of policymaking we may think of as involving largely "inattentive publics"—and electoral outcomes through changes to taxes that are more likely to fall under the domain of rational retrospective voting.[28] Documenting this relationship is the first step in establishing a link between expansions in pension policy, bailouts of funds, and their electoral consequences. It also may explain why elected officials care so much about the financial health of state pension systems, and why some Republican state administrations have decided in the past decade that it may make more sense for them, electorally, to simply blow up the status quo political framework surrounding pension policymaking.

Governor Walker: How Wisconsin Learned to Stop Worrying and Love the Disorganized State

Scott Walker's Divide-and-Conquer Strategy

The first decade of the twenty-first century saw the loss of hundreds of thousands of factory jobs in Wisconsin, spurred by the postindustrial collapse of the regional economy and accelerated by globalization.[29] The strain on Wisconsin's once abundant union culture reached its apex during the Great Recession as manufacturing employment in the state went into a free fall and jobs shifted to the service sector. It was against this backdrop of dramatic economic dislocation that Walker, an openly anti-union Republican politician, was elected to the state's highest office.[30]

Although some argue that Walker was able to win office solely because of the gradual decline in union culture and support among Wisconsinites, this explanation fails to acknowledge the immense protests and pushback Walker experienced during and after his attempts to neuter the state's public sector unions.[31] Others, instead, argue that Walker was successful in winning the governorship only because of the deception he employed when running for office.[32] Walker explicitly claimed that he did not intend to transform Wisconsin into a right-to-work state or strip workers of collective bargaining rights. He had long asserted to support private sector unions, stating that he needed their help to create jobs.[33] But after his election, a videotaped interaction between Walker and a millionaire campaign donor was released in which Walker was heard promising the donor that he would "divide and conquer" the workers of Wisconsin as a first step to achieving right-to-work status.[34]

Walker likely meant that he intended to pit private and public labor against one another. By identifying public labor as the enemy, Walker could preserve the vote of those who held private-union membership while simultaneously appeasing those who wished to see him attack public unions, believing such an approach to be a steppingstone to more holistically business-friendly legislation. According to Mary Spicuzza and Steven Verburg, "At that time, he didn't want to antagonize the entire labor movement at once. . . . If he had come out for right-to-work, he would have lost a substantial amount of the labor vote."[35] Walker's overall electoral strategy was to preserve a considerable portion of the labor vote by hedging his position on whether he planned to push Wisconsin to adopt right-to-work legislation once he was in office. Even his—much clearer—position on reforms to public sector collective bargaining was portrayed as a mere "budget-balancing measure" rather than as a cornerstone of his long-term efforts to deconstruct the labor rights of public workers in Wisconsin.[36]

The dual nature of Walker the candidate and Walker the elected official also hinged on his finely tuned, nuanced messaging meant to distinguish race from labor. This messaging predated his run for the governor's mansion. As Hannah Walker and Dylan Bennett recount, Walker "fought the county's labor and African American constituency with a budget-reducing agenda [as Milwaukee County executive beginning in 2002]."[37] Although Walker's public policy work clearly depicted an anti-union agenda, his public messaging was less clear. Walker and Bennett continue:

> Due to the solidified political alliance of the Democratic Party, African Americans, and public sector unions, when Governor Walker campaigned against unions he simultaneously campaigned against Milwaukee and African Americans, even when posturing behind the familiar conservative language of austerity and flexibility. The history of race and labor means the exclusion of an alternative hypothesis that Governor Walker's appeals could contain a race-free message in a contest over economic policies. To alienate Milwaukee voters with a narrative

about urban union failure is to marginalize the poor and people of color while prompting working class whites to forsake class for race and support the Republican Party.[38]

In other words, Walker's campaign worked to denounce the performance or necessity of unions and to urge working-class whites to relinquish any ties they felt to Democratic candidates based purely on labor practices. In this sense, Walker divided and conquered not only by highlighting the distinctions between public and private labor but also by highlighting differences between Black and white labor.

Pensions Before and After Walker's Act 10

Wisconsin's public employees have received some form of retirement benefits since 1891, beginning with funds for police officers and firefighters. By the early 1900s, most municipalities throughout the state had established individual systems to provide pensions to their public workers. When the solvency of these local retirement programs became threatened by mismanagement and diseconomies of scale (a recurring story in the history of state pension systems), these systems were slowly consolidated into larger state-run programs. The most important of these were the State Teachers Retirement Board, established in 1911, and the Wisconsin Municipal Retirement Fund, established in 1943. Nevertheless, by the mid-1940s, more than seventy separate public retirement systems were in place across the state. Because of ongoing concerns about the difficulty of adequately supervising so many plans and continued fears over the solvency of some of the smallest plans, nearly all public retirement systems were rolled into the Wisconsin Retirement System (WRS) by 1981. With this merger, the WRS became one of the largest retirement systems in the United States and in the world.[39]

Several changes were made to the WRS between 1981 and Walker's election, all of which made benefits more generous for employees. By 1989, participants were granted portability and reciprocity for the benefits they had earned thus far when transferring between WRS and the Milwaukee County and City system (which, to this day, still remains a separate plan). Less than a decade later, a five-year vesting requirement was eliminated, meaning employees did not have a wait time before they could begin accruing their full benefits. In 1999, a cap on fixed fund participants was eliminated and variable funds became available to new participants in WRS. These benefits altered the yield that was possible for both older participants and new participants in the WRS program, making larger payouts possible. In 2003, the Wisconsin Department of Employee Trust Funds was given the ability to negotiate rates on annuities through a ruling process.[40]

On paper, the financial position of Wisconsin's pension system was not particularly distinct or noteworthy between 1998 and 2010. As figure 6.2 depicts, its unfunded liabilities as a percentage of assets bounced between quite low (falling below 6 percent in 2010—a consequence of historically unprecedented deflation) and moderate (reaching as high as 57 percent in 2009). These numbers, although much more variable from year to year as a result of Wisconsin's highly procyclical annual annuity adjustment, which allows annuities to be altered according to the year's market performance, are in line with New York's experience.[41] The performance of the WRS in the leadup to Walker's governorship is certainly not an example of a state pension in dire straits. Similarly, the payments being made by the state to the pension system as a percentage of state general expenditures remained

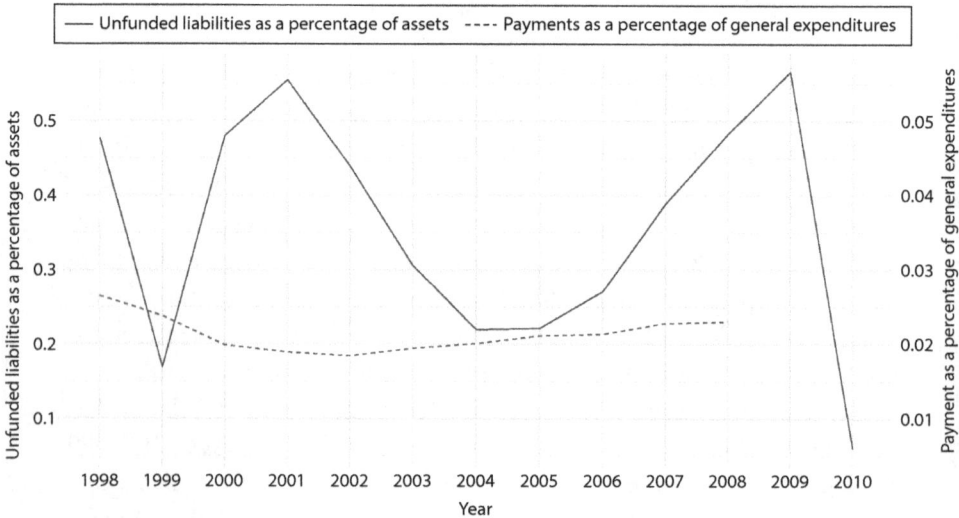

Figure 6.2 Wisconsin's unfunded liabilities and pension payments, over time. Unfunded liabilities as a percentage of assets is measured on the left-hand axis; payments as a percentage of general expenditures is measured on the right-hand axis.

Source: Author's dataset; U.S. Census Bureau, Census of Governments (1995–2012).

quite steady over this time frame, never exceeding 2.7 percent. Despite the state's comparably well-managed pension system, however, the rest of the state found itself in severe financial turmoil.

When Walker was inaugurated as governor of Wisconsin in January 2011, a $3.6 billion budget deficit awaited him, inherited from the previous administration but a culmination of decades of cyclical and structural budget shortfalls. Figure 6.3 plots the state's general fund balance—annual general revenue less annual general expenditures—over time. Although the state's general fund's balance had been falling swiftly since the beginning of my time series, it did not fall below zero—becoming a deficit—until 2001. These structural challenges to the state budget were largely a result of expanded spending—especially to local K–12 schools—and slashed taxes under Governor Thompson between 1992 and 2000. The state's budget never recovered from these reforms, despite rosy forecasts of swift economic growth that were believed would replenish the state's coffers.[42] As a result (according to Walker), Walker introduced Act 10 shortly after his inauguration. The bill made clear his plan to diminish the power of public sector unions and was promoted as a cure-all for the state's long-standing budget deficits. According to Walker, the bill was necessary because, "The

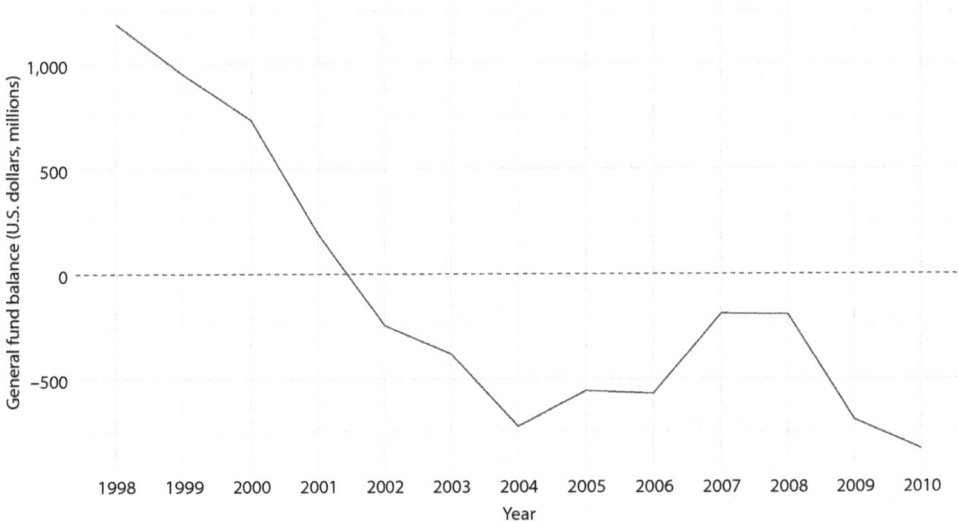

Figure 6.3 Wisconsin's general fund balance, over time.

Source: U.S. Census Bureau, Census of Governments (1995–2012).

state's broke. Local governments are broke. They don't have anything to offer."[43] After the election, Walker made clear that he felt that the state could not afford to negotiate with public unions because of the budget deficit. Act 10 required public sector workers, many of whom had previously not been responsible for contributing to the pension system, to start contributing nearly 6 percent of their salaries. Act 10 also doubled the required employee contributions for health care. Most significantly, however, Act 10 placed substantial limits on the ability of public sector unions to engage in efforts toward collective action. Although right-to-work legislation that would prohibit unions from collecting agency fees and union dues from workers who did not want to join the organization would come later in 2015, Act 10 immediately prohibited public employers from collectively bargaining with unions over wages and other essential workplace matters.[44] Research suggests that collective bargaining, far more than mandatory collection of agency fees, is the most crucial aspect of determining public worker organizational strength and the single most important condition for facilitating public employees to overcome the collective action problem.[45] Because Act 10 affected pensions and because it affected employee compensation and workplace conditions, it also affected public services. Teachers were no longer motivated to keep their jobs, now understanding that the state did not recognize their labor as essential. Act 10 cut the state's pension contributions, it cut its health-care contributions, and it outlawed the ability of workers to demand promises about workplace safety or the possibility that wage increases could ever outstrip inflation. At the same time, Walker's new budget incorporated $13 billion in tax cuts—an extra hard pill for workers to swallow when they were being told that these changes were necessary because of structural budget shortfalls. Finally, in an echo of Walker's divide-and-conquer strategy that pitted private against public labor and Black against white labor, Act 10 exempted uniformed public sector workers—fire services and nearly all police—from any and all changes prompted by the law.[46]

Act 10 gutted nearly all of the expansive developments that had shaped WRS since 1981. Following its passage, public employees began contributing half of the total required contribution to the pension system. This was a break with the historic pattern of employers paying the majority—and in some cases, nearly all—of the required contribution. State and local employers were prohibited from contributing more than half of the required contribution except in the case of police officers and firefighters. The vesting period was also reinstated.[47] Most enraging to employees, however, was the loss of their ability to collectively bargain on essential labor issues like workplace conditions and salaries. Workers could now only bargain for raises that were capped at inflation, and they lost all other ability to discuss wages, benefits, and job conditions. The loss of large health-care subsidies—also a result of Act 10—and the increase in the diversion of wages toward pension contributions were immediately felt by government employees.[48]

In the way that it had been conceived by Governor Walker and his backers, Act 10 worked. It did not solve any structural issues with the state's persistent budget shortfalls.[49] But it did dismantle the powerhouse of public sector labor in Wisconsin. The union-busting Act 10 was complemented by the passage of Act 1, a statewide right-to-work law, in 2015, which prohibited any employer from requiring a worker to belong or pay dues to a union as a condition of employment.[50] The combination of these two laws dealt a powerful blow to the strength of both public and private sector unions in Wisconsin.[51] For many of Wisconsin's public employees, this meant leaving their job, their union, or even the state.[52] In 2010, 46.6 percent of public employees belonged to a union in Wisconsin. By 2023, that number had fallen to 20.1 percent.[53]

The 2011 Protests and Attempted Recall of Walker

Walter attempted to garner the support of workers left jobless and unionless as a result of economic dislocation, primarily through a populist agenda of scapegoating urban public sector workers of color, but he met considerable resistance from those who continued to cling to the state's historic prolabor culture. Unsurprisingly, Walker and his Act 10 were met with disapproval by many public workers and, in some cases, public employers who believed unions were the best way to motivate high performance of their staff.[54] Indeed, beginning in February 2011, protestors convened across Wisconsin to express this disapproval, with hundreds of thousands gathering at universities, government buildings, and the state capitol. Walker even put the Wisconsin National Guard on alert as he anticipated violent resistance to the passage of the bill.[55] The unrest culminated in an attempted recall of the governor in 2012, which ultimately failed by a small margin. Although Walker was ultimately reelected as governor in 2014, he was narrowly defeated in 2018 by Democrat Tony Evers. Evers, the state schools superintendent, received 49.6 percent of the vote compared with Walker's 48.5 percent.[56] Despite Walker's loss, Act 10 remains the law of the land.[57]

Scott Walker's experience with public sector labor—and his success with most of the rest of Wisconsin's electorate—did not go unnoticed by neighbor states. A *New York Times* article from January 2012 predicting the fall of organized labor across the middle of the country, wrote that "after legislatures in Wisconsin and several other Republican-dominated states curbed the power of public sector unions, lawmakers are now turning their sights toward private sector unions, setting up what is sure to be another political storm. The thunderclouds are gathering first here in Indiana."[58] A month after the article was written, Indiana Governor Mitchell Daniels approved measures to make Indiana the first Midwestern right-to-work state—three years before Walker would get the chance to do so in Wisconsin.[59] Governor Daniels used his final term in office, knowing he would not be able to run for reelection, to push through the electorally unpopular measure.[60] Daniels, like Walker, did not run on an antilabor platform, and he certainly did not suggest that he would push to turn Indiana into a right-to-work state. It was Walker's political tenure and what was perceived as a referendum on the rights of public sector workers that enabled Governor Daniels to successfully pursue the radical change. That he had nothing to lose, politically, certainly helped as well.

Michigan underwent a similar transformation to its labor relations in 2012. A year prior, in 2011, Michigan boasted the fifth-largest union membership in the nation; the size of the state's organized labor force, along with its storied industrial history, could not prevent the momentum of the antiunion agenda, however. Republican Governor Rick Snyder—like Walker in Wisconsin and Daniels in Indiana—did not campaign on turning Michigan into a right-to-work state. In fact, Snyder claimed that it was the unions' fault for backing him into a corner by placing Proposal 2 on the ballot in 2012. Snyder, describing the ballot initiative's proposal to "grant public and private employees the constitutional right to organize and bargain collectively through labor unions" (among other statewide prolabor protections), recounted that he "asked them not to go forward. And the reason . . . is . . . [the unions] are going to start a very divisive discussion. It'll be about collective bargaining first, but it'll create a big stir about right-to-work in addition to collective bargaining."[61] With more than $45 million spent by both sides, Proposal 2 was the costliest ballot proposal in Michigan's history. The proposal was soundly rejected by voters, with 58 percent of the electorate voting against granting workers a state constitutional right to collective bargaining.[62] One month later, Snyder signed two bills into law that instituted right-to-work rules for both private and public sector labor. On the day that that bills were passed, one news story reported that "state police . . . [formed] a 'perimeter' outside the capitol . . . wearing riot gear . . . state troopers deploy[ed] pepper spray and other methods of crowd control as they . . . [tried] to calm the outrage being expressed by . . . union supporters."[63] In an unexpected twist, the Michigan legislature voted to repeal the private sector right-to-work law in March 2023. As of this writing, the repeal has not yet gone into effect.[64] Public workers in Michigan, however, are still subject to right-to-work rules as the Supreme Court ruling in *Janus v. AFSCME* made it illegal to require public sector workers to pay union dues or agency fees anywhere in the country beginning in 2018.

Ohio also pursued antilabor legislation in the wake of Walker's political success. Describing the state's antibargaining bill in 2011, the *New York Times* wrote that "[the Ohio bill] goes further than [Wisconsin's Act 10] . . . Ohio's law allows only limited bargaining: If management and union do not reach a settlement, then city councils and school boards can impose their side's final contract offer unilaterally. The Ohio law bans binding arbitration and bargaining on health coverage, pensions or staffing levels. It also requires government workers to pay at least 15 percent of their health insurance costs and pay 10 percent of their salaries toward their pensions."[65] Republican Governor John Kasich's success at union-busting was more ephemeral than that of his Republican colleagues in other states, however; the law was repealed by popular referenda eight months later with 62 percent of voters casting ballots in favor of overturning the law.[66]

Wisconsin's experience with public sector unions in the second decade of the twenty-first century, and its ensuing attempt to destroy the pluralist policymaking framework, reflects broader patterns and themes that have manifested across the country. From the vantage point of time, it is clear that Wisconsin was an important catalyst for changes to labor relations in the Midwest—changes that radically redesigned the government-labor framework that had been operating for more than half a century. As the original pioneer of union culture, neighboring states were eager to follow in Wisconsin's footsteps under their Republican-led governments and newly unfettered millionaire and billionaire donors. It is also evident that Wisconsin's influence over the rest of the Midwest—including Illinois and Republican Governor Rauner—would have reverberating effects on workers' rights that would extend well past the confines of the middle of the country and its former industrial heartland and into the rest of the nation. These secondary effects, although not wholly unexpected, were fervently hoped for by conservative lawmakers and advocates, as I discuss in the conclusion.

Conclusion

y central claim throughout the book has been that fiscal sustainability is intimately related to stable political coalitions. This
argument—simple on its face—has been made in other contexts,
often as an aside to explain other types of fiscal behavior. In this book's six
chapters, I have crystalized this contention through an in-depth analysis of
state pension plans from the end of the twentieth century to the beginning
of the twenty-first century. I found that well-organized public sector workers act as permanent components of Democratic Party coalitions through
their unions and that this promotes and encourages the internalization of
the costs of fiscal recklessness. Although public sector unions desire—and,
more important, have the organizational capacity to demand—increases to
pension benefits that are paid for by state taxpayers, unions also recognize
the electoral dangers posed to Democrats who unilaterally increase taxes
and expand pension benefits. This forces both the union and the Democratic
Party to strike a delicate balance that has favored fiscal sustainability, on net.
In contrast, under periods of Republican Party governance, public sector
unions transform into traditional interest groups working under a pluralist
framework in which they vie for fiscal resources in a competitive political
environment. Over the past decade, however, unified Republican control
has begun to present a potential existential risk to the very survival of public sector unions and the coalitional versus pluralist political framework
that has characterized strong union states. Eliminating the union removes

the coalitional relationship when Democrats are governing and removes the pluralist environment when Republicans are governing, leaving public sector workers on their own to navigate the disorganized state. This strategy has been most typified by Governor Scott Walker's crusade against public sector unions in Wisconsin, but his playbook has been copied by Republicans in other Midwest states, as well.

I also presented arguments that a centralized budgeting authority, like a political machine, plays an essential role in maintaining fiscal integrity. Ester Fuchs also found this to be the case in her work on Chicago and New York City during the twentieth century.[1] Political machines, with their inherent monopoly power and permanent electoral coalitions, have the luxury of centralizing policymaking and ensuring short- and medium-term fiscal stability.[2] Other types of strong coalitions can also embody this concept. This is in contrast to a more fractured political and policymaking apparatus in which there are "too many cooks in the kitchen" who all want to ensure that they get a piece of what they believe to be a limit-less pie. During periods of reform—in which political institutions move away from the strong party or party machine apparatus and typically are characterized by weak party rule—fiscal crises often arise because of competing and unconstrained demands from various interest groups. We have seen this pattern play out time and time again at the state and local level in the United States.[3]

Finally, there is very likely a perception among voters and, possibly, certain policymakers that states have a softer budget constraint than they actually do.[4] In reality, however, states face a much harder budget constraint than the federal government as they have more limited access to policy tools that might soften financial constraints like printing money. States' budget con-straints are far more similar to local governments' constraints than to those of the federal government, despite the fact that state political conflict has become considerably nationalized whereas local political conflict has not (as of this writing, at least).[5] As discussed in the next section, there has also been movement to reverse this trend and "state-ify" national politics—that is, bring state issues into the national policymaking arena, particularly with regard to public labor policy issues. The Midwest's attempt to reduce the power of public sector unions—and essentially eliminate them altogether—coalesced into a nationwide movement that culminated in a landmark policy decision made by the U.S. Supreme Court.

Public Sector Labor Politics Post-*Janus*

In 2015, as one of his first acts in office, Republican Governor of Illinois Bruce Rauner issued an executive order prohibiting the collection of "fair share" fees from nonunion state workers. Rauner had felt that public sector unions wielded a disproportionate and inappropriate influence on state finances even though his election was the direct result of the failure of his Democratic predecessor to cave to public sector union demands over pensions (and the Illinois unions' grave mistake in their refusal to compromise and the withdrawal of their support from Democratic Governor Pat Quinn).[6] Rauner's executive order faced legal challenges from the outset, however, and the governor attempted to move the American Federation of State, County, and Municipal Employees' (AFSCME's) pending lawsuit from state to federal court as soon as it was filed to challenge the fair share (also called "agency") fees on First Amendment grounds.[7] Although the federal District Court judge ruled that Rauner had no standing in the lawsuit, the judge allowed the suit to continue with three state employees as plaintiffs in lieu of Rauner. One of these employees was an Illinois child support specialist named Mark Janus.[8]

At the same time, *Friedrichs v. California Teachers Association*, which revolved around a similar First Amendment complaint (compelling political speech through the mandatory collection of union fees), was working its way up the federal court hierarchy.[9] The Ninth Circuit ruled against the plaintiffs, citing precedent set by *Abood v. Detroit Board of Education* that established the constitutionality of maintaining a union shop in a public sector workplace through mandatory agency fees.[10] As circumstances would have it, however, Justice Antonin Scalia died after the Supreme Court heard the appeal but before a decision could be issued. His death and vacant seat on the court resulted in a 4–4 split that left the appellate court's decision in place.[11] This set of events allowed the case in Illinois to proceed. In 2017, once Justice Neil Gorsuch was appointed and confirmed to fill Justice Scalia's seat, the plaintiffs in *Janus* applied for and were granted a writ of certiorari from the Supreme Court to appeal the Seventh Circuit's decision to dismiss the case on the basis of the *Abood* precedent.[12]

In June 2018, the Supreme Court, in a 5–4 decision, sided with the plaintiffs and declared that the mandatory collection of agency fees from nonunion public employees was unconstitutional. The decision, authored by Justice Samuel Alito, effectively overturned *Abood*, marking a significant shift in the Court's stance on union fees in the public sector. As one scholar noted, "Nothing really changed between *Abood* and *Janus* but the Court."[13] The decision overturned countless collective bargaining agreements around the nation in which agency fees had been enshrined. Public sector unions could no longer forcibly collect dues from workers who chose to not belong to the union and AFSCME's nonmember agency fees declined by 98 percent after the ruling.[14] Contrary to the predictions of many, however, the number of active, dues-paying union members only marginally declined from 1,114,128 in 2017 to 1,075,480 in the year after *Janus* was decided—a relatively small loss of 6 percent.[15] By 2022, that number stood at 1,050,013, representing an additional loss of 2 percent of membership spread out over three years.[16] This was not the doomsday scenario conservative groups had been hoping for.

Although the activities of public sector unions had a clear financial impact—fee-paying nonmembers disappeared almost entirely once they were no longer obligated to contribute agency fees—there were fewer challenges in maintaining membership than had been anticipated. This was largely due to the fact that the ban on agency fees turned out to *not* be the greatest threat to public sector unions. Instead, the broader attack on collective bargaining and exclusive representation rights—as described in chapter 5's depiction of the Midwest and as nationally repudiated, for now, by the Supreme Court's denial of certiorari to a case that had been heard at the Sixth Circuit upholding the right to exclusive representation—poses a more significant danger to the stability, existence, and efficacy of public sector unions.[17]

The reasons for this are twofold. First, collective bargaining is the cornerstone of labor unions' power and effectiveness, enabling unions to negotiate fair wages, benefits, and working conditions on behalf of their members. Without the ability to collectively bargain, unions lose their primary mechanism to advocate for workers' interests. If they cannot negotiate effectively (their raison d'être), unions will struggle to attract and retain members. Indeed, as we examined in chapter 5, this has proven to be the case in Wisconsin.

Second, collective bargaining provides unions with a seat at the table in discussions about workplace policies and decisions. Without this bargaining power, unions are often marginalized and excluded from crucial decision-making processes. This loss of influence diminishes unions' ability to shape policies that affect their members' livelihoods. In the public sector context, this loss of influence would also extend to the political arena. As Patrick Flavin and Michael Hartney recount in their important work on the role of collective bargaining in political mobilization, "the political power of teachers unions (and public employee unions more generally) would likely be much less if mandatory bargaining laws were never enacted by state governments."[18] This is because of the manner in which collective bargaining laws subsidize the operations of the union and lessen costs associated with overcoming the collective action problem. One example the authors provide is the manner in which teachers unions are provided, by the school district, a list of all district employees—regardless of whether the employee is a member of the union—and their contact information. Teachers unions in states with mandatory collective bargaining laws are also typically given privileges to use school facilities to conduct union business. Most important, however, is that collective bargaining protections have been shown to causally and materially increase union membership across the states, presumably because of the lower cost to mobilization and the greater reward to solidarity.[19]

The Future of Public Sector Unionism and Public Sector Pensions

Much has been made of the precipitous decline in private sector unionization rates, but the challenges facing private sector workers are far different from those facing public sector workers. For one, the decline in the strength of organized workers in the private sector was largely due to structural changes to the economy (moving from a manufacturing-based economy to one more reliant on services) and a rapid movement toward large-scale globalization. The obstacles facing public sector unions have less to do with the economy—as it is unlikely, at this point, that we will offshore teachers' jobs to countries with lower labor costs—and far more to do with the political and ideological climate. Although public sector unions experienced rapid growth in the mid to late twentieth century, leading to substantial gains in wages, benefits, and working conditions, the political landscape for public unions began to shift in the beginning of the twenty-first century. Conservative politicians and interest groups sought to limit the power and influence of unions first at the state level and then at the national level. Many claimed that this attempt to restrain the power of public sector unions originated from a desire to balance the budget and regain fiscal sustainability, but my findings throw this assertion into doubt. Even if true, however, conservatives also knew that destruction of the public sector union would decimate the power of the Democratic Party and allow Republicans to more easily hold onto the reins of power. As a result, the spate of antilabor legislation that has emerged in several states and policy decisions that have been made by the U.S. Supreme Court are far and away the largest challenge to public sector unionism in the immediate future.

In response to continued legal challenges and changes to labor law, the divide between public sector unions and their detractors is likely to become even more politically fraught. The response to the passage of Act 10 in Wisconsin was met with weeks of protesting and Capitol sit-ins and even an attempt by the state Democrats to prevent a key legislative vote by fleeing to Illinois.[20] As public sector unions face ever-growing pressure, they are also likely to increase their political activism. Changes in labor laws may lead to shifts in union membership and representation patterns around the country. Some states have always had far lower public sector unionization rates than others, but antilabor legislation is likely to reorganize these dynamics among the states. Many public workers in states that have purposively weakened unions through legislation, for instance, have left the public sector workforce or decamped for other, more labor-friendly states altogether.[21] I discussed the impact of these political and legal decisions on the management of human resources and the supply of public labor in chapter 5 within the context of Kentucky's disorganized state. Many others, however, have also recognized the urgency of retaining or recruiting public sector workers in a politically hostile environment—especially and most crucially, teachers.[22]

A more complex prediction to make is about the trajectory of public sector pensions. Since the end of my dataset's sample period, state pensions have rebounded to their most funded levels since before the Great Recession. But where the finances of public sector pensions are headed depends on a variety of factors—not only demographic trends but also economic conditions, investment returns, policy changes, and broader fiscal developments in state budgets.

Demographic shifts are important because of the way that public pensions are funded. In many states, current pension contributions go almost entirely to fund current annuitants' benefits. This means that pension plans are not yet finding it necessary to touch the assets that are tied up in investments like the stock market but also in far more illiquid vehicles like private equity.[23] As the population ages, however, and the dynamics of the workforce shift, this funding strategy will no longer work. Nevertheless, in many states, public employers have begun offering employees defined contribution plans in lieu of pensions—and many have taken their employers up on their offer. As a result, it is still unclear whether the shrinking workforce or the shift away from traditional defined benefit plans will be more impactful on the long-run fiscal sustainability of state pensions.

The other especially large source of uncertainty revolves around investment performance and economic conditions, more generally. Although cyclical economic downturns typically lead to lower investment returns (and pension contribution holidays)—as the country saw during the Great Recession in 2008—structural changes to the economy hold the potential to reduce more long-term returns as well. Pew forecasts that the typical public pension fund will earn a yearly return of around 6 percent on their investments. This is below most plans' assumptions of 7 percent and does not take into account the increased risk, volatility, and illiquidity pensions have assumed since the pandemic by more aggressively moving into alternative investments.[24]

Opposition to the optics of austerity—shrouded in what some have considered fearmongering over pension sustainability—has argued that public pensions were never in immediate crisis and are not likely to be at any point in the near future.[25] Other work has forcefully argued that any approach to full or near-full funding of public sector pensions would be disastrous for both governments and the economy—a type of forced savings that would require large cuts in government goods and services, increases in taxes, or both.[26] Amanda Kass, Andrew Crosby, and Brenda Parker, for instance, found that an Illinois law requiring municipalities to shore up their own pensions—at the local level—triggered extreme austerity measures and was particularly harmful for majority-Black communities.[27] Although these voices have gained steam and attention, they are still relatively isolated. Many agree that state pensions are now on a footing that makes them likely to be sustainable in the near term (as of 2024), but few would necessarily concur that their funding is adequate to fully alleviate the fears of a fiscal crisis over the next half-century.

Good Government Groups and the Governmental Accounting Standards Board Reforms

Good government groups have been instrumental in pressing for reforms of public pensions over the past decade. Groups like Pew Charitable Trusts, the Center for Retirement Research at Boston College, the Center for State and Local Government Excellence, and the Volcker Alliance have been active in advocating for specific types of pension reform, in promoting more transparency and better disclosure practices, and—perhaps most importantly—in educating the public about fiscal issues surrounding pension management. Without their advocacy—which in and of itself is often fueled by ideological concerns, as most government reform efforts are—the Governmental Accounting Standards Board (GASB) would have almost certainly not undertaken the task of revising their guidelines surrounding pension reporting.

Beginning in 2012, GASB issued several new rules that changed the manner in which public pension finances are reported. These new standards were meant to enhance transparency and accountability in public pension financial reporting and—hopefully—make the sort of data collection and construction I did for this book unnecessary going forward. The most important of these reporting standard changes were GASB Statements No. 67 and 68.

Statement No. 67 focused on pension plans' financial statements, requiring more detailed disclosures about plan assets, liabilities, and net position. The rule change also required plans to measure their pension liabilities using a prescribed method, known as the projected benefit obligation method.[28] This method is used to calculate the present value of future pension benefit payments expected to be paid to plan participants, taking into account various factors, such as salary levels, years of service, and expected retirement ages. The statement also introduced guidelines for choosing the discount rate used to calculate the present value of liabilities. Whereas pension plans typically chose a discount rate equivalent to the chosen expected rate of return on plan assets (which has no economic or financial rationale whatsoever)—vastly and inappropriately discounting the size of the liability—GASB now recommends that the discount rate be uncoupled from the expected rate of return on assets if certain conditions are not met. In those circumstances, GASB requires that the plan use "a tax-exempt, high-quality municipal bond rate."[29] My liability measure used the ten-year Treasury yield as a discount rate, likely decreasing the liability I constructed relative to a liability measure that uses a discount rate pegged to a municipal bond, but the ethos of the calculations is nevertheless quite similar.[30] Overall, GASB No. 67 aimed to standardize and improve the quality of financial reporting for pension plans, which would—ideally—help stakeholders make more informed decisions about plan funding, investment, and sustainability. Additionally, the establishment of clear guidelines for measurement, presentation, and disclosure now allows for better comparability and reliability of pension plan financial information across different jurisdictions and periods of time.

Statement No. 68 addressed reporting by employers participating in pension plans, requiring them to recognize their proportionate share of pension liabilities and expenses on their financial statements. The most important change introduced by GASB No. 68 was the requirement that state and local governments recognize a net pension liability (NPL) on their balance sheets. The NPL represents the difference between the total pension liability of the government's pension plan and the plan's assets available to cover those liabilities. This change provided a clearer picture of the government's long-term financial obligations related to pensions. No longer would governments be able to treat the pension liability—or pension debt—as off-budget.[31]

Although the guidance issued by GASB in 2012 in the wake of the Great Recession and what was perceived as the depths of the pension crisis was roundly lauded as correcting course, challenges have remained. Sheila Weinberg and Eileen Norcross, skeptical of the likelihood of enforcement by a nongovernmental agency like the GASB, wrote:

> Based on a review of these 144 plans as of June 2014 we find that the implementation of GASB 67 resulted in little change in the reported liability, contrary to the expectation of scholars . . . only a small fraction of plans applied GASB 67's recommended "blended discount rate" in FY 2014, leading to almost no discernable change in the size of unfunded liabilities for the majority of plans, and a slight improvement in the case of Illinois, a state among the most distressed pension plans in the nation. Secondly, we find that GASB 68, while revealing more of plans' underfunding in financial reports continues to conceal total amount of underfunding.[32]

From my perspective, this should be anything but surprising. Even after GASB's revised guidance, states remain responsible for reporting their pension finances and for choosing which actuarial assumptions they make. The temptation to manipulate data in a subjective reporting environment is just too much for states to resist, particularly if they exhibit characteristics that are linked to underreporting liabilities: union control of pension boards, poor funding, and easily accessible financial documents. The only way that this can be addressed in the long term is by having the federal government assume a formal role in the administration and governance of state pension plans, much in the way that the doomed public version of the Employee Retirement Income Security Act (ERISA) proposed in 1975.[33]

The overreliance on financial documents, while tempting because of their supposed and apparent objectivity, can often lead to a skewed understanding of a government's fiscal health. This is not limited to public sector pensions. In late 2023, for example, Mayor Eric Adams of New York City warned of massive budget cuts because of the costs of housing and feeding an unprecedented influx of asylum seekers. New York City Schools was told to cut $100 million from their 2024 budget (5 percent of 2023 expenditures); even the New York Police Department (NYPD), a pet department of the former-police officer mayor, was warned that there would be a hiring freeze and that no new recruits would be trained.[34] In January 2024, however, the shortfalls magically disappeared: all funding to the NYPD and the Fire Department of New York would be restored.[35] The cuts to the schools would be lessened, although early education was still severely curtailed. Public library service was reduced by 15 percent by being forced to close their doors on Sundays, but some programs were reinstated. Composting in public parks was eliminated but curbside composting pickup was allowed to remain. Mayor Adams attempted to spin the budget magic as something he had been responsible for, specifically, to save New Yorkers from drastic decreases in quality of life. Political opponents, however, countered that the mayor had been lying. Although they could not find incontrovertible evidence in financial reports, experts understood that the assumptions made for projecting things like revenue and mandatory spending—like costs to house migrants under the obligatory, constitutional *right to shelter* in New York—were inherently mushy and manipulable for political purposes.[36] Nathan Gusdorf, for example, mused:

When the mayor's office initially released its estimated costs for aid to migrants and its low revenue projections . . . these were too pessimistic by a considerable margin. The city regularly underestimates future revenues, and in this case . . . their projections were inconsistent with current economic indicators and recent revenue trends . . . they were [also] not accounting for operating efficiencies in asylum-seeker costs, such as negotiating better deals with shelter providers. . . . We can't speculate on why the city managed its fiscal forecasts in this way, but we think this outcome was predictable.[37]

Both in pension and other types of public sector financial reporting, it is essential to employ a critical analysis of the underlying data and assumptions when making decisions and recommendations. This advice extends to both academics and policymaking practitioners. One of my central arguments revolves around the idea that policy decisions based solely off of self-reported financial documents are likely to overlook broader policy implications, trade-offs, and the true impact on various stakeholders.

Final Thoughts

In this book, I have (I hope) returned to a central claim over and over: Fiscal sustainability is intricately linked to stable political coalitions. Through a comprehensive analysis of state pension plans spanning the end of the twentieth and beginning of the twenty-first century, I have provided evidence for my claim, shedding light on the complex relationship between organized public sector workers, political parties, and policy and budgetary decisions.

I have shown how well-organized public sector workers, primarily through their unions, form a vital component of the Democratic Party. This alliance has served as a bulwark against fiscal recklessness, as unions and Democrats navigate the delicate balance between advocating for workers' interests and recognizing the electoral risks of unilaterally redistributing resources to state employees. Conversely, under Republican governance, public sector unions transition into more traditional interest groups, vying for fiscal resources in a competitive political landscape.

The pivotal role of centralized budgeting authority, as in a political machine, has also been emphasized throughout the book. Political machines, characterized by their monopoly power and permanent electoral coalitions, have historically promoted fiscal stability through centralized policymaking. Conversely, periods of reform, marked by weak party rule and fractured policymaking apparatuses, often lead to fiscal crises—primarily in the form of acute short- and medium-term solvency concerns—because of competing interest group demands.

Finally, I have highlighted the misperception among voters and policy-makers regarding states' budget constraints, which are often perceived as softer than they truly are. This misperception, combined with nationalized political conflict, poses significant challenges to fiscal sustainability. Although the risk of underfunded public pensions to overall fiscal stability has been mostly overstated by certain advocacy groups, it is essential to understand that pension debt, legally speaking, is comparable to any other form of public debt. From a political perspective, however, pension debt carries additional weight as it represents a solemn promise from one generation to another to ensure financial security in old age, much like Social Security.

Importantly, most public pensions in the United States are on firmer financial ground than Social Security. The real question moving forward is whether voters and policymakers will continue to honor this generational commitment through the maintenance and support of public pensions and Social Security. As we navigate the complexities of fiscal policy in the second half of the twenty-first century, the decisions we make will determine the stability and sustainability of these crucial social contracts. By recognizing and addressing these fiscal challenges with clarity and foresight, we can work toward a more secure financial future for all generations.

Methodological Appendix

A. Description of Data Sources

Table A.1 includes the data used in the book and their sources.

TABLE A.1

Data sources

Variable	Source
Count of net expansionary legislation	National Conference of State Legislatures (NCSL) (1999–2011)
Contributions FROM public employers, employees, and state	Pew Center on the States (2010); and Public Plans Data (2001–2022)
Self-reported liability estimates	Public Plans Data (2001–2022)
Revised liability and funding ratio estimates and salary estimates	Author's calculations from CAFR data
Per capita tax revenue	U.S. Census Bureau (1977–2012)
Partisan composition of legislature	Klarner (2013c); and NCSL (1999–2011, 2011)
Partisanship of governors and dates of gubernatorial elections	Klarner (2013b); and NCSL (1999–2011)
State worker unionization and concentration rates	U.S. Census Bureau and Bureau of Labor Statistics (1995–2012); and Hirsch, Macpherson, and Vroman (2001)
Public sector union donations to state campaigns	National Institute on Money in State Politics (1995–2012)
Public sector labor laws	Valletta and Freeman (1988)
State unemployment rate (consumer price index, CPI)	U.S. Bureau of Labor Statistics (1995–2012)

(continued)

TABLE A.1

(*Continued*)

Variable	Source
Gross state product and personal income	U.S. Bureau of Economic Analysis (1995–2012)
Federal transfers, expenditures, population, debt, surplus, and interest	U.S. Census Bureau (1977–2012)
Balanced budget requirements	Hou and Smith (2006)
Partisan voter index	Wolf (2015)
Days to state Comprehensive Annual Financial Reports (CAFR) release	Institute for Truth in Accounting (2013); and Jones et al. (2012)
Pension board composition	Author's calculations from pension documents
Credit ratings	Prah, Rotmil, and Fehr (2014)
Polarization	Shor and McCarty (2011)
Traditional party organization	Mayhew (1986)
Strong party organization	Clark and Hoffmann-Martinot (1998)

B. Revised Pension Liabilities and Assets

B.1. Constructing the Revised Data

The greatest data challenges of this book project was constructing a dataset that accurately reflected the liability and asset status of states' public pension plans. With the help of Nolan McCarty and a grant from the Russell Sage Foundation, I set out to collect the Comprehensive Annual Financial Reports (CAFRs) of 128 state-funded pension plans over seventeen years.[1] Following a procedure outlined by Novy-Marx and Rauh that they used to revise liabilities from 2009, I used these CAFRs to hard-code data on benefit levels, cost of living adjustments, salary structure, employee age and experience distributions, and current annuitant numbers and allowances.[2] Using these (comparably) few data, I was then able to construct a standardized measure of liabilities across pension membership tiers, plans, states, and years. Again following Novy-Marx and Rauh, I used the accumulated benefit obligation (ABO) as a measure of plan liability, the most conservative of the standard actuarial formulations. This obligation is essentially a measure of what the plan would owe if all of the employees stopped working today. An easy analogy would be if the employer (i.e., the school system in the case of a teachers pension plan) closed up shop and dissolved *today* but was still responsible for paying off the pension benefits that their employees had accrued. This construction of the liability is convenient because it makes the minimum number of assumptions necessary to get a picture of the plan's obligations—I do not need to guess about termination rates or wage increases, for instance. Current annuitants would continue to receive what they receive today, while active employees would receive only what they have earned to date, beginning when they reach normal retirement age.[3]

Once the data were collected, I constructed the ABO in four stages:

1. Calculate averages of active workers and annuitants by age and years of service per year across regions (west, midwest, south, northeast) or across plan types (judges, general/mixed, teachers, police and firefighters, elected officials) and collect data on plan-year benefit factors (typically between 1 percent and 5 percent), salary, and average annuitant benefits
2. Construct distributions (weights)
3. Calculate individual ABOs
   - Match plan-year to weights by region and year or plan types and year
   - ABO for active members = plan-year benefit factor × years of service × weight for age-service salary cell × plan-year average salary
   - ABO for annuitants = weight for age benefit cell × plan-year average benefit
4. Calculate discounted plan ABOs
   - Obtain life expectancy data (mortality tables)
   - Calculate expected years of remaining annuity payments
   - Pick discount rate and cost-of-living adjustment (COLA)[4]
   - Calculate individual discounted ABOs
   - Plan discounted ABO = (discounted individual ABO × weight for age-service employee cell × plan-year total active workforce size) + (discounted annuitant ABO × weight for age annuitant cell × plan-year total annuitants)

Depending on the level of analysis, the plan ABO can be left as is or again aggregated to the state level with other plan ABOs.

I also readjusted pension assets such that their actuarial value reflected a more reasonable expected rate of return. I collected the market value of net plan assets for each pension-year and then calculated their adjusted actuarial value such that

$$A_t = A_{t-1} + rA_{t-1} + s\,(M_t - (A_{t-1} + rA_{t-1}))$$

where A_t is the actuarial value in period t, M_t is the market value in period t, r is the expected rate of return on the assets, and s is the smoothing factor (the percent of the difference between market value and expected actuarial value that is incorporated into the current actuarial value). For the calculations employed in the book, I used a 6.5 percent rate of return and the standard actuarial assumption of a 20 percent smoothing rate.

All of the assumptions made to revise the actuarial value of pension liabilities and assets are essentially *subjective*. Some assumptions are more reasonable (i.e., lowering the discount rate) than others (i.e., raising the discount rate), but I cannot claim I am more justified in picking the ten-year Treasury rate over a high-grade tax-exempt municipal bond rate, especially when the conversation is still ongoing.[5] As such, the project does not seek to establish an authoritative measure of state pension liabilities, assets, or overall funding levels; I never make any claim that plan x needs to raise y dollars in revenue to avert financial collapse. What I *do* establish, however, is a pecking order of plans' financial health. Although I cannot say with certainty that Texas's state pensions were funded at only a woeful 37.8 percent in 2011 (versus the more reasonable 83.0 percent the state claimed), I can say with certainty that it was (1) *not* funded as well as the state claimed, (2) better funded than Kentucky (the worst offender for that year, with a revised 20.6 percent funding level versus a 50.6 percent state-reported funding level), and (3) *not* as well funded as Hawaii (52.2 percent revised funding level, 59.4 percent self-reported). By standardizing assumptions and calculations across plans, states, and years and preserving an ordinal relationship between liabilities, assets, and funding levels, I may not be able to say with absolute certainty how bad a state's financial position is, but I am able to draw conclusions about why some states are in more precarious financial positions than others.

B.2. Constructing the Annual Required Contribution

Self-reported annual required contribution (ARC) and contribution rates were first obtained from the Pew Center on the States for all fifty states and the years 1997–2008.[6] Using this data, I was then able to back out exactly how much public employers, employees, and the state legislature paid into the pension system in a given year: ARC × Contribution Rate = Actual Payment.

Next, I used my revised liability and asset data to construct a measure of what I call the aggregate unfunded actuarial accrued liability (UAAL), which is simply the sum of the UAALs for all pension plans in a given state. This is mathematically constructed as UAAL = Liabilities − Assets and is an indicator of how much the state needs to meet its future and current obligations.

To get a sense of how many dollars would need to be contributed on a yearly basis over thirty years to pay off this UAAL, I then calculated the revised ARC. This number is calculated much in the same way a prospective homeowner would calculate a possible mortgage payment. The interest rate that the state is "borrowing" at is the rate of return that the assets would have received had the UAAL not existed—the opportunity cost of not having enough assets, in other words. For this calculation, I used the rate of return that was equal to the rate of return I assumed to revise the actuarial value of assets calculations (rather than the plans' assumed rate of return), or 6.5 percent. To construct the revised ARC, then,

$$\text{Revised ARC} = \text{UAAL} \times \frac{i(1+i)^n}{(1+i)^n - 1}$$

$$= \text{UAAL} \times \frac{0.065(1.065)^{30}}{(1.065)^{30} - 1}.$$

$$\approx \text{UAAL} \times 0.077$$

From here, calculating the *actual* contribution rates of state legislatures over my sample period is straightforward. I simply divided the actual payment amount (backed out from Pew's data) by the revised ARC, so that Revised Contribution Rate = Actual Payment/Revised ARC.

To isolate the contribution rate of the state legislature, I supplemented Pew's data with data from Public Plans Database that broke down plan contributions by employer, employee, and the state. Then,

$$\text{Revised State Contribution Rate} = \frac{\text{State Payment}}{\text{Revised ARC - Employer and Employee Payments}}$$

C. Full Liability Models Broken Down by Plan Type

Table C.1. shows the linear regression on change in pension obligations, per capita, by type of employment plan.

D. Alternative Models

I next offer additional specifications of the legislation models contained in chapter 2.

D.1. Ordered Probit with Random Effects

Because most data observations take on a value of zero in the data (approximately 80 percent) and because no good statistical models of zero-inflated count data with negative values exist, I use an ordered probit model for the following analysis. The results of this robustness check is largely in line with findings from the linear probability model in the main text.

The probit is estimated as follows, where y_{st} is the measured outcome and z_{st} is the latent variable:

$$
y_{st} = \begin{cases}
-4 \text{ if } z_{st} \leq \mu_1 \\
-3 \text{ if } \mu_1 < z_{st} \leq \mu_2 \\
-2 \text{ if } \mu_2 < z_{st} \leq \mu_3 \\
-1 \text{ if } \mu_3 < z_{st} \leq \mu_4 \\
0 \text{ if } \mu_4 < z_{st} \leq \mu_5 \\
1 \text{ if } \mu_5 < z_{st} \leq \mu_6 \\
2 \text{ if } \mu_6 < z_{st} \leq \mu_7 \\
3 \text{ if } \mu_7 < z_{st}
\end{cases}
$$

where $z_{st} = \beta_1 \times \text{Union Strength}_{st} + \beta_2 \times \text{Dem Gov}_{st} + \beta_3 \times \text{Avg Dems}_{st}$
$+ \beta_4 \times \text{Union Strength}_{st} \times \text{Dem Gov}_{st} + \beta_5 \times \text{Union Strength}_{st}$
$\times \text{Avg Dems}_{st}$
$+ \beta_6 \times \text{State Worker Concentration}_{st} + \beta_7 \cdot \text{Bargaining Index}_s$
$+ \gamma \mathbf{X}_{st} + \delta_s + \kappa_t + \varepsilon_{st}$

$\mathbf{X}_{st}$ is a vector of control variables that vary by state; and year and δ_s and κ_t are random effects attributable to state and year, respectively.[7] *Union Strength*

TABLE C.1

Linear regression on change in pension obligations, per capita, by type of employment plan

	General (1)	Police (2)	Teachers (3)	Judges (4)
Union strength	−108.465	71.810	−239.908	−37.401
	(290.131)	(75.932)	(344.419)	(42.744)
Change in democratic seats	3, 287.534	3, 236.991**	19,782.020***	−1, 755.057
	(6, 760.843)	(1, 439.024)	(5,765.570)	(1,866.399)
Lagged democratic seats	−765.275**	6.215	475.942	88.160
	(378.208)	(128.730)	(460.462)	(187.276)
Total taxes, p.c.	0.274***	−0.084*	0.126**	−0.025
	(0.066)	(0.050)	(0.051)	(0.067)
Logged general expenditures	−109.873	427.437*	427.614	−210.184
	(364.998)	(257.131)	(324.118)	(161.797)
State worker rate	3, 300.410	2,721.719**	882.410	768.956
	(5,040.710)	(1,064.290)	(3, 569.893)	(900.218)
Logged population	1, 944.245***	−27.004	823.751	175.334
	(586.337)	(183.003)	(614.667)	(213.999)
Personal income, p.c.	0.076***	0.007*	0.049**	0.007
	(0.020)	(0.004)	(0.024)	(0.010)
Logged nominal gross state product	−1,21.156***	−276.382**	−1,143.083	14.442
	(642.924)	(128.540)	(728.204)	(151.361)
Unemployment rate	−212.096***	−64.261**	−169.581***	−2.983
	(31.002)	(26.851)	(22.681)	(7.379)
Lagged plan liabilities, p.c.	0.004	0.032**	−0.030	0.078***
	(0.015)	(0.013)	(0.024)	(0.018)
Democratic governor	114.633	0.236	−61.331	−48.430
	(121.408)	(31.921)	(107.218)	41.999)
Union strength × chg. in dems.	−12, 260.850	−3,46.577**	−26,72.530***	1,719.321
	(8,507.855)	(1,708.625)	(7,461.376)	(1,936.068)
No. obs.	599	316	322	140
R²	0.095	0.082	0.128	0.314
Adj. R²	0.075	0.042	0.092	0.243

Source: Klarner (2013a, 2013b); U.S. Census Bureau and Bureau of Labor Statistics (1995–2012); Hirsch and Macpherson (2011); Author's dataset; U.S. Bureau of Labor Statistics (1995–2012); U.S. Bureau of Economic Analysis (1995–2012); U.S. Census Bureau, U.S. Census of Governments (1995–2012); Hou and Smith (2006); Valletta and Freeman (1988); Shor and McCarty (2011).

Note: This table reports the full model results depicted in figure 2.4 in chapter 2. Intercept not reported. ***$p < 0.01$, **$p < 0.05$, *$p < 0.01$.

is an index of state-level unionization rates and campaign contributions, *Dem Gov* is an indicator variable for whether the governorship is controlled by a Democrat, and *Avg Dems* is the average percent of seats held by Democrats in both legislative houses. *State Worker Concentration* is the percent of full-time workers employed by the state government, and *Bargaining Index* is an index of public sector laws that includes collective bargaining rights, the right to strike, and right-to-work laws. The results of the ordered probit are reported in table D.1.

To see how the raw coefficients from the probits translate into probabilities of policy change, consider figure D.1, which plots the likelihood of observing a net policy change as union strength increases. The left plot shows the effect of unions in an unfavorable partisan environment in which Republicans hold a majority of legislative seats (here, around 65 percent). The right plot shows what happens if Democrats gain control (also around 65 percent). Although policy changes are in both cases relatively rare (long dashed line), increases in union strength are associated with an increasing likelihood of expanding pension benefits (and with a decreasing likelihood of contracting benefits) under Republican control, whereas the reverse is true under Democratic control.

Changes in the likelihood of policy change are also strongly related to changes in the percent of Democrats in the legislature, but only when unions are strong. Consider figure D.2. The left panel shows probabilities from a model in which unions are relatively weak. There is essentially no relationship between the presence of Democrats in the state legislature and the likelihood of passing expansionary pension policy. Neutral and no policy changes are again the most probable outcome, regardless of partisan control. The likelihood of passing expansionary or contractionary legislation is largely unresponsive to changes in the partisan composition of the legislature. In contrast, the right panel shows that partisans can have a strong impact on policy if state workers are well organized and politically powerful. As more Democrats populate the legislature under regimes of high unionization rates and union campaign activity, the more likely it is that the government will pass contractionary pension policy, and the less likely that it will pass expansions.

D.2. Rare Events Logit

Tables D.2 and D.3 present an analysis using a rare events framework.[8] Here I split the outcome variable into two groups: those with negative

TABLE D.1

Ordered probit regression on net expansionary pension legislation

	(1)	(2)	(3)	(4)	(5)
Avg. dems.	0.20	0.19	0.07	−0.09	0.68
	(0.65)	(0.65)	(0.65)	(1.07)	(1.17)
Union strength	0.75★★	0.72★	0.67★	0.84★★	1.34★★★
	(0.37)	(0.37)	(0.38)	(0.42)	(0.50)
Democratic governor	−0.30	−0.31	−0.30	−0.16	−.020
	(0.19)	(0.19)	(0.19)	(0.39)	(.040)
Bargaining index	−0.01	−0.01	0.07	−0.02	−0.06★
	(0.02)	(0.02)	(0.65)	(0.03)	(0.03)
State worker concentration	2.43	2.54	3.24	3.88	8.27★★
	(2.75)	(2.76)	(2.80)	(2.96)	(4.08)
Avg. dems. × union strength	−1.41★★	−1.36★★	−1.23★	−1.42★	−2.34★★★
	(0.66)	(0.66)	(0.68)	(0.77)	(0.86)
Dem. gov. × union strength	0.13	0.15	0.16	0.08	0.14
	(0.20)	(0.20)	(0.20)	(0.21)	(0.22)
Std. dev. of dems. in state legislature				−1.13	−1.70
				(9.39)	(10.18)
No. of gov. party switches since 1963				−0.05	−0.03
				(0.04)	(0.05)
Lagged pension policy				0.00	−0.05
				(0.08)	(0.08)
Std. dev. dems. × avg. dems.				8.15	7.17
				(17.62)	(19.05)
Party switches × dem. gov.				−.01	−0.02
				(0.07)	(0.07)
No. obs.	547	547	547	487	487
State random effects		✓	✓	✓	✓
Post-2008 dummy		✓	✓	✓	✓
Year random effects			✓	✓	✓
Economic controls					✓

Source: National Conference of State Legislatures (1999–2011); Klarner (2013a, 2013b); U.S. Census Bureau and Bureau of Labor Statistics (1995–2012); Hirsch and Macpherson (2011); Author's dataset; U.S. Bureau of Labor Statistics (1995–2012); U.S. Bureau of Economic Analysis (1995–2012); U.S. Census Bureau, U.S. Census of Governments (1995–2012); Hou and Smith (2006); Valletta and Freeman (1988); Shor and McCarty (2011).

Note: Control variables and intercept not reported for purposes of brevity. ★★★$p < 0.01$, ★★$p < 0.05$, ★$p < 0.01$.

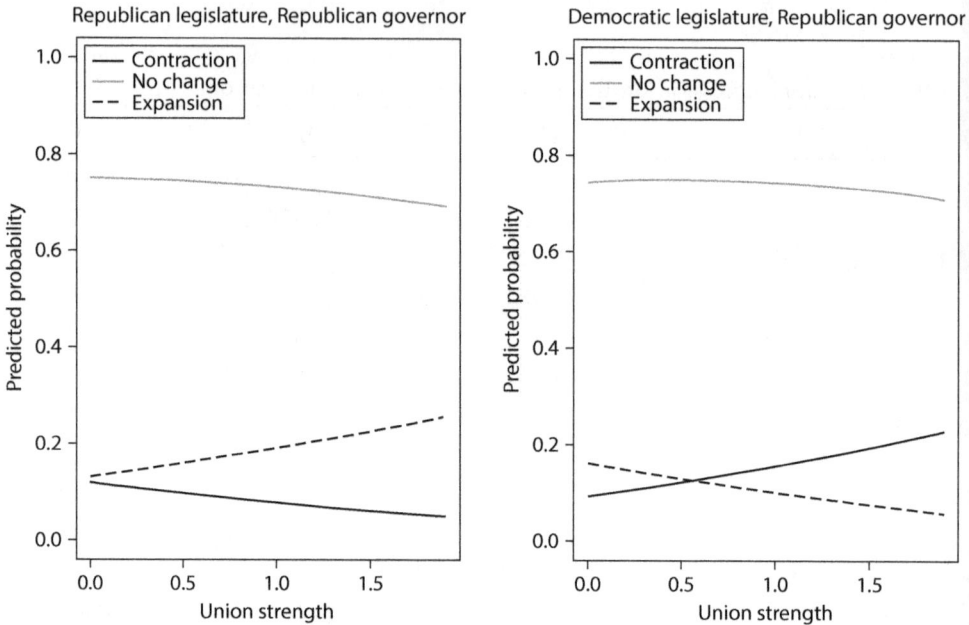

Republican legislature, Republican governor

Democratic legislature, Republican governor

Figure D.1 Predicted probability of pension policy change versus union strength. Effects plotted from model 1 of table D.1, using a collapsed dependent variable. The figure on the left plots probabilities from a model with a low percentage (bottom quarter of the sample) of Democrats in the state legislature, and the figure on the right does so with a high percentage (third quarter of the sample) of Democrats. The party of the governor takes on the median value in the sample, which is Republican. Other variables are held at their mean.

Source: National Conference of State Legislatures (1999–2011, 2011); Klarner (2013a, 2013b); U.S. Census Bureau and Bureau of Labor Statistics, Current Population Survey (1995–2012); Hirsch and Macpherson (2023); Author's dataset; U.S. Bureau of Labor Statistics (1995–2012); U.S. Bureau of Economic Analysis (1995–2012); U.S. Census Bureau, Census of Governments (1995–2012); Hou and Smith (2006); Valletta and Freeman (1988); Shor and McCarty (2011).

values and zeroes, and those with positive values and zeroes. Using this method, I can contrast action to inaction, but I cannot contrast contraction to expansion. Although less than ideal, it is true that most states are probably not weighing all of the paired choices between contraction, expansion, and neutrality (or inaction), but they are instead considering either to contract or not contract, or to expand or not expand. The advantage of using this design, however, is that I can account for inflated zeroes in the data and focus on the likelihood of contracting unfunded benefits

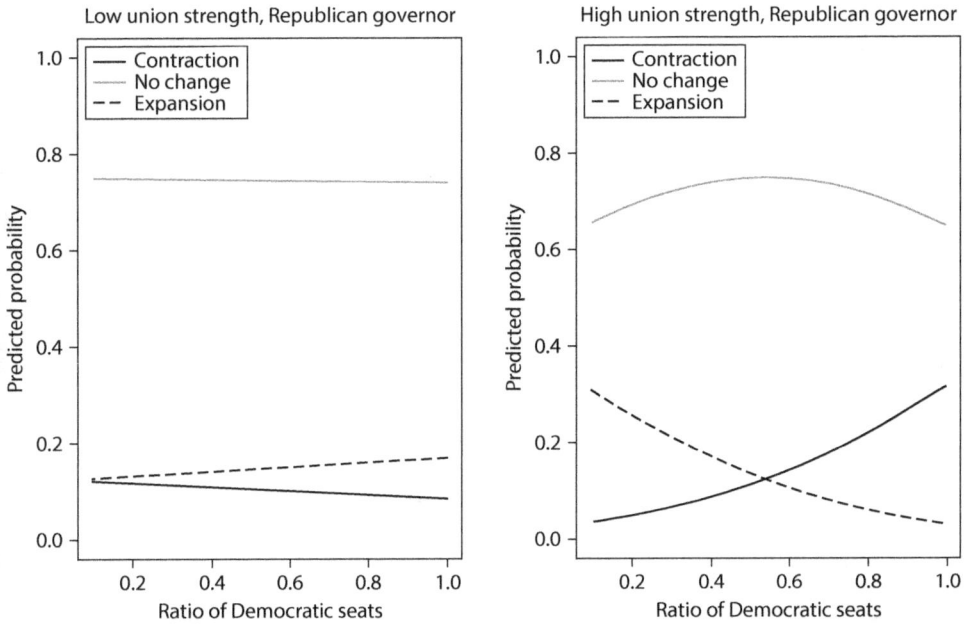

Figure D.2 Predicted probability of pension policy change versus democratic legislative seats. Effects plotted from model 1 of table D.1, using a collapsed dependent variable. The figure on the left plots probabilities from a model with low union strength (bottom quarter of the sample), and the figure on the right does so with high union strength (third quarter of the sample). The party of the governor takes on the median value in the sample, which is Republican. Other variables are held at their mean.

Source: National Conference of State Legislatures (1999–2011, 2011); Klarner (2013a, 2013b); U.S. Census Bureau and Bureau of Labor Statistics, Current Population Survey (1995–2012); Hirsch and Macpherson (2023); Author's dataset; U.S. Bureau of Labor Statistics (1995–2012); U.S. Bureau of Economic Analysis (1995–2012); U.S. Census Bureau, Census of Governments (1995–2012); Hou and Smith (2006); Valletta and Freeman (1988); Shor and McCarty (2011).

(table D.2)—regardless of the degree—and on the likelihood of expanding unfunded benefits (table D.3). The results are slightly different from the linear regression in chapter 2 and the previous ordered probit. Most of the variables in table D.2 are statistically insignificant, while those in table D.3 are more important in determining whether the state passes new or non-neutral legislation. It appears that unions and Democrats are much more active in working together to prevent expansions of unfunded benefits, rather than working together to actively contract pensions.

TABLE D.2

Rare events logit regression on net contractions of pension legislation

	(1)	(2)	(3)	(4)	(5)
Avg. dems.	−0.50	−5.34	−3.32	−1.51	−2.20
	(1.54)	(3.03)	(3.66)	(2.41)	(2.89)
Union strength	−1.17	−2.92	−2.02	−1.76★	−2.58★★
	(0.90)	(2.28)	(2.36)	(0.99)	(1.20)
Democratic governor	0.48	0.34	0.23	−0.01	0.14
	(0.45)	(0.54)	(0.57)	(0.97)	(1.04)
Bargaining index	0.03			0.05	0.15★
	(0.06)			(0.06)	(0.08)
State worker concentration	1.29	21.56	8.56	−2.29	8.23
	(6.48)	(21.27)	(22.26)	(6.93)	(10.94)
Ratio of dems. × union strength	1.81	−4.12	1.75	2.48	3.08
	(1.55)	(3.78)	(3.91)	(1.75)	(2.08)
Dem. gov. × union strength	−0.45	−0.24	−0.29	−0.21	−0.25
	(0.47)	(0.56)	(0.58)	(0.50)	(0.48)
Std. dev. of dems. in state legislature				−6.90	−3.02
				(20.29)	(22.76)
No. of gov. party switches since 1963				0.18★	0.11
				(0.11)	(0.11)
Lagged pension policy				−0.23	−0.09
				(0.18)	(0.18)
Std. dev. dems. × ratio of dems.				15.24	−3.02
				(37.57)	(22.76)
Party switches × dem. gov.				0.02	0.01
				(0.02)	(0.17)
No. obs.	482	482	482	427	427
State fixed effects		✓	✓		
Post-2008 dummy		✓			
Time trend			✓		
Year fixed effects				✓	✓
Region fixed effects					✓
Controls					✓

Source: National Conference of State Legislatures (1999–2011); Klarner (2013a, 2013b); U.S. Census Bureau and Bureau of Labor Statistics (1995–2012); Hirsch and Macpherson (2011); Author's dataset; U.S. Bureau of Labor Statistics (1995–2012); U.S. Bureau of Economic Analysis (1995–2012); U.S. Census Bureau, U.S. Census of Governments (1995–2012); Hou and Smith (2006); Valletta and Freeman (1988); Shor and McCarty (2011).

Note: Control variables and intercept not reported for purposes of brevity. ★★★$p < 0.01$, ★★$p < 0.05$, ★$p < 0.01$.

TABLE D.3

Rare events logit regression on net expansions of pension legislation

	(1)	(2)	(3)	(4)	(5)
Avg. dems.	0.97	4.28	3.21	−2.05	−0.68
	(1.66)	(3.64)	(3.78)	(3.14)	(3.65)
Union strength	1.41	3.95★	3.19	1.72	2.61★
	(1.03)	(2.32)	(2.37)	(1.16)	(1.37)
Democratic governor	−0.56	−0.72	−0.55	−1.76★	−2.15★
	(0.52)	(0.64)	(0.65)	(1.07)	(1.10)
Bargaining index	0.03			0.05	0.07
	(0.06)			(0.07)	(0.09)
State worker concentration	9.04	33.89	45.16★	12.66★	39.15★★★
	(7.12)	(25.04)	(25.28)	(7.65)	(13.49)
Ratio of dems. × union strength	−3.65★	−10.54★★	−8.86★★	−4.33★	−7.33★★★
	(2.02)	(4.41)	(4.55)	(2.35)	(2.78)
Dem. gov. × union strength	0.07	−0.07	−0.11	0.20	0.42
	(0.58)	(0.78)	(0.81)	(0.61)	(0.63)
Std. dev. of dems. in state legislature				−30.09	−38.80
				(27.00)	(28.27)
No. of gov. party switches since 1963				−0.12	−0.08
				(0.11)	(0.12)
Lagged pension policy				−0.28	−0.35
				(0.21)	(0.22)
Std. dev. dems. × ratio of dems.				82.32	92.62★
				(53.06)	(55.02)
Party switches × dem. gov.				0.24	0.25
				(0.18)	(0.20)
No. obs.	468	468	468	410	410
State fixed effects		✓	✓		
Post-2008 dummy		✓			
Time trend			✓		
Year fixed effects				✓	✓
Region fixed effects					✓
Controls					✓

Source: National Conference of State Legislatures (1999–2011); Klarner (2013a, 2013b); U.S. Census Bureau and Bureau of Labor Statistics (1995–2012); Hirsch and Macpherson (2011); Author's dataset; U.S. Bureau of Labor Statistics (1995–2012); U.S. Bureau of Economic Analysis (1995–2012); U.S. Census Bureau, U.S. Census of Governments (1995–2012); Hou and Smith (2006); Valletta and Freeman (1988); Shor and McCarty (2011).

Note: Control variables and intercept not reported for purposes of brevity. ★★★$p < 0.01$, ★★$p < 0.05$, ★$p < 0.01$.

E. Why Some States Might Bias
Funding Data Downward

As discussed in section B, the construction of the revised funding ratios are not objective in the sense that they are "true." The difference in the revised and self-reported funding ratio does not indicate that a given pension plan is reporting x percentage points above the true rate. What the difference *does* tell us is how far a given pension plan is reporting from an established point of comparison. Given the methodology and discount rate chosen and supported by much of the mathematical pension literature, I can say that a given pension plan reports x percentage points above my established standard and that it is overstating its funding *relative to my standard* by y percentage points more than another plan.

In practice, this may mean that some pension plans *underreport* their funding ratios in relation to my measure. This, more than anything, is likely due to the fact that I am using one of the most conservative accrual methods in the literature to construct the revised liabilities. This methodology understates the "true" discounted value of liabilities, if anything. Some pension plans may be more concerned about not understating this value, relative to other plans. Because my measure of disclosure (the distance between self-reported and revised funding ratios) is continuous and not truncated at zero, the same incentives that work to encourage plans to overreport funding ratios will work in the opposite direction to underreport funding ratios. The greatest difference between pension plans that overreport versus underreport their funding ratios, however, is that underreporting plans are far more likely to have higher revised funding ratios. Pension boards and governments keep their pensions well-funded by telling voters that they are poorly funded, and by preventing unions from making grabs at the relatively large pension surplus. This is confirmed in table E.1. Both underreporting and overreporting pension plans look strikingly similar otherwise (with the exception that fewer mixed pension plans underreport funding ratios relative to those that overreport their funding ratios). Even if we believe that pensions that underreport their funding ratios relative to my standardized measure *are* fundamentally different from those that overreport, I show in section F.3 that accounting for these observations leaves my results relatively robust.

TABLE E.1

Summary statistics

	y < 0		y ≥ 0		All values of y	
	Mean	**S.D.**	**Mean**	**S.D.**	**Mean**	**S.D.**
Days to CAFR release	192.33	37.91	226.10	87.21	205.92	67.36
Lagged funding ratio (%)	98.82	36.16	52.71	17.94	55.69	30.91
Union strength	0.97	0.54	0.82	0.52	0.86	0.52
Employees on board (%)	69.12	17.48	68.35	26.11	64.98	27.63
Percent gen./mixed plan	31.15		61.65		58.70	
Percent uniformed plan	21.31		4.73		6.33	
Percent teachers plan	47.54		33.63		34.97	
Number of members	86,344	125,934	194,465	206,433	122,120	194,569
Democratic governor	0.64	0.48	0.51	0.50	0.50	0.50
Dems. in legislature (%)	49.42	13.67	50.56	14.75	50.17	13.44
Average polarization	1.65	0.47	1.45	0.48	1.47	0.52
Electoral competition	0.92	0.07	0.93	0.05	0.92	0.06
Fund balance, p.c. ($)	166.22	792.61	61.15	778.42	82.93	576.40
Balanced budget req.	0.39	0.49	0.60	0.49	0.63	0.48
Total debt, p.c. ($)	3,821.1	2.136.7	3,280.5	2,004.3	3,004.7	1,871.6
Tax capacity (%)	7.18	2.12	6.48	1.91	6.62	1.60
No. obs.	61	61	571	571	632	632

Source: Author's dataset; Institute for Truth in Accounting (2013); National Association of State Auditors, Comptrollers, and Treasurers (2005–2011); U.S. Bureau of Labor Statistics (1995–2012); U.S. Bureau of Economic Analysis (1995–2012); U.S. Census Bureau, U.S. Census of Governments (1995–2012); U.S. Census Bureau and Bureau of Labor Statistics (1995–2012); Hirsch and Macpherson (2011).

Note: y is the difference between the plan's self-reported funding ratio and my revised funding ratio such that $y < 0$ indicates that the plan is underreporting funding status relative to my standardized measure. *Lagged Funding Ratio* is the revised measure.

F. Alternative Specifications to Chapter 3 Models

F.1. Alternative Dependent Variables

The negative effect union strength has on disclosure practices, and its increasingly negative effect as transparency increases, is robust to a number of alternative specifications of the dependent variable. Although the main analysis used the distance between the self-reported and revised funding ratios as a proxy for the degree of dishonest reporting, table F.1 instead uses

TABLE F.1

Linear regression on difference between revised and self-reported unfunded liabilities per capita ($)

	Full sample	Timely	Tardy
Union strength	−18.04	1789.72★★	−133.05
	(621.10)	(846.66)	(502.24)
Lagged unfunded liabilities per capita ($)	0.56★★★	1.00★★★	0.43★★
	(0.18)	(0.15)	(0.18)
Union strength × lagged unfunded liabilities	−0.06	0.35★★	0.01
	(0.12)	(0.12)	(0.10)
No. obs.	615	228	386
Year fixed effects	✓	✓	✓
State fixed effects	✓	✓	✓
Economic and demographic controls	✓	✓	✓

Source: Author's dataset; Institute for Truth in Accounting (2013); National Association of State Auditors, Comptrollers, and Treasurers (2005–2011); U.S. Bureau of Labor Statistics (1995–2012); U.S. Bureau of Economic Analysis (1995–2012); U.S. Census Bureau, U.S. Census of Governments (1995–2012); U.S. Census Bureau and Bureau of Labor Statistics (1995–2012); Hirsch and Macpherson (2011).

Note: The dependent variable is the difference between two distance measures: revised liabilities less revised assets, per capita, and self-reported liabilities less self-reported assets, per capita. Robust standard errors clustered by pension plan in parentheses. Estimated intercept is not reported. Controls include unemployment rate, per capita personal income, logged population, and federal transfers as a fraction of general revenue. ★★★$p < 0.01$, ★★$p < 0.05$, ★$p < 0.01$.

the distance between the revised and self-reported unfunded liabilities per capita.[9] As in previous analyses, an increase in the dependent variable is an increase in overreporting of the pension's financial position, and a decrease in accurate and full disclosure. Tables F.2 and F.3 examine the effect of transparency and pension board composition on the disclosure of the funding ratio's constituent pieces, liabilities (per capita) and assets (per capita).

F.2. Alternative Transparency Measures

In this section, I present results from the full model using data on government website transparency from the Sunshine Review and an index of fiscal transparency from James E. Alt, David Dreyer Lassen, and Shanna Rose in lieu of the timeliness of the CAFR release.[10] As shown in table F.4, results are largely in line with my previous analyses. Figures F.1 and F.2 demonstrate the role that union strength plays in disclosure decisions, as transparency increases.

TABLE F.2

Linear regression on difference between revised and self-reported liabilities per capita ($)

	Full sample	Timely	Tardy
Chair elected by board	1439.04	−1180.77	−655.86
	(27.70)	(2744.80)	(751.12)
Employee chair	2509.70*	7862.70*	6816.08★★★
	(1341.64)	(4493.88)	(2418.45)
Percent employees on board (%)	38.13	144.57★★★	29.08
	(31.37)	(48.20)	(62.65)
Lagged funding ratio (%)	11.02	−54.75	−65.57★★
	(27.70)	(56.06)	(32.29)
Chair elected by board × lagged ratio	−19.98	−47.59	26.94
	(19.36)	(35.94)	(0.252)
Employee chair × lagged ratio	−20.50	78.86	−87.726★★
	(19.12)	(61.31)	(37.35)
Percent employees × lagged ratio	−0.30	−0.57	0.69
	(0.53)	(0.84)	(0.76)
No. obs.	552	192	359
Year fixed effects	✓	✓	✓
State fixed effects	✓	✓	✓
Economic and demographic controls	✓	✓	✓

Source: Author's dataset; Institute for Truth in Accounting (2013); National Association of State Auditors, Comptrollers, and Treasurers (2005–2011); U.S. Bureau of Labor Statistics (1995–2012); U.S. Bureau of Economic Analysis (1995–2012); U.S. Census Bureau, U.S. Census of Governments (1995–2012); U.S. Census Bureau and Bureau of Labor Statistics (1995–2012); Hirsch and Macpherson (2011).

Note: Robust standard errors clustered by pension plan in parentheses. Estimated intercept is not reported. Controls include unemployment rate, per capita personal income, logged population, and federal transfers as a fraction of general revenue. ★★★$p < 0.01$, ★★$p < 0.05$, *$p < 0.01$.

F.3. Alternative Tests of the Full Model

Because we may believe that the distance between the self-reported and revised funding ratios should never be less than zero, I present two alternative models that take this into account. Table F.5 presents results of a fully specified model with all controls. The first column of table F.5 reports Tobit estimates of the coefficients. This model is correct if we believe that all values of the funding ratio distance below zero (i.e., cases

Linear regression on difference between revised and self-reported assets per capita ($)

	Full sample	Timely	Tardy
Chair elected by board	674.30	6063.00★★★	123.44
	(672.81)	(1231.17)	(219.45)
Employee chair	−1428.30★★	2806.11	−1333.25
	(593.83)	(1907.19)	(817.51)
Percent employees on board (%)	48.89★★★	−40.38	33.37★★
	(16.60)	(31.03)	(16.67)
Lagged funding ratio (%)	8.84	−4.52	9.70
	(11.44)	(25.72)	(9.09)
Chair elected by board × lagged ratio	10.93	10.93	3.59
	(7.04)	(12.91)	(5.40)
Employee chair × lagged ratio	−43.70	−43.70	13.79
	(9.37)	(28.92)	(11.61)
Percent employees × lagged ratio	−0.58★★	0.83	−0.29
	(0.28)	(0.62)	(0.21)
No. obs.	552	192	359
Year fixed effects	✓	✓	✓
State fixed effects	✓	✓	✓
Economic and demographic controls	✓	✓	✓

Source: Author's dataset; Institute for Truth in Accounting (2013); National Association of State Auditors, Comptrollers, and Treasurers (2005–2011); U.S. Bureau of Labor Statistics (1995–2012); U.S. Bureau of Economic Analysis (1995–2012); U.S. Census Bureau, U.S. Census of Governments (1995–2012); U.S. Census Bureau and Bureau of Labor Statistics (1995–2012); Hirsch and Macpherson (2011).

Note: Robust standard errors clustered by pension plan in parentheses. Estimated intercept is not reported. Controls include unemployment rate, per capita personal income, logged population, and federal transfers as a fraction of general revenue. ★★★$p < 0.01$, ★★$p < 0.05$, ★$p < 0.01$.

in which pension boards report lower funding ratios than my revised estimates would otherwise suggest) should be censored at zero—that is, we are observing erroneous cases that were miscalculated. The second column of the table reports truncated regression estimates of the coefficients. This model is appropriate if we believe we observe two different data generating processes—one data generating process for observed values equal to or greater than zero, and one process for observed values less than zero. Here, instead of censoring the data at zero, I throw out all observations of

TABLE F.4

Linear regression on difference between revised and self-reported funding ratio using alternative transparency measures

	Sunshine transparency grade	Alt-lassen index
Sunshine grade	−3.36	
	(2.17)	
Alt-lassen index		−7.55
		(4.99)
Lagged funding ratio (%)	−0.42★	−0.94★★
	(0.22)	(0.38)
Union strength	−15.29★★	−27.43★★
	(6.59)	(11.72)
Employees on pension board	0.08	0.02
	(0.07)	(0.08)
Uniformed plan	10.35	14.73
	(9.349)	(10.60)
Teachers plan	−9.89★★★	−7.21★
	(3.47)	(3.71)
Logged no. of members	2.62	2.93
	(2.28)	(2.37)
Democratic governor	−0.55	−0.54
	(2.32)	(1.94)
Share of dems. in legislature (%)	−0.31★★★	−0.35★★★
	(0.09)	(0.09)
Avg. polarizations across chambers	−5.46	2.86
	(4.12)	(3.91)
Electoral competition	2.26	9.55
	(19.72)	(18.55)
Sunshine grade × funding ratio	−0.02	
	(0.00)	
Sunshine grade × union strength	4.43★★★	
	(1.48)	(0.02)
Alt-lassen × funding ratio		0.07
		(0.07)
Alt-lassen × union strength		5.83★★
		(2.37)
No. obs.	532	532
Year fixed effects	✓	✓
Region fixed effects	✓	✓
Economic and demographic controls	✓	✓

Source: Author's dataset; Institute for Truth in Accounting (2013); National Association of State Auditors, Comptrollers, and Treasurers (2005–2011); U.S. Bureau of Labor Statistics (1995–2012); U.S. Bureau of Economic Analysis (1995–2012); U.S. Census Bureau, U.S. Census of Governments (1995–2012); U.S. Census Bureau and Bureau of Labor Statistics (1995–2012); Hirsch and Macpherson (2011); Sunshine Review (2011); Alt, Lassen, and Rose (2006); Klarner (2013a, 2013b, 2013c).

Note: Increases in *Sunshine Transparency Grade* and *Alt-Lassen Index* indicate improvements in state-level transparency. Robust standard errors clustered by pension plan in parentheses. Estimated intercept is not reported. Controls include unemployment rate, per capita personal income, logged population, and federal transfers as a fraction of general revenue. Budgetary variables are not included for purposes of brevity, and are not statistically significant. ★★★$p < 0.01$, ★★$p < 0.05$, ★$p < 0.01$.

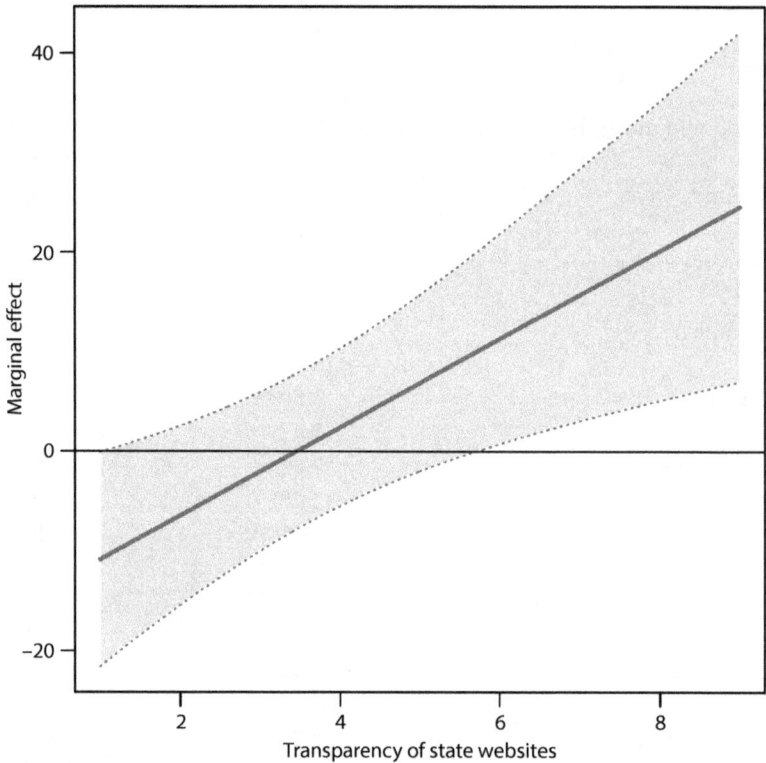

Figure F.1 Marginal effect of union strength on disclosure as transparency increases, using the Sunshine Review transparency measure. This figure shows the effect of a marginal increase in union strength on the discrepancy in reporting behavior, as the state becomes less transparent. When a state is relatively transparent, an increase in union strength worsens the disclosure behavior of the pension plan by increasing the distance between self-reported and revised funding ratios. The impact that a strong union has on generous reporting behavior decreases as a state's transparency practices worsen. Calculations come from first column of table F.4.

Source: Author's dataset; Institute for Truth in Accounting (2011); National Association of State Auditors, Comptrollers, and Treasurers (2005–2011); U.S. Bureau of Labor Statistics (1995–2012); U.S. Bureau of Economic Analysis (1995–2012); U.S. Census Bureau and Bureau of Labor Statistics, Current Population Survey (1995–2012); Hirsch and Macpherson (2023); Sunshine Review (2011).

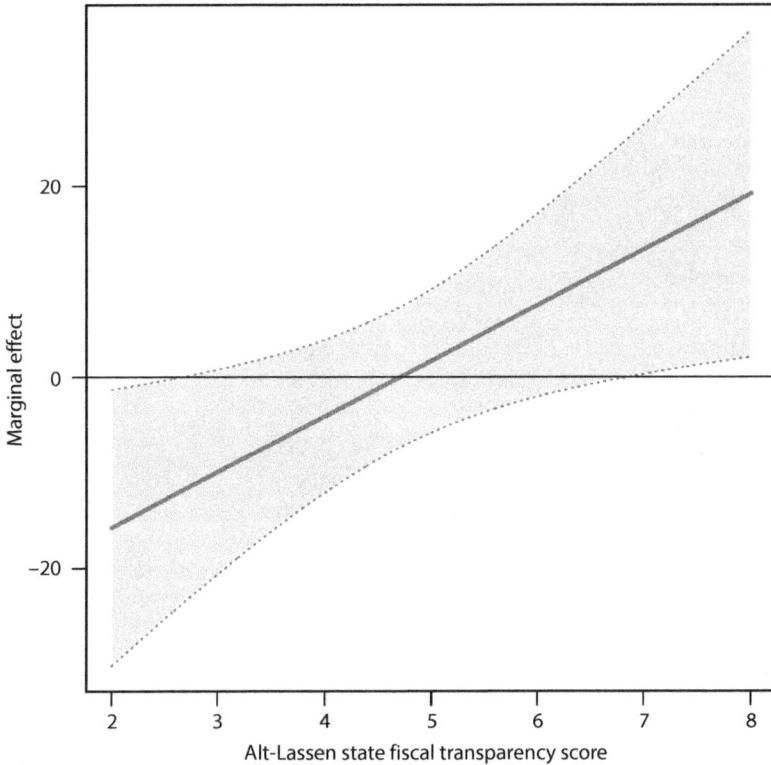

Figure F.2 Marginal effect of union strength on disclosure as transparency increases, using the Alt-Lassen transparency index. This figure shows the effect of a marginal increase in union strength on the discrepancy in reporting behavior, as the state becomes less transparent. When a state is relatively transparent, an increase in union strength worsens the disclosure behavior of the pension plan by increasing the distance between self-reported and revised funding ratios. The impact that a strong union has on generous reporting behavior decreases as a state's transparency practices worsen. Calculations come from second column of table F.4.

Source: Author's dataset; Institute for Truth in Accounting (2011); National Association of State Auditors, Comptrollers, and Treasurers (2005–2011); U.S. Census Bureau and Bureau of Labor Statistics, Current Population Survey (1995–2012); U.S. Census Bureau and Bureau of Labor Statistics, Current Population Survey (1995–2012); Hirsch and Macpherson (2023); Alt, Lassen, and Rose (2006).

TABLE F.5

Censored (Tobit) and truncated regression on difference between revised and self-reported funding ratio

	Tobit (censored from below at $y = 0$)	Truncated regression
Days to CAFR release	−0.08*	0.00
	(0.04)	(0.05)
Lagged funding ratio (%)	−0.81***	−0.44**
	(0.13)	(0.18)
Union strength	10.14**	12.56**
	(5.14)	(5.69)
Employees on pension board (%)	0.04	0.05
	(0.03)	(0.03)
Uniformed plan	11.45***	13.84***
	(4.29)	(4.68)
Teachers plan	−8.67***	−7.18***
	(1.56)	(1.74)
Logged no. of members	2.17*	2.01
	(1.21)	(1.33)
Democratic governor	−1.92	−1.65
	(1.33)	(1.43)
Share of dems. in legislature (%)	−0.15***	−0.18**
	(0.05)	(0.06)
Avg. polarization across chambers	−4.93***	−4.84***
	(1.72)	(1.84)
Electoral competition	−5.44	−5.48
	(17.57)	(19.02)
Days × funding ratio	0.00***	0.00
	(0.00)	(0.00)
Days × union strength	−0.07***	−0.09***
	(0.02)	(0.02)
Fund balance, per capita ($)	−0.00	−0.00**
	(0.00)	(0.00)
Balanced budget req.	−2.93	−3.25**
	(1.53)	(1.63)
Total debt, per capita ($)	−0.00	0.00
	(0.00)	(0.00)
Tax capacity (%)	0.00***	0.00***
	(0.00)	(0.00)
No. obs.	532	488
Economic and demographic controls	✓	✓

Source: Author's dataset; Institute for Truth in Accounting (2013); National Association of State Auditors, Comptrollers, and Treasurers (2005–2011); U.S. Bureau of Labor Statistics (1995–2012); U.S. Bureau of Economic Analysis (1995–2012); U.S. Census Bureau, U.S. Census of Governments (1995–2012); U.S. Census Bureau and Bureau of Labor Statistics (1995–2012); Hirsch and Macpherson (2011); Sunshine Review (2011); Alt, Lassen, and Rose (2006); Klarner (2013a, 2013b, 2013c).

Note: Robust standard errors clustered by pension plan in parentheses. Estimated intercept is not reported. Controls include unemployment rate, per capita personal income, logged population, and federal transfers as a fraction of general revenue. ***$p < 0.01$, **$p < 0.05$, *$p < 0.01$.

TABLE F.6

Linear regression on difference between revised and self-reported funding ratio, with partisanship measures

	Model 1	Model 2	Model 3	Model 4
Democratic governor	−2.31	−2.01	−0.95	−3.71*
	(1.42)	(1.48)	(1.14)	(2.15)
Share of dems. in legislature (%)	−0.05	−0.00	−0.06	−0.11
	(0.16)	(0.15)	(0.13)	(0.15)
Union strength		−4.68	−2.74	−9.01
		(3.87)	(2.68)	(8.74)
Electoral competitiveness		−4.61	7.29	9.71
		(27.60)	(15.41)	(15.24)
Average polarization		−8.78	−8.05	−6.63
		(8.18)	(8.79)	(8.74)
Lagged funding ratio (%)			−0.57***	−0.57***
			(0.14)	(0.14)
Union strength × dem. gov.				3.42
				(2.12)
Union strength × share of dems.				0.09
				(0.16)
No. obs.	627	542	540	540
Year fixed effects	✓	✓	✓	✓
State fixed effects	✓	✓	✓	✓
Economic and demographic controls	✓	✓	✓	✓

Source: Author's dataset; Institute for Truth in Accounting (2013); National Association of State Auditors, Comptrollers, and Treasurers (2005–2011); U.S. Bureau of Labor Statistics (1995–2012); U.S. Bureau of Economic Analysis (1995–2012); U.S. Census Bureau, U.S. Census of Governments (1995–2012); U.S. Census Bureau and Bureau of Labor Statistics (1995–2012); Hirsch and Macpherson (2011); Sunshine Review (2011); Alt, Lassen, and Rose (2006); Klarner (2013a, 2013b, 2013c).

Note: Robust standard errors clustered by pension plan in parentheses. Estimated intercept is not reported. Controls include unemployment rate, per capita personal income, logged population, and federal transfers as a fraction of general revenue. ***$p < 0.01$, **$p < 0.05$, *$p < 0.01$.

the data in which the dependent variable is negative. As evidenced next, both models report strikingly similar coefficients. The results are also in line with the fixed effects regressions in chapter 3.

F.4 Partisan Effects

Table F.6 shows that state partisanship and electoral pressure cannot explain the variation in disclosure practices within pension plans over time.

G. Distributions of the Administrative Structures of Pension Boards

Pension boards vary considerably in their administrative structure and composition. The following are summaries of how they vary across states and years.

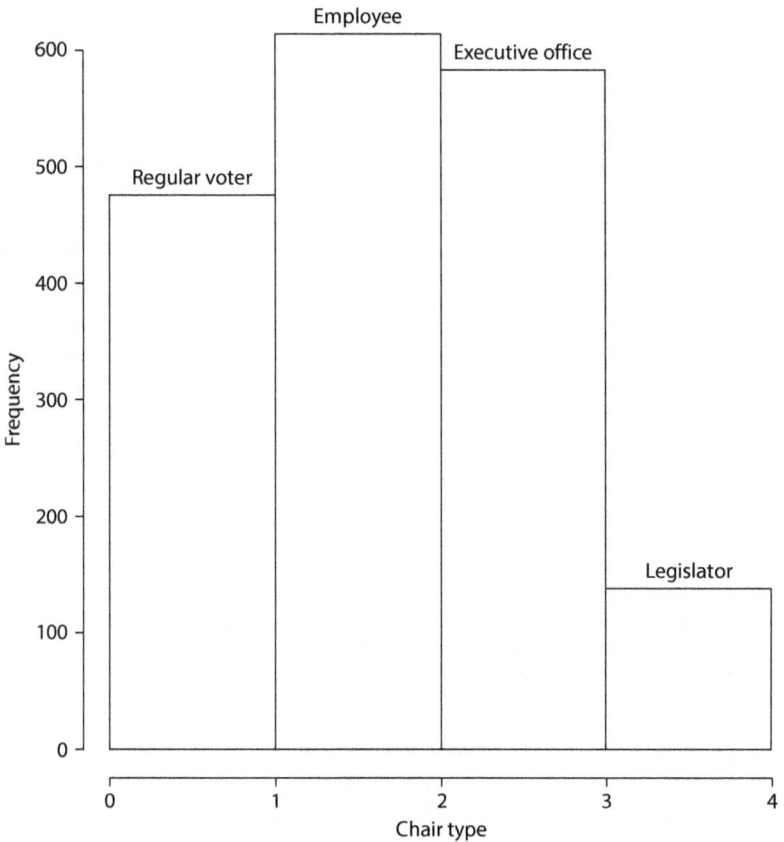

Figure G.1 Distribution of pension board chair types, by plan-year.

Source: Author's dataset.

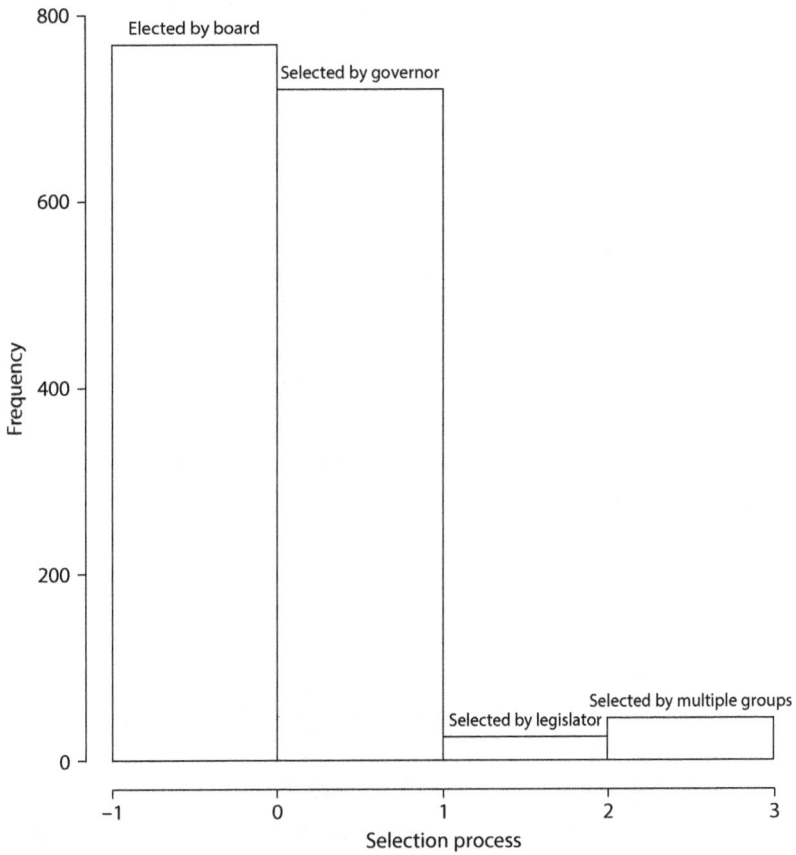

Figure G.2 Distribution of pension board chair selection process, by plan-year.

Source: Author's dataset.

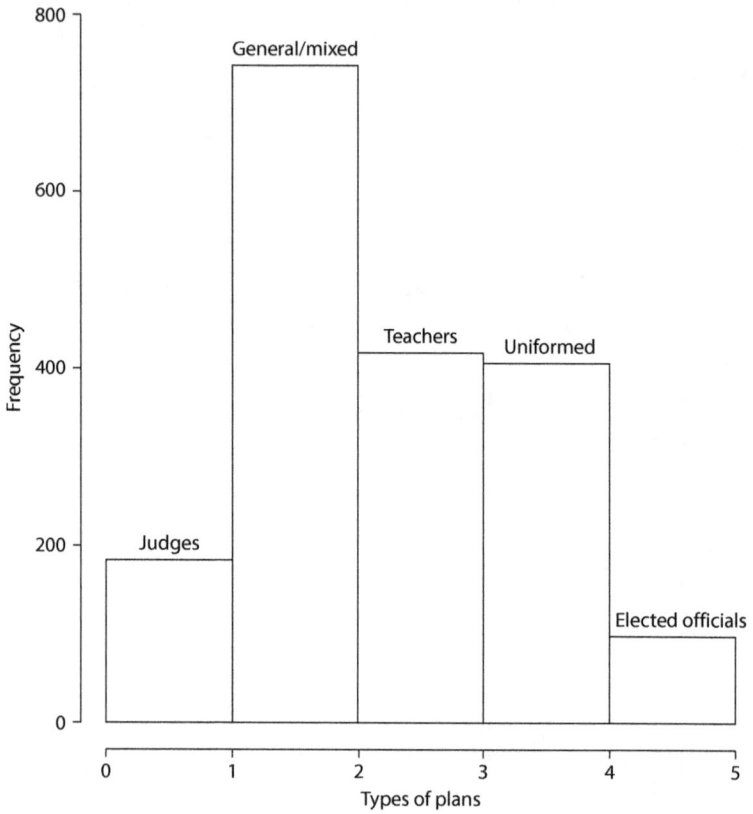

Figure G.3 Distribution of pension plan types, by plan-year.

Source: Author's dataset.

H. State Worker Concentration Versus Union Strength

A corollary to my first hypothesis states that the organization of workers is important to achieving policy goals and that unorganized workers will be less efficient at doing so. In all of the analyses contained within this book, the sheer size of the state public sector workforce has no impact on the likelihood of passing expansionary pension legislation. The variable *State Worker Concentration*, which is the percentage of full-time workers employed by the state, is statistically insignificant in all models. Furthermore,

TABLE H.1

Linear probability model of net expansionary legislation using state
worker labor force concentration as predictor (in lieu of union strength)

	(1)
Avg. dems.	−0.35
	(2.09)
State worker concentration	2.98
	(10.14)
Democratic governor	−0.20
	(0.27)
Union strength	0.02
	(0.33)
Avg. dems. × state worker concentration	−4.63
	(22.03)
Dem. gov. × state worker concentration	−0.62
	(2.97)
Lagged pension policy	−0.09
	(0.07)
Std. dev. dems. × avg. dems.	4.29
	(14.73)
Party switches × dem. gov.	0.03
	(0.04)
No. obs.	486
State fixed effects	✓
Year fixed effects	✓
Economic controls	✓

Source: National Conference of State Legislatures (1999–2011, 2011); Klarner (2013b, 2013c); U.S. Census Bureau and Bureau of Labor Statistics (1995–2012); Hirsch and Macpherson (2011); Author's dataset; U.S. Bureau of Labor Statistics (1995–2012); U.S. Bureau of Economic Analysis (1995–2012); U.S. Census Bureau, U.S. Census of Governments (1995–2012); Hou and Smith (2006); Valletta and Freeman (1988); Shor and McCarty (2011).

Note: Control variables have not been reported for purposes of brevity. Robust clustered standard errors reported in parentheses. ★★★$p < 0.01$, ★★$p < 0.05$, ★$p < 0.01$.

swapping out the state worker variable for the union strength variable
in table H.1 does not make any of the independent variables statistically
significant. The only statistically significant relationship in the regression is
the control variable *Unemployment*'s strongly negative influence on policy
(which is standard across all models).

TABLE H.2

Linear regression on disclosure discrepancy using state worker labor force concentration as predictor (in lieu of union strength)

	Funding ratio (%)
Days to CAFR release	−0.26★★★
	(0.09)
Lagged funding ratio (%)	−1.11★★★
	(0.28)
State worker rate (% of working pop.)	−3.95
	(4.06)
Percent employees on board (%)	0.08
	(0.07)
Uniformed plan	11.97
	(9.30)
Teachers plan	−9.93★★★
	(3.345)
Total debt, per capita ($)	0.00
	(0.00)
Fund balance, per capita ($)	−0.00
	(0.00)
Tax capacity (%)	0.00
	(0.00)
Logged total members	1.52
	(2.04)
Democratic governor	1.23
	(2.33)
Share of democrats in state legislature (%)	−0.36★★★
	(0.12)
Average polarization	−0.17
	(4.24)
Electoral competition	9.25
	(19.91)
Balanced budget req.	−2.14
	(4.08)
Days × lagged ratio	0.00★★
	(0.00)
Days × state worker rate	0.02
	(0.02)
No. obs.	521
Year fixed effects	✓
Region fixed effects	✓
Economic and demographic controls	✓

Source: Author's dataset; Institute for Truth in Accounting (2013); National Association of State Auditors, Comptrollers, and Treasurers (2005–2011); U.S. Bureau of Labor Statistics (1995–2012); U.S. Bureau of Economic Analysis (1995–2012); U.S. Census Bureau, U.S. Census of Governments (1995–2012); U.S. Census Bureau and Bureau of Labor Statistics (1995–2012); Hirsch and Macpherson (2011).

Note: Robust standard errors clustered by pension plan in parentheses. Estimated intercept is not reported. Controls include unemployment rate, per capita personal income, logged population, and federal transfers as a fraction of general revenue. ★★★$p < 0.01$, ★★$p < 0.05$, ★$p < 0.01$.

The organizational and financial strength of unions is the source from which state employees draw their power to influence pension policy. The sheer size of the workforce employed by the state government is inadequate to explain how workers get preferred policy passed. Table H.2 emphasizes this point by demonstrating the lack of relationship between state workers and the disclosure gap when their unionization status is not taken into account.

I. Further Evidence of Coalitional Politics

If coalitional politics is a better way to describe pension policymaking in the U.S. states it must also be true that (1) unions prefer to have Democrats over Republicans in office and (2) that Democrats are likely to lose elections if they vote for generous pension benefits that decrease the welfare of regular voters through changes in the rest of the budget. The fact that American Federation of State, County, and Municipal Employees and the National Education Association donates overwhelmingly and disproportionately to state Democratic candidates and parties suggests that (1) is true.[11] I next offer suggestive evidence of (2), showing that Democratic lawmakers suffer electorally when engaging in policymaking in ways that are consistent with the coalitional politics hypothesis.

The evidence for informed, retrospective voting is mixed, particularly at the state level. Early studies argued that citizens did not meet the criteria needed to hold state-level elected officials accountable; they did not have the attention span or knowledge necessary to make informed decisions.[12] Other work has found that less than 20 percent of voters can correctly identify their state legislator.[13] Nevertheless, the contemporary research on state retrospective voting has found strong and clear links between constituent preferences and policy outcomes. Beginning with Robert Erikson, Gerald Wright, and John McIver's finding that the most liberal states tend to have the most liberal constituents, scholars have found that state policy is highly responsive to voter opinion over specific domain issues, that more liberal legislative districts are represented by state legislators who vote more liberally, and that voters are capable of attributing policy responsibility to the correct level of government.[14] Finally, Leah Stokes's study of wind turbine locations in Ontario provides considerable evidence of subnational retrospective voting in action: Voters in Canada punished incumbent provincial

TABLE I.1

Logistic regression on likelihood of switch in partisan control of legislature

	Lower chamber	Upper chamber
Pension policy (election year)	2.00★★	2.28★★
	(0.98)	(0.98)
Pension policy (one-period lag from election)	0.36	0.63
	(0.51)	(0.82)
Pension policy (two-period lag from election)	−0.36	−0.63
	(0.65)	(0.69)
Percent change in general expenditures, p.c.	−3.38	27.41
	(14.78)	(16.98)
Percent change in total taxes, p.c.	−6.61	9.98
	(9.50)	(12.61)
Percent change in total debt, p.c.	5.09	0.65
	(5.12)	(4.41)
Change in S&P's credit rating	−2.43	0.29
	(2.22)	(1.24)
Democratic control of chamber (in election year)	0.73	3.82★★
	(0.93)	(1.79)
Switch in partisan control of governor	−2.95★★	−0.15
	(1.34)	(1.02)
No. obs.	107	107
Region fixed effects	✓	✓
Year fixed effects	✓	✓
Controls	✓	✓

Source: National Conference of State Legislatures (1999–2011, 2011); Klarner (2013b, 2013c); U.S. Census Bureau and Bureau of Labor Statistics (1995–2012); U.S. Bureau of Labor Statistics (1995–2012); U.S. Bureau of Economic Analysis (1995–2012); U.S. Census Bureau, U.S. Census of Governments (1995–2012); Prah, Rotmil, and Fehr (2014).

Note: Values reported are raw coefficients. Dependent variable is measured after a state's legislative election. Estimated intercept not reported. Control variables include lagged policy and economic indicators and have not been reported for purposes of brevity. ★★★$p < 0.01$, ★★$p < 0.05$, ★$p < 0.01$.

legislators if the machines were placed within three kilometers of their homes, often leading to incumbent defeat.[15]

While chapter 6 provided evidence of the importance of pension policy in retrospective voting, tables I.1 and I.2 offer additional insight using logistic regression models. Table I.1 investigates the electoral consequences of passing expansionary pension policy for Democratic legislators. The table

TABLE I.2

Logistic regression on likelihood of democratic gubernatorial winner

	(1)	(2)	(3)
Percent change in total taxes, p.c.	−0.07	0.08	0.08
	(0.05)	(0.07)	(0.07)
Pension policy (election year)		0.02	0.04
		(0.43)	(0.62)
Pension policy (one-period lag from election)		0.08	−0.05
		(0.42)	(0.61)
Pension policy (two-period lag from election)		0.44	0.09
		(0.42)	(0.41)
Percent change in general expenditures, p.c.		0.08	0.08
		(0.10)	(0.13)
Percent change in total debt, p.c.		−0.01	−0.01
		(0.03)	(0.04)
Change in S&P's credit rating		−0.53	−1.08
		(0.87)	(1.14)
Presidential partisan voter index		0.07	0.06
		(0.05)	(0.05)
Democratic governor in office (in election year)	2.11★★	1.55★★	1.66
	(0.46)	(0.71)	(1.09)
Democratic governor × percent change in taxes	−0.17★★★	−0.29★★★	−0.28★★★
	(0.06)	(0.11)	(0.10)
Democratic governor × pension policy			0.29
			(0.84)
Democratic governor × change in expenditures			−0.03
			(0.17)
Democratic governor × debt			−0.00
			(0.06)
Democratic governor × change in credit rating			2.04
			(2.20)
No. obs.	158	111	111
Region fixed effects	✓	✓	✓
Year fixed effects	✓	✓	✓
Controls		✓	✓

Source: National Conference of State Legislatures (1999–2011, 2011); Klarner (2013b, 2013c); U.S. Census Bureau and Bureau of Labor Statistics (1995–2012); U.S. Bureau of Labor Statistics (1995–2012); U.S. Bureau of Economic Analysis (1995–2012); U.S. Census Bureau, U.S. Census of Governments (1995–2012); Prah, Rotmil, and Fehr (2014); Wolf (2015).

Note: Values reported are raw coefficients. Dependent variable is measured after a state's gubernatorial election. Estimated intercept not reported. Control variables include lagged policy and economic indicators and have not been reported for purposes of brevity. Presidential Partisan Voter Index is a proxy for the partisanship of the state, and is measured by comparing the state's Democratic share of the two-party presidential vote against the national average. ★★★$p < 0.01$, ★★$p < 0.05$, ★$p < 0.01$.

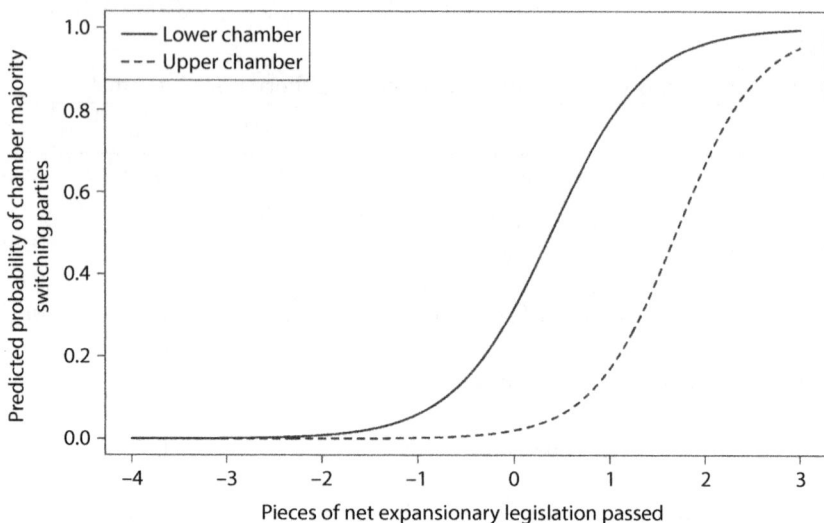

Figure I.1 Predicted probability of losing partisan control of legislative chamber. Predicted probability of the likelihood of partisan control of the lower or upper legislative chamber switching after a gubernatorial election and a given number of statutory changes to pension generosity. Calculations made using table I.1 for a state in 2007 in the Midwest. Other variables are held at their mean.

Source: National Conference of State Legislatures (1999–2011, 2011); Klarner (2013b, 2013c); U.S. Census Bureau and Bureau of Labor Statistics, Current Population Survey (1995–2012); U.S. Bureau of Economic Analysis (1995–2012); U.S. Census Bureau, Census of Governments (1995–2012); Prah, Rotmil, and Fehr (2014).

provides logistic regression estimates of the impact of passing one piece of expansionary legislation on the probability of losing partisan control of the lower or upper chamber of the state legislature after an election. Passing expansionary legislation has a strong and statistically significant impact on this likelihood, even after controlling for a host of other variables. As depicted in figure I.1, one piece of expansionary legislation passed in the year of a gubernatorial election is associated with a nearly 40 percentage point increase in the likelihood of the majority party losing control of the chamber relative to not passing any legislation at all.

Table I.2 uses a logistic regression to show that the electoral fortunes of governors are more closely tied to direct changes in tax policy. Although there are second-order effects of pension policy through tax changes, there

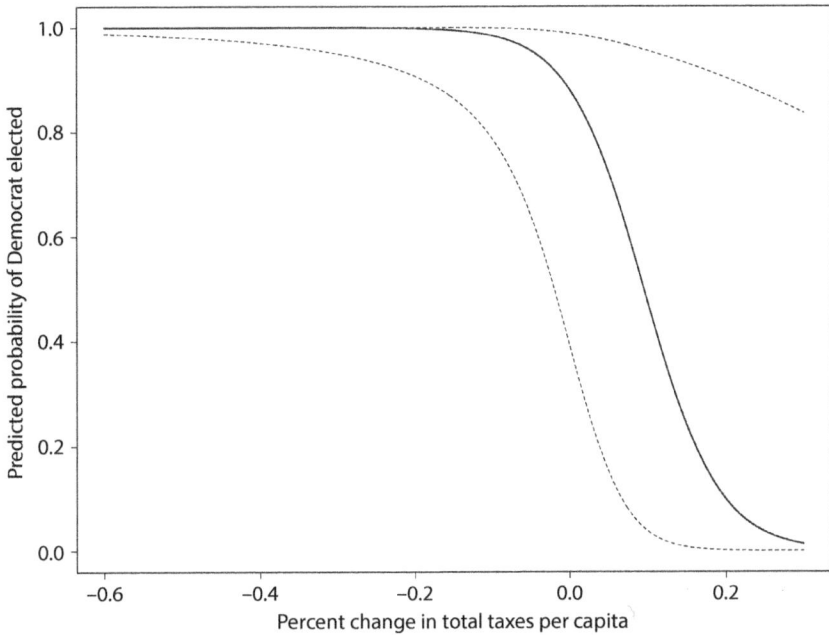

Figure I.2 Predicted probability of retaining Democratic control of governorship. Predicted probability of the likelihood of Democrats retaining the governorship after a given change in taxes during an election year. Calculations made using model 2 of table I.2 for a state in 2007 in the Midwest. Other variables are held at their mean. Dashed lines indicate 95 percent confidence intervals.

Source: National Conference of State Legislatures (1999–2011, 2011); Klarner (2013b, 2013c); U.S. Census Bureau and Bureau of Labor Statistics, Current Population Survey (1995–2012); U.S. Bureau of Economic Analysis (1995–2012); U.S. Census Bureau, Census of Governments (1995–2012); Prah, Rotmil, and Fehr (2014); Wolf (2015).

are no first-order consequences to governors that oversee expansionary pension legislation while in office (model 3 of table I.2). Figure I.2 plots the predicted probability of a Democratic incumbent retaining control of the governorship after overseeing a given change in the tax burden.

Notes

Introduction

1. Lincoln Chafee held the governorship from 2011 to mid-2013 as an independent but converted to the Democratic Party in May 2013. He was a registered Republican until 2007 and became a registered Libertarian in 2019. Gina Raimondo became governor of Rhode Island in 2015 as a Democrat.
2. Across the nation, the average state worker unionization rate was 29 percent during this period. Sarah Anzia and Terry Moe, "Polarization and Policy: The Politics of Public-Sector Pensions," *Legislative Studies Quarterly* 42, no. 1 (February 2017): 33–62.
3. Except for those its own making—that is, failing to raise the debt limit ceiling fast enough to avoid a credit downgrade in 2011.
4. Governments can also drawdown savings from a "rainy day" fund, but this fund assumes that revenue was once greater than spending. Rainy day funds are typically used for consumption smoothing over business cycles rather than mitigating structural, long-term budget imbalances. Some small governments who do not have easy access to capital markets may also use sinking funds to pay for capital projects. Neither of these budgetary methods are discussed in the book as they are not used—nor are they appropriate from a good government perspective—in the financing of state public sector pensions.
5. Anzia and Moe, "Polarization and Policy," 34; and Daniel DiSalvo, *Government Against Itself: Public Union Power and Its Consequences* (New York: Oxford University Press, 2015).

6. John Aldrich, *Why Parties? The Origin and Transformation of Political Parties in America* (Chicago: University of Chicago Press, 1995); and Jessica Trounstine, "All Politics Is Local: The Reemergence of the Study of City Politics," *Perspectives on Politics* 7, no. 3 (2009): 611–18.

7. Harold D. Lasswell, *Politics: Who Gets What, When, How.* Pickle Partners, 2018.

8. Taxpayer utility may suffer if, instead, a decrease in pension generosity was offset by an increase in wages or a decrease in worker productivity.

9. As a case in point, the reader is referred to Senator Mitch McConnell's (R–KY) COVID-19 pandemic-era statements promoting the idea of creating a legal avenue for state bankruptcy along with his pension policy suggestions for alleviating fiscal crises: David Frum, "Why Mitch McConnell Wants States to Go Bankrupt," *The Atlantic*, April 25, 2020, https://www.theatlantic.com/ideas/archive/2020/04/why-mitch-mcconnell-wants-states-go-bankrupt/610714/.

10. "Statement No. 67: Financial Reporting for Pension Plans," Governmental Accounting Standards Board, GASB Home, June 2012, https://gasb.org/page/ShowPdf?path=GASBS67.pdf&title=GASBS+67; and "Statement No. 68: Accounting and Financial Reporting for Pensions," Governmental Accounting Standards Board, GASB Home, June 2012, https://gasb.org/page/document?pdf=GASBS%2B68.pdf&title=GASBS%2B68.

11. This inconsistency is largely due to the lack of authority and enforceability of the GASB, which is a private, nongovernmental organization. This is discussed in more depth in the conclusion.

12. Terry M. Moe, "Political Control and the Power of the Agent," *Journal of Law, Economics, and Organization* 22, no. 1 (2006): 1–29.

13. Micky Tripathi, Stephen Ansolabehere, and James M. Snyder, "Are PAC Contributions and Lobbying Linked? New Evidence from the 1995 Lobby Disclosure Act," *Business and Politics* 4, no. 2 (2002): 131–55.

14. Joseph A. McCartin, "Bringing the State's Workers In: Time to Rectify an Imbalanced U.S. Labor Historiography," *Labor History* 47, no. 1 (2006): 73–94.

15. Mike Davis, "The Barren Marriage of American Labour and the Democratic Party," *New Left Review*, no. 124 (1980): 43.

16. McCartin, "Bringing the State's Workers In," 79.

17. Martin Shefter, *Political Crisis/Fiscal Crisis: The Collapse and Revival of New York City* (New York: Columbia University Press, 1992).

18. Ester Fuchs, *Mayors and Money: Fiscal Policy in New York and Chicago* (Chicago: University of Chicago Press, 1992); Shefter, *Political Crisis/Fiscal Crisis*; and Jessica Trounstine, "All Politics Is Local."

19. Robert Novy-Marx and Joshua Rauh, "The Liabilities and Risks of State-Sponsored Pension Plans," *Journal of Economic Perspectives* 23, no. 4 (2009): 191–210; and Robert Novy-Marx and Joshua Rauh, "Public Pension Promises: How Big Are They and What Are They Worth?," *Journal of Finance* 66, no. 4 (2011): 1211–49.

Although financial economists and public administration scholars have not settled on an objectively "optimal" way to calculate unfunded liabilities, my dataset standardizes this data and removes the biases inherent in self-reporting. Both of these improvements are absolutely essential to compare pensions across space and time.

20. For example, Anzia and Moe, "Polarization and Policy," 34.
21. Sarah Anzia and Terry Moe, "Public Sector Unions and the Cost of Government," *Journal of Politics* 77, no. 1 (January 2015): 114–27; and Qiushi Wang and Jun Peng, "Political Embeddedness of Public Pension Governance: An Event History Analysis of Discount Rate Changes," *Public Administration Review* 78, no. 5 (2018): 785–94.
22. On the state economy, see Charles Steindel, "Public Pension Shortfalls and State Economic Growth: A Preliminary Examination," *National Association for Business Economics* 55, no. 3 (2020): 138–49; and Wang and Peng, "Political Embeddedness of Public Pension Governance." On the national economy, see Ugo Panizza and Andrea Presbitero, "Public Debt and Economic Growth: Is There a Causal Effect?," *Journal of Macroeconomics* 41 (2014): 21–41. For an exception, see D. Roderick Kiewiet, "The Day After Tomorrow: The Politics of Public Employee Retirement Benefits," *California Journal of Politics and Policy*, no. 2 (2010): 1–30; and Roderick Kiewiet and Mathew McCubbins, "State and Local Government Finance: The New Fiscal Ice Age," *Annual Review of Political Science* 17, no. 1 (2014): 105–22.
23. The ability of a government to fulfill its public obligations to its constituents, either through service provision or service efficiency. For a more thorough description of this concept, see Carolyn Abott and Akheil Singla, "Service Solvency and Quality of Life After Municipal Bankruptcy," *Journal of Political Institutions and Political Economy* 2, no. 2 (2021): 249–80, https://doi.org/10.1561/113.00000037.
24. Republicans did not control all three branches of Kentucky state government until 2017 and lost that control in 2020; many may be surprised to learn that this is not uncharacteristic of many southern and historically conservative states.
25. *Janus v. American Federation of State, County, and Municipal Employees, Council 31, et al.*, 2018, https://www.supremecourt.gov/opinions/17pdf/16-1466_2b3j.pdf.
26. Patrick Flavin and Michael T. Hartney, "When Government Subsidizes Its Own: Collective Bargaining Laws as Agents of Political Mobilization," *American Journal of Political Science* 59, no. 4 (2015): 896–911, https://doi.org/10.1111/ajps.12163.

1. Public Sector Unions, Pensions, and Partisanship

1. Elmer E. Schattschneider, *The Semi-Sovereign People: A Realist's View of Democracy in America* (Hinsdale, IL: Dryden, 1975).

2. Regarding benefits, see R. Douglas Arnold, *The Logic of Congressional Action* (New Haven, CT: Yale University Press, 1992); about disadvantaged voters, see David P. Baron, "Electoral Competition with Informed and Uninformed Voters," *American Political Science Review* 88, no. 1 (1994): 33–47; and Susanne Lohmann, "An Information Rationale for the Power of Special Interests," *American Political Science Review* 92, no. 4 (1998): 809–27; and about legislatures, see Richard L. Hall and Alan V. Deardorff, "Lobbying as Legislative Subsidy," *American Political Science Review* 100, no. 1 (2006): 69–84.

3. For example, Alexander Hertel-Fernandez, *State Capture: How Conservative Activists, Big Businesses, and Wealthy Donors Reshaped the American States—and the Nation* (New York: Oxford University Press, 2019).

4. Kathleen Bawn et al., "A Theory of Political Parties: Groups, Policy Demands and Nominations in American Politics," *Perspectives on Politics* 10, no. 3 (2012): 571–97; and Marty Cohen, David Karol, Hans Noel, and John Zaller, *The Party Decides: Presidential Nominations Before and After Reform* (Chicago: University of Chicago Press, 2009).

5. John H. Aldrich, *Why Parties? The Origin and Transformation of Political Parties in America* (Chicago: University of Chicago Press, 1995).

6. Raymond J. La Raja and Brian F. Schaffner, *Campaign Finance and Political Polarization: When Purists Prevail* (Ann Arbor: University of Michigan Press, 2015).

7. Jessica Trounstine, *Political Monopolies in American Cities: The Rise and Fall of Bosses and Reformers* (Chicago: University of Chicago Press, 2009).

8. Terry M. Moe, "Political Control and the Power of the Agent," *Journal of Law, Economics, and Organization* 22, no. 1 (2006): 1–29.

9. Paul Frymer, *Uneasy Alliances: Race and Party Competition in America* (Princeton, NJ: Princeton University Press, 2010).

10. For example, this was likely the case in Daniel DiSalvo, "Unions, Parties, and the Politics of State Government Legacy Cost," *Policy Studies Journal* 46, no. 3 (2018): 573–97.

11. For civil service requirements, see Pamela S. Tolbert and Lynne G. Zucker, "Institutional Sources of Change in the Formal Structure of Organizations: The Diffusion of Civil Service Reform, 1880–1935," *Administrative Science Quarterly* 28, no. 1 (1983): 22–39; for more on the demands of business interests and social groups, see Frances Fox Piven, "The Urban Crisis: Who Got What and Why," in *The Fiscal Crisis of American Cities*, ed. Roger E. Alacaly and David Mermelstein (New York: Random House, 1977), 197–216; and Ester R. Fuchs, *Mayors and Money: Fiscal Policy in New York and Chicago* (Chicago: University of Chicago Press, 1992).

12. Trounstine, *Political Monopolies in American Cities*, 7

13. Sarah F. Anzia and Terry M. Moe, "Public Sector Unions and the Costs of Government," *Journal of Politics* 77, no. 1 (2015): 114–27; Sarah F. Anzia and Terry M.

Moe, "Do Politicians Use Policy to Make Politics? The Case of Public-Sector Labor Laws," *American Political Science Review* 110, no. 4 (2016): 763–77; Sarah F. Anzia and Terry M. Moe, "Polarization and Policy: The Politics of Public-Sector Pensions," *Legislative Studies Quarterly* 42, no. 1 (2017): 33–62; Daniel DiSalvo, *Government Against Itself: Public Union Power and Its Consequences* (New York: Oxford University Press, 2015); and Terry M. Moe, *Special Interest: Teachers Unions and America's Public Schools* (Washington, DC: Brookings Institution, 2011).

14. Anzia and Moe, "Do Politicians Use Policy," 763–780.

15. Dean Baker, "Origins and Severity of the Public Pension Crisis" (Center for Economic and Policy Research, Washington, DC, 2011).

16. Anzia and Moe, "Polarization and Policy," examines the individual legislator's decision to vote for or against an expansion or contraction, but does not examine the actual passage or failure of a policy change.

17. Others have spent good and considerable time explaining the details, terminology, and processes through which pensions function. For a fuller treatment of those issues than I can provide here, I direct the reader to Alicia H. Munnell, *State and Local Pensions: What Now?* (Washington, DC: Brookings Institution, 2012); Olivia S. Mitchell and Edwin C. Hustead, eds., *Pensions in the Public Sector* (Philadelphia: University of Pennsylvania Press, 2001); and Robert Novy-Marx and Joshua D. Rauh, "The Liabilities and Risks of State-Sponsored Pension Plans," *Journal of Economic Perspectives* 23, no. 4 (2009): 191–210.

18. As in D. Roderick Kiewiet and Mathew D. McCubbins, "State and Local Government Finance: The New Fiscal Ice Age," *Annual Review of Political Science* 17 (2014): 105–22.

19. Or liabilities per worker.

20. Truth in Accounting, *The Truth About Balanced Budgets: A Fifty State Study* (Glencoe, IL: Truth in Accounting, 2009), 30.

21. The Greek government debt crisis of 2009–2015 is a case in point.

22. Though Republicans might also hold an ideological commitment to pushing specific sectors of the government out of business.

23. Thad Kousser and Justin H. Phillips, *The Power of American Governors: Winning on Budgets and Losing on Policy* (Cambridge: Cambridge University Press, 2012).

24. Anzia and Moe, "Polarization and Policy"; Erick M. Elder and Gary A. Wagner, "Political Effects on Pension Underfunding," *Economics and Politics* 27, no. 1 (2015): 1–27; and Rod Kiewiet, "The Day After Tomorrow: The Politics of Public Employee Benefits," *California Journal of Politics and Policy* 2, no. 3 (2010): 1–30.

25. Anzia and Moe, "Polarization and Policy," 33–62

26. Alicia H. Munnell, J. Aubry, and Mark Cafarelli, "How Did State/Local Plans Become Underfunded?," *State and Local Pension Plans* 42 (2015): 1–7.

27. Munnell, Aubry, and Cafarelli, "How Did State/Local Plans Become Underfunded?"

28. Moe, "Political Control and the Power of the Agent."

29. That public sector unions contribute overwhelmingly to state Democrats and virtually not at all to Republicans (National Institute on Money in State Politics, "Follow the Money, 1995–2012," https://www.followthemoney.org/) is evidence in support of the latter claim, as is the storied history of private sector union voting behavior; see Richard B. Freeman, "What Do Unions Do . . . to Voting?" (National Bureau of Economic Research, Cambridge, MA, 2003).

30. Anzia and Moe, "Do Politicians Use Policy," 763–780; Patrick Flavin and Michael T. Hartney, "When Government Subsidizes Its Own: Collective Bargaining Laws as Agents of Political Mobilization," *American Journal of Political Science* 59, no. 4 (2015): 896–911; and Jacob S. Hacker and Paul Pierson, "After the Master Theory: Downs, Schattschneider, and the Rebirth of Policy-Focused Analysis," *Perspectives on Politics* 12, no. 3 (2014): 643–62.

31. As in Terry M. Moe, "The Politics of Bureaucratic Structure," in *Can the Government Govern?*, ed. John E. Chubb and Paul E. Peterson (Washington, DC: Brookings Institution, 1989), 267–329.

32. Anzia and Moe, "Polarization and Policy," 33–62; Kiewiet, "The Day After Tomorrow"; and DiSalvo *Government Against Itself.*

33. Anzia and Moe, "Polarization and Policy," 33–62

34. Schattschneider, *The Semi-Sovereign People.*

35. As I show in chapter 2, I find no evidence for a difference between before and after 2008 because the funding of public sector pensions has *always* been contentious.

36. As in a group identity setting à la Michael C. Dawson, *Behind the Mule: Race and Class in African-American Politics* (Princeton, NJ: Princeton University Press, 1994).

37. See, for example, Peter J. Katzenstein, *Small States in World Markets: Industrial Policy in Europe* (Ithaca, NY: Cornell University Press, 1985); and Torben Iversen and David Soskice, "Electoral Institutions and the Politics of Coalitions: Why Some Democracies Redistribute More than Others," *American Political Science Review* 100, no. 2 (2006): 165–81.

38. Anzia and Moe, "Polarization and Policy," 33–62

39. Clarence Stone, *Regime Politics: Governing Atlanta, 1946–1988* (Lawrence: University Press of Kansas, 1989).

40. Fuchs, *Mayors and Money.*

41. David M. Primo and James M. Snyder, "Party Strength, the Personal Vote, and Government Spending," *American Journal of Political Science* 54, no. 2 (2010): 354–70; and Christopher R. Berry, *Imperfect Union: Representation and Taxation in Multilevel Governments* (Cambridge: Cambridge University Press, 2009).

42. As in Arnold, *Logic of Congressional Action.*

43. Labor market effects are neglected here. Although it is possible that increasing pension benefits at the expense of taxpayer income is a net benefit for taxpayers as they are able to attract higher-quality workers, the size of this effect is likely

to be small if not zero, given the discourse around public sector largesse and the fact that there is no longer a comparable retirement option in the private sector. Furthermore, the fact that pension financial reporting is—across the board—distorted in ways meant to underplay the size of liabilities suggests that voters would prefer smaller rather than larger pension benefits for workers. Last, the slow but steady movement toward defined contribution (versus defined benefit) plans for public sector workers suggests that elected officials and voters want to get pension plans off of their balance sheets.

44. As a reference point, consider that average nonpension debt grew at a similar rate, but remained at only a fraction of the size of unfunded liabilities—39 percent of expenditures in 1995 and 51 percent in 2011.

45. Morris P. Fiorina, "Economic Retrospective Voting in American National Elections: A Micro-Analysis," *American Journal of Political Science*, no. 72 (1978): 426–43.

46. Anzia and Moe, "Polarization and Policy," 33–62. See Moe, "Politics of Bureaucratic Structure," for the political insulation of bureaucracies, generally, and see Jonathan Rodden, *Hamilton's Paradox: The Promise and Peril of Fiscal Federalism* (Cambridge: Cambridge University Press, 2006) for a model of fiscal bailouts, specifically.

47. As the empirical chapters will show, however, most public (and private) union political activity is concentrated on campaign expenditures rather than lobbying.

48. Flavin and Hartney, "When Government Subsidizes Its Own."

49. David R. Mayhew, *Placing Parties in American Politics: Organization, Electoral Settings, and Government Activity in the Twentieth Century* (Princeton, NJ: Princeton University Press, 1986).

50. I always think of the way in which reporters still describe the Andrew Cuomo–era politics of New York: "three men in a room in Albany" making all budgetary and policy decisions for the state. According to Bennett Liebman, "'Three Men in a Room' and Albany: Where Did the Phrase Come From?," *Government Reform* (blog), March 11, 2015, https://governmentreform.wordpress.com/2015/03/11/three-men-in-a-room-and-albany-where-did-the-phrase-come-from/, the term was first used by a reporter at Newsday in 1988 and was meant to be imply that machine bosses—and thus, machine parties—never actually disappeared in the way that many of us think that they did. This is a point that has been argued by John Mollenkopf at least as early as 1994; see John H. Mollenkopf, *A Phoenix in the Ashes: The Rise and Fall of the Koch Coalition in New York City Politics* (Princeton, NJ: Princeton University Press, 1994).

51. Regarding one-party states, as in the Democrat-dominated South, see V. O. Key, *Southern Politics in State and Nation* (New York: Knopf, 1949); on intraparty conflict, see Devin Caughey, *The Unsolid South* (Princeton, NJ: Princeton University Press, 2018); Peter Bucchianeri, "Party Competition and Coalitional Stability: Evidence from American Local Government," *American Political Science Review*

114, no. 4 (2020): 1055–70; and Robert Mickey, *Paths Out of Dixie: The Democratization of Authoritarian Enclaves in America's Deep South, 1944–1972* (Princeton, NJ: Princeton University Press, 2015).

52. Austin Ranney, "Parties in State Politics," in *Politics in the American States: A Comparative Analysis*, ed. Herbert Jacobs and Kenneth N. Vines (Boston: Little, Brown, 1965), 45–88; and T. M. Holbrook and E. Van Dunk, "Electoral Competition in the American States," *American Political Science Review* 87, no. 4 (1993): 955–62.

53. Such as Berry, *Imperfect Union*; and Terry Nichols Clark and Vincent Hoffmann-Martinot, eds., *The New Political Culture* (Boulder, CO: Westview, 1998).

54. Most state pension plans use a formula like the following:

$$Annual\ Benefit = Years\ of\ Service \times Benefit\ Multipler \times Final\ Average\ Salary$$

where the benefit multiplier is a percentage typically between 1 percent and 5 percent. Increasing the benefit multiplier (via statute) and increasing salaries of workers has the effect of increasing a beneficiary's annual pension benefit.

55. The actuarial assumptions include mortality rates, salary projections, separation rates, discount rates, and inflation expectations.

56. Funding can also come from the issuance of pension obligation bonds (POBs), but these are relatively rare and simultaneously create additional liabilities.

57. All of these bankruptcies occurred at the local level. States do not have access to the federal bankruptcy code.

58. Diane Lourdes Dick, "Bondholders vs. Retirees in Municipal Bankruptcies: The Political Economy of Chapter 9," *American Bankruptcy Law Journal* 92 (2018): 73–103.

59. Bruce Bartlett, "Starve the Beast: Origins and Development of a Budgetary Metaphor," *Independent Review* 12, no. 1 (2007): 5–26.

60. Carolyn Abott and Akheil Singla, "Helping or Hurting? The Efficacy of Municipal Bankruptcy," *Public Administration Review* 81, no. 3 (2021): 428–45.

61. Center for Responsive Politics, "We Are Open Secrets," 2019, https://www.opensecrets.org/. For the history of private sector union voting behavior see Freeman, *What Do Unions Do. . . to Voting?*.

62. We do know, however, that even the police are overwhelmingly registered Democrats, according to Bocar Ba et al., "Who Are the Police? Descriptive Representation in the Coercive Arm of Government" (working paper, Princeton University, October 28, 2022).

63. Emma Fitzsimmons and Ashley Wong, "Unions in New York Bristle After de Blasio Issues Testing Mandate," *New York Times*, July 28, 2021, A14.

64. Joseph A. Schlesinger, "The Primary Goals of Political Parties: A Clarification of Positive Theory," *American Political Science Review* 69, no. 3 (1975): 840–49.

65. Aaron Wildavsky, "The Goldwater Phenomenon: Purists, Politicians, and the Two-Party System," *Review of Politics* 27, no. 3 (1965): 386–413.

66. Aldrich, *Why Parties?*

67. Randolph H. Boehm and Dan C. Heldman, *Public Employees, Unions, and the Erosion of Civic Trust: A Study of San Francisco in the 1970s* (Lanham, MD: University Publications of America, 1983); Joshua B. Freeman, *Working-class New York: Life and Labor Since World War II* (New York: The New Press, 2001); Mark Maier, *City Unions: Managing Discontent in New York City* (New Brunswick, NJ: Rutgers University Press, 1987); Adolph L. Reed, *Stirrings in the Jug: Black Politics in the Post-Segregation Era* (Minneapolis, MN: Choice, 1999); Michael Spear, "A Crisis in Urban Liberalism: The New York City Municipal Unions and the 1970s Fiscal Crisis," PhD diss., City University of New York, 2005.

68. Martin Shefter, *Political Crisis/Fiscal Crisis: The Collapse and Revival of New York City* (New York: Columbia University Press, 1992).

69. Rauner, it must be said, was subsequently responsible for the most devastating court case for public sector unions in U.S. history, *Janus v AFSCME* (2018), which stripped public sector unions of the right to collect agency fees.

2. The Size and Fiscal Sustainability of State Pensions

1. Roderick Kiewiet, "The Day After Tomorrow: The Politics of Public Employee Benefits," *California Journal of Politics and Policy* 2, no. 3 (2010): 1–30.

2. Daniel DiSalvo and Jeffrey Kucik, "Unions, Parties, and the Politics of State Government Legacy Cost," *Policy Studies Journal* 46, no. 3 (2018): 573–97.

3. Ester R. Fuchs, *Mayors and Money: Fiscal Policy in New York and Chicago* (Chicago: University of Chicago Press, 1992), most specifically.

4. Alabama pension data proved impossible to obtain, even after repeated FOIA requests. For the years, 1995–2011: 130 plans across seventeen years resulted in 1,845 observations—a slightly unbalanced panel.

5. Sarah F. Anzia and Terry M. Moe, "Interest Groups on the Inside: The Governance of Public Pension Funds," *Perspectives on Politics* 17, no. 4 (2019): 1059–78.

6. Robert Novy-Marx and Joshua Rauh, "The Liabilities and Risks of State-Sponsored Pension Plans," *Journal of Economic Perspectives* 23, no. 4 (2009): 191–210; and Robert Novy-Marx and Joshua Rauh, "Public Pension Promises: How Big Are They and What Are They Worth?," *Journal of Finance* 66, no. 4 (2011): 1211–49.

7. Novy-Marx and Rauh, "Public Pension Promises."

8. Sarah F. Anzia and Terry M. Moe, "Polarization and Policy: The Politics of Public-Sector Pensions," *Legislative Studies Quarterly* 42, no. 1 (2017): 33–62.

9. This analysis does not assume that benefit and contribution changes are of comparable magnitude. Given the data requirements, it would be incredibly difficult if not impossible to forecast numerical estimates of unfunded liabilities that are a result of statutory changes. What I focus on, instead, are perceived shifts in the pension burden. Elected officials, for instance, will find the political constraints

of passing pension benefit increases to be lessened if they also increase the employee contribution rate, regardless of whether or not the increased contributions are adequate to fully offset the increased benefits over the next thirty years.

10. B. Hirsch and D. Macpherson, "Union Membership, Coverage, Density and Employment by Occupation, 2008," *Union Membership and Coverage Database from the CPS* (2023).

11. Data collected from National Institute on Money in State Politics, "Follow the Money, 1995–2012," https://www.followthemoney.org/.

12. I have also analyzed the data using these two indicators separately with qualitatively similar results.

13. Olle Folke, Shigeo Hirano, and James Snyder, "Patronage and Elections in U.S. States," *American Political Science Review* 105, no. 3 (2011): 567–85; and DiSalvo and Kucik, "Unions, Parties, and the Politics."

14. B. Shor and N. McCarty, "The Ideological Mapping of American Legislatures," *American Political Science Review* 105, no. 3 (2011): 530–51.

15. David R. Mayhew, *Placing Parties in American Politics: Organization, Electoral Settings, and Government Activity in the Twentieth Century* (Princeton, NJ: Princeton University Press, 1986); and Terry Nichols Clark and Vincent Hoffmann-Martinot, *The New Political Culture* (Boulder, CO: Westview, 1998).

16. Sarah F. Anzia and Terry M. Moe, "Public Sector Unions and the Costs of Government," *Journal of Politics* 77, no. 1 (2015): 114–27.

17. Anzia and Moe, "Public Sector Unions," operationalize unionization as a binary variable. As discussed, I construct an index of union strength that incorporates the percentage of unionized workers and how much unions contribute to electoral campaigns.

18. The Massachusetts State Employees Retirement System, for instance, was able to provide me with financial documents for years 2005–2007 and 2009–2011 but simply could not locate documents for 2008.

19. Frank R. Baumgartner et al., *Lobbying and Policy Change* (Chicago: University of Chicago Press, 2009).

20. This is true for legislatures that are controlled by both Republicans and Democrats, although I lose too much power by splitting the sample this way to detect a statistically significant effect.

21. Recall that this measure of the dependent variable does not take any forward-looking reforms into account. Legislation that decreases pension benefit generosity for new hires, for instance, will not be reflected in the liability data for many years. I look directly at legislation in the subsequent section.

22. The State of Washington.

23. Uniformed workers generally include fire safety and public safety workers (i.e., police, corrections officers). Many states also have plans that cover elected

officials, but I remove these plans from my analysis as the politics of these plans is likely to be much different.

24. Hirsch and Macpherson, "Union Membership, Coverage, Density, and Employment," provides data on state-level public sector unionization rates. These data cannot be disaggregated into public sector occupation. Although data from the National Institute on Money in State Politics, "Follow the Money," would allow me to make a rough estimate of how much different public sector unions are contributing to state-level races, the lack of unionization data would make the analysis too suspect.

25. National Institute on Money in State Politics, "Follow the Money."

26. Jason Stein, "Why Scott Walker Still Has Some Union Support," *Milwaukee Journal Sentinel*, February 19, 2015, https://www.governing.com/topics/mgmt/why-scott-walker-still-has-some-union-support.html.

27. James J. Heckman, "The Incidental Parameters Problem and the Problem of Initial Conditions in Estimating a Discrete Time-Discrete Data Stochastic Process," in *Structural Analysis of Discrete Data with Econometric Applications*, ed. Charles F. Manski and Daniel McFadden (Cambridge, MA: MIT Press, 1981), 179–95.

28. Although it would bolster the results to use a one-tailed test, a more stringent two-tailed test is used here.

29. Mayhew, *Placing Parties in American Politics*.

30. Christopher R. Berry, *Imperfect Union: Representation and Taxation in Multilevel Governments* (Cambridge: Cambridge University Press, 2009); and David M. Primo and James M. Snyder, "Party Strength, the Personal Vote, and Government Spending," *American Journal of Political Science* 54, no. 2 (2010): 354–70.

31. In reality, Democrats controlled 62 percent of legislative seats in New York in 2011 and unions were about as strong as in the previous example. That year, Democrats passed neither contractionary nor expansionary legislation.

32. Clark and Hoffmann-Martinot, *New Political Culture*; and F. R. Baumgartner et al., *Lobbying and Policy Change*.

33. Alicia H. Munnell, Jean-Pierre Aubry, and Mark Cafarelli, "How Did State/Local Plans Become Underfunded?," *State and Local Pension Plans* 42 (2015): 1–7.

34. Munnell et al., "How Did State/Local Plans Become Underfunded?"

35. West Virginia is one of the rare exceptions. A provision in the state's constitution going back to 1872 forbid the state from investing in the stock market (see Bond Buyer, "A Court Closes Off West Virginia's Route to Equities Investment," December 16, 1996, https://www.bondbuyer.com/news/a-court-closes-off-west-virginias-route-to-equities-investment). This was amended to allow equity investment in 1997: West Virginia Consolidated Public Retirement Board, *Comprehensive Annual Financial Report for the Fiscal Years Ended June 30, 2017 and 2016* (2018).

36. Jean-Pierre Aubry and Kevin Wandrei, "Internal vs. External Management for State and Local Pension Plans," *State and Local Pension Plans*, no. 75 (Center for Retirement Research at Boston College, Chestnut Hill, MA, November 2020).

37. D. Roderick Kiewiet and Mathew D. McCubbins, "State and Local Government Finance: The New Fiscal Ice Age," *Annual Review of Political Science* 17 (2014): 105–22.

38. Payment data are available only at the state level. Some states have several different state-administered pension plans and others may have only one, but pension funding data have been aggregated to the state level to make them comparable, without loss of information.

39. Thad Kousser and Justin H. Phillips, *The Power of American Governors: Winning on Budgets and Losing on Policy* (Cambridge: Cambridge University Press, 2012).

40. Kousser and Phillips, *Power of American Governors*.

41. Jamie Lenney, Bryon Lutz, and Louise Sheiner, "The Sustainability of State and Local Government Pension Plans: A Public Finance Approach," *Brookings Papers on Economic Activity* 2021, no. 1 (2021): 1–48, https://cepr.net/wp-content/uploads/2015/11/pension-funding-2015-11.pdf; and Charles Steindel, "Public Pension Shortfalls and State Economic Growth: A Preliminary Examination," *Business Economics* 55, no. 3 (2020): 138–49.

42. Kiewiet and McCubbins, "State and Local Government Finance."

43. Charles Steindel, "New Jersey's Pension Problems: Turning the Corner?" (unpublished manuscript, 2021).

44. William Glaberson, "N.Y. Judges, Angry on Pay, Seek Union-Like Group," *New York Times*, January 11, 2011, https://www.nytimes.com/2011/01/12/nyregion/12judges.html.

3. The Paradox of Financial Transparency

1. James E. Alt, David Dreyer Lassen, and Shanna Rose, "The Causes of Fiscal Transparency: Evidence from the US States," *IMF Staff Papers* (2006): 30–57; and Brandice Canes-Wrone, Michael C. Herron, and Kenneth W. Shotts, "Leadership and Pandering: A Theory of Executive Policymaking," *American Journal of Political Science* 45 (2001): 532–50.

2. Andrea Prat, "The Wrong Kind of Transparency," *American Economic Review* 95, no. 3 (2005): 862–77.

3. Justin Fox, "Government Transparency and Policymaking," *Public Choice* 131 (2007): 23–44.

4. Scott Ashworth and Kenneth W. Shotts, "Does Informative Media Commentary Reduce Politicians' Incentives to Pander?," *Journal of Public Economics* 94, no. 11 (2010): 838–47.

5. R. Douglas Arnold, *The Logic of Congressional Action* (New Haven, CT: Yale University Press, 1990); David P. Baron, "Electoral Competition with Informed and Uninformed Voters," *American Political Science Review* 88, no. 1 (1994): 33–47; Gene M. Grossman and Elhanan Helpman, *Special Interest Politics* (Cambridge, MA: MIT

Press, 2001); and Susanne Lohmann, "An Information Rationale for the Power of Special Interests," *American Political Science Review* 92, no. 4 (1998): 809–27.

6. Dan Amiram, Edward Owens, and Oded Rozenbaum, "Do Information Releases Increase or Decrease Information Asymmetry? New Evidence from Analyst Forecast Announcements," *Journal of Accounting and Economics* 62, no. 1 (2016): 121–38; and Marco DiMaggio and Marco Pagano, "Financial Disclosure and Market Transparency with Costly Information Processing," *Review of Finance* 22, no. 1 (2018): 117–53.

7. Arnold, *Logic of Congressional Action*; and Lohmann, "Information Rationale," 809–27.

8. This, however, naturally raises separate questions about accountability mechanisms.

9. Mary Williams Walsh, "A Sour Surprise for Public Pensions: Two Sets of Books," *New York Times*, September 18, 2016, BU1; Institute for Truth in Accounting, "The 2011 Financial State of the States" (Institute for Truth in Accounting, Northbrook, IL, 2013); and Michelle Surka and Elizabeth Ridlington, "Following the Money: How 50 States Rate in Providing Online Access to Government Spending Data" (2016).

10. Mark Baldassare, *When Government Fails: The Orange County Bankruptcy* (Berkeley: University of California Press, 1998); and Steven Erie, Vladimir Kogan, and Scott MacKenzie, *Paradise Plundered: Fiscal Crisis and Governance Failures in San Diego* (Stanford, CA: Stanford University Press, 2011).

11. "Statement No. 68: Accounting and Financial Reporting for Pensions." Governmental Accounting Standards Board." GASBS Home, June 2012. https://gasb .org/page/document?pdf=GASBS%2B68.pdf&title=GASBS%2B68.

12. GASB recommendations are not binding law. Although many states have passed legislation codifying the recommendations into law, the only way to enforce these laws are through the auditors that are employed by the state. Having employees or contractors hired by the state to enforce laws passed by the state, on the state, does little to instill confidence in the bite of GASB recommendations. For a similar argument about why good practices governing private sector accounting are also woefully underenforced, see Abigail Allen and Karthik Ramanna, "Towards an Understanding of the Role of Standard Setters in Standard Setting," *Journal of Accounting and Economics* 55, no. 1 (2013): 66–90.

13. Former Senator Orrin Hatch's (R-UT) multiple failed attempts to wrest control of the pensions from the states notwithstanding.

14. Public Plans Data, Center for Retirement Research at Boston College, Mission Square Research Institute, National Association of State Retirement Administrators, and the Government Finance Officers Association, 2001–2022. https:// publicplansdata.org/public-plans-database/.

15. Alt et al., "Causes of Fiscal Transparency."

16. On transparency versus disclosure, see Alessandro Gavazza and Alessandro Lizzeri, "Transparency and Economic Policy," *Review of Economic Studies* 76, no. 3 (2009):

1023–48; and George Kopits and J. D. Craig, "Transparency in Government Operations" (Occasional Paper 158, International Monetary Fund, Washington, DC, 1998). On disclosure as a substitute, see DiMaggio and Pagano, "Financial Disclosure and Market Transparency."

17. By "accurate," I assume that inaccurate disclosure would exaggerate how well funded the pension is. Unions have strong incentives to be dishonest in this direction, rather than the reverse.

18. Erie et al., *Paradise Plundered*, offers a rich case study in how San Diego duped the bond market and the credit rating agencies by misrepresenting the size of their pension funding gap.

19. Marc Joffee, "OpenGov Voices: A Transparent Approach to Understanding Local Government Debt" (Sunlight Foundation, Washington, DC, 2013).

20. Fiscal transparency decisions cannot, at least in the short term, be manipulated by individual agents. Increased availability of fiscal and budgetary data and other efforts at increasing "sunshine" have only come about as a result of long-standing pressure from good government groups (and to a lesser extent, markets), and only very slowly over time. Alt et al., "Causes of Fiscal Transparency," developed a panel of fiscal transparency in the states and found that states increased transparency only over time (no state decreased their transparency) and that any movement in a given state's transparency index was excruciatingly slow. Nevertheless, following Alt et al.'s attempt to identify the predictors of the evolution of fiscal transparency, I include what may reasonably be assumed to be possible determinants of transparency in my analysis (including the absolute size of pension and general budgetary expenditures, electoral competition and turnover, Democratic control, and economic conditions). The inclusion of these control variables has no impact on the forgoing analysis.

21. Gavazza and Lizzeri, "Transparency and Economic Policy."

22. Gavazza and Lizzeri claim that increased revenue transparency increases wasteful transfers, but this point is a bit more sensitive to their assumptions about tax efficiencies and distortions.

23. For ease of exposition, I assume that the likelihood of voters receiving a signal about policy is the same as that of public sector workers and unions.

24. In a way analogous to public debt.

25. Gavazza and Lizzeri, despite not distinguishing between disclosure and transparency, present a fitting story of how Greece more or less made up budget and deficit numbers to gain access to the European Union only after more data were demanded from them.

26. As in Gavazza and Lizzeri, "Transparency and Economic Policy."

27. Please see the Methodological Appendix for a discussion of why some states might bias their funding ratios downward.

28. Richard F. Dye, Nancy W. Hudspeth, and David F. Merriman, "Transparency in State Budgets: A Search for Best Practices" (Institute of Government and Public Affairs at the University of Illinois, 2011).

29. Institute for Truth in Accounting, "2011 Financial State of the States."

30. Ronald L. Jones et al., "Charting a Course Through Stormy Seas: State Financial Executives in 2012" (NASACT–AGA 2012 Survey of State Financial Executives, 2012); and D. M. Mead, "The Timeliness of Financial Reporting by State and Local Governments Compared with the Needs of Users" (research brief, Governmental Accounting Standards Board, Norwalk, CT, 2011).

31. As Bill Bergman, head of research at the Institute for Truth in Accounting, relayed in a phone call (May 13, 2016): "States can be fast, but it doesn't mean the information is right."

32. Sunshine Review, "State Transparency Checklist" (2011).

33. Alt et al., "Causes of Fiscal Transparency."

34. A decrease in fiscal transparency is indicated by an *increase* in *Avg. Days to CAFR Release*.

35. Jones et al., "Charting a Course Through Stormy Seas"; and Mead, "Timeliness of Financial Reporting."

36. Regarding the manipulation of actuarial assumptions, see Sarah F. Anzia and Terry M. Moe, "Interest Groups on the Inside: The Governance of Public Pension Funds," *Perspectives on Politics* 17, no. 4 (2019): 1059–78. For deferred payments, see Erie et al., *Paradise Plundered*. For the importance of the composition of pension boards, see John Brooks, "Board on the Job: Public-Pension Governance in the United States (US) States." *Journal of Public Policy* 39, no. 1 (2019): 1–34.

37. I rerun these analyses using the distance between revised liabilities per capita and self-reported liabilities per capita and the distance between self-reported assets per capita and revised assets per capita with the expectation that transparency will play a smaller role. These results are presented in the Methodological Appendix.

38. As is implied, a pension board composed completely of employees or annuitants would report funding ratios 80 percentage points above my revised measure. Although no pension in my sample is composed completely of employees, during my sample period, Colorado's Public Employees Retirement Association was chaired by a board composed of fourteen employee members out of a total of fifteen. Other pensions, like the General Assembly Retirement System of Illinois, may have boards composed 100 percent of employees (state legislators) but my data do not include enough observations of these plans to reasonably include them in the analysis.

39. Sarah F. Anzia and Terry M. Moe, "Polarization and Policy: The Politics of Public-Sector Pensions," *Legislative Studies Quarterly* 42, no. 1 (2017): 33–62; and Rod Kiewiet, "The Day After Tomorrow: The Politics of Public Employee Benefits," *California Journal of Politics and Policy* 2, no. 3 (2010): 1–30.

40. Gavazza and Lizzeri, "Transparency and Economic Policy."

4. What Does Pension Debt Mean for What States Can Do?

1. Carolyn Abott and Akheil Singla, "Helping or Hurting? The Efficacy of Municipal Bankruptcy," *Public Administration Review* 81, no. 3 (2021): 428–45.
2. Carolyn Abott and Akheil Singla, "Service Solvency and Quality of Life After Municipal Bankruptcy," *Journal of Political Institutions and Political Economy* 2, no. 2 (2021): 249–80.
3. CBS News, "Court Hit with Sad Stories from Detroit Retirees Objecting to Bankruptcy Cuts," *CBS News*, accessed July 9, 2024, https://www.cbsnews.com /detroit/news/court-hit-with-sad-stories-from-detroit-retirees-objecting-to -bankruptcy-cuts/.
4. Monica Davey and Mary Williams Walsh, "Billions in Debt, Detroit Tumbles Into Insolvency," *New York Times*, July 19, 2013, A1.
5. For an argument in favor of allowing states to have access to federal bankruptcy protection, see David A. Skeel, "The Education of Detroit's Pension and Bond Creditors," *Wharton School of the University of Pennsylvania Issue Brief* 2, no. 1 (2014).
6. Brian K. Collins, "Credit and Credibility: State Government Bond Ratings, 1975–2002," *American Review of Public Administration* 44, no. 1 (2014): 112–23.
7. For directly calculating interest costs, see Craig L. Johnson and Kenneth A. Kriz, "Fiscal Institutions, Credit Ratings, and Borrowing Costs," *Public Budgeting and Finance* 25, no. 1 (2005): 84–103. For the use of surveys that poll bond traders, see Robert C. Lowry and James E. Alt, "A Visible Hand? Bond Markets, Political Parties, Balanced Budget Laws, and State Government Debt," *Economics and Politics* 13, no. 1 (2001): 49–72; James M. Poterba and Kim S. Rueben, "Fiscal News, State Budget Rules, and Tax-Exempt Bond Yields," *Journal of Urban Economics* 50, no. 3 (2001): 537–62; and James M. Poterba and Kim S. Rueben, "State Fiscal Institutions and the US Municipal Bond Market," in *State Fiscal Institutions and the US Municipal Bond Market* (Chicago: University of Chicago Press, 1999), 181–208. For a look at bond ratings, see Collins, "Credit and Credibility," 112–23; Craig A. Depken and Courtney L. Lafountain, "Fiscal Consequences of Public Corruption: Empirical Evidence from State Bond Ratings," *Public Choice* 126, no. 1–2 (2006): 75–85; Benedict S. Jimenez, "Management Quality and State Bond Ratings: Exploring the Links between Public Management and Fiscal Outcomes," *International Journal of Public Administration* 34, no. 12 (2011): 783–99; Johnson and Kriz, "Fiscal Institutions," 84–103; Skip Krueger and Robert W. Walker, "Divided Government, Political Turnover, and State Bond Ratings," *Public Finance Review* 36, no. 3 (2008): 259–86; Skip Krueger and Robert W. Walker, "Management Practices and State Bond Ratings," *Public Budgeting and Finance* 30, no. 4 (2010): 47–70; and Judith I. Stallmann, Steven Deller, Lindsay Amiel,

and Craig Maher, "Tax and Expenditure Limitations and State Credit Ratings," *Public Finance Review* 40, no. 5 (2012): 643–69.

8. Krueger and Walker, "Divided Government," 259–86; James C. Clingermayer and Dan B. Wood, "Disentangling Patterns of State Debt Financing," *American Political Science Review* 89, no. 1 (1995): 108–20; Michael A. Ellis and D. Eric Schansberg, "The Determinants of State Government Debt Financing," *Public Finance Review* 27, no. 6 (1999): 571–87; and D. Roderick Kiewiet and Kristin Szakaty, "Constitutional Limitations on Borrowing: An Analysis of State Bonded Indebtedness," *Journal of Law, Economics, and Organization* 12, no. 1 (1996): 62–97.

9. Johnson and Kriz, "Fiscal Institutions," 84–103.

10. Unlike the federal government, however, most U.S. subnational governments must put the issue to a popular vote first.

11. Standard and Poor's, *U.S. Public Finance: U.S. State Ratings Methodology* (2011).

12. S&P has changed its published criteria several times over a short period of time, and no longer lists the UAAL as the operative measure when evaluating pensions' role in credit grades, but it instead claims to use unfunded pension liabilities per capita and unfunded liabilities as a percentage of personal income. Because of space constraints and because of the fact that S&P's criteria listed UAAL during the years that these credit grades were actually reported, I do not include the other measures in my analysis.

13. For issues with lower ratings, Pu Liu and Anjan V. Thakor, "Interest Yields, Credit Ratings, and Economic Characteristics of State Bonds: An Empirical Analysis," *Journal of Money, Credit and Banking* 16, no. 3 (1984): 344–51; and Daniel Rubinfeld, "Credit Ratings and the Market for General Obligation Municipal Bonds," *National Tax Journal* 26, no. 1 (1973): 17–27. For the relationship with the cost of borrowing, see Johnson and Kriz, "Fiscal Institutions," 84–103.

14. Pamela M. Prah, Adam Rotmil, and Stephen C. Fehr, "Infographic: S&P State Credit Ratings, 2001–2014," Pew Trusts, June 2014, http://www.pewtrusts.org/en/research-and-analysis/blogs/stateline/2014/06/09/sp-ratings-2014.

15. No state has defaulted since 1933. Additionally, U.S. states cannot legally declare bankruptcy, which makes this hypothetical restructuring even more difficult to sort through.

16. Steven Church, "Calpers No Better Than Bondholders in Stockton Bankruptcy," Bloomberg, 2014, https://www.bloomberg.com/news/articles/2014-10-01/calpers-denied-special-protection-in-stockton-bankruptcy; and Skeel, "Education of Detroit's Pension and Bond Creditors."

17. Of course, as interest and other borrowing costs increase for high debt entities, the difficulty of paying off loans will only accelerate.

18. Stallmann et al., "Tax and Expenditure Limitations," 643–69.

19. Standard and Poor's, *U.S. Public Finance*.

20. On tax and expenditure limits, see Johnson and Kriz, "Fiscal Institutions," 84–103; and Stallmann et al., "Tax and Expenditure Limitations," 643–69. On public management quality, see Jimenez, "Management Quality and State Bond Ratings," 783–99; and Krueger and Walker, "Management Practices," 47–70. On political uncertainty, see Jimenez, "Management Quality and State Bond Ratings," 783–99; and Krueger and Walker, "Divided Government," 259–86. On political corruption, see Depken and Lafountain, "Fiscal Consequences of Public Corruption," 311–26.

21. On the impact of private pension management on corporate debt ratings, see for instance, Thomas J. Carroll and Greg Niehaus, "Pension Plan Funding and Corporate Debt Ratings," *Journal of Risk and Insurance* 65, no. 3 (1998): 427–43; and John J. Maher, "Pension Obligations and the Bond Credit Market: An Empirical Analysis of Accounting Numbers," *Accounting Review* 62, no. 4 (1987): 785–98. On the relationship between public pensions and public credit ratings, see Alicia H. Munnell, Jean-Pierre Aubry, and Laura Quinby, "The Impact of Pensions on State Borrowing Costs," Issue in Brief 14 (Center for Retirement Research, Chestnut Hill, MA, 2011).

22. Prah, Rotmil, and Fehr, "Infographic."

23. Mark D. Robbins and Bill Simonsen, "Do Debt Levels Influence State Borrowing Costs?," *Public Administration Review* 72, no. 4 (2012): 498–505.

24. Pew Center on the States, *The Trillion Dollar Gap: Underfunded State Retirement Systems and the Roads to Reform* (Washington, DC: Pew Charitable Trust, 2010).

25. The unemployment rate for each state-year was obtained from the U.S. Bureau of Labor Statistics, "BLS Statistics on Unemployment," 1995–2012, http://www.bls.gov/bls/unemployment.htm; per capita personal income and gross state product (GSP) growth comes from the U.S. Bureau of Economic Analysis, "Regional Economic Accounts," 1995–2012, http://www.bea.gov/regional/. For state government partisan composition, see Carl Klarner, "State Partisan Balance Data, 1937–2011," *Harvard Dataverse* 1 (2013c), https://doi.org/10.7910/DVN/LZHMG3; for state polarization data, see Boris Shor and Nolan McCarty, "The Ideological Mapping of American Legislatures," *American Political Science Review* 105, no. 3 (2011): 530–51; for budgetary data, see U.S. Census Bureau. "Census of Governments Annual Survey of State Government Finances," 1995–2012, https://www.census.gov/govs/state/; and for indicators of legal limits on debt, see Yilin Hou and Daniel L. Smith, "A Framework for Understanding State Balanced Budget Requirement Systems: Reexamining Distinctive Features and an Operational Definition," *Public Budgeting and Finance* 26, no. 3 (2006): 22–45.

26. BBB, BBB+, A–, A, A+, AA–, AA, AA+, or AAA.

27. Joshua D. Angrist, "Estimation of Limited Dependent Variable Models with Dummy Endogenous Regressors," *Journal of Business and Economic Statistics* 19, no. 1 (2001): 2–28.

28. The peculiarity of the GSP growth rate's negative relationship to credit ratings remains, however.

29. Lawrence J. White, "Credit Rating Agencies: An Overview," *Annual Review of Financial Economics* 5, no. 1 (2013): 93–122; Anil K. Kashyap and Natalia Kovrijnykh, "Who Should Pay for Credit Ratings and How?," *Review of Financial Studies* 29, no. 2 (2016): 420–56; Han Xia, "Can Investor-Paid Credit Rating Agencies Improve the Information Quality of Issuer-Paid Rating Agencies?," *Journal of Financial Economics* 111, no. 2 (2014): 450–68; and Jess Cornaggia, Kimberly J. Cornaggia, and Ryan D. Israelsen, "Credit Ratings and the Cost of Municipal Financing," *Review of Financial Studies* 31, no. 6 (2018): 2038–79.

30. The level of liabilities and assets, not reported for brevity, is not statistically related to interest costs.

31. Regression analysis, although harder conceptually to model, shows that a positive relationship exists between pension contributions and all of the budgetary line items discussed in the text (most, but not all, of these relationships are also statistically significant). This implies that pension payments and expenditures on other items in the budget increase or decrease at the same time because of larger, external influences that shape the general budget and state economy (results not reported but available upon request).

32. American Society of Civil Engineers, "Failure to Act: Closing the Infrastructure Investment Gap for America's Economic Future" (American Society of Civil Engineers, 2016); and Jerry Zhirong Zhao, Camila Fonseca-Sarmiento, and Jie Tan, "America's Trillion-Dollar Repair Bill" (working paper, Volcker Alliance, November 2019).

33. These results are nearly identical if I use the share of total expenditures rather than general expenditures.

5. The Pluralist State, the Coalitional State, and the Disorganized State: Three Examples of Pension Politics

1. Relative to the rest of the country. Compared with the rest of the South, however, Kentucky's unionization rates are actually relatively high.

2. Only forty-eight miles of which is on land; New Jersey Geological and Water Survey, "Geoscience Information in New Jersey," *Out of the Rock* 2, no. 2 (1996): 1–8, https://www.nj.gov/dep/njgs/enviroed/newsletter/v2n2.pdf.

3. Urban Institute, "New Jersey State Fiscal Brief," October 2024, https://www.urban.org/policy-centers/cross-center-initiatives/state-and-local-finance-initiative/projects/state-fiscal-briefs/new-jersey; and Urban Institute, "New York State Fiscal Brief," October 2024, https://www.urban.org/policy-centers

/cross-center-initiatives/state-and-local-finance-initiative/projects/state
-fiscal-briefs/new-york.

4. Urban Institute, "New Jersey State Fiscal Brief"; and Urban Institute, "New York State Fiscal Brief,".

5. Urban Institute, "New Jersey State Fiscal Brief,"; and Urban Institute, "New York State Fiscal Brief."

6. Jim Brennan, Gotham Gazette, "New York City Residents and Economy Are Generating an Increasingly Large Share of State Government Resources," October 19, 2018, https://www.gothamgazette.com/130-opinion/8002-new-york-city-s -residents-and-economy-are-generating-an-increasingly-large-share-of-state -government-resources.

7. Citizens Budget Commission, "Facing Tough Challenges: What to Look for in New York State's Fiscal Year 2025 Budget," press release, January 11, 2024, https:// cbcny.org/newsroom/cbc-releases-facing-tough-challenges-what-look-new -york-states-fiscal-year-2025-budget; and Nikita Biryukov, "New Jersey Faces Steep Deficits in Coming Years, Group Warns," *New Jersey Monitor*, February 13, 2024, https://newjerseymonitor.com/2024/02/13/new-jersey-faces-steep-deficits -in-coming-years-group-warns/.

8. Carl Klarner, "State Partisan Balance Data, 1937–2011," *Harvard Dataverse* 1 (2013c), https://doi.org/10.7910/DVN/LZHMG3.

9. U.S. Census Bureau, "Annual Survey of Public Employment and Payroll," https://www.census.gov/programs-surveys/apes.html.

10. New York State Public Employment Relations Board, "Taylor Law," https:// www.nysenate.gov/legislation/laws/CVS/A14.

11. New Jersey Public Employment Relations Commission, "Chapter 13A—Public Employment Relations Act," current as of March 31, 2022, accessed July 15, 2024, https://www.nj.gov/perc/documents/Chapter%2013A.pdf?ver=20220404.

12. Barry Hirsch and David Macpherson, "Union Membership, Coverage, and Earnings from the CPS," UnionStats.com, https://www.unionstats.com/.

13. Right-to-work laws allow both public and private sector workers to choose whether or not to join a union and whether or not to pay union dues—even if wages, benefits, and work rules are determined by a union contract.

14. For an overview of how this happened and an excellent explanation for why it happened (and why it was inevitable that it happened), see pages 408–411 of Amy B. Monahan, "When a Promise Is Not a Promise: Chicago-Style Pensions," *UCLA Law Review* 64 (2017): 356–413.

15. An astute observer may point out that the gap in self-reported ARC and revised ARC is considerably smaller in New Jersey than New York, even though New Jersey has paid much less of its ARC on average using either metric. This is a political choice and a point addressed in chapter 4.

16. Public Plans Data, Center for Retirement Research at Boston College, Mission Square Research Institute, National Association of State Retirement Administrators, and the Government Finance Officers Association, 2001–2022, accessed July 20, 2024, https://publicplansdata.org/public-plans-database/.

17. Tom Bryan, "The New Jersey Pension System," in *Pensions in the Public Sector*, ed. Olivia S. Mitchell and Edwin C. Hustead (Philadelphia: University of Pennsylvania Press, 2001), 327–53.

18. Mike Lilley, "Job Number One: NJEA's Leading Role in New Jersey's Pension Crisis" (Sunlight Policy Center, New Jersey, June 17, 2019).

19. New Jersey League of Municipalities, "Pension Systems," https://www.njlm.org/884/Pension-Systems.

20. William N. Thompson, "Public Pension Plans: The Need for Scrutiny and Control," *Public Personnel Management* 6, no. 4 (1977): 203–24.

21. H.R. 9155, 94th Cong., 1st sess., introduced July 31, 1975.

22. *Abbott v. Burke*, 119 N.J. 287, 575 A.2d 359 (1990).

23. Robert Hanley, "Trenton Assails Florio Proposal for School Aid," *New York Times*, May 31, 1990.

24. Randy Diamond, "Read Florio's Lips: New State Taxes," *Christian Science Monitor*, June 22, 1990.

25. Peter Kerr, "Florio Facing Revolt by 4 on Tax Plan," *New York Times*, November 14, 1990.

26. Iver Peterson, "New Jersey Teachers Flex Muscles, but Carefully," *New York Times*, April 19, 1994, https://www.nytimes.com/1994/04/19/nyregion/new-jersey-teachers-flex-muscles-but-carefully.html; and Karen Diegmueller, "Whitman Confronts N.J. Union on Divisive Issues," *Education Week*, February 23, 1994.

27. Peter Kerr, "Florio School-Aid Package Gains Final Approval," *New York Times*, June 22, 1990.

28. Wayne King, "Old Friends Break Up: Trenton Democrats and Angry Unions," *New York Times*, May 7, 1991.

29. Joseph P. Fried, "Jim Florio, New Jersey Governor Undone by Tax Hike, Dies at 85," *New York Times*, September 26, 2022.

30. Brigid Callahan Harrison, "We Should Have Listened to Florio," NorthJersey.com, July 17, 2016, https://www.northjersey.com/story/opinion/2016/07/17/harrison-we-should-have-listened-to-florio/94944728/.

31. Jerry Gray, "Pension Deal Announced in Trenton," *New York Times*, June 16, 1994.

32. Alicia H. Munnell, Jean-Pierre Aubry, and Mark Cafarelli, "An Update on Pension Obligation Bonds," Center for Retirement Research at Boston College, July 2014; and Rod Kiewiet, "The Day After Tomorrow: The Politics of Public Employee Benefits," *California Journal of Politics and Policy* 2, no. 3 (2010): 1–30.

33. Lilley, "Job Number One."

34. Iver Peterson, "On Politics; Is McGreevey Squeezing Until Everyone Yells 'Taxes'?," *New York Times*, February 2, 2003.

35. National Governors Association, "James E. McGreevey," https://www.nga.org /governor/james-e-mcgreevey/.

36. National Conference of State Legislatures, "Pension and Retirement Plan Enactments in State Legislatures," 1999–2010, https://www.ncsl.org/?tabid=13399.

37. National Conference of State Legislatures, "Pension and Retirement Plan Enactments."

38. The Court wrote that the law "cannot constitutionally create a legally binding, enforceable obligation on the state to annually appropriate funds as [the pension reform legislation] purports to require." *Burgos v. New Jersey*, 221 N.J. 258, 111 A.3d 96 (2015).

39. Robert Steyer, "New Jersey Fully Funds Pension System for Third Straight Fiscal Year," *Pensions and Investments*, July 5, 2023.

40. Bryan, "New Jersey Pension System," 327–53.

41. John Albert Holbritter, "A History of the New York State Teachers Retirement System, 1921–1959" (PhD diss., New York University, 1960), ProQuest (301861307).

42. State legislature would go on to remove the statutorily required contributions from employees in 1966 (for ERS members) and 1968 (for TRS members) and then reinstate them in 1976: Howard Martin Greenberg, "A History of the New York State Teachers Retirement System: 1960–1979" (PhD diss., New York University, 1980), ProQuest (303033211).

43. Andria L. Bentley, "The New York State Comptroller as Sole Trustee of the Common Retirement Fund: A Constitutional Guarantee," *Albany Law Review* 72, no. 3 (2009): 761–88.

44. On the noncontributory plan for ERS, see Greenberg, "History of the New York State Teachers Retirement System"; and on the noncontributory plan for TRS, see *Laws of the State of New York Passed at the Sessions of the Legislature*, Session 191.2, chap. 498–1096 (1968), chap. 1084. In 1966 and 1968, New York State had a Republican governor, Republican-controlled State Senate, and a slim Democratic majority in the State Assembly.

45. Tier 2 eliminated the ability of an employee to apply out of state service to the calculation of pension benefits and slightly changed the way the retirement age and requirements were calculated but altered little else.

    New York State Teachers' Retirement System, "Learning About NYSTRS," https://www.nystrs.org/NYSTRS/media/PDF/LearningAboutNYSTRS.pdf.

46. Greenberg, "History of the New York State Teachers Retirement System." In 1976, New York State had a Democratic governor, a slim Republican majority in the State Senate, and a Democratic-controlled State Assembly. Republicans held a majority in the State Senate for nearly all of 1927–2009 except for a brief

period during the Great Depression. This was largely due to districts that were drawn in such a way as to violate the "one-person, one-vote."

47. Richard Pérez-Peña, "Legislators Back Pension Rises for Retired Public Employees," *New York Times*, June 14, 2000.

48. Tier 4 was introduced in 1983 under Governor Mario Cuomo (D–NY), but there are no discernible differences between Tier 3 and Tier 4. They are always combined when discussed in any official state literature about the pension system.

49. James Dao, "Comptroller Sues to Block Pataki Pension Fund Plan," *New York Times*, July 6, 1995.

50. On Comptroller Hevesi's schemes, see Michael Rothfeld and Chad Bray, "'Pay to Play' Probe Gets Key Guilty Plea; Focus on Rattner," *Wall Street Journal*, October 8, 2010. James C. McKinley Jr., "Hevesi Rejects Pataki Pension Fund Plans," *New York Times*, January 20, 2004, https://www.nytimes.com/2004/01/20/nyregion/hevesi-rejects-pataki-pension-fund-plans.html?searchResultPosition=1.

51. "Spitzer Resigns After Sex Scandal, Pressure," *NPR*, March 12, 2008, https://www.npr.org/2008/03/12/88134976/spitzer-resigns-after-sex-scandal-pressure.

52. For a recent and thorough treatment see David Schleicher, *In a Bad State: Responding to State and Local Budget Crises* (New York: Oxford University Press, 2023).

53. In addition to hiring freezes, pay cuts, and decreases in government services.

54. Danny Hakim, "Paterson and Unions Agree on Limits for New Pensions," *New York Times*, June 5, 2009.

55. Danny Hakim, "Paterson Vetoes Pension Bill, Drawing Union's Fire," *New York Times*, June 3, 2009.

56. Thomas Kaplan, "Major New York Unions Angry at Pension Vote, Plan to Boycott Hispanic Conference," *New York Times*, March 22, 2012, https://www.nytimes.com/2012/03/23/nyregion/major-new-york-unions-angry-at-pension-vote-plan-to-boycott-hispanic-conference.html?searchResultPosition=9.

57. Richard W. Johnson, Owen Haaga, and Benjamin G. Southgate, "Understanding the Growth in Government Contributions to New York State's Public Pension Plans" (Urban Institute, Washington, DC, June 2016).

58. Danny Hakim, John Eligon, and Thomas Kaplan, "Cuomo, Admitting Setbacks, Says He Asked for the Moon," *New York Times*, March 16, 2012, https://www.nytimes.com/2012/03/16/nyregion/cuomo-admits-setbacks-but-says-he-asked-for-the-moon.html?searchResultPosition=6.

59. Thomas Kaplan, "Angry at Pension Vote, Unions Plan to Skip Hispanic Event," *New York Times*, March 22, 2012, https://www.nytimes.com/2012/03/23/nyregion/major-new-york-unions-angry-at-pension-vote-plan-to-boycott-hispanic-conference.html.

60. James Dao, "Cuomo Appeals to Union Leaders for Help in Campaign," *New York Times*, August 4, 1994.

61. Kaplan, "Angry at Pension Vote."

62. Gerald Benjamin and Elizabeth Benjamin, "New York's Governorship 'Restored'?," in *Governing New York State*, ed. Robert F. Pecorella and Jeffrey M. Stonecash (Albany: SUNY Press, 2006), 117–42.

63. Bennett Liebman, "'Three Men in a Room' and Albany: Where Did the Phrase Come From?" *Government Reform* (blog), March 11, 2015, https://governmentreform.wordpress.com/2015/03/11/three-men-in-a-room-and-albany-where-did-the-phrase-come-from/.

64. Shane Goldmacher and Jesse McKinley, "Flexing Their Support for Cuomo, Key Unions Leave Working Families Party," *New York Times*, April 13, 2018, https://www.nytimes.com/2018/04/13/nyregion/cuomo-nixon-wfp-labor-governor-election.html.

65. The infamous Independent Democratic Conference (and its precursor, the "Four Amigos") handed State Senate control over to the Republicans more than once and was responsible for a number of scandals and protracted budget fights between 2009 and 2018. See Danny Hakim, "After a Rebellion That Shook Albany, Three Falls From Grace," *New York Times*, May 9, 2012; and Vivian Wang, "How 3 Little Letters (I.D.C.) Are Riling Up New York Progressives," *New York Times*, September 11, 2018.

66. Urban Institute, "Kentucky State Fiscal Brief," accessed July 16, 2024, https://www.urban.org/policy-centers/cross-center-initiatives/state-and-local-finance-initiative/projects/state-fiscal-briefs/kentucky.

67. Klarner, "State Partisan Balance Data"; and National Conference of State Legislatures (NCSL), "State Partisan Composition," updated October 29, 2024, https://www.ncsl.org/about-state-legislatures/state-partisan-composition.

68. Hirsch and Macpherson, "Union Membership, Coverage, and Earnings."

69. Kentucky Chamber of Commerce, "Right to Work 2017," https://www.kychamber.com/issues/2019-priorities/rtw.

70. Klarner, "State Partisan Balance Data"; NCSL, "State Partisan Composition."

71. Kentucky Teachers' Retirement System, "History," https://trs.ky.gov/home/history/.

72. Maria O'Brien, "The Case for Public Pension Reform: Early Evidence from Kentucky," Boston University School of Law, accessed July 16, 2024, https://scholarship.law.bu.edu/cgi/viewcontent.cgi?article=1194&context=faculty_scholarship; and Kentucky Chamber of Commerce, "Pension Crisis," February 25, 2024, https://www.kychamber.com/sites/default/files/pdfs/Pension%20Crisis%20-%20Feb%2025%20Edits.pdf.

73. Jacob S. Hacker, "Privatizing Risk Without Privatizing the Welfare State: The Hidden Politics of Social Policy Retrenchment in the United States." *American Political Science Review* 98, no. 2 (2004): 243–60.

74. Rick Howlett, "Pension Reform Bill 'A Great Beginning'," *Louisville Public Media*, July 1, 2008.

75. Pew Trusts, "Kentucky's Successful Public Pension Reform," September 27, 2013, accessed July 16, 2024, https://www.pewtrusts.org/en/research-and-analysis/issue-briefs/2013/09/27/kentuckys-successful-public-pension-reform.

76. O'Brien, "Case for Public Pension Reform."

77. Tom Loftus, "Kentucky Supreme Court Strikes Down Pension Reform Law," *Courier Journal*, December 13, 2018.

78. Olivia Krauth, "Kentucky Legislature Overrides Teacher Pension Veto, Putting New Hires on 'Hybrid' Plan," *Courier Journal*, March 29, 2021.

79. Sarah F. Anzia and Terry M. Moe, "Public Sector Unions and the Costs of Government," *Journal of Politics* 77, no. 1 (2015): 114–27.

6. Blowing Up the Pluralist Framework: Republicans and Twenty-First Century Labor Politics

1. Uniformed workers—police and fire—were not affected by Act 10 and Wisconsin public employers are still mandated to engage in collective bargaining with unions that represent these workers.

2. Barry T. Hirsch, David A. Macpherson, and Wayne G. Vroman, "Estimates of Union Density by State," *Monthly Labor Review* 124, no. 7 (July 2001): 51–55; and Public Employee Collective Bargaining Act, Pub. L. No. 86–257, 73 Stat. 519 (1959).

3. Perhaps ironically, AFSCME was founded to prevent a Democratically controlled state legislature in Wisconsin from eliminating the civil service and returning to a system of patronage in which Republican employees would be fired from the state.

4. Barry T. Hirsch and David A. Macpherson, "Union Membership and Coverage Database from the CPS," UnionStats, https://www.unionstats.com/.

5. David Nack, Michael Childers, Alexia Kulwiec, and Armando Ibarra, "The Recent Evolution of Wisconsin Public Worker Unionism Since Act 10," *Labor Studies Journal* 45, no. 2 (2020): 147–65.

6. Francis Capria, "Right-to-Work or Right-to-Free Ride?," *Marquette University Law School Faculty* (blog), April 19, 2018, https://law.marquette.edu/facultyblog/2018/04/right-to-work-or-right-to-free-ride/.

7. Peter Rachleff, "The Right-to-Work Offensive: Tracking the Spread of the Anti-Union Virus," *New Labor Forum* 21, no. 1 (2012): 22–29, https://doi.org/10.4179/NLF.211.0000005.

8. "Labor Unions in Wisconsin History," Wisconsin Historical Society, https://www.wisconsinhistory.org/Records/Article/CS1709#:~:text=Wisconsin's%20first%20labor%20unions%20were,working%20conditions%20through%20collective%20action.

9. "Labor Unions in Wisconsin History."

10. "AFSCME 2412 History," AFSCME Wisconsin Local 2412, accessed July 17, 2024, https://www.afscme32.org/afscme-wisconsin-local-2412/about-us/afscme -2412-history.

11. "AFSCME 2412 History."

12. Joseph E. Slater, "State Legislation as a Fulcrum for Change: Wisconsin's Public Sector Labor Law, and the Revolution in Politics and Worker Rights," *bepress Legal Repository* (2005): 516.

13. "A Short History of the Statute," Federal Labor Relations Authority, accessed July 17, 2024, https://www.flra.gov/resources-training/resources/statute-and-regulations /statute/short-history-statute.

14. Laura Dresser, Joel Rogers, and Pablo Aquiles-Sanchez, *The State of Working Wisconsin 2023* (Madison: University of Wisconsin–Madison, COWS [High Road Strategy Center], September 2023), https://highroad.wisc.edu/wp-content /uploads/sites/1368/2023/09/SOWW2023-FINAL-REPORT-1.pdf.

15. Wisconsin Policy Forum, "Focus 22–04: Unions in Wisconsin," February 2022, https://wispolicyforum.org/wp-content/uploads/2022/02/Focus_22_04_Unions .pdf.

16. Since the 2010 elections that ushered in Walker as governor, Republicans have enjoyed control of both chambers of the state legislature, but the governor's mansion was returned to a Democrat after Tony Evers beat Scott Walker in the 2018 election. National Conference of State Legislatures, "State Partisan Composition," updated October 29, 2024, https://www.ncsl.org/about-state-legislatures /state-partisan-composition.

17. Cameron Joseph, "Thompson's Work with Unions as Governor Could Hurt His Senate Campaign," *The Hill*, December 20, 2011, https://thehill.com/blogs /ballot-box/senate-races/100888-thompsons-work-with-unions-as-governor -could-hurt-his-senate-campaign/.

18. Joseph, "Thompson's Work with Unions."

19. Alexander Hertel-Fernandez, *State Capture: How Conservative Activists, Big Businesses, and Wealthy Donors Reshaped the American States—and the Nation* (New York: Oxford University Press, 2019); Alexander Hertel-Fernandez, Theda Skocpol, and Jason Sclar. "When Political Mega-Donors Join Forces: How the Koch Network and the Democracy Alliance Influence Organized U.S. Politics on the Right and Left," *Studies in American Political Development* 32, no. 2 (2018): 127–65.

20. Steven Rogers, *Accountability in State Legislatures* (Chicago: University of Chicago Press, 2023).

21. Carl Klarner, "State Partisan Balance Data, 1937–2011," *Harvard Dataverse* 1 (2013c), https://doi.org/10.7910/DVN/LZHMG3; and U.S. Census Bureau, "Annual Survey of State and Local Government Finances," 1977–2012.

22. Results not reported but available upon request.

23. V. O. Key, *The Responsible Electorate: Rationality in Presidential Voting 1936–1960* (Cambridge, MA: Harvard University Press, 1966).

24. On complex federal system, see Steven Rogers, "Electoral Accountability for State Legislative Roll Calls and Ideological Representation," *American Political Science Review* 111, no. 3 (2017): 555–71; Steven Rogers, "National Forces in State Legislative Elections," *ANNALS of the American Academy of Political and Social Science* 667, no. 1 (2016): 207–25; and Justin de Benedictis-Kessner and Christopher Warshaw, "Accountability for the Local Economy at All Levels of Government in United States Elections," *American Political Science Review* 114, no. 3 (2020): 660–76. On attentive audiences, see Sarah F. Anzia, *Timing and Turnout: How Off-Cycle Elections Favor Organized Groups* (Chicago: University of Chicago Press, 2013); and Robert S. Erikson, Michael MacKuen, and James A. Stimson, *The Macro Polity* (Cambridge: Cambridge University Press, 2002).

25. Thad Kousser and Justin H. Phillips, *The Power of American Governors: Winning on Budgets and Losing on Policy* (Cambridge: Cambridge University Press, 2012).

26. Kousser and Phillips, *Power of American Governors*

27. Larry M. Bartels, *Unequal Democracy: The Political Economy of the New Gilded Age* (Princeton, NJ: Princeton University Press, 2016), 1–424.

28. On "inattentive publics," see R. Douglas Arnold, *The Logic of Congressional Action* (New Haven, CT: Yale University Press, 1992); and Morris P. Fiorina, *Economic Retrospective Voting in American National Elections: A Micro-Analysis* (New Haven, CT: Yale University Press, 1981).

29. Roger Bybee, "Sorry, Your Job's Been Outsourced!," Isthmus, November 2, 2007, https://isthmus.com/news/cover-story/sorry-your-jobs-been-outsourced/.

30. "Wisconsin Labor History: An Epic Story," School for Workers, April 9, 2020, https://schoolforworkers.wisc.edu/wisconsin-labor-history-an-epic-story/.

31. Katherine J. Cramer, *The Politics of Resentment: Rural Consciousness in Wisconsin and the Rise of Scott Walker* (Chicago: University of Chicago Press, 2016).

32. William Finnegan, "The Storm," *New Yorker*, February 27, 2012; and Bill Glauber and Patrick Marley, "Scott Walker's Eight Years as Governor Ushered in Profound Change in Wisconsin," *Milwaukee Journal Sentinel*, January 4, 2019, https://www.jsonline.com/story/news/politics/2019/01/04/scott-walkers-eight-years-wisconsin-governor-were-consequential/2473616002/.

33. Mary Spicuzza and Steven Verburg, "From a 'Distraction' to Fast-Tracked to His Desk: Scott Walker Poised to Sign Right-to-Work Bill," *Wisconsin State Journal*, February 26, 2015, https://wiscnews.com/news/local/government-politics/from-a-distraction-to-fast-tracked-to-his-desk-scott-walker-poised-to-sign-right/article_be51da88-a2cb-5ed4-9d6e-1da1d289edba.html.

34. John Nichols, "Scott Walker Promised $500K Donor He Would 'Divide and Conquer' Unions," *The Nation*, May 11, 2012, https://www.thenation.com/article/archive/scott-walker-promised-500k-donor-he-would-divide-and-conquer-unions/.

35. Spicuzza and Verburg, "From a 'Distraction' to Fast-Tracked to His Desk."

36. "Video: Walker Explains 'Divide and Conquer' Strategy," News 8 Now, May 11, 2012, accessed at https://www.news8000.com/news/local-news/video-walker -explains-divide-conquer-strategy/article_5cbf4739-f02c-5edf-80a8-31538a417853 .html.

37. Hannah Walker and Dylan Bennett, "The Whiteness of Wisconsin's Wages: Racial Geography and the Defeat of Public Sector Labor Unions in Wisconsin," *New Political Science* 37, no. 2 (2015): 181–203.

38. Walker and Bennett, "Whiteness of Wisconsin's Wages," 189.

39. "History of Employee Trust Funds," Wisconsin Department of Employee Trust Funds, accessed July 17, 2024, https://etf.wi.gov/boards/joint/history-etf/direct.

40. "History of Employee Trust Funds."

41. Anthony Randazzo and Scott Alexander, "Calm Amid the Chaos: Wisconsin's Pension System and the 2008 Financial Crisis," Equable Institute, January 31, 2020, https://equable.org/wisconsin-pension-system-and-the-2008-financial -crisis/.

42. James K. Conant, "Wisconsin's Budget Deficit: Size, Causes, Remedies, and Consequences," *Public Budgeting and Finance* 23 (2003): 5–25, https://doi-org .remote.baruch.cuny.edu/10.1111/1540-5850.2302002.

43. "Wisconsin Gov. Scott Walker Says National Guard Ready for Any Unrest Over Anti-Union Bill," Wisconsin Situation, May 22, 2011, https://wisconsinsituation .wordpress.com/2011/05/22/wisconsin-gov-scott-walker-says-national-guard -ready-for-any-unrest-over-anti-union-bill/.

44. Krishnadev Calamur, "Wisconsin Gov. Scott Walker Signs Right-To-Work Bill," NPR, March 9, 2015, https://www.npr.org/sections/thetwo-way/2015/03/09 /391901732/wisconsin-gov-scott-walker-sighs-right-to-work-bill

45. Patrick Flavin and Michael T. Hartney, "When Government Subsidizes Its Own: Collective Bargaining Laws as Agents of Political Mobilization," *American Journal of Political Science* 59, no. 4 (2015): 896–911.

46. Martin H. Malin, "Life After Act 10: Is There a Future for Collective Representation of Wisconsin Public Employees," *Marquette Law Review* 96 (2012): 623–50; and Paul M. Secunda, "The Wisconsin Public-Sector Labor Disputes of 2011," *ABAJ Labor and Employment Law Journal* 27 (2011): 293.

47. "Wisconsin Pension Laws," Equable Institute, November 20, 2021. https://equable .org/wisconsin-pension-laws/.

48. "Scott Walker's Act 10 Caused an Uproar, but Things Are Mostly Back to Normal," Fordham Institute, August 25, 2015, https://fordhaminstitute.org/national /commentary/scott-walkers-act-10-caused-uproar-things-are-mostly-back -normal.

49. James K. Conant, "State of Wisconsin Budgeting After the Great Recession," *Municipal Finance Journal* 40 (2019): 37–58; Secunda, "The Wisconsin Public-Sector

Labor Disputes of 2011," 293; and Aimee Pernsteiner, D'Arcy Becker, Matthew Fish, William F. Miller, and Dawna Drum, "Budget Repair or Budget Spectacle? The Passage of Wisconsin's Act 10," *Public Money and Management* 36, no. 7 (2016): 507–14.

50. "Information Memo 2015–04," Wisconsin Legislative Council, accessed July 17, 2024, https://docs.legis.wisconsin.gov/misc/lc/information_memos/2015/im_2015 _04.

51. "Scott Walker's Act 10 Caused an Uproar," Fordham Institute.

52. E. Jason Baron, "The Effect of Teachers' Unions on Student Achievement in the Short Run: Evidence from Wisconsin's Act 10," *Economics of Education Review* 67 (2018): 40–57.

53. Hirsch and Macpherson, "Union Membership and Coverage Database."

54. Malin, "Life After Act 10," 623.

55. "Wisconsin Gov. Scott Walker Says National Guard Ready."

56. Daniel Strauss, "Democrat Tony Evers Ousts Wisconsin Gov. Scott Walker," Politico, November 7, 2018, https://www.politico.com/story/2018/11/07/scott -walker-vs-tony-evers-wisconsin-governor-race-results-2018-965594.

57. Secunda, "The Wisconsin Public-Sector Labor Disputes of 2011," 293.

58. Steven Greenhouse, "A Gathering Storm Over 'Right to Work' in Indiana," *New York Times*, January 2, 2012.

59. National Right to Work Committee, "State Right to Work Timeline," accessed July 17, 2024, https://nrtwc.org/facts/state-right-to-work-timeline-2016/.

60. Monica Davey, "Indiana Governor Signs a Law Creating a 'Right to Work' Stat," *New York Times*, February 1, 2012.

61. Senate Fiscal Agency, "Senate Fiscal Agency Analysis of Proposal 12–2," November 2012, https://www.senate.michigan.gov/SFA/Publications/BallotProps/Proposal12 -2.pdf; and Kevin Robillard, "Gov: Unions Sparked Right-to-Work," Politico, December 11, 2012, https://www.politico.com/story/2012/12/michigan-right-to -work-rick-snyder-084918

62. Dave Murray, "Proposal 2: Unions Lose Big-Money, High-Profile Effort to Restore Clout in Michigan," MLive, November 7, 2012, https://www.mlive.com /politics/2012/11/post_88.html.

63. Mark Memmott and Korva Coleman, "Michigan Governor Signs Right-To-Work Bills Into Law," NPR, December 11, 2012, https://www.npr.org/sections /thetwo-way/2012/12/11/166946294/michigan-lawmakers-poised-to-pass -right-to-work-bill-outraging-union-protesters.

64. PBS NewsHour, "Michigan Becomes 1st State in Decades to Repeal Right-to-Work Law," March 24, 2023, https://www.pbs.org/newshour/politics/michigan -becomes-1st-state-in-decades-to-repeal-right-to-work-law.

65. Steven Greenhouse, "Ohio Wages Fierce Fight on Collective Bargaining," *New York Times*, October 15, 2011.

66. Rachel Weiner, "Issue 2 Falls, Ohio Collective Bargaining Law Repealed," *Washington Post*, November 8, 2011. Missouri also overturned a legislatively enacted antilabor bill through referendum in 2018. Although the bill focused on right-to-work rather than collective bargaining, it was a noteworthy development in the evolution of the Midwest's political relationship with labor. Ballotpedia, "Missouri Proposition A, Right to Work Referendum (August 2018)," accessed July 17, 2024, https://ballotpedia .org/Missouri_Proposition_A,_Right_to_Work_Referendum_(August_2018).

Conclusion

1. Ester R. Fuchs, *Mayors and Money: Fiscal Policy in New York and Chicago* (Chicago: University of Chicago Press, 1992).
2. Jessica Trounstine, *Political Monopolies in American Cities: The Rise and Fall of Bosses and Reformers* (Chicago: University of Chicago Press, 2009).
3. For an example of this dynamic in New York City, see Martin Shefter, *Political Crisis/Fiscal Crisis: The Collapse and Revival of New York City* (New York: Columbia University Press, 1992).
4. Survey results indicate that 42 percent of respondents believe that their state government is "spending more money than it collects." Carolyn Abott, Matthew Incantalupo, and Akheil Singla, "Voter Responsiveness to Signals of Local Government Financial Health" (unpublished manuscript, February 14, 2024), typescript.
5. Jacob Grumbach, *Laboratories Against Democracy: How National Parties Transformed State Politics*, vol. 184 (Princeton, NJ: Princeton University Press, 2022); and Sarah F. Anzia, *Local Interests: Politics, Policy, and Interest Groups in US City Governments* (Chicago: University of Chicago Press, 2022).
6. John S. Jackson, *The 2014 Illinois Governor Race: Quinn vs. Rauner* (Paul Simon Public Policy Institute, Southern Illinois University, Carbondale, 2015).
7. Rauner referred to these fees as "unfair share fees" in the press release touting the executive order: "Illinois Government News Release," Illinois.gov, February 9, 2015, https://www.illinois.gov/news/press-release.13216.html. See also "Rauner Move on Fair Share Fees Flops in Federal Court," AFSCME Council 31, March 25, 2015, https://m.afscme31.org/news/rauner-move-on-fair-share-fees-flops-in -federal-court.
8. Rick Pearson, "Judge Drops Rauner Fair Share Suit, Lets Non-Union Workers' Case Proceed," *Chicago Tribune*, May 25, 2019, https://www.chicagotribune.com /2015/05/19/judge-drops-rauner-fair-share-suit-lets-non-union-workers-case -proceed/.
9. *Friedrichs v. California Teachers Association*, 578 U.S. ___ (2016).
10. *Abood v. Detroit Board of Education*, 431 U.S. 209 (1977).

11. Rick Pearson, Kim Geiger, and Monique Garcia, "U.S. Supreme Court Gives Rauner Major Victory Over Labor, in Ruling That Could Undercut Public Worker Unions Nationwide," *Chicago Tribune*, May 15, 2019, https://www .chicagotribune.com/2018/06/27/us-supreme-court-gives-rauner-major -victory-over-labor-in-ruling-that-could-undercut-public-worker-unions -nationwide/.

12. "Appeals Court Ruling Clears Path for U.S. Supreme Court to Hear Lawsuit to End Mandatory Union Fees," *Illinois Policy*, March 21, 2017, https://www .illinoispolicy.org/press-releases/appeals-court-ruling-clears-path-for-u-s -supreme-court-to-hear-lawsuit-to-end-mandatory-union-fees/.

13. Ann C. Hodges, "The US Labor Relations System After *Janus v. AFSCME*: An Early Assessment," *Employee Responsibilities and Rights Journal* 33 (2021): 49–60.

14. Robert Iafolla, "Mass Exodus of Public Union Fee Payers After High Court Ruling," *Bloomberg Law*, April 5, 2019, https://news.bloomberglaw.com/daily-labor-report /mass-exodus-of-public-union-fee-payers-after-high-court-ruling.

15. Heather Gies, "Supreme Court Decision in *Janus* Case Deals a Blow to Public Sector Unions," *In These Times*, March 27, 2019, https://inthesetimes.com /article/janus-afscme-supreme-court-union-labor-agency-fees.

16. Jarrett Skorup, "AFSCME Has Lost 200K Plus Members and Fee Payers Nationwide Since *Janus* Decision," Mackinac Center for Public Policy, May 10, 2023, https://www.mackinac.org/blog/2023/afscme-has-lost-200k-plus-members -and-fee-payers-nationwide-since-janus-decision.

17. *Thompson v. Marietta Education Association*, No. 19–4217 (6th Cir. 2020); and Michael M. Oswalt, "The Doomed Constitutional Attacks on Exclusive Representation" (issue brief, American Constitution Society, June 2021), https:// www.acslaw.org/wp-content/uploads/2021/06/Constitutional-Attacks-on -Exclusive-Representation-Oswalt.pdf.

18. Patrick Flavin and Michael T. Hartney, "When Government Subsidizes Its Own: Collective Bargaining Laws as Agents of Political Mobilization," *American Journal of Political Science* 59, no. 4 (2015): 908.

19. Gregory M. Saltzman, "Bargaining Laws as a Cause and Consequence of the Growth of Teacher Unionism," *ILR Review* 38, no. 3 (1985): 335–51; and Gregory M. Saltzman, "Public Sector Bargaining Laws Really Matter: Evidence from Ohio and Illinois," in *When Public Sector Workers Unionize*, ed. Richard B. Freeman and Casey Ichniowski (Chicago: University of Chicago Press, 1988), 41–80.

20. "WI Democratic Lawmakers Flee to Prevent Vote," *NPR*, February 17, 2011, https:// www.npr.org/2011/02/17/133847336/wis-democratic-lawmakers-flee-to-prevent -vote.

21. E. Jason Baron, "The Effect of Teachers' Unions on Student Achievement in the Short Run: Evidence from Wisconsin's Act 10," *Economics of Education Review* 67 (2018): 40–57.

22. Eunice S. Han, "The Myth of Unions' Overprotection of Bad Teachers: Evidence from the District–Teacher Matched Data on Teacher Turnover," *Industrial Relations: A Journal of Economy and Society* 59, no. 2 (2020): 316–52.

23. Amy B. Resnick, "Things Look Good for Public Sector Pensions," Government Finance Research Center, January 25, 2022, https://gfrc.uic.edu/the-government-finance-research-blog/things-look-good-for-public-sector-pensions/.

24. Resnick, "Things Look Good for Public Sector Pensions."

25. "Public Pension Shortfalls and State Economic Growth: A Preliminary Examination," *Center for Retirement Research at Boston College*, April 2023, https://crr.bc.edu/wp-content/uploads/2023/04/IB_23-8.pdf; and Charles Steindel, "Public Pension Shortfalls and State Economic Growth: A Preliminary Examination," *Business Economics* 55, no. 3 (2020): 138–49.

26. Jamie Lenney, Finn Schüle, Byron Sheiner, and Louise Lutz, "The Sustainability of State and Local Pensions: A Public Finance Approach," *Brookings Papers on Economic Activity* 2021, no. 1 (2021): 1–48, https://cepr.net/wp-content/uploads/2015/11/pension-funding-2015-11.pdf.

27. Amanda Kass, Andrew Crosby, and Brenda Parker, "A Vicious Cycle: Fiscal Intervention, Pension Underfunding, and Instability in (Re) Making Racialized Geographies," *Environment and Planning A: Economy and Space* 55, no. 7 (2023): 1780–98.

28. This method is similar to the one I use in this book, the accumulated benefit obligation (ABO), but it generally results in a higher overall liability because it projects the effect of future salary increases. It is more difficult to construct and requires more assumptions, as it considers what the liability will look like in the future rather than what it would like if the entire workforce retired today.

29. "Statement No. 67: Financial Reporting for Pension Plans," Governmental Accounting Standards Board, June 2012, https://gasb.org/page/ShowPdf?path=GASBS67.pdf.

30. Although Treasury bonds are considered the safest of all investments, the yield is typically higher than municipal bonds with the same maturity because of the preferred tax treatment of municipal bonds. According to J. P. Morgan, the yield on municipal bonds was, on average, 84 percent of the yield on Treasury bonds between 2017 and 2022. In 2023, that percentage fell to 75 percent. "J.P. Morgan Insights: A Rare Municipal Bond Opportunity—Equity-Like Yields," J.P. Morgan Private Bank, accessed July 29, 2024, https://privatebank.jpmorgan.com/nam/en/insights/markets-and-investing/ideas-and-insights/a-rare-municipal-bond-opportunity-equity-like-yields#fn9.

31. "Statement No. 68: Accounting and Financial Reporting for Pensions," Governmental Accounting Standards Board, June 2012, https://gasb.org/page/ShowPdf?path=GASBS+68.pdf.

32. Sheila Weinberg and Eileen Norcross, "A Judge in Their Own Cause: GASB 67/68 and the Continued Mismeasurement of Public Sector Pension Liabilities," *Journal of Law, Economics and Policy* 14 (2017): 62.

33. The Public Employee Retirement Income Security Act (PERISA) was introduced in Congress in 1975 and every year thereafter until 1985. Scott Ridgeley, "Misuse of Public Pension Assets: White Collar Crimes and Other Offenses," *Indiana Law Review* 26 (1992): 589–629.

34. On the New York City Schools budget, see Michael Elsen-Rooney and Alex Zimmerman, "Eric Adams School Funding Cuts Less Than Expected," *Chalkbeat*, January 17, 2024, https://www.chalkbeat.org/newyork/2024/01/17/eric-adams -school-funding-cuts-less-than-expected. On the New York Police Department, see William K. Rashbaum, "Adams Plans to Cut N.Y.P.D. Budget by $1 Billion," *New York Times*, January 10, 2024, https://www.nytimes.com/2024/01/10/nyregion /budget-adams-nypd.html.

35. Ayana Harry, "Mayor Adams Announces Reversal for Some Budget Cuts," *NY1*, January 10, 2024, https://ny1.com/nyc/manhattan/politics/2024/01/11/mayor -adams-announces-reversal-for-some-budget-cuts.

36. Bradley R. Haywood, "The Right to Shelter as a Fundamental Interest Under the New York State Constitution," *Columbia Human Rights Law Review* 34 (2002): 157.

37. Ralph R. Ortega, "How Did New York City Reverse Its 2024 Budget Cuts?," City and State NY, January 18, 2024, https://www.cityandstateny.com/policy /2024/01/how-did-new-york-city-reverse-its-2024-budget-cuts/393450/.

Methodological Appendix

1. Plans that were at least partially funded by contributions from the state legislature were included in the collection. Municipal plans that receive no revenue from the state government were not included, even if they were administered by the state. Many large and prominent plans were excluded using this standard (including the Teachers' Retirement System of New York City and Detroit's municipal pension funds), but the idea was to look at funds that are the direct and clear responsibility of the state legislature, even if there are scenarios in which the state bails out local funds.

2. Robert Novy-Marx and Joshua Rauh, "Public Pension Promises: How Big Are They and What Are They Worth?," *Journal of Finance* 66, no. 4 (2011): 1211–49.

3. Assumed here to be sixty. Rerunning the simulations assuming that police and firemen retire at fifty-five, teachers at sixty-five, and everyone else at sixty does not qualitatively change the results.

4. For the discount rate, I used the contemporaneous year average of the ten-year Treasury rate, but this is a hotly contested issue. Most plans use the expected return on their assets as a discount rate on their liabilities—which has no basis in economic theory or actuarial practice, but was encoded in the Governmental

Accounting Standards Board's (GASB's) list of recommendations until 2012—often at a much-too-high rate of 7 or 8 percent. The GASB recently revised their recommendations to suggest that state pension plans use a discount rate (and expected rate of return) that at least partially reflects a high-quality tax-exempt municipal bond rate. For COLA, I used annual consumer price index (CPI) inflation.

5. Douglas J. Elliott, "State and Local Pension Funding Deficits: A Primer" (Brookings Institution, Washington, DC, 2010).

6. Pew Center on the States, *The Trillion Dollar Gap: Underfunded State Retirement Systems and the Roads to Reform* (Washington, DC: Pew Charitable Trust, 2010).

7. Using random effects assumes that state and year effects are uncorrelated with my independent variables. Although this is a heroic assumption to make, it is one that has to be made when using nonlinear models because of the incidental parameter problem posed by fixed effects; see James J. Heckman, "The Incidental Parameters Problem and the Problem of Initial Conditions in Estimating a Discrete Time-Discrete Data Stochastic Process," in *Structural Analysis of Discrete Data with Econometric Applications*, ed. C. F. Manski and D. McFadden (Cambridge, MA: MIT Press, 1981), 179–95.

8. Gary King and Langche Zeng, "Logistic Regression in Rare Events Data," *Political Analysis* 9, no. 2 (2001): 137–63.

9. $\left(\left(Liabilities_{revised} - Assets_{revised} \right) - \left(Liabilities_{self-reported} - Assets_{self-reported} \right) \right)$

10. For the full model using data on government website transparency, see Sunshine Review, "State Transparency Checklist," 2011. For the index of fiscal transparency, see James E. Alt, David Dreyer Lassen, and Shanna Rose, "The Causes of Fiscal Transparency: Evidence from the US States," *IMF Staff Papers* 53 (2006): 30–57.

11. This pattern is also observed in the giving behavior of public sector unions to federal candidates.

12. Jack M. Treadway, *Public Policymaking in the American States* (New York: Praeger, 1985).

13. Steven Rogers, "National Forces in State Legislative Elections," *ANNALS of the American Academy of Political and Social Science* 667, no. 1 (2016): 207–25.

14. On liberal states, see Robert S. Erikson, Gerald C. Wright, and John P. McIver, *Statehouse Democracy: Public Opinion and Policy in the American States* (Cambridge: Cambridge University Press, 1993). On responsiveness to voter opinion, see Jeffrey R. Lax and Justin H. Phillips, "The Democratic Deficit in the States," *American Journal of Political Science* 56, no. 1 (2012): 148–66; and Jeffrey R. Lax and Justin H Phillips, "Gay Rights in the States: Public Opinion and Policy Responsiveness," *American Political Science Review* 103, no. 3 (2009): 367–86. On liberal legislative districts, see Chris Tausanovitch and Christopher Warshaw, "Measuring Constituent Policy Preferences in Congress, State Legislatures, and Cities,"

Journal of Politics 75, no. 2 (2013): 330–42. On attributing policy responsibility, see Kevin Arceneaux, "Does Federalism Weaken Democratic Representation in the United States?," *Publius: Journal of Federalism* 35, no. 2 (2005): 297–311.

15. Leah C. Stokes, "Electoral Backlash Against Climate Policy: A Natural Experiment on Retrospective Voting and Local Resistance to Public Policy," *American Journal of Political Science* 60, no. 4 (2016): 958–74.

References

Abood v. Detroit Board of Education, 431 U.S. 209 (1977).

Abott, Carolyn, Matthew Incantalupo, and Akheil Singla. "Voter Responsiveness to Signals of Local Government Financial Health." Unpublished manuscript, February 14, 2024. Typescript.

Abott, Carolyn, and Akheil Singla. "Helping or Hurting? The Efficacy of Municipal Bankruptcy." *Public Administration Review* 81, no. 3 (2021): 428–45.

Abott, Carolyn, and Akheil Singla. "Service Solvency and Quality of Life After Municipal Bankruptcy." *Journal of Political Institutions and Political Economy* 2, no. 2 (2021): 249–80. https://doi.org/10.1561/113.00000037.

"AFSCME Local 2412 History." AFSCME Wisconsin Local 2412. Accessed July 17, 2024. https://www.afscme32.org/afscme-wisconsin-local-2412/about-us/afscme-2412-history/.

Aldrich, John H. *Why Parties? The Origin and Transformation of Political Parties in America.* Chicago: University of Chicago Press, 1995.

Allen, Abigail, and Karthik Ramanna. "Towards an Understanding of the Role of Standard Setters in Standard Setting." *Journal of Accounting and Economics* 55, no. 1 (2013): 66–90.

Alt, James E., David Dreyer Lassen, and Shanna Rose. "The Causes of Fiscal Transparency: Evidence from the US States." *IMF Staff Papers* 53 (2006): 30–57.

American Society of Civil Engineers. "Failure to Act: Closing the Infrastructure Investment Gap for America's Economic Future." American Society of Civil Engineers, 2016.

Amiram, Dan, Edward Owens, and Oded Rozenbaum. "Do Information Releases Increase or Decrease Information Asymmetry? New Evidence from Analyst

Forecast Announcements." *Journal of Accounting and Economics* 62, no. 1 (2016): 121–38.

Angrist, Joshua D. "Estimation of Limited Dependent Variable Models with Dummy Endogenous Regressors." *Journal of Business and Economic Statistics* 19, no. 1 (2001): 2–28.

"Angry at Pension Vote, Unions Plan to Skip Hispanic Event." *New York Times*, March 22, 2012. https://www.nytimes.com/2012/03/23/nyregion/major-new -york-unions-angry-at-pension-vote-plan-to-boycott-hispanic-conference .html?searchResultPosition=9.

Anzia, Sarah F. *Local Interests: Politics, Policy, and Interest Groups in US City Governments.* Chicago: University of Chicago Press, 2022.

Anzia, Sarah F. *Timing and Turnout: How Off-Cycle Elections Favor Organized Groups.* University of Chicago Press, 2013.

Anzia, Sarah F., and Terry M. Moe. "Do Politicians Use Policy to Make Politics? The Case of Public-Sector Labor Laws." *American Political Science Review* 110, no. 4 (2016): 763–77.

Anzia, Sarah F., and Terry M. Moe. "Interest Groups on the Inside: The Governance of Public Pension Funds." *Perspectives on Politics* 17, no. 4 (2019): 1059–78.

Anzia, Sarah F., and Terry M. Moe. "Polarization and Policy: The Politics of Public-Sector Pensions." *Legislative Studies Quarterly* 42, no. 1 (2017): 33–62.

Anzia, Sarah F., and Terry M. Moe. "Public Sector Unions and the Costs of Government." *Journal of Politics* 77, no. 1 (2015): 114–27.

"Appeals Court Ruling Clears Path for U.S. Supreme Court to Hear Lawsuit to End Mandatory Union Fees." *Illinois Policy*, March 21, 2017. https://www.illinoispolicy .org/press-releases/appeals-court-ruling-clears-path-for-u-s-supreme-court-to -hear-lawsuit-to-end-mandatory-union-fees/.

Arceneaux, Kevin. "Does Federalism Weaken Democratic Representation in the United States?" *Publius: Journal of Federalism* 35, no. 2 (2005): 297–311.

Arnold, R. Douglas. *The Logic of Congressional Action.* New Haven, CT: Yale University Press, 1990.

Ashworth, Scott, and Kenneth W. Shotts. "Does Informative Media Commentary Reduce Politicians' Incentives to Pander?" *Journal of Public Economics* 94, no. 11 (2010): 838–47.

Aubry, Jean-Pierre, and Kevin Wandrei. "Internal vs. External Management for State and Local Pension Plans." *State and Local Pension Plans*, no. 75. Center for Retirement Research at Boston College, Chestnut Hill, MA, November 2020.

Baker, Dean. "Origins and Severity of the Public Pension Crisis." Center for Economic and Policy Research, Washington, DC, 2011.

Baldassare, Mark. *When Government Fails: The Orange County Bankruptcy.* Berkeley: University of California Press, 1998.

Ballotpedia. "Missouri Proposition A, Right to Work Referendum (August 2018)." Accessed July 17, 2024. https://ballotpedia.org/Missouri_Proposition_A,_Right _to_Work_Referendum_(August_2018).

Baron, David P. "Electoral Competition with Informed and Uninformed Voters." *American Political Science Review* 88, no. 1 (1994): 33–47.

Baron, E. Jason. "The Effect of Teachers' Unions on Student Achievement in the Short Run: Evidence from Wisconsin's Act 10." *Economics of Education Review* 67 (2018): 40–57.

Bartels, Larry M. *Unequal Democracy: The Political Economy of the New Gilded Age.* Princeton, NJ: Princeton University Press, 2016.

Bartlett, Bruce. "Starve the Beast: Origins and Development of a Budgetary Metaphor." *Independent Review* 12, no. 1 (2007): 5–26.

Baumgartner, Frank R., Jeffrey M. Berry, Marie Hojnacki, Beth L. Leech, and David C. Kimball. *Lobbying and Policy Change: Who Wins, Who Loses, and Why.* Chicago: University of Chicago Press, 2009.

Bawn, Kathleen, Martin Cohen, David Karol, Seth Masket, Hans Noel, and John Zaller. "A Theory of Political Parties: Groups, Policy Demands and Nominations in American Politics." *Perspectives on Politics* 10, no. 3 (2012): 571–97.

Benjamin, Gerald, and Elizabeth Benjamin. "New York's Governorship 'Restored'?" In *Governing New York State*, ed. Robert F. Pecorella and Jeffrey M. Stonecash, 117–42. Albany: SUNY Press, 2006.

Bentley, Andria L. "The New York State Comptroller as Sole Trustee of the Common Retirement Fund: A Constitutional Guarantee." *Albany Law Review* 72, no. 3 (2009): 761–88. https://heinonline.org/HOL/P?h=hein.journals/albany72&i=767.

Berry, Christopher R. *Imperfect Union: Representation and Taxation in Multilevel Governments.* Cambridge: Cambridge University Press, 2009.

Biryukov, Nikita. "New Jersey Faces Steep Deficits in Coming Years, Group Warns." *New Jersey Monitor*, February 13, 2024. https://newjerseymonitor.com/2024/02/13 /new-jersey-faces-steep-deficits-in-coming-years-group-warns/.

Ba, Bocar, Jacob Kaplan, Dean Knox, Mayya Komisarchik, Rachel Mariman, Jonathan Mummolo, Roman Rivera, and Michelle Torres. "Who Are the Police? Descriptive Representation in the Coercive Arm of Government." Working paper. Princeton University, October 28, 2022.

Boehm, Randolph H., and Dan C. Heldman. *Public Employees, Unions, and the Erosion of Civic Trust: A Study of San Francisco in the 1970s.* Lanham, MD: University Publications of America, 1983.

Bond Buyer. "A Court Closes Off West Virginia's Route to Equities Investment." December 16, 1996. https://www.bondbuyer.com/news/a-court-closes-off-west -virginias-route-to-equities-investment.

Brennan, Jim. "New York City Residents and Economy are Generating an Increasingly Large Share of State Government Resources." Gotham Gazette, October 19,

2018. https://www.gothamgazette.com/130-opinion/8002-new-york-city-s-residents
-and-economy-are-generating-an-increasingly-large-share-of-state-government
-resources.

Brooks, John. "Board on the Job: Public-Pension Governance in the United States
(US) States." *Journal of Public Policy* 39, no. 1 (2019): 1–34.

Bryan, Tom. "The New Jersey Pension System." In *Pensions in the Public Sector*, ed.
Olivia S. Mitchell and Edwin C. Hustead, 327–53. Philadelphia: University of
Pennsylvania Press, 2001.

Bucchianeri, Peter. "Party Competition and Coalitional Stability: Evidence from
American Local Government." *American Political Science Review* 114, no. 4 (2020):
1055–70.

Bybee, Roger. "Sorry, Your Job's Been Outsourced!" Isthmus, November 2, 2007.
https://isthmus.com/news/cover-story/sorry-your-jobs-been-outsourced/.

Calamur, Krishnadev. "Wisconsin Gov. Scott Walker Signs Right-To-Work Bill." NPR,
March 9, 2015. https://www.npr.org/sections/thetwo-way/2015/03/09/391901732
/wisconsin-gov-scott-walker-sighs-right-to-work-bill.

Canes-Wrone, Brandice, Michael C. Herron, and Kenneth W. Shotts. "Leadership
and Pandering: A Theory of Executive Policymaking." *American Journal of Political
Science* 45, no. 3 (2001): 532–50.

Capria, Francis. "Right-to-Work or Right-to-Free Ride?" *Marquette University
Law School Faculty* (blog), April 19, 2018. https://law.marquette.edu/facultyblog
/2018/04/right-to-work-or-right-to-free-ride/.

Carroll, Thomas J., and Greg Niehaus. "Pension Plan Funding and Corporate Debt
Ratings." *Journal of Risk and Insurance* 65, no. 3 (1998): 427–43.

Caughey, Devin. *The Unsolid South.* Princeton, NJ: Princeton University Press, 2018.

CBS News. "Court Hit with Sad Stories from Detroit Retirees Objecting to Bankruptcy
Cuts." *CBS News*, accessed July 9, 2024. https://www.cbsnews.com/detroit/news
/court-hit-with-sad-stories-from-detroit-retirees-objecting-to-bankruptcy-cuts/.

Center for Responsive Politics. "We Are Open Secrets." 2019. https://www.opensecrets
.org/.

Church, Steven. "Calpers No Better Than Bondholders in Stockton Bankruptcy."
Bloomberg, 2014. https://www.bloomberg.com/news/articles/2014-10-01/calpers
-denied-special-protection-in-stockton-bankruptcy.

Citizens Budget Commission. "Facing Tough Challenges: What to Look for in New
York State's Fiscal Year 2025 Budget." Press release, January 11, 2024. https://
cbcny.org/newsroom/cbc-releases-facing-tough-challenges-what-look-new
-york-states-fiscal-year-2025-budget.

Clark, Terry Nichols, and Vincent Hoffmann-Martinot, eds. *The New Political Culture.* Boulder, CO: Westview, 1998.

Clingermayer, James C., and Dan B. Wood. "Disentangling Patterns of State Debt
Financing." *American Political Science Review* 89, no. 1 (1995): 108–20.

Cohen, Marty, David Karol, Hans Noel, and John Zaller. *The Party Decides: Presidential Nominations Before and After Reform.* Chicago: University of Chicago Press, 2009.

Collins, Brian K. "Credit and Credibility: State Government Bond Ratings, 1975–2002." *American Review of Public Administration* 44, no. 1 (2014): 112–23.

Conant, James K. "State of Wisconsin Budgeting After the Great Recession." *Municipal Finance Journal* 40 (2019): 37–58.

Conant, James K. "Wisconsin's Budget Deficit: Size, Causes, Remedies, and Consequences." *Public Budgeting and Finance* 23 (2003): 5–25. https://doi.org/10.1111/1540-5850.2302002.

Cornaggia, Jess, Kimberly J. Cornaggia, and Ryan D. Israelsen. "Credit Ratings and the Cost of Municipal Financing." *Review of Financial Studies* 31, no. 6 (2018): 2038–79.

Cramer, Katherine J. *The Politics of Resentment: Rural Consciousness in Wisconsin and the Rise of Scott Walker.* Chicago: University of Chicago Press, 2016.

Dao, James. "Comptroller Sues to Block Pataki Pension Fund Plan." *New York Times,* July 6, 1995.

Dao, James. "Cuomo Appeals to Union Leaders for Help in Campaign." *New York Times,* August 4, 1994.

Davey, Monica. "Indiana Governor Signs a Law Creating a 'Right to Work' Stat." *New York Times,* February 1, 2012.

Davey, Monica, and Mary Williams Walsh. "Billions in Debt, Detroit Tumbles Into Insolvency." *New York Times,* July 19, 2013, A1.

Davis, Mike. "The Barren Marriage of American Labour and the Democratic Party." *New Left Review,* no. 124 (1980): 43.

Dawson, Michael. *Behind the Mule: Race and Class in African-American Politics.* Princeton, NJ: Princeton University Press, 1994.

De Benedictis-Kessner, Justin, and Christopher Warshaw. "Accountability for the Local Economy at All Levels of Government in United States Elections." *American Political Science Review* 114, no. 3 (2020): 660–76.

Depken, Craig A., and Courtney L. Lafountain. "Fiscal Consequences of Public Corruption: Empirical Evidence from State Bond Ratings." *Public Choice* 126, no. 1–2 (2006): 75–85.

Diamond, Randy. "Read Florio's Lips: New State Taxes." *Christian Science Monitor,* June 22, 1990.

Dick, Donald L. "Bondholders vs. Retirees in Municipal Bankruptcies: The Political Economy of Chapter 9." *American Bankruptcy Law Journal* 92 (2018): 73–103.

Diegmueller, Karen. "Whitman Confronts N.J. Union on Divisive Issues." *Education Week,* February 23, 1994.

DiMaggio, Marco, and Marco Pagano. "Financial Disclosure and Market Transparency with Costly Information Processing." *Review of Finance* 22, no. 1 (2018): 117–53.

DiSalvo, Daniel. *Government Against Itself: Public Union Power and Its Consequences.* New York: Oxford University Press, 2015.

DiSalvo, Daniel, and Jeffrey Kucik. "Unions, Parties, and the Politics of State Government Legacy Cost." *Policy Studies Journal* 46, no. 3 (2018): 573–97.

Dresser, Laura, Joel Rogers, and Pablo Aquiles-Sanchez. *The State of Working Wisconsin 2023.* Madison: University of Wisconsin-Madison, COWS (High Road Strategy Center), September 2023. https://highroad.wisc.edu/wp-content/uploads /sites/1368/2023/09/SOWW2023-FINAL-REPORT-1.pdf.

Dye, Richard F., Nancy W. Hudspeth, and David F. Merriman. "Transparency in State Budgets: A Search for Best Practices." Institute of Government and Public Affairs at the University of Illinois, 2011.

Elder, Erick M., and Gary A. Wagner. "Political Effects on Pension Underfunding." *Economics and Politics* 27, no. 1 (2015): 1–27.

Elliott, Douglas J. "State and Local Pension Funding Deficits: A Primer." Brookings Institution, Washington, DC, 2010.

Ellis, Michael A., and D. Eric Schansberg. "The Determinants of State Government Debt Financing." *Public Finance Review* 27, no. 6 (1999): 571–87.

Elsen-Rooney, Michael, and Alex Zimmerman. "Eric Adams School Funding Cuts Less Than Expected." *Chalkbeat,* January 17, 2024. https://www.chalkbeat.org /newyork/2024/01/17/eric-adams-school-funding-cuts-less-than-expected.

Equable Institute. "Wisconsin Pension Laws." November 20, 2021. https://equable.org /wisconsin-pension-laws/.

Erie, Steven, Vladimir Kogan, and Scott MacKenzie. *Paradise Plundered: Fiscal Crisis and Governance Failures in San Diego.* Stanford, CA: Stanford University Press, 2011.

Erikson, Robert S., Michael MacKuen, and James A. Stimson. *The Macro Polity.* Cambridge: Cambridge University Press, 2002.

Erikson, Robert S., Gerald C. Wright, and John P. McIver. *Statehouse Democracy: Public Opinion and Policy in the American States.* Cambridge: Cambridge University Press, 1993.

Federal Labor Relations Authority. "A Short History of the Statute." Accessed July 17, 2024. https://www.flra.gov/resources-training/resources/statute-and-regulations /statute/short-history-statute.

Finnegan, William. "The Storm." *New Yorker,* February 27, 2012.

Fiorina, Morris P. "Economic Retrospective Voting in American National Elections: A Micro-Analysis." *American Journal of Political Science* 22, no. 2 (1978): 426–43.

Fiorina, Morris P. *Economic Retrospective Voting in American National Elections: A Micro-Analysis.* New Haven, CT: Yale University Press, 1981.

Fitzsimmons, Emma G., and Ashley Wong. "Unions in New York Bristle After de Blasio Issues Testing Mandate." *New York Times,* July 28, 2021, A14.

Flavin, Patrick, and Michael T. Hartney. "When Government Subsidizes Its Own: Collective Bargaining Laws as Agents of Political Mobilization." *American Journal of Political Science* 59, no. 4 (2015): 896–911.

Folke, Olle, Shigeo Hirano, and James Snyder. "Patronage and Elections in U.S. States." *American Political Science Review* 105, no. 3 (2011): 567–85.

Fox, Justin. "Government Transparency and Policymaking." *Public Choice* 131 (2007): 23–44.

Fox Piven, Frances. "The Urban Crisis: Who Got What and Why." In *The Fiscal Crisis of American Cities*, ed. Roger E. Alcaly and David Mermelstein, 197–216. New York: Random House, 1977.

Freeman, Joshua B. *Working-Class New York: Life and Labor Since World War II.* New York: New Press, 2001.

Freeman, Richard B. "What Do Unions Do . . . to Voting?" National Bureau of Economic Research, Cambridge, MA, 2003.

Fried, Joseph P. "Jim Florio, New Jersey Governor Undone by Tax Hike, Dies at 85." *New York Times*, September 26, 2022.

Friedrichs v. California Teachers Association, 578 U.S. ___ (2016).

Frum, David. "Why Mitch McConnell Wants States to Go Bankrupt." *The Atlantic*, April 25, 2020. https://www.theatlantic.com/ideas/archive/2020/04/why-mitch -mcconnell-wants-states-go-bankrupt/610714/.

Frymer, Paul. *Uneasy Alliances: Race and Party Competition in America.* Princeton, NJ: Princeton University Press, 2010.

Fuchs, Ester R. *Mayors and Money: Fiscal Policy in New York and Chicago.* Chicago: University of Chicago Press, 1992.

Gavazza, Alessandro, and Alessandro Lizzeri. "Transparency and Economic Policy." *Review of Economic Studies* 76, no. 3 (2009): 1023–48.

Gies, Heather. "Supreme Court Decision in Janus Case Deals a Blow to Public Sector Unions." *In These Times*, March 27, 2019. https://inthesetimes.com/article/janus -afscme-supreme-court-union-labor-agency-fees.

Glaberson, William. "N.Y. Judges, Angry on Pay, Seek Union-Like Group." *New York Times*, January 11, 2011. https://www.nytimes.com/2011/01/12/nyregion /12judges.html.

Glauber, Bill, and Patrick Marley. "Scott Walker's Eight Years as Governor Ushered in Profound Change in Wisconsin." *Milwaukee Journal Sentinel*, January 4, 2019. https://www.jsonline.com/story/news/politics/2019/01/04/scott-walkers -eight-years-wisconsin-governor-were-consequential/2473616002/.

Goldmacher, Shane, and Jesse McKinley. "Flexing Their Support for Cuomo, Key Unions Leave Working Families Party." *New York Times*, April 13, 2018. https:// www.nytimes.com/2018/04/13/nyregion/cuomo-nixon-wfp-labor-governor -election.html.

Gray, Jerry. "Pension Deal Announced in Trenton." *New York Times*, June 16, 1994.

Greenberg, Howard Martin. "A History of the New York State Teachers Retirement System: 1960–1979." PhD diss., New York University, 1980. ProQuest (303033211).

Greenhouse, Steven. "A Gathering Storm Over 'Right to Work' in Indiana." *New York Times*, January 2, 2012.

Greenhouse, Steven. "Ohio Wages Fierce Fight on Collective Bargaining." *New York Times*, October 15, 2011.

Grossman, Gene M., and Elhanan Helpman. *Special Interest Politics.* Cambridge, MA: MIT Press, 2001.

Grumbach, Jacob. *Laboratories Against Democracy: How National Parties Transformed State Politics.* Vol. 184. Princeton, NJ: Princeton University Press, 2022.

Hacker, Jacob S. "Privatizing Risk Without Privatizing the Welfare State: The Hidden Politics of Social Policy Retrenchment in the United States." *American Political Science Review* 98, no. 2 (2004): 243–60.

Hacker, Jacob S., and Paul Pierson. "After the Master Theory: Downs, Schattschneider, and the Rebirth of Policy-Focused Analysis." *Perspectives on Politics* 12, no. 3 (2014): 643–62.

Hakim, Danny. "After a Rebellion That Shook Albany, Three Falls From Grace." *New York Times*, May 9, 2012.

Hakim, Danny. "Paterson and Unions Agree on Limits for New Pensions." *New York Times*, June 5, 2009.

Hakim, Danny. "Paterson Vetoes Pension Bill, Drawing Union's Fire." *New York Times*, June 3, 2009.

Hakim, Danny, John Eligon, and Thomas Kaplan. "Cuomo, Admitting Setbacks, Says He Asked for the Moon." *New York Times*, March 16, 2012. https://www.nytimes.com/2012/03/16/nyregion/cuomo-admits-setbacks-but-says-he-asked-for-the-moon.html?searchResultPosition=6.

Hall, Richard L., and Alan V. Deardorff. "Lobbying as Legislative Subsidy." *American Political Science Review* 100, no. 1 (2006): 69–84.

Han, Eunice S. "The Myth of Unions' Overprotection of Bad Teachers: Evidence from the District–Teacher Matched Data on Teacher Turnover." *Industrial Relations: A Journal of Economy and Society* 59, no. 2 (2020): 316–52.

Hanley, Robert. "Trenton Assails Florio Proposal for School Aid." *New York Times*, May 31, 1990.

Harrison, Brigid Callahan. "We Should Have Listened to Florio." NorthJersey.com, July 17, 2016. https://www.northjersey.com/story/opinion/2016/07/17/harrison-we-should-have-listened-to-florio/94944728/.

Harry, Ayana. "Mayor Adams Announces Reversal for Some Budget Cuts." *NY1*, January 10, 2024. https://ny1.com/nyc/manhattan/politics/2024/01/11/mayor-adams-announces-reversal-for-some-budget-cuts.

Haywood, Bradley R. "The Right to Shelter as a Fundamental Interest Under the New York State Constitution." *Columbia Human Rights Law Review* 34 (2002): 157.

Heckman, James J. "The Incidental Parameters Problem and the Problem of Initial Conditions in Estimating a Discrete Time-Discrete Data Stochastic Process." In *Structural Analysis of Discrete Data with Econometric Applications*, ed. C. F. Manski and D. McFadden, 179–95. Cambridge, MA: MIT Press, 1981.

Hertel-Fernandez, Alexander. *State Capture: How Conservative Activists, Big Businesses, and Wealthy Donors Reshaped the American States—and the Nation*. New York: Oxford University Press, 2019.

Hertel-Fernandez, Alexander, Theda Skocpol, and Jason Sclar. "When Political Mega-Donors Join Forces: How the Koch Network and the Democracy Alliance Influence Organized U.S. Politics on the Right and Left." *Studies in American Political Development* 32, no. 2 (2018): 127–65.

Hirsch, Barry T., and David A. Macpherson. "Union Membership, Coverage, Density and Employment by Occupation, 2023." Union Membership and Coverage Database from the CPS, 2011. Unionstats. https://www.unionstats.com/.

Hirsch, Barry T., and David A. Macpherson. Union Membership and Coverage Database from the CPS. Unionstats. https://www.unionstats.com/.Hirsch, Barry T., David A. Macpherson, and Wayne G. Vroman. "Estimates of Union Density by State." *Monthly Labor Review* 124, no. 7 (July 2001): 51–55.

Hodges, Ann C. "The US Labor Relations System after *Janus* v. *AFSCME*: An Early Assessment." *Employee Responsibilities and Rights Journal* 33 (2021): 49–60.

Holbritter, John Albert. "A History of the New York State Teachers Retirement System, 1921–1959." PhD diss., New York University, 1960. ProQuest (301861307).

Holbrook, Thomas M., and Emily Van Dunk. "Electoral Competition in the American States." *American Political Science Review* 87, no. 4 (1993): 955–62.

Hou, Yilin, and Daniel L. Smith. "A Framework for Understanding State Balanced Budget Requirement Systems: Reexamining Distinctive Features and an Operational Definition." *Public Budgeting and Finance* 26, no. 3 (2006): 22–45.

Howlett, Rick. "Pension Reform Bill 'A Great Beginning.'" *Louisville Public Media*, July 1, 2008.

Iafolla, Robert. "Mass Exodus of Public Union Fee Payers After High Court Ruling." *Bloomberg Law*, April 5, 2019. https://news.bloomberglaw.com/daily-labor-report/mass-exodus-of-public-union-fee-payers-after-high-court-ruling.

"Illinois Government News Release." Illinois.gov, February 9, 2015. https://www.illinois.gov/news/press-release.13216.html.

Institute for Truth in Accounting. "The 2011 Financial State of the States." Institute for Truth in Accounting, Northbrook, IL, 2013. https://www.data-z.org/library/doclib/2011-FSOS.pdf.

"It All Comes Together." Government Law Center at Albany Law School. 2014. https://www.albanylaw.edu/centers/government-law-center/thought-leadership/three-men-room.

Iversen, Torben, and David Soskice. "Electoral Institutions and the Politics of Coalitions: Why Some Democracies Redistribute More than Others." *American Political Science Review* 100, no. 2 (2006): 165–81.

Jackson, John S. *The 2014 Illinois Governor Race: Quinn vs. Rauner.* Carbondale, IL: Paul Simon Public Policy Institute, 2015.

Janus v. American Federation of State, County, and Municipal Employees, Council 31, 2018. https://www.supremecourt.gov/opinions/17pdf/16-1466_2b3j.pdf.

Jimenez, Benedict S. "Management Quality and State Bond Ratings: Exploring the Links Between Public Management and Fiscal Outcomes." *International Journal of Public Administration* 34, no. 12 (2011): 783–99.

Joffee, Marc. "OpenGov Voices: A Transparent Approach to Understanding Local Government Debt." Sunlight Foundation, Washington, DC, 2013.

Johnson, Craig L., and Kenneth A. Kriz. "Fiscal Institutions, Credit Ratings, and Borrowing Costs." *Public Budgeting and Finance* 25, no. 1 (2005): 84–103.

Johnson, Richard W., Owen Haaga, and Benjamin G. Southgate. "Understanding the Growth in Government Contributions to New York State's Public Pension Plans." Urban Institute, Washington, DC, June 2016.

Jones, Ronald L., R. Kinney Poynter, Relmond Van Daniker, Kevin Johnson, Robert J. Shea, Thad Juszczak, and Robert Childtree. "Charting a Course Through Stormy Seas: State Financial Executives in 2012." NASACT–AGA 2012 Survey of State Financial Executives, 2012.

Joseph, Cameron. "Thompson's Work with Unions as Governor Could Hurt His Senate Campaign." *The Hill*, December 20, 2011. https://thehill.com/blogs/ballot -box/senate-races/100888-thompsons-work-with-unions-as-governor-could -hurt-his-senate-campaign/.

"J.P. Morgan Insights: A Rare Municipal Bond Opportunity—Equity-Like Yields." J.P. Morgan Private Bank. Accessed July 29, 2024. https://privatebank.jpmorgan .com/nam/en/insights/markets-and-investing/ideas-and-insights/a-rare -municipal-bond-opportunity-equity-like-yields#fn9.

Kaplan, Thomas. "Major New York Unions Angry at Pension Vote, Plan to Boycott Hispanic Conference." *New York Times*, March 22, 2012. https://www.nytimes.com /2012/03/23/nyregion/major-new-york-unions-angry-at-pension-vote-plan-to -boycott-hispanic-conference.html?searchResultPosition=9.

Kashyap, Anil K., and Natalia Kovrijnykh. "Who Should Pay for Credit Ratings and How?" *Review of Financial Studies* 29, no. 2 (2016): 420–56.

Kass, Amanda, Andrew Crosby, and Brenda Parker. "A Vicious Cycle: Fiscal Intervention, Pension Underfunding, and Instability in (Re) Making Racialized Geographies." *Environment and Planning A: Economy and Space* 55, no. 7 (2023): 1780–98.

Katzenstein, Peter J. *Small States in World Markets: Industrial Policy in Europe.* Ithaca, NY: Cornell University Press, 1985.

Kentucky Chamber of Commerce. "Pension Crisis." February 25, 2024. https://www.kychamber.com/sites/default/files/pdfs/Pension%20Crisis%20-%20Feb%2025%20Edits.pdf.

Kentucky Chamber of Commerce. "Right to Work 2017." https://www.kychamber.com/issues/2019-priorities/rtw.

Kentucky Teachers' Retirement System. "History." https://trs.ky.gov/home/history/.

Kerr, Peter. "Florio Facing Revolt by 4 on Tax Plan." *New York Times*, November 14, 1990.

Kerr, Peter. "Florio School-Aid Package Gains Final Approval." *New York Times*, June 22, 1990.

Key, V. O. *The Responsible Electorate: Rationality in Presidential Voting 1936–1960*. Cambridge, MA: Harvard University Press, 1966.

Key, V. O. *Southern Politics in State and Nation*. New York: Knopf, 1949.

Kiewiet, D. Roderick. "The Day After Tomorrow: The Politics of Public Employee Retirement Benefits." *California Journal of Politics and Policy* 2, no. 3 (2010): 1–30.

Kiewiet, D. Roderick, and Mathew D. McCubbins. "State and Local Government Finance: The New Fiscal Ice Age." *Annual Review of Political Science* 17 (2014): 105–22.

Kiewiet, D. Roderick, and Kristin Szakaty. "Constitutional Limitations on Borrowing: An Analysis of State Bonded Indebtedness." *Journal of Law, Economics, and Organization* 12, no. 1 (1996): 62–97.

King, Gary, and Langche Zeng. "Logistic Regression in Rare Events Data." *Political Analysis* 9, no. 2 (2001): 137–63.

King, Wayne. "Old Friends Break Up: Trenton Democrats and Angry Unions." *New York Times*, May 7, 1991.

Klarner, Carl. "Competitiveness Measures: Ranney Index & Holdbrook & Van Dunk Index." *Harvard Dataverse* 1 (2013a). http://hdl.handle.net/1902.1/22519.

Klarner, Carl. "Governors Dataset." *Harvard Dataverse* 1 (2013b). http://hdl.handle.net/1902.1/20408.

Klarner, Carl. "State Partisan Balance Data, 1937–2011." *Harvard Dataverse* 1 (2013c). https://doi.org/10.7910/DVN/LZHMG3.

Kopits, George, and J. D. Craig. "Transparency in Government Operations." Occasional Paper 158, International Monetary Fund, Washington, DC, 1998.

Kousser, Thad, and Justin H. Phillips. *The Power of American Governors: Winning on Budgets and Losing on Policy*. Cambridge: Cambridge University Press, 2012.

Krauth, Olivia. "Kentucky Legislature Overrides Teacher Pension Veto, Putting New Hires on 'Hybrid' Plan." *Courier Journal*, March 29, 2021.

Krueger, Skip, and Robert W. Walker. "Divided Government, Political Turnover, and State Bond Ratings." *Public Finance Review* 36, no. 3 (2008): 259–86.

Krueger, Skip, and Robert W. Walker. "Management Practices and State Bond Ratings." *Public Budgeting and Finance* 30, no. 4 (2010): 47–70.

La Raja, Raymond J., and Brian F. Schaffner. *Campaign Finance and Political Polarization: When Purists Prevail*. Ann Arbor: University of Michigan Press, 2015.

Lasswell, Harold D. *Politics: Who Gets What, When, How*. Pickle Partners, 2018.

Laws of the State of New York Passed at the Sessions of the Legislature, Sess. 191.2, chap. 498–1096 (1968), chap. 1084.

Lax, Jeffrey R., and Justin H. Phillips. "The Democratic Deficit in the States." *American Journal of Political Science* 56, no. 1 (2012): 148–66.

Lax, Jeffrey R., and Justin H. Phillips. "Gay Rights in the States: Public Opinion and Policy Responsiveness." *American Political Science Review* 103, no. 3 (2009): 367–86.

Lenney, Jamie, Bryon Lutz, and Louise Sheiner. "The Sustainability of State and Local Government Pension Plans: A Public Finance Approach." *Brookings Papers on Economic Activity* 2021, no. 1 (2021): 1–48. https://cepr.net/wp-content/uploads/2015/11/pension-funding-2015-11.pdf.

Liebman, Bennett. "'Three Men in a Room' and Albany: Where Did the Phrase Come From?" *Government Reform* (blog), March 11, 2015. https://governmentreform.wordpress.com/2015/03/11/three-men-in-a-room-and-albany-where-did-the-phrase-come-from/.

Lilley, Mike. "Job Number One: NJEA's Leading Role in New Jersey's Pension Crisis." Sunlight Policy Center, New Jersey, June 17, 2019.

Liu, Pu, and Anjan V. Thakor. "Interest Yields, Credit Ratings, and Economic Characteristics of State Bonds: An Empirical Analysis: Note." *Journal of Money, Credit and Banking* 16, no. 3 (1984): 344–51.

Loftus, Tom. "Kentucky Supreme Court Strikes Down Pension Reform Law." *Courier Journal*, December 13, 2018.

Lohmann, Susanne. "An Information Rationale for the Power of Special Interests." *American Political Science Review* 92, no. 4 (1998): 809–27.

Lowi, Theodore J. *The End of Liberalism: The Second Republic of the United States*. New York: Norton, 1969.

Lowry, Robert C., and James E. Alt. "A Visible Hand? Bond Markets, Political Parties, Balanced Budget Laws, and State Government Debt." *Economics and Politics* 13, no. 1 (2001): 49–72.

Maher, John J. "Pension Obligations and the Bond Credit Market: An Empirical Analysis of Accounting Numbers." *Accounting Review* 62, no. 4 (1987): 785–98.

Maier, Mark. *City Unions: Managing Discontent in New York City*. New Brunswick, NJ: Rutgers University Press, 1987.

Malin, Martin H. "Life After Act 10: Is There a Future for Collective Representation of Wisconsin Public Employees?" *Marquette Law Review* 96 (2012): 623–50.

Mayhew, David R. *Placing Parties in American Politics: Organization, Electoral Settings, and Government Activity in the Twentieth Century*. Princeton, NJ: Princeton University Press, 1986.

McCartin, Joseph A. "Bringing the State's Workers In: Time to Rectify an Imbalanced US Labor Historiography." *Labor History* 47, no. 1 (2006): 73–94.

McKinley Jr., James C. "Hevesi Rejects Pataki Pension Fund Plans." *New York Times*, January 20, 2004. https://www.nytimes.com/2004/01/20/nyregion/hevesi-rejects -pataki-pension-fund-plans.html?searchResultPosition=1.

Mead, D. M. "The Timeliness of Financial Reporting by State and Local Governments Compared with the Needs of Users." Research Brief. Governmental Accounting Standards Board, Norwalk, CT, 2011.

Memmott, Mark, and Korva Coleman. "Michigan Governor Signs Right-To-Work Bills Into Law." NPR, December 11, 2012. https://www.npr.org/sections/the -two-way/2012/12/11/166946294/michigan-lawmakers-poised-to-pass-right -to-work-bill-outraging-union-protesters.

Mickey, Robert. *Paths Out of Dixie: The Democratization of Authoritarian Enclaves in America's Deep South, 1944–1972.* Princeton, NJ: Princeton University Press, 2015.

Mitchell, Olivia S., and Edwin C. Hustead, eds. *Pensions in the Public Sector.* Philadelphia: University of Pennsylvania Press, 2001.

Moe, Terry M. "Political Control and the Power of the Agent." *Journal of Law, Economics, and Organization* 22, no. 1 (2006): 1–29.

Moe, Terry M. "The Politicized Presidency." In *The New Direction in American Politics*, ed. John E. Chubb and Paul E. Peterson, 235–71. Washington, DC: Brookings Institution Press, 1985.

Moe, Terry M. "The Politics of Bureaucratic Structure." In *Can the Government Govern?*, ed, John E. Chubb and Paul E. Peterson, 267–329. Washington, DC: Brookings Institution, 1989.

Moe, Terry M. *Special Interest: Teachers Unions and America's Public Schools.* Washington, DC: Brookings Institution Press, 2011.

Mollenkopf, John H. *A Phoenix in the Ashes: The Rise and Fall of the Koch Coalition in New York City Politics.* Princeton, NJ: Princeton University Press, 1994.

Monahan, Amy B. "When a Promise Is Not a Promise: Chicago-Style Pensions." *UCLA Law Review* 64 (2017): 356–82.

Munnell, Alicia H. *State and Local Pensions: What Now?* Washington, DC: Brookings Institution, 2012.

Munnell, Alicia H., Jean-Pierre Aubry, and Mark Cafarelli. "How Did State/Local Plans Become Underfunded?" *State and Local Pension Plans* 42 (2015): 1–7.

Munnell, Alicia H., Jean-Pierre Aubry, and Laura Quinby. "The Impact of Pensions on State Borrowing Costs." Issue in Brief 14 Center for Retirement Research, Chestnut Hill, MA, 2011.

Munnell, Alicia H., Jean-Pierre Aubry, and Mark Cafarelli. "An Update on Pension Obligation Bonds." Center for Retirement Research at Boston College, July 2014.

Murray, Dave. "Proposal 2: Unions Lose Big-Money, High-Profile Effort to Restore Clout in Michigan." MLive, November 7, 2012. https://www.mlive.com/politics /2012/11/post_88.html.

Nack, David, Michael Childers, Alexia Kulwiec, and Armando Ibarra. "The Recent Evolution of Wisconsin Public Worker Unionism Since Act 10." *Labor Studies Journal* 45, no. 2 (2020): 147–65.

National Association of State Auditors, Comptrollers, and Treasurers. "Time to Complete the States' CAFRs." Lexington, KY, 2005–2011.

National Conference of State Legislatures. "Pension and Retirement Plan Enactments in State Legislatures." 1999–2011. https://www.ncsl.org/?tabid=13399.

National Conference of State Legislatures. "State Partisan Balance Data, 1999–2011." *Harvard Dataverse*, 2011. http://hdl.handle.net/1902.1/12650 V2.

National Conference of State Legislatures. "State Partisan Composition." Updated October 29, 2024. https://www.ncsl.org/about-state-legislatures/state-partisan -composition.

National Governors Association. "James E. McGreevey." https://www.nga.org /governor/james-e-mcgreevey/.

National Institute on Money in State Politics. "Follow the Money, 1995–2012." https:// www.followthemoney.org/.

National Right to Work Committee. "State Right to Work Timeline." Accessed July 17, 2024. https://nrtwc.org/facts/state-right-to-work-timeline-2016/.

New Jersey Geological and Water Survey. "Geoscience Information in New Jersey." Out of the Rock 2, no. 2 (1996): 1–8. https://www.nj.gov/dep/njgs/enviroed /newsletter/v2n2.pdf

New Jersey League of Municipalities. "Pension Systems." https://www.njlm.org/884 /Pension-Systems.

New Jersey Public Employment Relations Commission. "Chapter 13A—Public Employment Relations Act." Current as of March 31, 2022. https://www.nj.gov /perc/documents/Chapter%2013A.pdf?ver=20220404.

New York State Public Employment Relations Board. "Taylor Law." https://www .nysenate.gov/legislation/laws/CVS/A14.

Nichols, John. "Scott Walker Promised $500K Donor He Would 'Divide and Conquer' Unions." *The Nation*, May 11, 2012. https://www.thenation.com/article/archive /scott-walker-promised-500k-donor-he-would-divide-and-conquer-unions/.

Novy-Marx, Robert, and Joshua Rauh. "The Liabilities and Risks of State-Sponsored Pension Plans." *Journal of Economic Perspectives* 23, no. 4 (2009): 191–210.

Novy-Marx, Robert, and Joshua Rauh. "Public Pension Promises: How Big Are They and What Are They Worth?" *Journal of Finance* 66, no. 4 (2011): 1211–49.

O'Brien, Maria. "The Case for Public Pension Reform: Early Evidence from Kentucky." Boston University School of Law. Accessed July 16, 2024. https://scholarship .law.bu.edu/cgi/viewcontent.cgi?article=1194&context=faculty_scholarship.

Ortega, Ralph R. "How Did New York City Reverse Its 2024 Budget Cuts?" City and State NY, January 18, 2024. https://www.cityandstateny.com/policy/2024/01/how-did-new-york-city-reverse-its-2024-budget-cuts/393450/.

Oswalt, Michael M. "The Doomed Constitutional Case Against Exclusive Representation." Issue Brief, American Constitution Society, June 2021. https://www.acslaw.org/wp-content/uploads/2021/06/Constitutional-Attacks-on-Exclusive-Representation-Oswalt.pdf.

Panizza, Ugo, and Andrea Presbitero. "Public Debt and Economic Growth: Is There a Causal Effect?" *Journal of Macroeconomics* 41 (2014): 21–41.

PBS NewsHour. "Michigan Becomes 1st State in Decades to Repeal Right-to-Work Law." March 24, 2023. https://www.pbs.org/newshour/politics/michigan-becomes-1st-state-in-decades-to-repeal-right-to-work-law.

Pearson, Rick. "Judge Drops Rauner Fair Share Suit, Lets Non-Union Workers' Case Proceed." *Chicago Tribune*, May 25, 2019. https://www.chicagotribune.com/2015/05/19/judge-drops-rauner-fair-share-suit-lets-non-union-workers-case-proceed/.

Pearson, Rick, Kim Geiger, and Monique Garcia. "U.S. Supreme Court Gives Rauner Major Victory Over Labor, in Ruling That Could Undercut Public Worker Unions Nationwide." *Chicago Tribune*, May 15, 2019. https://www.chicagotribune.com/2018/06/27/us-supreme-court-gives-rauner-major-victory-over-labor-in-ruling-that-could-undercut-public-worker-unions-nationwide/.

Pérez-Peña, Richard. "Legislators Back Pension Rises for Retired Public Employees." *New York Times*, June 14, 2000.

Pernsteiner, Aimee, D'Arcy Becker, Matthew Fish, William F. Miller, and Dawna Drum. "Budget Repair or Budget Spectacle? The Passage of Wisconsin's Act 10." *Public Money and Management* 36, no. 7 (2016): 507–14.

Peterson, Iver. "New Jersey Teachers Flex Muscles, but Carefully." *New York Times*, April 19, 1994. https://www.nytimes.com/1994/04/19/nyregion/new-jersey-teachers-flex-muscles-but-carefully.html.

Peterson, Iver. "On Politics; Is McGreevey Squeezing Until Everyone Yells 'Taxes'?" *New York Times*, February 2, 2003.

Pew Trusts. "Kentucky's Successful Public Pension Reform." September 27, 2013. https://www.pewtrusts.org/en/research-and-analysis/issue-briefs/2013/09/27/kentuckys-successful-public-pension-reform.

Pew Trusts. "The Trillion Dollar Gap: Underfunded State Retirement Systems and the Roads to Reform." February 18, 2010. https://www.pewtrusts.org/en/research-and-analysis/reports/2010/02/10/the-trillion-dollar-gap.

Poterba, James M., and Kim S. Rueben. "Fiscal News, State Budget Rules, and Tax-Exempt Bond Yields." *Journal of Urban Economics* 50, no. 3 (2001): 537–62.

Poterba, James M., and Kim S. Rueben. "State Fiscal Institutions and the US Municipal Bond Market." In *State Fiscal Institutions and the US Municipal Bond Market*, 181–208. Chicago: University of Chicago Press, 1999.

Prah, Pamela M., Adam Rotmil, and Stephen C. Fehr. "Infographic: S&P State Credit Ratings, 2001–2014." Pew Trusts, 2014. http://www.pewtrusts.org/en/research -and-analysis/blogs/stateline/2014/06/09/sp-ratings-2014.

Prat, Andrea. "The Wrong Kind of Transparency." *American Economic Review* 95, no. 3 (2005): 862–77.

Primo, David M., and James M. Snyder. "Party Strength, the Personal Vote, and Government Spending." *American Journal of Political Science* 54, no. 2 (2010): 354–70.

"Public Pension Shortfalls and State Economic Growth: A Preliminary Examination." Center for Retirement Research at Boston College, April 2023. https:// crr.bc.edu/wp-content/uploads/2023/04/IB_23-8.pdf.

Public Plans Data. Center for Retirement Research at Boston College, Mission Square Research Institute, National Association of State Retirement Administrators, and the Government Finance Officers Association, 2001–2022. https:// publicplansdata.org/public-plans-database/.

Rachleff, Peter. "The Right-to-Work Offensive: Tracking the Spread of the Anti-Union Virus." *New Labor Forum* 21, no. 1 (2012): 22–29. https://doi.org/10.4179 /NLF.211.0000005.

Randazzo, Anthony, and Scott Alexander. "Calm Amid the Chaos: Wisconsin's Pension System and the 2008 Financial Crisis." Equable Institute, January 31, 2020. https://equable.org/wisconsin-pension-system-and-the-2008-financial-crisis/.

Ranney, Austin. "Parties in State Politics." In *Politics in the American States: A Comparative Analysis*, ed. Herbert Jacobs and Kenneth N. Vines, 45–88. Boston: Little, Brown, 1965.

Rashbaum, William K. "Adams Plans to Cut N.Y.P.D. Budget by $1 Billion." *New York Times*, January 10, 2024. https://www.nytimes.com/2024/01/10/nyregion /budget-adams-nypd.html.

"Rauner Move on Fair Share Fees Flops in Federal Court." AFSCME Council 31, March 25, 2015. https://m.afscme31.org/news/rauner-move-on-fair-share-fees -flops-in-federal-court.

Reed, Adolph L. *Stirrings in the Jug: Black Politics in the Post-Segregation Era*. Minneapolis, MN: Choice, 1999.

Resnick, Amy B. "Things Look Good for Public Sector Pensions." Government Finance Research Center, January 25, 2022. https://gfrc.uic.edu/the-government -finance-research-blog/things-look-good-for-public-sector-pensions/.

Ridgeley, Scott. "Misuse of Public Pension Assets: White Collar Crimes and Other Offenses." *Indiana Law Review* 26 (1992): 589–629.

Robbins, Mark D., and Bill Simonsen, "Do Debt Levels Influence State Borrowing Costs?" *Public Administration Review* 72, no. 4 (2012): 498–505.

Robillard, Kevin. "Gov: Unions Sparked Right-to-Work." Politico, December 11, 2012. https://www.politico.com/story/2012/12/michigan-right-to-work-rick -snyder-084918.

Rodden, Jonathan. *Hamilton's Paradox: The Promise and Peril of Fiscal Federalism*. Cambridge: Cambridge University Press, 2006.

Rogers, Steven. *Accountability in State Legislatures*. Chicago: University of Chicago Press, 2023.

Rogers, Steven. "Electoral Accountability for State Legislative Roll Calls and Ideological Representation." *American Political Science Review* 111, no. 3 (2017): 555–71.

Rogers, Steven. "National Forces in State Legislative Elections." *Annals of the American Academy of Political and Social Science* 667, no. 1 (2016): 207–25.

Rothfeld, Michael, and Chad Bray. "'Pay to Play' Probe Gets Key Guilty Plea; Focus on Rattner." *Wall Street Journal*, October 8, 2010.

Rouse, Cecilia Elena, and Lisa Barrow. "School Vouchers and Student Achievement: Recent Evidence and Remaining Questions." *Annual Review of Economics* 1, no. 1 (2009): 17–42.

Rubinfeld, Daniel. "Credit Ratings and the Market for General Obligation Municipal Bonds." *National Tax Journal* 26, no. 1 (1973): 17–27.

Saltzman, Gregory M. "Bargaining Laws as a Cause and Consequence of the Growth of Teacher Unionism." *ILR Review* 38, no. 3 (1985): 335–51.

Saltzman, Gregory M. "Public Sector Bargaining Laws Really Matter: Evidence from Ohio and Illinois." In *When Public Sector Workers Unionize*, ed. Richard B. Freeman and Casey Ichniowski, 41–80. Chicago: University of Chicago Press, 1988.

Schattschneider, Elmer E. *The Semi-Sovereign People: A Realist's View of Democracy in America*. Hinsdale, IL: Dryden, 1975.

Schleicher, David. *In a Bad State: Responding to State and Local Budget Crises*. New York: Oxford University Press, 2023.

Schlesinger, Joseph A. "The Primary Goals of Political Parties: A Clarification of Positive Theory." *American Political Science Review* 69, no. 3 (1975): 840–49.

School for Workers. "Wisconsin Labor History: An Epic Story." April 9, 2020. https://schoolforworkers.wisc.edu/wisconsin-labor-history-an-epic-story/.

"Scott Walker's Act 10 Caused an Uproar, but Things Are Mostly Back to Normal." The Fordham Institute, August 25, 2015. https://fordhaminstitute.org/national/commentary/scott-walkers-act-10-caused-uproar-things-are-mostly-back-normal.

Secunda, Paul M. "The Wisconsin Public-Sector Labor Disputes of 2011." *ABAJ Labor and Employment Law Journal* 27 (2011): 293–310.

Senate Fiscal Agency. "Senate Fiscal Agency Analysis of Proposal 12–2." November 2012. https://www.senate.michigan.gov/SFA/Publications/BallotProps/Proposal12-2.pdf.

Shefter, Martin. *Political Crisis/Fiscal Crisis: The Collapse and Revival of New York City*. New York: Columbia University Press, 1992.

Shelly, Bryan. "Rebels and Their Causes: State Resistance to National Government." *American Politics Research* 36, no. 4 (2008): 591–621.

Shor, Boris. "Aggregate State Legislator Shor-McCarty Ideology Data, July 2020 Update." *Harvard Dataverse* 1, 2020. https://doi.org/10.7910/DVN/AP54NE.

Shor, Boris. "July 2014 Update: Aggregate Data for Ideological Mapping of American Legislatures." *Harvard Dataverse*, July 2014.

Shor, Boris, and Nolan McCarty. "The Ideological Mapping of American Legislatures." *American Political Science Review* 105, no. 3 (2011): 530–51.

Skeel, David A. "The Education of Detroit's Pension and Bond Creditors." *Wharton School of the University of Pennsylvania Issue Briefs* 2, no. 1 (2014).

Skorup, Jarrett. "AFSCME Has Lost 200K Plus Members and Fee Payers Nationwide Since Janus Decision." Mackinac Center for Public Policy, May 10, 2023. https://www.mackinac.org/blog/2023/afscme-has-lost-200k-plus-members-and-fee-payers-nationwide-since-janus-decision.

Slater, Joseph E. "State Legislation as a Fulcrum for Change: Wisconsin's Public Sector Labor Law, and the Revolution in Politics and Worker Rights." *bepress Legal Repository* (2005): 516.

Spicuzza, Mary, and Steven Verburg. "From a 'Distraction' to Fast-Tracked to His Desk: Scott Walker Poised to Sign Right-to-Work Bill." *Wisconsin State Journal*, February 26, 2015. https://wiscnews.com/news/local/government-politics/from-a-distraction-to-fast-tracked-to-his-desk-scott-walker-poised-to-sign-right/article_be51da88-a2cb-5ed4-9d6e-1da1d289edba.html.

"Spitzer Resigns After Sex Scandal, Pressure." NPR, March 12, 2008. https://www.npr.org/2008/03/12/88134976/spitzer-resigns-after-sex-scandal-pressure.

Stallmann, Judith I., Steven Deller, Lindsay Amiel, and Craig Maher. "Tax and Expenditure Limitations and State Credit Ratings." *Public Finance Review* 40, no. 5 (2012): 643–69.

Standard and Poor's. *U.S. Public Finance: U.S. State Ratings Methodology*. 2011.

"Statement No. 67: Financial Reporting for Pension Plans." Governmental Accounting Standards Board. GASB Home, June 2012. https://gasb.org/page/ShowPdf?path=GASBS67.pdf&title=GASBS+67.

"Statement No. 68: Accounting and Financial Reporting for Pensions." Governmental Accounting Standards Board. GASB Home, June 2012. https://gasb.org/page/document?pdf=GASBS%2B68.pdf&title=GASBS%2B68.

Stein, Jason. "Why Scott Walker Still Has Some Union Support." *Milwaukee Journal Sentinel*, February 19, 2015. https://www.governing.com/topics/mgmt/why-scott-walker-still-has-some-union-support.html.

Steindel, Charles. "New Jersey's Pension Problems: Turning the Corner?" Unpublished manuscript, 2021.

Steindel, Charles. "Public Pension Shortfalls and State Economic Growth: A Preliminary Examination." *Business Economics* 55, no. 3 (2020): 138–49.

Steyer, Robert. "New Jersey Fully Funds Pension System for Third Straight Fiscal Year." *Pensions and Investments*, July 5, 2023.

Stokes, Leah C. "Electoral Backlash Against Climate Policy: A Natural Experiment on Retrospective Voting and Local Resistance to Public Policy." *American Journal of Political Science* 60, no. 4 (2016): 958–74.

Stone, Clarence N. *Regime Politics: Governing Atlanta, 1946–1988.* Lawrence: University Press of Kansas, 1989.

Strauss, Daniel. "Democrat Tony Evers Ousts Wisconsin Gov. Scott Walker." Politico, November 7, 2018. https://www.politico.com/story/2018/11/07/scott-walker-vs -tony-evers-wisconsin-governor-race-results-2018-965594.

Sunshine Review. "State Transparency Checklist." 2011.

Surka, Michelle, and Elizabeth Ridlington. "Following the Money: How 50 States Rate in Providing Online Access to Government Spending Data." 2016.

Tausanovitch, Chris, and Christopher Warshaw. "Measuring Constituent Policy Preferences in Congress, State Legislatures, and Cities." *Journal of Politics* 75, no. 2 (2013): 330–42.

Thompson v. Marietta Education Association, No. 19–4217, 6th Cir. (2020).

Thompson, William N. "Public Pension Plans: The Need for Scrutiny and Control." *Public Personnel Management* 6, no. 4 (1977): 203–24.

Tolbert, Pamela S., and Lynne G. Zucker. "Institutional Sources of Change in the Formal Structure of Organizations: The Diffusion of Civil Service Reform, 1880–1935." *Administrative Science Quarterly* 28, no. 1 (1983): 22–39.

Treadway, Jack M. *Public Policymaking in the American States.* New York: Praeger, 1985.

Tripathi, Micky, Stephen Ansolabehere, and James M. Snyder. "Are PAC Contributions and Lobbying Linked? New Evidence from the 1995 Lobby Disclosure Act." *Business and Politics* 4, no. 2 (2002): 131–55.

Trounstine, Jessica. "All Politics Is Local: The Reemergence of the Study of City Politics." *Perspectives on Politics* 7, no. 3 (2009): 611–18.

Trounstine, Jessica. *Political Monopolies in American Cities: The Rise and Fall of Bosses and Reformers.* Chicago: University of Chicago Press, 2009.

Truth in Accounting. *The Truth About Balanced Budgets: A Fifty State Study.* Glencoe, IL: Truth in Accounting, 2009.

Urban Institute. "Kentucky State Fiscal Brief." Accessed July 16, 2024. https://www .urban.org/policy-centers/cross-center-initiatives/state-and-local-finance -initiative/projects/state-fiscal-briefs/kentucky.

Urban Institute. "New Jersey State Fiscal Brief." October 2024. https://www.urban .org/policy-centers/cross-center-initiatives/state-and-local-finance-initiative /projects/state-fiscal-briefs/new-jersey.

Urban Institute. "New York State Fiscal Brief." October 2024. https://www.urban .org/policy-centers/cross-center-initiatives/state-and-local-finance-initiative /projects/state-fiscal-briefs/new-york.

U.S. Bureau of Economic Analysis. "Regional Economic Accounts." 1995–2012. http:// www.bea.gov/regional/.

U.S. Bureau of Labor Statistics. "BLS Statistics on Unemployment." 1995–2012. http://www.bls.gov/bls/unemployment.htm.

U.S. Census Bureau. "Annual Survey of Public Employment and Payroll." https://www.census.gov/programs-surveys/apes.html.

U.S. Census Bureau, Census of Governments. "Annual Survey of State Government Finances." 1995–2012. https://www.census.gov/programs-surveys/gov-finances.html.

U.S. Census Bureau and Bureau of Labor Statistics. "Current Population Survey (CPS)." 1995–2012. http://www.census.gov/cps/.

Valletta, R. G., and R. B. Freeman. "When Public Employees Unionize." In *The NBER Public Sector Collective Bargaining Law Data Set*, ed. Richard B. Freeman and Casey Ichniowski. Chicago: NBER/University of Chicago Press, 1988.

"Video: Walker Explains 'Divide and Conquer' Strategy." News 8 Now, May 11, 2012. https://www.news8000.com/news/local-news/video-walker-explains-divide-conquer-strategy/article_5cbf4739-f02c-5edf-80a8-31538a417853.html.

Walker, Hannah, and Dylan Bennett. "The Whiteness of Wisconsin's Wages: Racial Geography and the Defeat of Public Sector Labor Unions in Wisconsin." *New Political Science* 37, no. 2 (2015): 181–203.

Walsh, Mary Williams. "A Sour Surprise for Public Pensions: Two Sets of Books." *New York Times*, September 18, 2016, BU1.

Wang, Qiushi, and Jun Peng. "Political Embeddedness of Public Pension Governance: An Event History Analysis of Discount Rate Changes." *Public Administration Review* 78, no. 5 (2018): 785–94.

Wang, Vivian. "How 3 Little Letters (I.D.C.) Are Riling Up New York Progressives." *New York Times*, September 11, 2018.

Weinberg, Sheila, and Eileen Norcross. "A Judge in Their Own Cause: GASB 67/68 and the Continued Mismeasurement of Public Sector Pension Liabilities." *Journal of Law, Economics and Policy* 14 (2017): 62.

Weiner, Rachel. "Issue 2 Falls, Ohio Collective Bargaining Law Repealed." *Washington Post*, November 8, 2011.

West Virginia Consolidated Public Retirement Board. "Pension Trust Funds of the State of West Virginia: Comprehensive Annual Financial Report for the Fiscal Years Ended June 30, 2017 and 2016, 2018."

White, Lawrence J. "Credit Rating Agencies: An Overview." *Annual Review of Financial Economics* 5, no. 1 (2013): 93–122.

"WI Democratic Lawmakers Flee to Prevent Vote." NPR, February 17, 2011. https://www.npr.org/2011/02/17/133847336/wis-democratic-lawmakers-flee-to-prevent-vote.

Wildavsky, Aaron. "The Goldwater Phenomenon: Purists, Politicians, and the Two-Party System." *Review of Politics* 27, no. 3 (1965): 386–413.

Wisconsin Department of Employee Trust Funds. "History of Employee Trust Funds." Accessed July 17, 2024. https://etf.wi.gov/boards/joint/history-etf/direct.

Wisconsin Historical Society. "Labor Unions in Wisconsin History." https://www
.wisconsinhistory.org/Records/Article/CS1709#:~:text=Wisconsin's%20
first%20labor%20unions%20were,working%20conditions%20through%20
collective%20action.

Wisconsin Legislative Council. "Information Memo 2015–04." Accessed July 17, 2024.
https://docs.legis.wisconsin.gov/misc/lc/information_memos/2015/im_2015_04.

Wisconsin Policy Forum. "Focus 22–04: Unions in Wisconsin." February 2022. https://
wispolicyforum.org/wp-content/uploads/2022/02/Focus_22_04_Unions.pdf.

Wisconsin Situation. "Wisconsin Gov. Scott Walker Says National Guard Ready for
Any Unrest Over Anti-Union Bill." May 22, 2011. https://wisconsinsituation
.wordpress.com/2011/05/22/wisconsin-gov-scott-walker-says-national-guard
-ready-for-any-unrest-over-anti-union-bill/.

Wolf, Stephen. "US Presidential Results & PVIs by State 1828–2012." 2015. https://
docs.google.com/spreadsheets/d/1rR9wSLHn2nC5oJyyF2gzfcA4JS4VNgI
qcj_wAPc-XzE/edit?gid=1370551484#gid=1370551484.

Wright, John R. *Interest Groups and Congress: Lobbying, Contributions, and Influence.*
Boston: Allyn and Bacon, 1996.

Xia, Han. "Can Investor-Paid Credit Rating Agencies Improve the Information
Quality of Issuer-Paid Rating Agencies?" *Journal of Financial Economics* 111, no. 2
(2014): 450–68.

Zhao, Jerry Zhirong, Camila Fonseca-Sarmiento, and Jie Tan. "America's Trillion-
Dollar Repair Bill." Working Paper. Volcker Alliance, 2019.

Index

Page numbers in *italics* refer to figures or tables.

AssetGrowth, 104–5

assets: contract, 19–20; pension, 57, 189–90; in public sector pensions, 20; valuation of, 72–73

assets/liabilities, 104–5

Aubry, Jean-Pierre, 100, 106, 110

average liabilities, 147–48

bankruptcy, states filing for, 34, 96–97, 228n57, 237n15

Bennett, Dylan, 166

Berry, Christopher, 28, 57

Beshear, Steve, 149

Bevin, Matt, 149

bondholders, 101

bonds: GO, 97–101, *102*, 124; government's issuing, 97–98; low-rated, 97; municipal, 252n30; ratings of, 97; revenue, 100–101; states using markets in, 125; top-rated, 97; Treasury, 252n30

borrowing, 97–99, 102, 124

budgets: gimmicks used for, 71; governor's decisions on, 60–62, 160; interest costs in, 121–24, *123*; pension funds debt and spending influencing, 120–24; pension plans resources in, 67; pension policy with data for, 164–65; public sector pensions and, 21; state's constraints of, 176, 186; transparency of, 73, 82–83; United State's constraints of, 2; voters and crowd-out of, 65–68; S. Walker inheriting deficit in, 169–70

Burgos v. New Jersey, 139, 242n38

Bush, George W., 138

CAFRs. *See* Comprehensive Annual Financial Reports

calculation: of ABO, 189; of ARC, 190–91

California Public Employees Retirement System (CalPERS), 70

campaign activity, of unions, 54–55

campaign contributions, 44

captured government, 90–93

"Causes of Fiscal Transparency" (Alt), 234n20

centralized policymaking, 39

CERS. *See* County Employees Retirement System

Chafee, Lincoln, 221n1

chair elected board, 92–93

Christie, Chris, 131, 138–39

Citizens United v. Federal Election Commission, 154–55

Civil Service Employees Association, 143

Clark, Terry, 45, 57

clientelistic competition, 82–90

coalitional partners, 28

coalitional politics, 60, 68, 215–19

Coalitional Politics Hypothesis, 25, 35; examples of, 28; expected fiscal behaviors under, *127*; fiscal behaviors of, *27*; pension benefits predicted by, 29–30; pension fund bailouts in, 65; political parties and, *27*; reality from, 53; scholarly work on, 39

coalitions, 39–40

COBA NYC. *See* Correction Officers' Benevolent Association

Codey, Richard, 138

COLAs. *See* cost-of-living adjustments

collective bargaining, 155–56, 170, 178–79, 245n1

Colorado, *9*

Colorado's Public Employees Retirement Association, 235n38

Comprehensive Annual Financial Reports (CAFRs), 72, 75, 188; dishonest reporting in, 93–95;

fixed effects regression, *116–19, 123*
Flavin, Patrick, 15, 30, 179
Fletcher, Ernie, 149
Florio, Jim, 135, 139, 149
Folke, Olle, 44
Fox, Justin, 69
Friedrichs v. California Teachers Association, 177
Frymer, Paul, 17
Fuchs, Ester, 28, 176
full disclosure, 78–80
fundedness: on credit ratings, *107–8, 111–12,* 113; of unfunded liabilities, 41–42
funding: pension plans levels of, 6–7, 59, 80–82; of public pensions, 33; public pensions rates of, 21; public sector pension's contentious, 226n35
FundingRatio, 104–5
funding ratios: in ordered probit model, 110; pension board reporting, 235n38; pension plans with underreported, 200–201. *201;* revised, *81, 84–86, 88, 92, 116,* 200, 203–9, *204–5, 208–9;* self-reported, *81, 84, 86–87, 92, 118,* 200–201, 203–9, *204–5, 208–9;* of state pension plans, 1, 62–63, 113, 120, 188; transparency of, *83, 205;* union strength and, *86,* 86–90, *88;* union strength and lagged, *90–91*
fusion ballot, 145

game theoretic model, 76
Garvey, Ed, 157
GASB. *See* Governmental Accounting Standards Board
Gavazza, Alessandro, 76–77
general obligation (GO) bonds, 97–98; credit ratings of, 100–101, *102;*

pension funds competition with, 99; self-reported pension data and, 124
Gorsuch, Neil, 177
government: bonds issued by, 97–98; captured, 90–93; monopolistic, 39; New York and control of, 242n46; political parties control of, 31–32; public pension plans of, 73; rainy day fund of, 221n4; services, 66; state, 5–6, 34, 96–97, 228n57, 237n15; S. Walker with balanced, 156
Governmental Accounting Standards Board (GASB), 6, 15, 40; *Accounting and Financial Reporting for Pensions* from, 71–72; discount rates recommended by, 253n4; legal enforcement of, 233n12; reforms of, 182–85; statement No. 67 of, 182–83; statement No. 68 of, 183; unfunded liabilities results after, 183–84
government-labor framework, 173–74
governors: budgetary decisions of, 60–62, 160; contribution rates increased by Democratic, 63–65, *64;* likelihood of democratic, *217, 219;* pension legislation from, 65; political party changes and, *161;* R. Snyder as Michigan, 172–73; tax revenue changes by, 162
Great Financial Crisis (2008), 138
Great Recession, 33, 96, 142–43, 180–81
Greek financial crisis, 225n21, 234n25
gross state product (GSP), 38, *66–67,* 239n28
Gusdorf, Nathan, 184

Hartney, Michael, 15, 30, 179
Hatch, Orrin, 233n13
Hevesi, Alan, 142

New York: ARC payments by, 133, 240n15; Democratic Party in, 132, 231n31; elected comptroller in, 142; government control in, 242n46; New Jersey's similarities with, 128–30; pension reforms in, 151–52; pension system of, 14, 132–33, 140–46; political party controlling, 126–28, 130–33; public sector unionization in, *132*; regime type of, 130–33; tiered pension system in, 150; unfunded liabilities in, *148*

New York City, 128–29, 184

New York City Police Benevolent Association (NYC PBA), 35

New York Police Department (NYPD), 184

New York State Public Employees Federation, 143

Nixon, Cynthia, 145

Nixon, Richard, 156

NJEA. *See* New Jersey Education Association

nonlinear statistical model, 52, 254n7

nonpension debt, 227n44

nonpension debt interest costs, 120

Norcross, Eileen, 183

North Carolina, 130

Novy-Marx, Robert, 40–41, 188

NPL. *See* net pension liability

NYC PBA. *See* New York City Police Benevolent Association

NYPD. *See* New York Police Department

occupations, public sector, 34–35

OLS. *See* ordinary least squares

OPEB. *See* other postemployment benefit

ordered probit model, 106–10, *107–9*, 192–94, *195*

ordinary least squares (OLS), 105; of revised excess liabilities, *117*; of revised funding ratio, *116*; of self-reported excess liabilities, *119*; of self-reported funding ratio, *118*

Orr, Kevyn, 96

other postemployment benefit (OPEB), 39

PACs. *See* political action committees

Paradise Plundered (Erie), 234n18

Parker, Brenda, 181

partisan control. *See* political parties

Pataki, George, 129, 142

Paterson, David, 143

pay-to-play schemes, 142

pension assets, 57, 189–90

pension benefits: Coalitional Politics Hypothesis predicting, 29–30; of Democratic Party, 24, 26, 158, 175; employee contributions and, 78; legislation reducing, 230n21; political parties and, 25, 27–28, 175–76; of Republican Party, 24, 26, 137–38, 175–76; Special Interest Group Politics Hypothesis differences in, 29–30; taxpayer income and, 226n43

pension boards: administrative structure of, 91–92; chair types on, *210*; disclosure amount by, 92–93; employees on, 92–93; funding ratios reported by, 235n38; members, 79; selection process for, *211*; state regulation of, 75

pension data, Alabama, 229n4

pension debt, *66–67*

pension fund finances: credit grades, 237n12; honest reporting of, 89; management of, 101; transparency of, 78–79; unions and, 78–79 pension funds: balances of, 108; burden of, 229n9; contributions to, 60–62; credit rating from, *108*; debt and spending of, 120–24; federal law not governing, 40; GO bonds competition with, 99; legislation controlling, 21; net pension legislation in, 52; pay-to-play schemes involving, 142; states ratios of, 113, 120; state's spending on, 121–24; transparency of, 72; union dishonesty on, 234n17; Wisconsin's general balance in, *169*

pension legislation, 4; back-room deals for, 144–45; Democratic seats changing, *54*; expansionary, *53*, *195*, *213*, *218*; from governors, 65; net, 52; partisan control of, 158; rare events logit on, *198–99*; union strength in, 52–57, *55*

pension liability: calculating size of, 41, 45–65; data, 40–45, 103–4; Democratic and Republican governors payment of, 68; employees accumulating, 32; linear probability model of, *56*; net present value with, 72; revised, 120; risks of, 98; self-reported data on, 103–4; union strength impact on, 46

pension obligation bonds (POBs), 137, 228n56

pension plans, 126; Act 10 influence on, 167–71; assets and liabilities of, 188–90; benefit changes of, *43*; budgets with resources for, 67; contribution rates for, *63*, 73; as contributory plan, 141, 242n42; costs of borrowing in, 99; credit ratings and, 125; employee contributions to, 32, 62, 138;

financial estimations of, 73; financial sustainability of, 42–44; formula for, 228n54; funding levels of, 6–7, 59, 80–82; government and, 73; Great Recession and rebounding of, 180–81; linear regressions of contributions to, *61*; obligations, *193*; obligations and assets of, *58*; payments for, 67; politics of, 139; state-administered, 232n38; states funding ratio of, 1, 62–63, 113, 120, 188; for state workers, 49; sustainability of, 139; transparency and disclosure of, 74–76; underreported funding ratios of, 200–201. *201*; unfunded liabilities in, 41–42; of union members, 75–76; union strength and, *206–7*; voters preferring smaller, 226n43; worker types of, *212*

pension policy, 14–15; budgetary data and, 164–65; consequences of, 13; data on public, 5–6; electoral outcomes and, 157–62; national, 66–67; per capita tax changes and, *164*; of political parties, 12; politics influencing, 29; predicted probability of, *197*; public sector unions and, 55–56; taxes and, 162–65; union outcomes on, 45, *196*; voter's attention of, 28–29; voter's interest in, 158

pension reforms, 131, 150–52

Pension Revaluation Act, 136

pension system: health of, 137–38; of Kentucky, 14, 146–49; Kentucky's crisis in, 150, 152; of New Jersey, 14, 133–40, 149–50; of New York, 14, 132–33, 140–46; New York's tiered, 150; of states, 14; unfunded liabilities and, *168*, 168–69

per capita liabilities: Democratic
legislative seats and, *50–51*, 50–52;
lagged union strength and, *50–51*;
standardized, *8–9*; unfunded
liabilities and, 7; unfunded liabilities
and standardized, *8*, *10*; unions
influence on, 47–48, *48*
per capita tax, 162–63, *163–64*
percent employees on board, 92–93
PERISA. *See* Public Employee
Retirement Income Security Act
PERS. *See* Public Employees'
Retirement System
PFRS. *See* Police and Firemen's
Retirement System
pluralist political parties, 26
POBs. *See* pension obligation bonds
polarization politics, 24–25
Police and Firemen's Retirement
System (PFRS), 134
police officers, 35, 124, *193*
political action committees
(PACs), 30
political monopolies, 17
political parties: campaign contributions
of, 44; Coalitional Politics
Hypothesis and, *27*; disorganized
or pluralist, 26; election result
concerns of, 19; expansionary
pension legislation control by,
218; expected fiscal behaviors
with, *127*; government control by,
31–32; governors and change of,
161; interest groups same as, 17;
Kentucky controlled by, 126–28, 147;
legislative seats held by, 44; New
York and New Jersey controlled
by, 126–28, 130–33; partisan control
of legislatures by, *216*, *218*; pension
benefit policies and, 25, 27–28,
175–76; pension legislation control

of, 158; pension policy of, 12; per
capita tax changes by, 162–63, *163*;
polarization politics by, 24–25;
solvency approach of, 33–34; Special
Interest Group Politics Hypothesis
and, 25, *26*; state legislature control
by, *159*; states controlled by, 126–28;
strength of, 30–31; tax increases
by, 162; unions and, *197*; unions
sabotaging policy ambitions of,
· 22–23
politics: coalitional, 60, 68, 215–19;
pension policy influenced by, 29;
polarization, 24–25; of public
pension plans, 139; of public sector
labor, 177–79; reforms in, 11; union's
activities in, 227n47; voters ignorant
of state, 157–58; WFP influence on,
145–46
Prat, Andrea, 69
predicted probability, *197*
Primo, David, 28
private sector unions, 10–11
private-union membership, 166
property taxes, 140
Proposal 2, in Michigan, 172–73
protesters, 171–72
public employee pensions, 4
Public Employee Retirement Income
Security Act (PERISA), 134
Public Employees Fair Employment
Act (1967), 130
Public Employees Federation, 145
Public Employees' Retirement System
(PERS), 134
public pensions, 1; fiscal sustainability
of, 6; funding rates of, 21, 33;
interstate variations of, 6; in United
States, 3
public sector labor: in Kentucky, 146,
152; laws against, 14–15; occupations

in, 34–35; politics of, 177–79; S. Walker and, 172, 176

public sector pensions: assets and liabilities in, 20; changes to, 153; funding contentious for, 226n35; state budgets and, 21; unions future and, 179–81; in United States, 3, 186

public sector unions, 9, 130; Act 10 influencing, 180–81; concerns influencing behaviors of, 23; Democratic Party and, 3, 11, 18, 21–22, 27–28, 36–37; financial impact of, 178; interest groups and, 5; membership rates of, 30; in New Jersey, *131*; in New York, *132*; pension policy and, 55–56; Republican Party and, 3, 18, 150, 185; strength measurements of, 44

public sector workers, 19, 25, 185

public welfare, 121

Quality Education Act, 135, 150
Quinby, Laura, 100, 106, 110
Quinn, Pat, 37, 177

Raimondo, Gina, 1, 221n1
rainy day fund, of government, 221n4
random effects, 254n7
rare events logit, 194–99, *198–99*
rate of return, 41
Rauh, Joshua, 41, 188
Rauner, Bruce, 37, 154, 174, 177
recall attempt, on Walker, S., 171–72
regime types, 126–28
regression analysis, 52–53, 106, 239n31
Relative Value survey, 97
representative democracy, 18
Republican governors, 68, 160
Republican Party: enemies of, 31; Great Recession and, 142–43; Kentucky control by, 223n24;

New Jersey legislature controlled by, 129, 151; NJEA endorsed by, 135; pension benefit policies of, 24, 26, 137–38, 175–76; pension policy generosity of, 12; Pension Revaluation Act by, 136; pension solvency by, 33–34; public sector unions and, 3, 18, 150, 185

resource allocation, 94–95
retirement plans, 68, 144, 167
retrospective voters, 29
revenue: bonds, 100–101; states capacity for raising, 16–17; tax, 160–62; transparency, 234n22
revised contribution rates, *63*
revised excess liabilities, *114, 117*
revised fundedness, *111*
revised funding ratios, *81, 84, 116*, 200, 203–9; administrative structure and, *92*; CAFRs and, *85*; CAFRs with lagged, *88*; differences with, *208–9*; linear regression of, *204–5*; with union strength, *86*
revised liabilities, 80, *203*, 235n37
revised pension liabilities, 120
revised-reported pension data, 106
revised unfunded liabilities, *202*
Rhode Island, 1
right to shelter, 184
right-to-work laws, 154, 170, 250n66; Act 1 law on, 171; employees and unions in, 240n13; in Kentucky, 146; Wisconsin and, 155, 165–66
Rockefeller, Nelson, 129, 141
Roosevelt, Franklin D., 155
Rose, Shanna, 83, 202

Scalia, Antonin, 177
scarce resources, 16–17
Schaffner, Brian, 17
Schattschneider, Elmer, 16, 25

State Teachers Retirement Board, 167
state workers, 1
Steindel, Charles, 65, 67
stock market, 231n35
Stokes, Leah, 215
strong party organizations (SPO), 57
supermajorities, in states, 31
Supreme Court, 177–78; *Janus v. AFSCME* decision, 15; Kentucky, 149; New Jersey, 139; U.S., 176
Surplus-to-Expenditures, 110

tardiness, in self-reported funding ratios, *87*
taxes, 2–3; Democratic governor likelihood and, *217*, *219*; Democratic governor's revenue from, 160–62; Democratic Party increasing, 5; governor's changes in revenue from, 162; increases in, 15; pension policy and, 162–65; political parties increase of, 162; property, 140; Republican governor's revenue from, 160; S. Walker cutting, 170; Whitman lowering, 136–37
taxpayers: pension benefits and, 226n43; public employee pensions support by, 4; utility, 222n8
Taylor Law. *See* Public Employees Fair Employment Act
teachers, 35, 49, *193*
Teachers' Pension and Annuity Fund (TPAF), 133–34
Teachers' Retirement Fund, 133
Teachers' Retirement System (TRS), 140–41, 149, 253n1
Thompson, Tommy, 156–57, 169
tier 2, of tiered pension system, 242n45
tier 4, of tiered pension system, 243n48

tiered pension system, 141; in New York, 150; tier 2 of, 142, 242n45; tier 4 of, 243n48; tier 5 of, 143
timeliness: of CAFRs, *83*, 83–90; of self-reported funding ratios, *87*
top-rated bonds, 97
TPAF. *See* Teachers' Pension and Annuity Fund
Traditional Party Organizations (TPOs), 31, 56–57
transparency, 70; *Accounting and Financial Reporting for Pensions* and, 71–72; of budgets, 73; CAFRs states of, *83*; clientelistic competition and, 82–90; disclosure compared to, 74–76, 87–90; dishonest reporting and, 93–95; of fiscal budgets, 73, 82–83; of funding ratios, *83*, *205*; imperfect, 77; negative effects of, 84; of pension finances, 72, 78–80; of pension fund finances, 78–79; of pension funds, 72; of public pension plans, 74–76; revenue, 234n22; revised and self-reported liabilities, 235n37; state's fiscal, 234n20; state website, *206*; union strength and, 202, *203*
Treasury bonds, 252n30
Treasury rates, 253n4
Trounstine, Jessica, 18
TRS. *See* Teachers' Retirement System

UAAL. *See* unfunded actuarial accrued liability
UFT. *See* United Federation of Teachers
unfunded actuarial accrued liability (UAAL), 191, 237n12
unfunded benefits, 163
unfunded liabilities: calculating, 222n19; debt burden of, 99–100; Democratic

unfunded liabilities (*continued*)
union regimes and, 57; fundedness
or solvency of, 41–42; GASB results
of, 183–84; in Kentucky, 148, *148*,
150; in Kentucky, New Jersey, New
York, *148*; nonpension debt and,
227n44; pension payments and, *168*;
pension system and, *168*, 168–69;
per capita liabilities and, 7; revised
and self-reported, *202*; standardized
per capita, *8*, *10*; union strength and,
57–59
unfunded pensions, 15
uniformed workers, 49, 143, 230n23,
245n1
union leaders, 18
unions, 1; campaign activity of, 54–55;
collective bargaining with, 245n1;
demands by, 130–31; financial
behavior of, 35; financial position
of, 20; interest groups influencing,
179–80; Kentucky's rate of, 239n1;
member's pension plans of, 75–76;
New Jersey's public sector, *131*; New
York's public sector, *132*; partisan
policy ambitions sabotaged by,
22–23; pension fund finances and,
78–79; pension funds dishonesty of,
234n17; pension liability impact by,
46; pension plans and strength of,
206–7; pension policy outcomes
of, 45, *196*; per capita liabilities and
lagged strength of, *50–51*; per capita
liabilities influenced by, 47–48, *48*;
policy outcomes from, 45; political
activities of, 227n47; political
parties and, *197*; public sector, 130;
public sector pensions and future
of, 179–81; right-to-work laws
and, 240n13; state-level public
sector, 231n24; state's with lower

activity of, 150–51; transparency and
strength of, 202, *203*; Wisconsin
workers in, 153–54
union strength: CAFRs and, *90–91*;
funding ratios and, *86*, 86–90, *88*;
in pension legislation, 52–57, *55*;
pension liability impacted by, 46;
pension plans and, *206–7*; per capita
liabilities and lagged, *50–51*; revised
and self-reported funding ratios
with, *86*; transparency and, 202, *203*;
unfunded liabilities and, 57–59
United Federation of Teachers (UFT),
36, 144
United States: budget constraints
of, 2; political monopolies in, 17;
public pensions in, 3; public sector
pensions in, 3, 186

Verburg, Steven, 166
voters: budgetary crowd-out and,
65–68; diverse base of, 129;
information obtained by, 77–78;
pension policy interest of, 158;
public pension policies attention
of, 28–29; retrospective, 29; smaller
pension plans preferred by, 226n43;
state politics ignorance of, 157–58.
See also elections

Wagner, Robert, 156
Wagner Act (1935), 156
Walker, Hannah, 166
Walker, Scott, 49, 153–54; Act 10 from,
167–71; balanced government
before, 156; Black and white labor
differences from, 166–67; budget
deficit inherited by, 169–70;
divide-and-conquer strategy of,
165–67; Evers beating, 246n16;
labor as enemy to, 166; labor

unions destroyed by, 157, 165; manufacturing employment decline from, 165; public sector labor and, 172, 176; recall attempted on, 171–72; tax cuts by, 170

Walsh, Mary, 70

website transparency, *206*

Weinberg, Sheila, 183

West Virginia, 231n35

WFP. *See* Working Families Party

Whitman, Christine Todd, 136–37

Wisconsin: AFSCME formed in, 155, 245n3; collective bargaining law in, 156; general fund balance in, *169*; government-labor framework changed in, 173–74; industries, 153; labor-hostile state transformation of, 153–55; manufacturing employment decline in, 165; as right-to-work state, 155, 165–66; unionized workers in, 153–54

Wisconsin Budget Repair Bill (Act 10), 153; employees bargaining abilities influenced by, 171; public sector unions influenced by, 180–81; WRS gutted by, 170–71

Wisconsin Department of Employee Trust Funds, 168

Wisconsin Municipal Retirement Fund, 167

Wisconsin Retirement System (WRS), 167–68, 170–71

Wisconsin State Employees Association, 155

worker's rights, 174

workforce, local, 129–30

Working Families Party (WFP), 145–46

Wright, Gerald, 215

WRS. *See* Wisconsin Retirement System

Yilin Hou, 104

GPSR Authorized Representative: Easy Access System Europe, Mustamäe tee
50, 10621 Tallinn, Estonia, gpsr.requests@easproject.com

www.ingramcontent.com/pod-product-compliance
Lightning Source LLC
Chambersburg PA
CBHW032116020426
42334CB00016B/976